PERSONAL SELLING
How to Succeed in Sales

PERSONAL SELLING
How to Succeed in Sales

CHARLES FUTRELL
TEXAS A&M UNIVERSITY

BUSINESS ONE IRWIN
Homewood, IL 60430

Cover Illustration: *John Howard*

Photo Research for Part Openers: *Laurel Anderson/PHOTOSYNTHESIS*
Part I: *Jim Pickerell*
Part II: *David Shaefer/The Picture Cube*
Part III: *FourByFive Inc.*
Part IV: *Jim Pickerell*
Part V: *Comstock*

© RICHARD D. IRWIN, INC., 1992

All rights reserved. No part of this publication may be
reproduced, stored in a retrieval system, or transmitted,
in any form or by any means, electronic, mechanical,
photocopying, recording, or otherwise, without the prior
written permission of the publisher.

This publication is designed to provide accurate and
authoritative information in regard to the subject matter
covered. It is sold with the understanding that neither the
author nor the publisher is engaged in rendering legal, accounting,
or other professional service. If legal advice or other expert
assistance is required, the services of a competent
professional person should be sought.

*From a Declaration of Principles jointly adopted by a Committee
of the American Bar Association and a Committee of Publishers.*

Sponsoring editor:	*Cynthia A. Zigmund*
Project editor:	*Margaret Haywood*
Production manager:	*Irene H. Sotiroff*
Jacket designer:	*Michael Finkelman*
Compositor:	*Better Graphics, Inc.*
Typeface:	*10/12 Bembo*
Printer:	*R. R. Donnelley & Sons Company*

Library of Congress Cataloging-in-Publication Data

Futrell, Charles.
    Personal selling : how to succeed in sales / Charles Futrell.
        p.   cm.
    ISBN 1-55623-651-4
    1. Selling.   2. Sales management.   3. Selling—Case studies.
    4. Sales management—Case studies.   I. Title.
HF5438.25.F876   1992
    658.8′5—dc20   91–25798

Printed in the United States of America
1 2 3 4 5 6 7 8 9 0 DOC 8 7 6 5 4 3 2 1

To my wife—the lady who role-played as my buyer when I carried the sales bag

ABOUT THE AUTHOR

Charles Futrell is Professor of Marketing at Texas A&M University in College Station, Texas. He received his undergraduate and M.B.A. degrees from The University of North Texas and his Ph.D. from The University of Arkansas. Charles is a salesperson turned professor.

Before beginning his academic career, Professor Futrell worked in sales and marketing capacities for eight years with the Colgate Company, The Upjohn Company, and Ayerst Laboratories. During that time, he developed and gave thousands of sales presentations to retailers, wholesalers, and industrial buyers.

Dr. Futrell serves as a frequent reviewer for several academic journals including the *Journal of Marketing,* the *Journal of Marketing Research,* and the *Journal of Personal Selling and Sales Management.* His research in sales and marketing management has appeared in numerous national and international journals. This work has earned him several research awards and resulted in his being the only academic elected to the national Bank Marketing Association's Sales and Professional Development Council for a three-year term. Charles has spoken to thousands of bankers across America on how to sell. Most recently he served on the Direct Selling Education Foundation's Board of Directors.

Charles has written or cowritten seven successful texts for the college and professional audience. These books are used in hundreds of American and international schools.

Professor Futrell has 20 years of teaching experience. Noted for being an excellent classroom instructor, he has developed numerous innovative instructional materials including computer simulations, computerized classroom materials, and video exercises. His classes are fun and educational—often with over 1,000 students a year. He has also participated in numerous executive development programs, always earning high marks for his classes.

This broad and rich background has resulted in his being used as a frequent speaker, researcher, and consultant to industry. Charles enjoys writing, jogging, photography, fishing, and music, plus watching movies and television.

There is no place in our society for high pressure, manipulative selling. The salesperson is a problem-solver, a helper, and an advisor for the customer. If the customer has no need, the salesperson should accept it and move on to help another person or firm. If the customer has a need, however, the salesperson should and must go for the sale. All successful salespeople I know feel that once they determine that the customer is going to buy someone's product and their product will satisfy that customer's needs, it is their job to muster all their energy, skill, and know-how to make that sale. That's what it's all about!

Personal Selling: How to Succeed in Sales was written by a salesperson turned professor. For many years I worked in sales with Colgate, Upjohn, and Ayerst. As both an educator and student of sales, I have thoroughly explored all areas of sales and sales management. Using these findings, industry experience, and educational learning pedagogy, I have developed a book that will help you succeed in sales.

As a student of sales, you should understand the fundamentals—the basics of personal selling. All of them. I do not advocate one way of selling as the best route to success; there are many roads to reaching personal and professional success. I do feel a salesperson should have an assortment of selling skills and should be very knowledgeable, even expert, in the field. Based on the situation faced, the salesperson determines the appropriate actions to take for that particular prospect or customer. No matter what situation is faced, however, the

basic fundamentals of selling can be applied.

It is my sincere hope that after you have read this book, you will say, "There's a lot more to selling than I ever imagined." It is my hope that after reading this book, you will feel this material can help you earn a living at sales while showing you that selling is a great occupation and career.

Finally, I hope each reader realizes that these new communication skills can be applied to all aspects of life. Once learned and internalized, selling skills can help a person be a better communicator throughout life regardless of his or her occupation.

ORGANIZATION OF TEXT

This book is based on fact; it is not an educational treatise. Many features have been included to show you how to succeed in sales: chapters include many buyer-seller dialogues, industry examples, comments from successful salespeople and sales managers, as well as profiles of sales personnel from Fortune 500 companies and smaller businesses. Each salesperson profiled in this book was selected by his or her company as an outstanding salesperson who has made an extraordinary sales contribution to the corporation. Additionally, selling materials and photographs were provided by numerous companies, making this both a practical and comprehensive guide to selling.

Profiles of successful salespeople are included to illustrate how individuals can succeed in sales: people like the Fingerhuts, who left teaching in public schools to create a multi-million dollar company, and Jack Pruitt who previously drove a Pepsi-Cola delivery truck and now sells $1 million worth of jewelry out of a retail store. The people profiled in this book are incredible individuals in their achievements who achieved success through a mix of hard work and sales talent.

The publisher and I worked hard to ensure that you were provided with the basics of successful selling and their applications. The 17 chapters contained in this book are divided into five parts:

I. "Selling as a Profession" shows how the career, rewards, and duties of the professional salesperson relate to the organization's overall success.

II. "Preparation for Successful Selling" shows salespeople how to develop a sales presentation.

III. "The Dynamics of Selling" shows the reader how the entire selling process works from prospecting to follow-up; it is the heart of the book. State-of-the-art selling strategies, tips, and techniques are presented in a how-to fashion.

IV. "Special Selling Topics" discussed the selling challenge and myriad of career opportunities in both retailing and industrial selling. The chapter shows the salesperson how to organize and manage his or her time and sales territory and includes the social, ethical, and issues a salesperson may encounter.

V. "Functions of the Sales Manager" focuses on the challenging job of managing salespeople. It represents a good introduction to the newly promoted salesperson as well as the salesperson aspiring to a management position.

I hope you learn from and enjoy this book as much as I enjoyed writing it. If you have any comments about the book, I would love to hear from you. My greatest wish is for your success in selling. Remember, it's the salesperson who gets the customer's orders that keeps the wheels of industry turning. America cannot do without you!

Charles Futrell

ACKNOWLEDGMENTS

I have had the good fortune of having reviewers who were a big help on this revision. My sincere thanks go to:

- Marjorie Caballero, *Baylor University*
- Brian Meyer, *Mankato State University*
- Robert Piacenza, *Madison Area Technical College*
- Dee Smith, *Lansing Community College*
- Jack Taylor, *Portland State University*
- Bruce Worsleys, *Trend Colleges*
- Dan Weilbaker, *Bowling Green State University*

Several friends also provided suggestions:

- Jeff Sager, *University of North Texas*
- Sid Dudley, *East Carolina University*
- O.C. Ferrell, *Memphis State University*
- Neil Herndon, *Texas A&M University*
- Donna Kantak, *Texas A&M University*

I would also like to thank the many Texas A&M students who have used the book in their classes and provided feedback. Thanks also to the many instructors who call me each year to discuss the book and what they do in their classes. While we have never met face-to-face, I feel that I know you. Your positive comments, encouragement, and ideas have been inspirational to me.

Additionally, many of the profiled salespeople made content suggestions that were incorporated throughout the text. They also answered many of the end-of-the-chapter exercises and cases.

A very special thanks goes to the professional sales force who has done so much for the success of this text. Several Irwin salespeople have contributed to the material and illustrations for this edition: Kathy Shadburne Butler, Jeffrey Christopher, John Dorff, Julie Britt Jahn, Ray Lesikar, Gerald Mentor, Steve Patterson, Stan Sandes, Rosalie Skears, Cliff Ward, and Clark White. Also, numerous Irwin reps have written to tell me that instructors want certain topics added. For example, thanks to Bruce Powell, materials on negotiations were added to this edition.

For the use of their selling exercises and sales management cases, I am especially grateful to:

- Gerald Crawford, *University of North Alabama*
- Dick Nordstrom, *California State University—Fresno*
- Bill Stanton, *University of Colorado at Boulder*
- James L. Taylor, *University of Alabama*
- George Wynn, *James Madison University*

Finally, I wish to thank the sales trainers, salespeople, and sales managers who helped teach me the art of selling when I carried the sales bag full time. I hope I have done justice to their great profession of selling.

C.F.

A Special Thank You

Successful salespeople and sales managers profiled throughout this text greatly added to the educational value of the text and its lively, real-life examples. To these people—thanks!

- Michael Bevan, *Parbron International of Canada*
- Bill Frost, *AT&T Communications*
- Terry and Paul Fingerhut, *Steamboat Party Sales, Inc., Tupperware*
- Martha Hill, *Hanes Corporation*
- Mike Impink, *Aluminum Company of America ALCOA*
- Bob James, *American Hospital Supply Corporation*
- Jeff Christopher, *Richard D. Irwin, Inc.*

- Jim Mobley, *General Mills, Inc.*
- George Morris, *The Prudential Insurance Company of America*
- Vikki Morrison, *First Team Walk-In Realty, California*
- Jack Pruett, *Bailey Banks and Biddle*
- Emmett Reagan, *Xerox Corporation*
- Bruce Scagel, *M&M—Mars*
- Linda Slaby-Baker, *The Quaker Oats Company*
- Sandra Snow, *The Upjohn Company*
- Matt Suffoletto, *International Business Machines IBM*
- Ed Tucker, *Cannon Financial Group, Georgia*

CONTENTS

III

THE DYNAMICS OF SELLING   138

SPECIAL SELLING TOPICS 337

V

FUNCTIONS OF THE SALES MANAGER   433

PERSONAL SELLING

How to Succeed in Sales

I

Selling as a Profession

1

The Life and Times of the Professional Salesperson

My name is Matt Suffoletto. I joined IBM as a marketing representative in 1969, after earning a bachelor's degree in management science from Rensselaer Polytechnic Institute in Troy, N.Y. Since then, I have held a number of marketing line and staff positions. I am currently manager of U.S. channel operations, responsible for the selection for all remarketers of IBM products.

Matt Suffoletto
IBM

While in college, I decided that I wanted to pursue a sales career. My technical background led me to seek employment in a company with a high technology product line. In addition, I was looking for a growing company in a growth industry.

IBM was one of the companies that fit my criteria. They have a strong emphasis on marketing and customer service and offer a clear opportunity for advancement. I still believe that the first successful sales call of my professional career was selling myself to IBM.

Career opportunities for salespeople are unlimited. That statement is evidenced by the vast number of former salespeople who are in key executive positions with Fortune 500 companies. What young salesperson doesn't dream of becoming a corporate vice president of sales?

Within IBM, the first step in launching oneself into a sales management career is to establish a consistent sales performance and maintain it for several years. However, remember that you will be competing with other outstanding salespeople for job promotion, so sales performance just gets you into the running. Qualities such as leadership, creativity, adaptability, intelligence, and dedication are the real "difference makers."

When I started in sales, I had a narrow view of my possible career opportunities. Through exposure to positions other than direct sales, I learned of a multitude of attractive alternatives. Though career alternatives are numerous, several areas that are closely related to sales are product development, marketing research, advertising, administration, personnel, business planning, and marketing support.

The rewards of a successful sales career are unparalleled by any other business career. First and foremost is the personal satisfaction derived from the culmination of a sale. Personal recognition is high on the salesperson's list of motivational needs, and sales management responds to those needs with a wealth of recognition programs. Second, the financial rewards for a successful salesperson are outstanding. It is common for the best salespeople to earn incomes equivalent to top corporate managers. Finally, there is a wealth of personal gain to be realized through a commitment to excellence, for no career has a better yardstick of excellence than sales. Sales, more than any other vocation, offers a close relationship between effort and reward. •

He came on muleback, dodging Indians as he went, with a pack full of better living and a tongue full of charms. For he was the great American salesman, and no man ever had a better thing to sell.

He came by rickety wagon, one jump behind the pioneers, carrying axes for the farmer, fancy dress goods for his wife, and encyclopedias for the farmer's ambitious boy. For he was the great practical democrat, spreader of good things among more and more people.

He came by upper berth and dusty black coupe, selling tractors and radios, iceboxes and movies, health and leisure, ambition and fulfillment. For he was America's emissary of abundance, Mr. High-Standard-of-Living in person.

He rang a billion doorbells and enriched a billion lives. Without him there'd be no American ships at sea, no busy factories, no 60 million jobs. For the great American salesman is the great American civilizer, and everywhere he goes he leaves people better off.[1] •

The salesperson makes valuable contributions to our way of life by selling goods and services that benefit individuals and industry. Red Motley, who was a sales training consultant, once said, "Nothing happens until somebody sells something." Selling brings in the money and causes cash registers across the country to ring. For centuries, the salespeople of the world have been causing goods and services to change hands.

More than ever, today's salespeople are a dynamic power in the business world. They are responsible for generating more revenue in our economy than workers in any other profession. The efforts of salespeople have a direct impact on such diverse areas as:

- The success of new products.
- Keeping existing products on the retailer's shelf.
- Constructing manufacturing facilities.
- Opening businesses and keeping them open.
- Generating sales orders that result in the loading of trucks, trains, ships, airplanes, and pipelines that carry goods to customers all over the world.

The salesperson is engaged in a highly honorable, challenging, rewarding, and professional career. In this chapter, you are introduced to the career, rewards, and duties of the salesperson. The chapter begins by examining why people choose sales careers.

WHAT IS SELLING?

Many people consider selling and marketing synonymous terms. However, selling is actually only one of many marketing components. In business, **selling** refers to the personal communication of information to persuade a prospective customer to buy something—a good, service, idea, or something else—which satisfies that individual's needs.

This definition of selling involves a person helping another person. The salesperson often works with a prospect or customer to examine their needs, provide information, suggest a product to meet their needs, and provide after-the-sale service to ensure long-term satisfaction.

The definition also involves communications between seller and buyer. The salesperson and the buyer discuss needs and talk about the product relative to how it will satisfy the person's needs. If the product is what the person needs, then the salesperson attempts to persuade the prospect to buy it.

Everybody Sells!

If you think about it, everyone sells. From an early age, you develop communications techniques for trying to get your way in life. You are involved in selling when you want someone to do something. For example, if you want a date, a pay raise, to return merchandise, your professor to raise a grade, or a job—you are selling. You use personal communication skills to persuade someone to act. Your ability to communicate effectively is a key to success in life.

This is why so many people take sales courses. They want to improve their communication skills to be more successful in both their personal and business lives. The skills and knowledge gained from a selling course can be used by a student who plans to go into virtually any field, such as law, medicine, journalism, the military, or their own business.

Selling is not just for salespeople; it is a must for everyone. In today's competitive environment, where good interpersonal skills are so valued, the lack of selling capability can put anyone at a disadvantage. So as you read this book and progress through the course, think about how you can use the material both personally and in business.

WHY CHOOSE A SALES CAREER?

Five major reasons for choosing a sales career are: (1) the wide variety of sales jobs available; (2) the freedom of being on your own; (3) the challenge of selling; (4) the opportunity for advancement in a company; and (5) the rewards from a sales career.

A Variety of Sales Jobs Are Available

As members of a firm's sales force, salespeople are a vital element in the firm's effort to market goods and services profitably. Personal selling accounts for major expenditures by most companies, and presents a large number of career opportunities. It is estimated that American firms spend over $140 billion on their salespeople, which equals the amount spent on sales promotion and advertising. There are some 12.6 million people employed in selling jobs in the United States. By the year 2000, employment is projected to grow over 30 percent to 16.3 million sales jobs.[2]

Table 1.1 provides a glimpse of the American salesperson.[3] The data represent estimates of these characteristics and are not meant to be totally accurate but to provide general information. For example, a recent population census reports 68,694 women in product sales (other than retail sales) out of a total of 433,496 salespeople, or slightly less than 16 percent of the total. However, the service sector of the economy and other nonmanufacturing industries have high percentages of females. For example, the financial, publishing, and cosmetic industries are traditionally made up of 40 to 50 percent women.

The profile indicates that the sales position is professional in nature. Salespeople are well-educated, young, loyal, well-trained, and receive above-average pay. We also see that it is costly to operate a sales force. Salespeople work long hours and must be persistent in closing sales with their customers.

The Sales Force of the Future. Marketers mapping long-range sales strategies through the 1990s will have to deal with a sales force whose complexion will change markedly.[4] Mostly, marketers can expect to have

TABLE 1.1   Profile of the American salesperson

• Age: 33	• Earnings per year: trainee, $25,000; experienced salesperson, $40,000	• Hours per week in selling activities within the territory: 41
• Male: 75%	• Cost to train: $18,000	• Hours per week in nonselling activities, such as paperwork and planning sales calls: 10
• Female: 30%	• Length of training: 3 months	• Turnover rate: 20%
• Some college or degree: 82%	• Cost per sales call: $95 to $350	
• Graduate degree: 9%	• Sales calls per day: 6.5	
• Most likely to leave after: 4.3 years	• Number of calls to close: 5	
• Average length of service: 6.3 years	• Cost of field expenses: $20,000	
• Usual pay: salary, 20%; commission, 30%; combination, 50%	• Value of benefits: $14,000	
	• Average sales volume: $1 million	

more women calling on prospects and accounts. They will also benefit from healthy productivity gains by their salespeople and experience considerable difficulty in hiring younger trainees.

These trends will be triggered by the aging of the baby boom generation and the baby bust group that followed it. The effects of this maturation process are at the core of the federal government's new long-range projections developed by the Bureau of Labor Statistics' Office of Economic Growth and Employment Projections (OEGEP), which covers the economy, labor force, industry, and occupations.

While the total labor force (people with jobs plus people looking for work) will increase, two-thirds of the newcomers will be women. Considering that the total number of salespeople is projected to increase at a faster-than-average rate of 30 percent, this rapid growth implies that marketers will have to hire greater numbers of women to keep expanding their sales forces.[5]

Marketers can be encouraged by the changed age mix of tomorrow's work force. Nearly three-fourths of the 1995 labor force will be in the prime working ages (25 to 54 years), compared with *two-thirds* in 1984. In fact, prime-age workers will swell to 21 million, while younger (16 to 24) and older (55 and up) workers will decline 3.7 million and 1.6 million, respectively.[6]

Thus, the sales force of the 1990s will be older, more female, and more productive. Plus, there will be an above-average growth rate in the number of hired salespeople.

Types of Sales Jobs—Which Is for You? While there are numerous specific types of sales jobs, most salespeople work in one of three categories: either as a retail salesperson, a wholesaler's salesperson, or as a manufacturer's sales representative. These categories are classified according to the type of products sold and the salesperson's type of employer.[7]

A **retail salesperson** is often considered an order taker who operates inside a place of business. Selling clothing, shoes, jewelry, and sporting goods are all examples of retail sales jobs. These salespeople generally stay in the store and let the business "come to them." While this situation is common, it is not always the rule. At times, a retail salesperson is required to contact customers at their home or business. Furthermore, many retail salespeople are highly skilled professionals, commanding exceptionally high incomes for their ability to sell.

The **wholesaler's sales representative** works for a firm that carries the products of several different manufacturers. The wholesaler's salesperson sells these products to retail or industrial customers. There may be thousands of items available for customers to purchase. This salesperson may obtain orders in three ways. One way is to ask customers what products they need. Second, a salesperson may check customers' inventories and suggest that they reorder products that are in low supply. Finally, they sell *new* products.

The wholesale salesperson's main responsibility is to provide service to his or her customers. Customers should be contacted routinely, using a low-pressure sales approach. A friendly and service-oriented approach is better than an aggressive one. Sales typically come from orders rather than special selling techniques for persuading a customer to buy.

The types of **manufacturer's sales representative** positions range from the order taker who delivers milk and bread, to the specialized salesperson selling highly technical industrial products. Working for the firm that manufactures a salesperson's products is the most prestigious sales job available. The saleperson working for a manufacturer may sell to other manufacturers, wholesalers, retailers, or directly to consumers. There are five main types of manufacturer sales positions:

An **account representative** calls on a large number of already established customers in—for example—the food, textile, and apparel industries.

A **detail salesperson** concentrates on performing promotional activities and introducing new products rather than directly soliciting orders. The medical detail salesperson seeks to persuade doctors, the indirect customers, to specify a pharmaceutical company's trade name product for prescriptions. The actual sale is ultimately made through a wholesaler or is made directly to pharmacists and hospitals who fill prescriptions.

A **sales engineer** sells products that call for technical know-how and an ability to discuss technical aspects of the product. Expertise in identifying, analyzing, and solving customer problems is another critical factor. This type of selling is common in the oil, chemical, machinery, and heavy equipment industries because of the technical nature of their products.

An **industrial products salesperson, nontechnical,** sells a tangible product to industrial buyers. No high degree of technical knowledge is required. Packaging materials manufacturers and office equipment sales representatives are nontechnical salespeople.

A **service salesperson,** unlike the four preceding types of manufacturing salespeople, must sell the benefits of intangible or nonphysical products such as financial, advertising, or computer repair services. Services, like goods, are either technical or nontechnical in nature.

A few years ago, many manufacturers required salespeople to routinely contact their customers and take orders. It was felt that the company's reputation, quality products, and advertising sold their products. Today, manufacturers want a salesperson to be an **order-getter,** not simply an **order-taker.** Manufacturer's salespeople are trained in the most current techniques for selling **tangible products** (manufacturing equipment, computers, or copy machines) or **intangible services** (insurance and advertising services). Jobs are always available for qualified manufacturer's sales representatives.

Freedom of Action: You're on Your Own

A second reason why people choose a sales career is the freedom it offers. A sales job provides possibly the greatest relative freedom of any career. Experienced employees in outside sales usually receive little direct supervision and may go for days, even weeks, without seeing their bosses.*

Job duties and sales goals are explained by a boss. Salespeople are expected to carry out their job duties and achieve goals with minimum guidance. They usually leave home to contact customers around the corner or around the world.

Job Challenge Is Always There

Working alone with the responsibility of a territory capable of generating thousands (sometimes millions) of dollars in revenue for your company is a personal challenge. This environment adds great variety to a sales job. Salespeople often deal with hundreds of different people and firms over time. It is much like operating your own business, without the burdens of true ownership.

Opportunities for Advancement Are Great

Successful salespeople have many opportunities to move into top management positions. In many instances, this advancement comes quickly. Companies like General Mills and Quaker Oats may promote successful salespeople to managerial positions such as district sales managers after they have been with the company for only two years.

A sales personnel **career path,** as Figure 1.1 depicts, is the upward sequence of job movements during a sales career. Occasionally, people without previous sales experience are promoted into sales management positions. However, 99 percent of the time, a career in sales management begins with an entry-level sales position. Firms believe that an experienced sales professional has the credibility, knowledge, and background to assume a higher position in the company.

---

*Outside sales usually are made off the employer's premises and involve person-to-person contact. Inside sales occur on the premises, as in retail and telephone contact sales.

FIGURE 1.1   A sales personnel career path

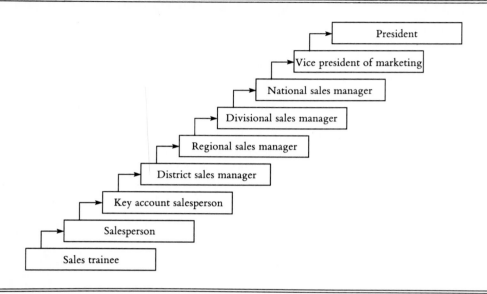

Most companies have two or three successive levels of sales positions, beginning at the junior or trainee level. Beginning as a salesperson allows a person to:

- Learn about the attitudes and activities of the company's salespeople.
- Become familiar with customer attitudes toward the company, its products, and its salespeople.
- Gain first-hand knowledge of products and their application, which is most important in technical sales.
- Become seasoned in the business world.

After training, a salesperson is given responsibility for a sales territory. The person then moves into a regular sales position. In a short time, the salesperson can earn the status and financial rewards of a senior sales position by contacting the larger, more important customers. Some companies refer to this function as a **key account** sales position.

There Are Two Career Paths.   Don't let Figure 1.1 mislead you—many salespeople prefer selling to managing people. They want to take care of themselves rather than others. In some companies, a salesperson may even earn more money than the manager.

Many companies have recognized the value of keeping some salespeople in their field for their entire sales career. They do a good job, know their customers, and love what they are doing—so why promote them if they do not want to move up within the organization? However, many people work hard to move into management.

You Can Move Quickly into Management

The first managerial level is usually the district sales manager's position. It is common for people to be promoted to this position within two to three years after joining the company. From district sales manager, a person may move into higher levels of sales management.

When asked why they like their jobs, first-line sales managers will say it is because of the rewards. By rewards, they mean both financial rewards and nonfinancial rewards, such as the great challenge and the feeling of making a valuable contribution to their salespeople and the company. Managers also frequently mention that this position represents their first major step toward the top. They have made the cut and are a member of the management team. Instead of having responsibility for $1 million in sales, like a salesperson, the manager is responsible for $10 million.

With success, many jobs throughout the sales force and in the corporate marketing department open up. This can include sales training, sales analysis, advertising, and product management. Frequently, traveling the upward career path involves numerous moves from field sales to corporate sales, back to the field, then to corporate, back to the field, etc. However, sales experience prepares people for more responsible jobs in the company.

Success also brings financial rewards. As shown in Table 1.2, the route to the top is typically through sales and marketing.[8] Thus, a beginning sales job is often a stepping stone to these higher positions. The larger a company's revenues, the heavier the responsibility of the chief executive, and the larger the compensation. Today, it's common for a CEO of a large national corporation to have total compensation of over $1 million annually.

Leaving aside compensation at the top echelons, both corporate and field sales managers typically receive higher salaries than others (such as production, advertising, product, or personnel managers) at the same organizational level. Salary is just one part of compensation. Many firms offer elaborate packages that include extended vacation and holiday periods; pension programs; health, accident, and legal insurance programs; automobiles and auto expenses; payment of professional association dues; educational assistance for themselves and sometimes for their families; financial planning assistance; company airplanes; home and entertainment expenses; and free country club membership. The higher the sales position, the greater the benefits offered.[9] Salary is also typically related to:

- Annual sales volume of units managed.
- Number of salespeople managed.

TABLE 1.2 Profile of a CEO

A composite of the chief executive officer (CEO) of a large U.S. corporation. Note the "route to the top" section in the career path below.

The position:
Title: Chairman and chief executive officer.
Compensation: $500,000 salary and bonus plus several benefits.
Workload: 60 or more hours in an average week.
Drawbacks: Insufficient time for family and outside interests.

The career path:
Route to the top: Sales/marketing.
Number of employers: 2.4.
Years with present company: 22
Number of locations with present company: No more than 2.

The person:
Age: 55 years.
Marital status: In first marriage.
Religion: Protestant.
Education: Advanced degree.
Ranking of priorities: Family first, then work, country, and community.

- Length of experience in sales.
- Annual sales volume of the firm.

Rewards: The Sky's the Limit

As a salesperson, you can look forward to two types of rewards—nonfinancial and financial.

Nonfinancial Rewards. Sometimes called psychological income or intrinsic rewards, **nonfinancial rewards** are generated by the individual, not given by the company. You know the job has been done well—for instance, when you have skillfully delivered a sales presentation.

Successfully meeting the challenges of the job produces a feeling of self-worth; you realize your job is important. Everyone wants to feel good about a job, and a selling career allows you to experience these good feelings and intrinsic rewards daily. Salespeople often report that the nonfinancial rewards of their jobs are just as important to them as financial rewards.

Financial Rewards. Many are attracted to selling because in a sales career **financial rewards** are usually based solely on performance. Many professional salespeople have opportunities to earn large salaries. These salaries average even higher than salaries for other types of workers at the same organizational level. People with no experience can find sales jobs paying $18,000 to $35,000. With several years' experience, their earnings can rise to $45,000 or more. In addition, employers furnish them with cars and allowances for travel, customer entertainment, and meals.[10]

Such practices indicate that employers recognize the importance of their salespeople and are willing to pay them an above-average salary year after year.

IS A SALES CAREER RIGHT FOR YOU?

It may be too early in life to determine if you really want to be a salesperson. The balance of this book will aid you in investigating sales as a career. Your search for any career begins with *you*. In considering a sales career, be honest and realistic. Ask yourself questions such as:

• What are my past accomplishments?
• What are my future goals?
• Do I want to have the responsibility of a sales job?
• Do I mind travel? How much travel is acceptable?
• How much freedom do I want in the job?
• Do I have the personality characteristics for the job?
• Am I willing to transfer to another city? Another state?

Your answers to these questions can help you analyze the various types of sales jobs and establish criteria for evaluating job openings. Determine the industries, types of products or services, and specific companies in which you have an interest.

College placement offices, libraries, and business periodicals offer a wealth of information on companies as well as sales positions in them. Conversations with friends and acquaintances who are involved in selling, or have been in sales, can give you realistic insight into what challenges, rewards, and disadvantages the sales vocation offers. To better prepare yourself to obtain a sales job, you must understand what companies look for in salespeople.

A Sales Manager's View of the Recruit

The following discussion of what sales managers consider when hiring a salesperson is based on a summary of a talk given by a sales manager to a sales class. It is reasonably representative of what companies look for when hiring salespeople.

> We look for outstanding applicants who are mature and intelligent. They should be able to handle themselves well in the interview, demonstrating good interpersonal skills. They should have a well-thought-out career plan and be able to discuss it rationally. They should have a friendly, pleasing personality. A clean, neat appearance is a must. They should have a positive attitude, be willing to work hard, be ambitious, and demonstrate a good

degree of interest in the employer's business field. They should have good grades and other personal, school, and business accomplishments. Finally, they should have clear goals and objectives in life. The more common characteristics on which applicants for our company are judged are (1) appearance, (2) self-expression, (3) maturity, (4) personality, (5) experience, (6) enthusiasm, and (7) interest in the job.

People often consider a sales career because they have heard that a person can earn a good salary selling. They think anyone can sell. These people have not considered all of the facts. A sales job has high rewards because it also has many important responsibilities. Companies do not pay high salaries for nothing. As you will see in this book, a sales career involves great challenges that require hard work by qualified individuals. Let us review the characteristics of a successful salesperson.

SUCCESS IN SELLING—WHAT DOES IT TAKE?

Throughout this book you will read comments from salespeople about their jobs. In order to answer the question, "What makes a salesperson successful?" I asked them what they felt was required to be successful salespeople. The eight most frequently mentioned characteristics were: (1) love of their job; (2) willingness to work hard; (3) need to achieve success; (4) optimistic outlook; (5) knowledge of their job; (6) careful use of selling time; (7) ability to listen to customers; and (8) customer service. Each of these characteristics is described more fully below.

Love of Selling

The successful salesperson is an individual who loves selling, finds it exciting, and is strongly convinced that the product being sold offers something of great value. Prudential Life Insurance salesman George Morris states it best by saying, "To be successful you need a very deep commitment to your product and what it will do."* In selling her Amway products, Bernice Hansen emphasizes that she "has wonderful products that everyone needs. . . . If you believe in what you are doing as strongly as I do, you have the self-confidence to be successful."[11]

To be sure, a love of selling itself is one characteristic of successful salespeople. Irving Rousso, who made a salary of $547,875 selling for the Russ Togs Corporation, says, "I'm still hungry and don't ask me why. I just know that it still gives me a thrill and a chill every time I get a reorder."[12] Other salespeople quoted throughout this book make similar comments about how their enthusiasm for their work helps them to be successful. They possess an eagerness to do the job well, which causes them to work hard at selling.

---

*A profile of George Morris appears in Chapter 10.

MAKING THE SALE

Don't Quit

When things go wrong, as they sometimes will,
When the road you're trudging seems all uphill,
When the funds are low and the debts are high,
And you want to smile, but you have to sigh,
When care is pressing you down a bit—
Rest if you must, but don't you quit.
Life is queer with its twists and turns,
As every one of us sometimes learns,
And many a person turns about
When they might have won had they stuck it out.

Don't give up though the pace seems slow—
You may succeed with another blow.
Often the struggler has given up
When he might have captured the victor's cup;
And he learned too late
When the night came down,
How close he was to the golden crown.
Success is failure turned inside out—
So stick to the fight when you're hardest hit—
It's when things seem worst that you mustn't quit.

Willingness to Work Hard

Successful salespeople will tell you that even though they enjoy it, selling requires long hours of hard work, day in and day out, to reach their personal goals. This usually means working at night to plan the next day's activities and working on many Saturdays and some Sundays.

A 10- to 12-hour work day is common. It is their love of work and their need for success that apparently motivates some salespeople to make this personal sacrifice. Matt Suffoletto of IBM says, "If you would make each sales call, presentation, or proposal as if it were the single event from which you will gain quota attainment, recognition, or promotion, you will always be miles in front of your competition." Underlying a tolerance for hard work, there is often a desire for success in life.

Need to Achieve

Each of us has a desire to be successful; yet some individuals seem to have a higher desire for success. Successful salespeople have, as part of their personality, a strong work ethic and a high need to strive for success. If people love their work, are willing to work hard, and have a strong desire to achieve success, do you think they will be successful?

Steve Gibson, a stockbroker for Smith Barney, finds "being second best is not good enough. I am personally challenged to be many customers' best broker. I want to excel. I've found that asking myself the simple question 'Did I do my best?' at the end of each business day is sufficient." "Second is not good enough," "Go beyond the call of duty," and "Make that second effort," are frequent comments of successful salespeople.

The need to achieve involves persistence. Consider former president Calvin Coolidge's following comments:

> Nothing in this world can take the place of *persistence*. Talent will not. Nothing is more common than unsuccessful men with talent. Genius will not. Unsuccessful genius is almost a proverb. Education will not. The world is full of educated derelicts. Persistence and determination alone are omnipotent. The slogan "press on" has solved and always will solve the problems of the human race.

The enthusiastic person who is willing to work hard in pursuit of a goal must be optimistic!

Have an Optimistic Outlook

Salespeople credit a positive attitude toward their companies, products, customers, themselves, and life as major reasons for their success. Successful salespeople are enthusiastic, confident, and constantly think of themselves as successful. Sure, salespeople have times when things do not go as they wish. Yet, their positive mental attitude helps overcome periodic problems. They continually look for methods to improve their attitude.

One method of maintaining a positive self-image is illustrated in the credo of Elbert Hubbard. At the age of 35, Hubbard retired as a highly successful soap salesperson. He went on to become successful as a magazine publisher, a marketer of books and furniture, and a direct-mail specialist. Elbert Hubbard's business credo was:

> I believe in myself.
> I believe in the goods I sell.
> I believe in the firm for whom I work.
> I believe in my colleagues and helpers.
> I believe in American business methods.
> I believe in producers, creators, manufacturers, distributors, and in all industrial workers of the world who have a job and hold it down.
> I believe that Truth is an asset.
> I believe in good cheer and in good health, and I recognize the fact that the first requisite in success is not to achieve the dollar, but to confer a benefit, and that the reward will come automatically and usually as a matter of course.
> I believe in sunshine, fresh air, spinach, applesauce, laughter, buttermilk, babies, bombazine, and chiffon, always remembering that the great word in the English language is *sufficiency*.
> I believe that when I make a sale, I make a friend.
> And I believe that when I part with a man, I must do it in such a way that when he sees me again, he will be glad and so will I.

I believe in the hands that work, and the brains that think, and in the hearts that love.

Amen, and Amen.

Although Mr. Hubbard's philosophy may sound a bit old-fashioned, it boils down to:

- Believing in yourself.
- Thinking of yourself as a success.
- Being enthusiastic when helping buyers—be service oriented.
- Being positive in your outlook on life and the job.

In no other career is the need to think positively more important than in sales. As a salesperson, examine your inner self, commonly referred to as self-concept, and make sure you have a positive, enthusiastic attitude toward yourself, your work, and your customers.

Optimism and hard work are building blocks for success. In addition, top salespeople believe job and product knowledge are also necessary for success in a sales career.

Be Knowledgeable

Successful salespeople place great emphasis on being thoroughly knowledgeable in all aspects of their business. This helps them to project a professional image and to build customer confidence.

When you read Mike Impink's profile at the beginning of Chapter 13, consider the product and customer knowledge he must have to sell $21 million of Alcoa aluminum products to developmental engineers, production managers, and corporate officers. The comments later in the book from salespeople representing such companies as General Mills, Century 21 Realtors, and The Upjohn Company discuss the need to be informed. Take, for example, Steve Gibson of Smith Barney who says:

> Successful salespeople gain a broad knowledge of their business through reading and observation. Learning through study, such as reading, does not end after college—it begins! Many professionals have extensive personal libraries. In general, sales professionals often are not coached or motivated by their companies to read enough. You may have to do it on your own. Subscribe to such publications as your industry's trade magazine, *The Wall Street Journal* and *Business Week*. Routinely visit your local bookstores and public and college libraries. Keep abreast of local, state, national, and international news. Take an evening course at a local college.

As goods and services become more complex, companies place greater emphasis on training their salespeople, and on salespeople training themselves. It is no wonder that corporate recruiters seek above-average individuals to fill their entry-level sales positions.

This knowledge characteristic also includes awareness of the most up-to-date ideas concerning selling skills. Successful salespeople are experts at developing and presenting talks that sell their products. They are constantly educating themselves on methods of better determining customers' needs and of effectively communicating the benefits of their products in order to satisfy their needs.

Salespeople read books and magazine articles on selling, and attend sales training courses to learn how to sell their products better. This knowledge is incorporated into their sales presentation, which is rehearsed until it sounds like a natural conversation between seller and buyer. Please remember that knowledge is power, but enthusiasm pulls the switch! Another characteristic found in good salespeople is the careful use of time.

Value Time

Since there is only so much time in the day for contacting customers and there are so many demands on their time, successful salespeople value time and use it wisely by carefully planning their day's activities. Effective time management is a must. What customer will be called on, what product will be presented, and how to present it must be planned carefully.

Ask Questions and Then Listen to Uncover Customer Needs

Joe Gandolfo, who sold over *$1 billion* of life insurance in a single year, has a sign on his office wall that reads: "God gave you two ears and one mouth, and He meant for you to do twice as much listening as talking."[13]

Good salespeople are good listeners. They ask questions to uncover prospects' needs and then listen as prospects answer the questions and state their needs. Then, they show how their products' benefits will fulfill these needs. The ability to identify and meet customer needs separates the successful salesperson from the average salesperson. To meet customers' needs successfully, you have to provide service.

Serve Your Customer

The most important characteristic for establishing a lasting sales relationship with a customer is willingness to provide service. Customers must believe that you care about them and their welfare. Successful salespeople respect their customers, treat them fairly, honestly like them, and develop a good working relationship with them much like a partnership. They provide outstanding service to each person.

These factors help them earn the respect of customers and to be considered professional businesspeople with high ethics. Steve Gibson says,

MAKING THE SALE

What Is a Customer?

- Customers are the most important people in any business.
- Customers are not dependent on us. We are dependent on them.
- Customers are not an interruption of our work. They are the purpose of it.
- Customers do us a favor in doing business with us. We aren't doing customers a favor by waiting on them.
- Customers are part of our business—not outsiders. Customers are not just money in the cash register. Customers are human beings with feelings, and they deserve to be treated with respect.

- Customers are people who come to us with needs and wants. It is our job to fill them.
- Customers deserve the most courteous attention we can give them.
- Customers are the lifeblood of this and every business. Customers pay your salary. Without customers we would have to close our doors.
- Don't ever forget it!

"I've found the Golden Rule of 'Do unto others . . .' always to be a basis of earning respect."

SALES JOBS ARE DIFFERENT FROM OTHER JOBS

Consultive-selling, counselor-selling, nonmanipulative-selling, and relationship-selling are terms commonly used to describe the role of today's salesperson. Salespeople are no longer adversaries who manipulate people for personal gain. They want to be a consultant, partner, and problem-solver for customers. Their goal is to build a long-term relationship with clients. Salespeople seek to benefit their employer, themselves, and customers.

In recent years, the distinction between a salesperson and a professional has blurred because the salesperson of today is a pro. Many salespeople know more about their field and product than the buyer. This expertise enables the seller to become the buyer's partner, their counselor on how to solve problems.

As you can see, sales jobs are different from other jobs in several ways. Here are some major differences:

- Salespeople represent their company to the outside world. Consequently, opinions of a company and its products are formed often from impressions left by the sales force. The public ordinarily will not judge a firm by its office or factory workers.

• Other employees usually work under close supervisory control, whereas the outside salesperson typically operates with little or no direct supervision. Moreover, to be successful, salespeople must often be creative, persistent, and show great initiative—all of this requires a high degree of motivation.

• Salespeople probably need more tact, diplomacy, and social poise than other employees in an organization. Many sales jobs require the salesperson to display considerable social intelligence in dealing with buyers.

• Salespeople are among the few employees authorized to spend company funds. They spend this money for entertainment, transportation, and other business expenses.

• Some sales jobs frequently require considerable traveling and time spent away from home and family. At times, salespeople deal with customers who seem determined not to buy the sellers' products. These challenges, coupled with the physical demands of long hours and traveling, require mental toughness and physical stamina rarely demanded in other types of jobs. Selling is hard work!

THE SALESPERSON'S ACTIVITIES AS A TERRITORIAL MANAGER

The salesperson's roles or activities can vary from company to company, depending on whether sales involve goods or services, the firm's market characteristics, and the location of customers. For example, a salesperson selling *Encyclopaedia Britannica* or Avon products performs similar, but somewhat different, job activities than the industrial salesperson making sales calls for General Electric or RCA.

Most people believe that a salesperson only makes sales presentations, but there is much more to the job than person-to-person selling. The salesperson functions as a **territory manager**—planning, organizing, and executing activities that increase sales and profits in a given territory. A sales territory is comprised of a group of customers assigned within a geographical area. Figure 1.2 indicates a few typical activities of a salesperson working for General Mills, Inc. As manager of a territory, the salesperson performs the following seven functions:

1. Provides Solutions to Customer's Problems. Customers have needs that can be met and problems that can be solved by purchasing goods or services. Salespeople seek to uncover potential or existing needs or problems and show how the use of their products or services can satisfy needs or solve problems.

2. Provides Service to Customers. Salespeople provide a wide range of services, including handling complaints, returning damaged merchandise, providing samples, suggesting business opportunities, and developing

FIGURE 1.2 Examples of a consumer goods salesperson's activities

• *General Mills' Becky Roy (1) reviews her customer sales call plan; (2) checks her shelf stock; (3) counts the merchandise in the back stockroom; (4) makes her sales presentation and plans an in-store promotion with the store manager; and (5) finally moves on to her next sales call.*

recommendations on how the customer can promote products purchased from the salesperson.

If necessary, salespeople may even occasionally work at the customer's business. For example, a salesperson selling fishing tackle may arrange an in-store demonstration of a manufacturer's products and offer to repair fishing reels as a service to the retailer's customers. Furthermore, a manufacturer may have its salespeople sell to distributors or wholesalers.

Then, the manufacturer's representative may make sales calls with the distributor's salespeople to aid them in selling and providing service for the distributor's customers.

3. Sells to Current and New Customers.   The acquisition of new accounts is the lifeblood of a business; it brings new revenues into the company. This important job must be done if a salesperson's territory is to grow.

While new accounts are crucial, salespeople also strive to increase the sales volume of their present customers by encouraging them to purchase additional items within the same product line along with any new product offerings.

4. Helps Customers Resell Products to Their Customers.   A major part of many sales jobs is for the salesperson to help wholesalers and retailers resell the products that they have purchased. The salesperson helps wholesale customers sell products to retail customers and helps retail customers sell products to consumers.

Consider the Quaker Oats salesperson selling a product to grocery wholesalers. Not only must the wholesaler be contacted, but also grocery retailers must be called on, sales made, and orders written up and sent to the wholesaler. In turn, the wholesaler sells and delivers the products to the retailers. The Quaker Oats salesperson also develops promotional programs to help the retailer sell the firm's products. These programs involve supplying advertising materials, conducting store demonstrations, and setting up product displays.

5. Helps Customers Use Products after Purchase.   The salesperson's job is not over after the sale is made. Often, customers must be shown how to obtain full benefit from the product. For example, after a customer buys an IBM computer system, technical specialists help the buyer learn how to operate the equipment.

6. Builds Goodwill with Customers.   A selling job is people-oriented, entailing face-to-face contact with the customer. Many sales are based, to some extent, on friendship and trust. The salesperson needs to develop a personal, friendly, businesslike relationship with everyone who may influence a buying decision. This is an ongoing part of the salesperson's job, and it requires integrity, high ethical standards, and a sincere interest in satisfying customers' needs.

7. Provides Company with Market Information.   Salespeople provide information to their companies on such topics as competitors' activities, customers' reactions to new products, complaints about products or policies, market opportunities, and their job activities. This information is so important for many companies that their salespeople are required to send

MAKING THE SALE

A Typical Day for a Xerox Salesperson

You are responsible for sales coverage, time, and budget. Help is available and you'll have plenty of marketing and service support; but you're expected to work independently, without constant direction.

Your day is devoted primarily to customer contact. Potential customers may phone the branch and ask to see a Xerox representative. More likely, however, you will acquire customers by making appointments or by visiting businesses to meet the decision makers, discuss their needs, and offer solutions to their problems. As part of your position, you'll make product presentations, either at the Xerox branch office or at the customer's office. You will also spend a fair amount of time on the telephone, following up leads, arranging appointments, and speaking with managers in a variety of businesses and organizations.

In working with customers, you'll need to solve a number of problems. What Xerox product best fits the customer's needs? How do Xerox products compare with the competition? Should the machine be purchased or leased? What's the total cash outlay—and per copy cost—for the machine and its service? How should the product be financed? Where should the machine be placed for maximum efficiency? What training is needed for employees? How can Xerox products meet future office needs?

You'll also be engaged in a number of customer support activities, such as expediting product deliveries, checking credit, writing proposals, and training customer employees in the use of the product. You might also refer customers to other Xerox sales organizations and make joint calls with representatives from these organizations.

Each day will bring you new challenges to face and problems to solve. Your days will be busy and interesting.[14]

---

in weekly or monthly reports on activities of the firm's competition in their territory. Salespeople are a vital part of their employers' information retrieval system.

When combined and properly implemented, these seven job activities produce a successful sales performance. An example of how a salesperson integrates these activities helps to better understand the sales job. See the insert, "A Typical Day for a Xerox Salesperson."

THE SALES PROCESS USED BY SUCCESSFUL SALESPEOPLE

Much of your course will revolve around the sales process. The **sales process** refers to a sequential series of actions by the salesperson that leads toward the customer taking a desired action and ends with a follow-up to ensure purchase satisfaction. This desired action by a prospect is usually buying, which is the most important action. Such desired actions can also include advertising, displaying, or reducing the price of the product.

Although many factors may influence how a salesperson makes a presentation in any situation, there is a logical, sequential series of actions

TABLE 1.3   There are 10 important steps in the selling process

1. **Prospecting:** Locating and qualifying prospects.
2. **Preapproach:** Obtaining interview; determining sales call objective; developing customer profile, customer benefit program, and sales presentation strategies.
3. **Approach:** Meeting prospect and beginning customized sales presentation.
4. **Presentation:** Further uncovering needs; relating product benefits to needs using demonstration, dramatization, visuals, and proof statements.
5. **Trial Close:** Asking prospects' *"opinion"* during and after presentation.
6. **Objections:** Uncovering objections.
7. **Meet Objections:** Satisfactorily answering objections.
8. **Trial Close:** Asking prospect's *"opinion"* after overcoming each objection and immediately before the close.
9. **Close:** Bringing prospect to the logical conclusion to buy.
10. **Follow-up and Service:** Serving customer after the sale.

that, if followed, can greatly increase the chances of making a sale. This selling process involves 10 basic steps as briefly listed in Table 1.3. Each of these steps will be discussed in greater detail in the following chapters.

Before a sales presentation is attempted, several important preparatory activities should occur. This involves prospecting and planning the sales presentation. Steps 3 through 9 compose the sales presentation itself. Step 10 involves the important follow-up phase of the selling process to ensure customer satisfaction.

Before discussing the sales process, we will examine where personal selling fits into a firm's marketing effort. Then, consideration is given to what a salesperson needs to know, such as why people buy.

SUMMARY OF MAJOR SELLING ISSUES

Personal selling is an old and honorable profession. It is responsible for helping to improve this country's standard of living and providing benefits to individual buyers through the purchase of products. Thousands of people have chosen a sales career because of the availability of sales jobs, the personal freedom it provides, its challenge, the multitude of opportunities for success, and its nonfinancial and financial rewards.

A person can become a successful salesperson through company and personal training and by the proper application of this knowledge in the development of skills and abilities for benefiting customers. It is also important to believe in the product or service being sold, work hard, want to succeed, and maintain a positive outlook toward both selling and oneself. In addition, a successful salesperson should be knowledgeable, should be able to plan, and should use selling time wisely. It is also important to be a good listener, and to provide service to customers.

The salesperson's job requires the planning, organization, and execution of activities that increase sales and profits. These involve selling to new customers, obtaining reorders, selling new products, helping customers find new uses for present products, helping customers use products properly, and suggesting ways wholesalers and retailers can sell to their customers.

The remainder of the book will expand on these topics to provide you with the background either to improve your present selling ability or to help you decide if a sales career is right for you.

2

Where Personal Selling Fits into the Firm

Bill Frost received his Bachelor of Science degree in engineering from Texas A&M University. He earned a Master of Science degree in management from Pace University in New York. Frost's career with the Bell System began in 1962 with Southwestern Bell. He was named to his current position as AT&T communications sales vice president in 1983— prior to the divestiture of AT&T and its operating companies.

Preparation, personal selling, and people management are the elements of Frost's success in the competitive telecommunications environment. "You've got to be out there in the marketplace. As a sales vice president with responsibility for 5 states and more than 300 employees, I am continually their support. I am there to help them in any way I can."

This Texas native doesn't believe in "howdy" calls—where you go out, shake hands, and tell a client to call if they ever need you. Frost maintains that planning before a contact is essential. "I go with a purpose. Whether it's a telephone call or a personal visit, you must think through the strategy and tactical plan. Then you go out and perform your plan."

The follow-up is just as crucial, Frost says. "After the contact is over, then you need to critique it. You ask yourself questions—like what went right or what didn't go well at all. You must be very honest with yourself and recognize whether or not you accomplished what you set out to do."

For Frost, building long-term personal relationships is another key element to successful selling. "It's important to be seen as a friend instead of a sales type who's simply there for personal gain." Frost works for this type of relationship at the bottom, the top, and every level in between in his client organizations. •

Bill Frost
AT&T

"Each year," one national sales manager said, "our corporate marketing group gives us a selling program for existing and new products, and I am instructed in which months of the year to have my salespeople place special effort on products with our customers. We are given product, competitive, and market information, along with sales presentation materials. This information is used to develop sales plans and presentations for our customers.

"We hold sales meetings to present this program to all of our field sales personnel. As the sales force begins to sell a product, our national product advertising, sampling, and couponing begins. This process results in a coordinated marketing effort aimed at selling a single product both to consumers and to our retail customers all over America. Sales quotas are established for each salesperson for each product we are selling in a particular sales period (such as for a two-month period). Salespeople who reach their quotas earn bonus money and sales contest prizes as well as corporate recognition of their selling ability." •

This sales manager's comments and the remarks of AT&T's Bill Frost show that a firm's sales force is one part of its total marketing effort. This chapter introduces the purpose and components of a firm's marketing efforts, along with the role and importance of the sales force in a firm's total marketing effort. The chapter ends with a discussion of sales objectives and quotas to illustrate their importance to the firm and their salespeople.

MARKETING SELLS A FIRM'S GOODS AND SERVICES

What does a business do in our economy? Reduced to basics, businesses have two major functions: *production* of goods or creation of services and *marketing* goods and services.

To be successful in today's competitive marketplace, people in business realize that they must first determine people's needs, and then produce goods and services to satisfy them. A company, whether it is General Motors or a small retailer, is in business to create want-satisfying products and services for its customers. In today's competitive business environment, the success of goods and services is determined by the consumers who buy them. Goods and services that do not satisfy consumers will be forced from the market, since consumers will not buy them.

If you asked the general public what the term *marketing* means, many would say *selling*. Selling, in turn, usually implies advertising and personal selling to the public. Yet, the act of selling is only one part of a firm's marketing activities.

The role of the marketing function in a business is basically to generate sales or revenues for the company. The firm's customers exchange something of value (such as money, credit, or other goods) for the firm's goods and services. Thus, marketing is an *exchange* process.

Marketing is a total system of business activities designed to plan, price, promote, and distribute want-satisfying products, services, and ideas to target markets in order to achieve organizational objectives.[1] These activities involve the development, pricing, promotion, and distribution of want-satisfying goods and services to consumers and industrial users. Marketing activities are therefore very important both to the individual company and to our economy as a whole. This has not always been the case.

Business Has Changed over the Years

American business has gone through many changes of philosophy and direction. These changes were largely caused by the ultimate realization that the "consumer is king." However, this has not always been the viewpoint of business. Several major nonconsumer marketing phases existed prior to the emergence of today's consumer-oriented attitude.

Production-Oriented Stage Was First. Before the Great Depression of the 1930s, a common saying in industry was, "Build a better mousetrap, and the world will beat a path to your door." Companies were basically production-oriented. "We know what people want—they want our product," or "I like this product and so will others" were phrases often used by corporate presidents.

In those days, few firms had marketing departments, and many did not even have a formal sales department. An engineer would develop a product, have the production department make it, and then simply put it in the catalog and wait for people to order. Production and engineering shaped the company's objectives and planning. Products were sold at a price determined by production and financial executives. Henry Ford, for example, said that customers could have any color automobile they wanted as long as it was black. The automobile was a new, exciting product needed by consumers. America bought what was produced.[2]

Next Came the Sales-Oriented Stage. By the early 1940s, it became clear that the attitude and needs of the consumer had changed. The military requirements of World War II created a shortage of goods and services. This wartime deprivation resulted in a strong consumer demand when the war was over.

A few years after the war, consumers had many products to choose from and firms found they had to go to the consumer, instead of waiting for consumers to buy. Companies still produced goods with little regard for the consumer's needs. However, the use of personal selling and advertising began to be recognized as important selling methods. In the postwar era, firms placed most emphasis on advertising their product, expecting salespeople to contact customers and take their orders.

Salespeople, armed with very unsophisticated selling techniques, were asked to contact potential customers, show them their products, and take their orders. Training for salespeople consisted mainly of providing them with product knowledge. They had to rely on natural ability for developing and giving sales presentations. Few companies recognized the value of training their salespeople in selling techniques. However, as time passed, businesses found that they had to become market-oriented rather than sales-oriented.

Market-Oriented Stage: The Now Generation.   Today's marketing philosophy is market- or customer-oriented. No longer do companies manufacture a product and give it to salespeople to sell without first considering the customer. Firms developed complementary goals of both achieving a profitable sales volume *and* satisfying their customers. Marketing, rather than selling, became the focus of business sales activities.

As business people have come to recognize that marketing is vitally important to the success of a firm, an entirely new way of business thinking—a new philosophy—has evolved. It is called the *marketing concept,* and it is based on three fundamental beliefs, as shown in Figure 2.1. These beliefs are:

- All company planning and operations should be *customer-oriented.*
- The goal of the firm should be *profitable sales volume* and not just volume for the sake of volume alone.
- All marketing activities in a firm should be *organizationally coordinated.*

The **marketing concept** is a business philosophy that says the customers' want-satisfaction is the economic and social justification for a firm's existence. Consequently, all company activities should be devoted to determining customers' wants and then satisfying them, while still making a profit.

Difference between Selling and Marketing.   Unfortunately, many people, including some business executives, still do not understand the difference between selling and marketing. In fact, many people think the terms are synonymous. Instead, these concepts have opposite meanings. See Table 2.1.

Under the selling concept, a company makes a product and then uses various selling methods to persuade customers to buy the product. In effect, the company is bending consumer demand to fit the company's supply. Just the opposite occurs under the marketing concept. The company determines

FIGURE 2.1   The marketing concept is based on three fundamental beliefs

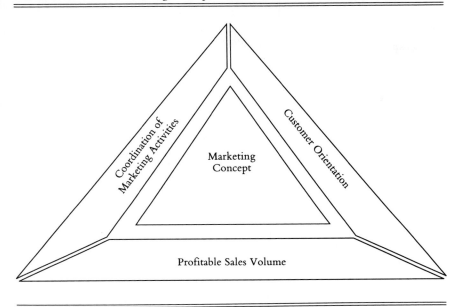

Coordination of Marketing Activities

Customer Orientation

Marketing Concept

Profitable Sales Volume

what the customer wants and then develops a product to satisfy that want and still yield a profit. Now, the company bends its supply to the will of consumer demand.

For a business enterprise to realize the full benefits of the marketing concept, that philosophy must be translated into action. This means that: (1) marketing activities must be fully coordinated and well managed, and (2) the chief marketing executive must be accorded an important role in company planning.

TABLE 2.1   What is the difference between selling and marketing?

Selling	Marketing
1. Emphasis is on the product.	1. Emphasis is on customers' wants.
2. Company first makes the product and then figures out how to sell it.	2. Company first determines customers' wants and then figures out how to make and deliver a product to satisfy those wants.
3. Management is sales-volume-oriented.	3. Management is profit-oriented.
4. Planning is short-run, in terms of today's products and markets.	4. Planning is long-run, in terms of new products, tomorrow's markets, and future growth.
5. Stresses needs of seller.	5. Stresses wants of buyers.

Marketing's Importance in the Individual Firm

Marketing considerations should be the most critical factor guiding all short-range and long-range planning in any organization, for two reasons. First, the core of marketing is customer want-satisfaction, and that is the basic social and economic justification for the existence of virtually all organizations. Second, while many departments in a company are essential to its growth, it is marketing's responsibility to generate revenues.

Too often, unfortunately, American business has been oriented toward production. Products are designed by engineers, manufactured by production people, priced by accountants, and then given to sales managers to sell. That procedure generally won't work in today's environment of intense competition and constant change. Just building a good product will not result in a company's success. The product must be marketed to consumers before its full value is realized.

Research findings published in two nationally acclaimed books, *In Search of Excellence* and *A Passion for Excellence,* identified about 50 companies that had a history of successful performance.[3] Included in this group were such well-known firms as:

- McDonald's
- 3M
- Marriott
- Procter & Gamble
- Delta Airplanes
- Hewlett-Packard
- Maytag
- Boeing Aircraft
- Wal-Mart Stores

Two traits that every one of these companies possessed were outstanding leadership and "turned-on" people. The workers' performance was the result of management's listening to workers and displaying a respect for the dignity and creativity of workers.

Two additional traits—"two edges of excellence"—found in each of these organizations were: (1) a drive to provide superior service and quality to customers and (2) a drive to innovate—to develop new products and services. In other words, every one of these companies was marketing-oriented. In dealings with their customers, these firms gave top priority to finding out what the customers wanted and then creatively developed products and services to satisfy those wants.

ESSENTIALS OF A FIRM'S MARKETING EFFORT

The essentials of a firm's marketing effort include their abilities: (1) to determine the needs of their customers and (2) to create and maintain an effective marketing mix that satisfies customer needs. As shown in Figure 2.2, a firm's **marketing mix** consists of four main elements—product, price, distribution or place, and promotion—used by a marketing manager to market goods and services. It is the marketing manager's responsibility to determine how best to use each element in the firm's marketing efforts.

FIGURE 2.2 Four elements to the marketing mix and four promotion activities

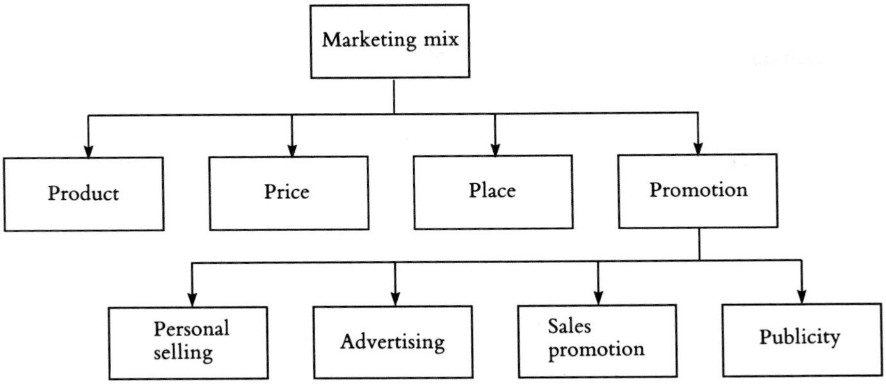

The Product

A **product** is a set of tangible and intangible attributes, including packaging, color, price, quality, and brand, plus the services and reputation of the seller. This definition says that consumers buy more than a set of physical attributes. They buy want-satisfaction in the form of product benefits, such as the brand name or service provided by the seller.

Today, firms spend enormous amounts of time and money creating the products they sell. They carefully research what customers want before developing a product. Consideration is given to the product and to its package design, trademarks, warranties, and service policies.

Research and development and strategies for selling new products are major corporate marketing department activities. Often, sales personnel have little input on what products should be produced. Their involvement in selling the product begins after the product has been produced.★

The Price

The corporate marketing department also determines each product's initial **price.** This process involves establishing each product's normal price and possible special discount prices. Since product price is often critical to customers, it is an important part of the marketing mix.

★Product, price, and distribution are discussed further in Chapter 5.

Companies develop varied pricing techniques and methods for their salespeople to use. For example, General Motors, Chrysler, and Ford have offered consumers cash rebates to increase automobile sales. Companies such as Quaker Oats, Kraft, and Lever Brothers send out discount coupons to consumers, and offer special price reductions to retailers on their products so that retailers will reduce their prices. Some salespeople use offers of price reductions in their sales presentations to entice the retailer to purchase large quantities of the product. Getting large shipments to retailers and other types of customers leads to another element of the marketing mix.

Distribution

The marketing manager also determines the best method of distributing the product. It is important to have the product available to customers in a convenient and accessible location.

Several examples of **distribution** channels for consumer and industrial products are shown in Figure 2.3. The manufacturer of consumer products may have its salespeople selling directly to the household consumer. Most consumer product manufacturers, however, sell directly to resellers— retailers or wholesalers. Two main distribution channels for manufacturers of industrial products are selling directly to the industrial user, such as another manufacturer, or selling to a wholesaler, who in turn sells to another manufacturer.

Promotion

Promotion, as part of the marketing mix, is designed to increase company sales by communicating product information to potential customers. The four basic parts of a firm's promotional effort are (1) **personal selling,** (2) **advertising,** (3) **publicity,** and (4) **sales promotion.** These are briefly explained in Table 2.2. The company's sales force is one segment of the firm's promotional effort.

In addition to informing people about a product's existence, promotion also is used to educate consumers about the product's features, advantages, and benefits; tell them where to buy it; and make them aware of its price versus value. The question arises as to "What is the best promotional element to use in selling a product?" This decision is made only after consideration of the type of product and the customers who will buy it.

The marketing manager determines what proportion of the firm's budget will be allocated to each product and how much emphasis on each of the promotional variables will be given to each product. As shown in Table 2.3, firms typically spend more money on their sales force than on advertising and promotion.[4] Organizations selling in industrial markets spend a higher percentage of the promotion budget on their sales force than

FIGURE 2.3   Examples of distribution channels for consumer and
             industrial products

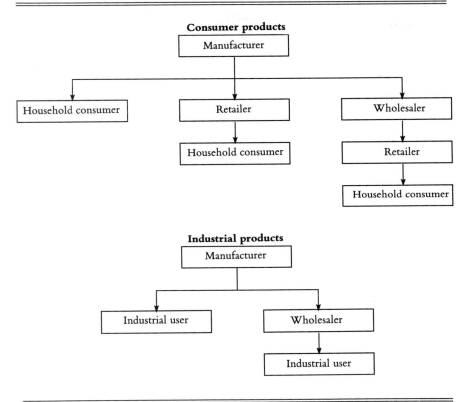

TABLE 2.2   Promotion activities

Personal selling: Personal communication of information to persuade a prospective
  customer to buy something—a good, service, idea, or something else—that satisfies
  an individual's needs.
Advertising: Nonpersonal communication of information paid for by an identified
  sponsor such as an individual or an organization. Modes of advertising include
  television, radio, direct mail, catalogs, newspapers, and outdoor advertising such as
  billboards.
Publicity: Nonpersonal communication of information that is not paid for by an
  individual or organization. Information appears in media such as television, radio, and
  newspapers.
Sales promotion: Involves activities or materials used to create sales for goods or
  services. The two types of sales promotion are consumer and trade sales promotion.
  Consumer sales promotion includes free samples, coupons, contests, and
  demonstrations to consumers. Trade sales promotion encourages wholesalers and
  retailers to purchase and to sell aggressively using devices such as sales contests,
  displays, special purchase prices, and free merchandise.

TABLE 2.3   Firms spend more on sales force than on advertising and promotion*

Advertising and Promotion		Sales Force	
Food products	4.0%	Food	8.1%
Textile mill products	1.4	Textile mill	3.9
Apparel products	3.8	Fabrics and apparel	4.5
Foundries	1.6	Iron and steel	3.0
Fabricated metals	2.3	Fabricated metals	4.7
Printed and publishing	3.4	Printing and publishing	10.0
Ethical drugs and toiletries	8.3	Ethical drugs and toiletries	9.4
Chemicals	1.5	Chemicals and petroleum	3.1
Autos and parts	4.7	Auto parts and accessories	5.4

*Figures are expenses as a percentage of company sales.

consumer goods manufacturers.[5] This is because industrial purchasing agents do not see advertisements for their products on television. Salespeople keep them informed.

No matter what promotional variables are used, they must be coordinated with other marketing mix elements, as shown in Table 2.4. The following example illustrates the importance of this coordination.

The original marketing of the Timex watch is an excellent example of how a firm determines consumers' needs and then develops a marketing mix for selling their product. Timex used five essential elements in their marketing plan. First, *product:* Timex recognized that a large market existed for a low-cost, functional watch. Second, *price:* low production costs made possible a low-priced, quality watch. The third element was *distribution:* they made the watch available through an innovative distribution system that largely excluded the traditional jewelry store channel in favor of mass

TABLE 2.4   Examples of each marketing mix element

Product	Price	Place	Promotion
Brand name	Credit terms	Channels	Advertising
Features	Discounts	Inventory	Coupons
Image	List price	Locations	Free samples
Packaging	Promotional	Retailers	Personal selling
Quality level	allowances	Transportation	Product displays
Returns		Wholesalers	Publicity
Services			Sales management
Sizes			Trade shows
Warranties			

merchandisers, drugstores, and grocery stores. Fourth, they used *nonpersonal promotion:* television advertising made potential customers aware of the watch and its advantages. Fifth, *personal promotion,* or aggressive personal selling at the wholesale and retail levels, convinced buyers to purchase and display Timex watches. Timex's marketing plan has made the company very successful!

THE ROLE OF THE SALES FORCE IN THE FIRM'S PROMOTIONAL EFFORTS

A major marketing strategy issue is determining the sales force's role. Firms use salespeople in many ways. However, there are four basic questions used as guidelines in defining the role of the sales force:

1. How much selling effort is necessary to gain and hold customers?
2. Is the sales force the best marketing tool, compared to advertising and other sales promotion methods, in terms of cost and results?
3. What type of sales activities—for example, technical assistance, frequent or infrequent sales calls—will be necessary?
4. Can the firm gain strength relative to its competition with its sales force?

The answers to these questions come largely from an analysis of competition, the target markets, and the firm's product offerings. This helps determine sales force objectives, the level of resources—such as personnel and money—allocated to sales force activities, and the importance of personal selling in the marketing mix.[6]

Why Is Personal Selling Important?

Personal selling is the "personal" communication of information to persuade a prospective customer to buy something—a good, service, idea, or something else. This is in contrast to the mass, "impersonal" communication of advertising, sales promotion, and other promotional tools.

Compared to other promotional tools, personal selling has the advantage of more flexibility in operation. Salespeople such as Quaker Oats' Linda Baker can tailor their sales presentations to fit the needs and behavior of individual customers. Also, salespeople can see the customer's reaction to a particular sales approach and then make the necessary adjustments on the spot. A second merit of personal selling is that it can focus on prospective customers, which minimizes wasted effort. By contrast, in most forms of advertising, much of the cost is devoted to sending the message to people who are not real prospects. In personal selling, a company has an opportunity to pinpoint its target market far more effectively than with any other promotional device.

In most instances, a third feature of personal selling is that it results in the actual sale. Advertisements can attract attention and arouse desire, but usually they do not arouse buying action or complete the sale.

The major limitation of personal selling is its high cost. It is true that the use of a sales force enables a business to reach its market with a minimum of wasted effort. However, the cost of developing and operating a sales force is high compared to advertising. This limitation is offset by the fact that a salesperson can contact the specific individuals and organizations who are the buyers. Advertising cannot do that.

The use of salespeople to promote a company's products is a necessity in today's competitive marketplace. In terms of cost effectiveness, many companies see the sales force as their best promotional tool. Companies have found that their customers want to be contacted by supplier representatives. For customers, the salesperson *is* the company. The salesperson provides the customer with product information and service and is the link between the company and its customers. The salesperson manages a territory and is responsible to the company for reaching assigned job objectives.

Sales Objectives Provide the Direction

The basic **sales objectives** of salespeople are to make profitable sales to customers and potential customers and to transmit information received from the firm's customers back to the firm. Given the general marketing and promotion plan, the sales manager's job is to coordinate the activities of the sales force in support of each product or group of products.

Typically, the sales force is urged to increase the company's total sales. They do so by increasing sales of particular products by specified dollar amounts or units. Once their sales objectives and quotas are established by corporate management, top field sales management develops strategies and tactics to attain them. AT&T's Bill Frost comments:

> For my organization, we put together annual sales strategies. It's an actual document about six pages long and outlines our strategies for achieving our sales goals. In the competitive environment we're in, of course, this type of material is proprietary information.
>
> We do a bottom-up forecast with people under me providing where they can go for the new year as far as achieving revenue. We do measure salespeople on revenue, not points or credits. That's a percent of increase over base. We also get a top-down view from our corporate offices. Our corporate financial types know what kind of revenue we must generate to meet corporate earnings objectives. Then, it's a matter of negotiation with your boss and your subordinates as to how the actual objectives are set.
>
> Our strategy then becomes focused toward meeting these objectives. We live with risk every day and in the selling world, we're really being measured on revenue. If I don't make my sales quota at year-end, then I can expect to suffer as far as my personal financial gain. I've never been in that

situation and don't plan to be because I think the sales organization gets where it's going as a team.

Individual salespeople's quotas are derived from the quotas given to the entire sales force. The **sales quota** is the specific quantitative share of the portion of work assigned to the sales group or individual toward which that group's or person's effort is directed. A salesperson may be given a quota of making six sales calls each day and increasing sales by 10 percent for the coming year. The strategies and tactics mentioned above are designed to aid the salesperson in achieving these quotas.

Strategies and Tactics Come Next

Strategies are plans that have been made to enable the sales force to reach its sales quotas. The number of salespeople to employ and which products to promote during a sales period are example of strategies. The **tactics** used to implement these strategies are the specific "how to's" of reaching objectives. For example, "what materials can we furnish our salespeople to help them develop a quality sales presentation?" This can include product samples and visual aids.

The sales manager considers the quotas for the sales force and then decides how much time and money salespeople should spend on selling the specific products sold to customers in the various markets served by the firm. Figure 2.4 is an example of how a consumer goods company allocates its salespeople's time by developing a 1990 sales promotion calendar. In April 1989, advertising, promotion, product, and sales personnel in the firm's marketing department determined which products they would promote in 1990. Also determined were the months of the year each product would be emphasized through promotion and sales force activities. They decided that March was the best time to introduce a new product (product N). It was determined that some products (such as products B, F, G, O, and Q) should receive heavier promotional efforts than others. In contrast, other products (such as products I, K, M, and P) will receive no promotional efforts for 1990.

Sales Presentations Are Developed

At sales meetings, field sales personnel for this company are told which products to emphasize for the coming sales period. Salespeople are given or must develop on their own the needed product information, selling skills, and materials for developing sales presentations.

In larger companies, this is often done for salespeople. However, sales personnel working for smaller firms may do this themselves. It is important for all salespeople to know how to develop their own sales presentations. Figure 2.4 shows that five products were singled out for special selling

FIGURE 2.4 1990 sales promotion calendar

XYZ Company* — 1990 SALES PROMOTION CALENDAR												
Product	**1**	**2**	**3**	**4**	**5**	**6**	**7**	**8**	**9**	**10**	**11**	**12**
A**			▓						▓			
B	▓				▓		▓		▓		▓	
C		▓		▓		▓		▓		▓		▓
D			▓					▓			▓	
E	▓			▓		▓		▓		▓		
F	▓		▓		▓		▓		▓		▓	
G	▓		▓		▓		▓		▓		▓	
H	▓		▓									
I												
J												
K												
L	▓			▓		▓		▓		▓		▓
M												
N+			▓	▓		▓		▓		▓		
O		▓		▓		▓		▓		▓		
P												
Q	▓			▓		▓		▓		▓		▓

Month

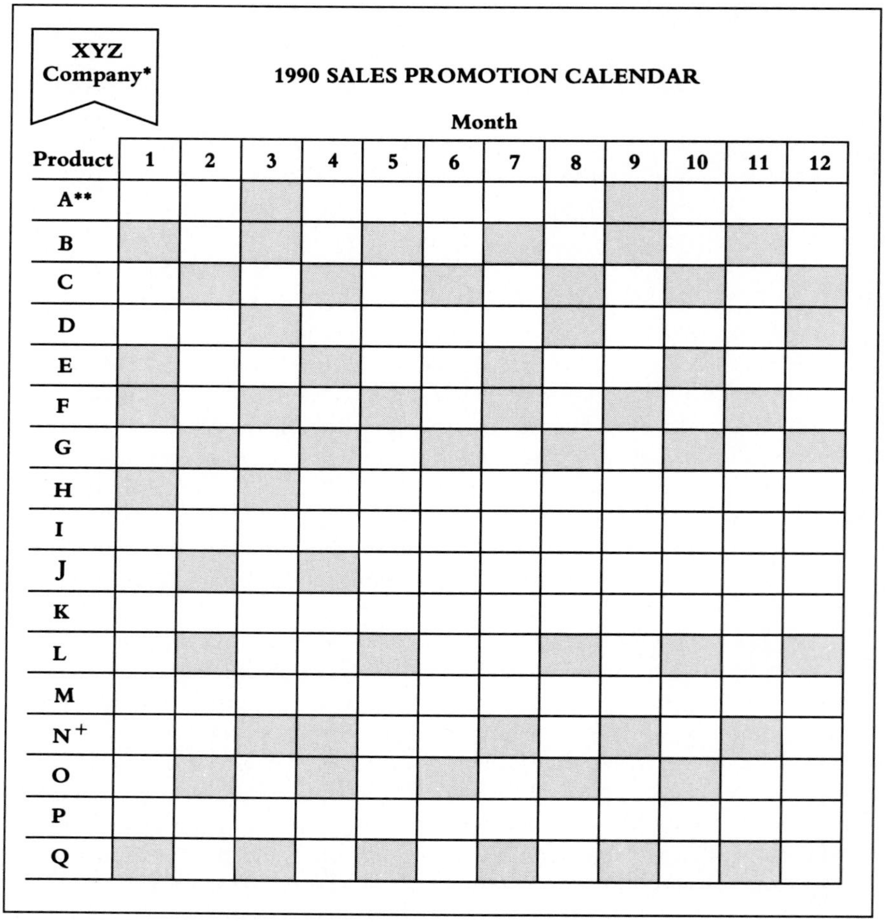

*Company name changed and actual yearly sales promotion program reduced at company request.
†Dark, shaded areas indicate months a product will be promoted.
‡New product introduction.

efforts for January. Thus, five sales presentations would need to be developed.

The next three chapters (Part II) examine major areas of selling knowledge that salespeople should possess to develop a successful sales presentation. Part III examines various elements of the sales process and the sales presentation used by successful salespeople.

SUMMARY OF MAJOR SELLING ISSUES

Most people today associate marketing with selling. Yet, the act of selling is only one part of the overall marketing activities of the firm. The task of providing products that satisfy consumer wants forms the basis for our current marketing system. Marketing is an exchange process between buyers and sellers, the purpose of which is to satisfy the buyer's needs and wants through the purchase of the seller's products.

This "marketing concept" evolved over the years, developing as American business matured. Initially, American business was production-oriented, assuming that people would buy whatever was efficiently proc. ced. This concept gradually evolved into a sales-oriented approach in which firms generally felt that an effective sales approach would stimulate consumer demand for a product. The marketing-oriented philosophy of today focuses on a firm's desire to increase sales while anticipating and satisfying consumer needs. Progressive businesses today are much more consumer-oriented than firms of the past.

The marketing mix consists of four variables—product, price, distribution, and promotion. The product variable encompasses the physical attributes of the product. Pricing involves the marketing manager in establishing each product's price as well as overall pricing policies. Getting that product to the right place at the right time is the distribution variable. The promotion variable is concerned with increasing demand through communicating information to potential customers via personal selling, advertising, publicity, and sales promotion.

Firms must carefully consider the role of the sales force in their promotional program or promotional aspect of the marketing mix. A firm has to decide if a sales force is a viable direct-marketing tool for them, and if so, what types of selling activities will optimally promote their product.

The basic objectives of salespeople are to make profitable sales to customers and potential customers, and also to transmit information received from customers back to the firm. Sales force performance is often evaluated on attainment of general and specific sales objectives and quotas. A quota is a portion of work assigned to an individual or group that serves as a guide for goals to be accomplished and as a means of evaluating how completely they are accomplished. Sales goals, or quotas, are established for certain products at specific times of the year. This requires sales presentations to be developed for each product.

II

Preparation for Successful Selling

3

The Psychology of Selling
Why People Buy

After graduating from Southern Methodist University in Dallas, Jim Mobley began his sales career in 1968 as a Dallas-area sales representative for General Mills, Inc., Grocery Products Sales Division. Over the years, Jim has advanced through several different sales positions within General Mills to his present assignment of district sales manager. He is responsible for six account managers, two territory managers, two shelf-management specialists, and for the sale of approximately 4,000,000 cases of products annually.

Jim Mobley
General Mills

"General Mills salespeople," says Jim, "are involved in selling approximately 200 different consumer food products and sizes directly to grocery wholesalers, who in turn supply the retail grocery industry. These salespeople then contact individual food retailers to persuade them to purchase and promote General Mills products.

"Why our customers buy is sometimes complicated by the fact that our customers normally stock a certain maximum number of products. The grocery industry operates on a small per-unit net profit and is restricted by both warehouse and retail shelf space. In the majority of our sales of new items to accounts, we're not only selling the new product but we must offer the account guidance in what similar product should be deleted. We also must show them where the new product fits into their product mix and where it will be placed on the retail grocery shelf.

"It is important that we make our presentations in a professional manner with documentation on potential benefits such as sales and profits. We make it as easy as possible for an account to consider and purchase our products. For example, we may sell a product using test market results, volume potential for the account, and anticipated customer demand for the product. We then lay out a merchandising plan for the new product that covers media support, couponing, consumer programs, and introductory price discounts.

"Using good business rationale will add credibility to your sales presentations and build customer rapport and trust. Giving your buyer this type of credible information will build stronger presentations in the future as well as maintain the oh-so-valuable customer rapport. We deal with the same buyers day in and day out, and it is very important in our industry that we build the rapport and trust that is necessary for continually successful sales presentations.

"As you can see, a sales career offers an opportunity to be competitive and can be an exciting and challenging career. I have found sales personally rewarding, an excellent opportunity for growth within the company. Sales provides the opportunity to be challenged on a daily basis. These are things that are not found in all career avenues." •

Joe Gandolfo has reportedly sold more life insurance than any other person in the world. His sales average has been over $800 million each year. In 1975, he sold an incredible $1 billion worth of insurance policies.

Joe's philosophy of selling is that "selling is 98 percent understanding human beings and 2 percent product knowledge." Do not let that statement mislead you, for Joe holds the Charter Life Underwriter (CLU) designation as a member of the American College of Life Underwriters. He is extremely knowledgeable about insurance, tax shelters, and pension plans. In fact, he spends several hours a day studying recent changes on pensions and taxation. *"But,"* Joe says, *"I still maintain that it's not product knowledge but understanding of human beings that makes a salesperson effective."*[1] •

Joe Gandolfo's philosophy toward selling is shared by all successful salespeople, such as Jim Mobley. In order to sell, you need to understand people's needs and behavior. Corporations spend millions of dollars each year training their salespeople how to determine a prospect's buying needs, what factors influence these needs, and how to convert this information into developing a sales presentation.

Part II examines major areas of selling knowledge that salespeople need to develop a successful sales presentation. This chapter examines why and how an individual buys.

There are numerous influences on why people buy one product rather than another. We will discuss these reasons and apply them to the various steps in the customer's buying process. This chapter presents a number of selling techniques that will aid you later with sales presentation.

TO BUY OR NOT TO BUY— A CHOICE DECISION

Salespeople realize that people buy a product because of a need, and that needs can be complex due to the influence of perceptions, attitudes, beliefs, and personality. Furthermore, perceptions, attitudes, and beliefs may differ from one purchase situation to another. How, then, is it possible to simply state why people buy one product and not another?

No, salespeople do not have to be psychologists to understand human behavior. Nor do they need to understand the material covered in the courses taken by a psychology major. Furthermore, the average salesperson cannot know all that is involved in the psychological and practical processes that a buyer goes through in making a purchase decision.

What the salesperson *does* need to understand are the various factors that can influence the buying decision, the fact that buyers actually examine various factors that influence these decisions, that buyers actually go through various steps in making decisions, and how to develop a sales presentation that persuades buyers to purchase the product to satisfy needs. To do this, the salesperson should consider the following questions before developing a sales presentation:

- What type of product is desired?
- What type of buying situation is it?
- How will the product be used?
- Who is involved in the buying decision?
- What practical factors may influence the buyer's decision?
- What psychological factors may influence the buyer's decision?
- What are the buyer's important buying needs?

Again, it seems necessary to know a great deal about a person's attitudes and beliefs to answer these questions. Can this be made simpler? Yes. Simply stated, to buy or not to buy is a choice decision. The person's choice takes one of two forms. First, a person has the choice of buying a product or not. Second, the choice can be between competing products. The question salespeople should ask themselves is, "How can I convince a person to choose my product?" The answer to this question involves five things; each is necessary to make the sale. People will buy if:

1. They perceive a need or problem.
2. They desire to fulfill a need or solve a problem.
3. They decide there is a high probability that your product will fulfill their needs or solve their problems better than your competitor's products.
4. They believe they should buy from you.
5. They have the resources and authority to buy.

What do you do if you know your product can reduce a prospect's manufacturing costs, saving the firm $5,000 a year, for a cost of $4,000, and the prospect says, "No thanks, I like my present equipment"? This buyer does not perceive a need, and will not buy. Suppose you make your point about reducing operating costs, but for some reason the prospect is not interested in reducing costs? Chances are, this person will not buy no matter how persuasively you present your product's benefits—because high costs are not seen as an important problem.

Furthermore, even customers who want to solve a problem, but do not like your product, will not buy. But, if you have convinced them, if they want to solve a problem, and if they perceive your product as solving this problem, the question is still: "Will these customers buy from you?" They will, if they believe you represent the best supplier. If they would rather buy from another supplier, you have lost the sale. Your job is to provide the necessary information so that customer's say yes to each of the five statements.

PSYCHOLOGICAL INFLUENCES ON BUYING

Since personal selling requires an understanding of human behavior, each salesperson must be concerned with a prospective customer's motivations, perceptions, learning, attitudes, and personality. Further, the salesperson should know how each type of behavior might influence a customer's purchase decision.

Motivation to Buy Must Be There

Human beings are motivated by needs and wants.[2] These needs and wants build up inside, causing people to desire to buy a product—a new car or a new duplicating machine. People's **needs** result from a "lack of something desirable." **Wants** are "needs learned by the person." For example, people need transportation, but some want a Cadillac, while others prefer a Ford Mustang.

This example illustrates that both practical or rational reasons (the need for transportation) and emotional or psychological reasons (the desire for the prestige of owning a Cadillac) influence the buying decision. Different individuals have different reasons for wanting to buy. The salesperson must determine a prospect's needs and then match the product's benefits to the particular needs and wants of that prospect.

Maslow's Need Hierarchy Provides Clues

Years ago, psychologist Abraham H. Maslow developed a widely accepted categorization of human needs which is referred to as **Maslow's need hierarchy.** Maslow based his hierarchy of needs on several major assumptions. First, all individuals have in common certain basic needs that are the origins of their motivation. Second, these needs are hierarchical, in that one level of need satisfaction must be met before an individual progresses to the next level. Third, an unsatisfied need serves as a motivator. Fourth, once a need has been satisfied, it no longer acts as a motivator. Maslow proposed five basic levels of needs and defined them as:

Level 1:

> *Physiological needs* are necessary to maintain health and normal well-being, including food, drink, clothing, and shelter. Sales example: Newlyweds contact a realtor about buying their first home.

Level 2:

> *Safety needs* are desires for factors that give a safe and secure environment and freedom from danger, such as health and home insurance or deadbolt locks for the doors of one's house. Sales example: An

elderly person enters a retail store asking about a security system for a house.

Level 3:

Social needs include a feeling of belonging, friendship, love, and acceptance from others. Sales example: A person wants to join a tennis club.

Level 4:

Ego needs are truly individual needs including self-esteem, personal reputation, and status. Fulfillment of esteem needs gives the individual a feeling of personal worth and self-confidence. Sales example: A new college graduate goes to buy a new sports car.

Level 5:

Self-actualization needs relate to the desire to attain one's full potential in life and work.[3] Sales example: A person wanting to open a business goes to a bank to discuss a commercial loan.

Maslow's research examined an individual's personal needs. These needs can influence a person's buying decision and provide clues as to why someone would buy. As a salesperson, recognize that people have needs and that unmet needs will motivate them to buy your product. It is sometimes difficult to determine the particular type of need people expect to fulfill by purchasing a product. However, we do know that most individuals are concerned about their economic needs.

Economic Needs: The Most Bang for the Buck

Economic needs are the buyer's need to purchase the most satisfying product for the money. Economic needs include price, quality (performance, dependability, durability), convenience of buying, and service. Some people's purchases are based primarily on economic need. However, most people consider the economic implications of all their purchases along with other reasons for buying.

Many salespeople mistakenly assume that people base their buying decision solely on price. This is not always correct. A higher product price relative to competing goods can often be offset by such factors as service, quality, better performance, friendliness of the salesperson, or convenience of purchase.

Whatever a person's need might be, it is important for a salesperson to uncover it. Once you determine the individual's need, you are better prepared to develop your sales presentation in a manner relating your product's benefits to that particular need. This is not always easy to do, since people may not be fully aware of their needs.

Awareness of Needs: Some Are Unsure

You have seen that people purchase products to satisfy various needs. Often, however, these needs are developed over such a long period that people may not be fully conscious of their reasons for buying or not buying a product. The buying decision can be complicated by their awareness level of needs. Three degrees or levels of need awareness have been identified— conscious, preconscious, and unconscious.

At the first level, the **conscious need level,** buyers are fully aware of their needs. These are the easiest people to sell to because they know what products they want and are willing to talk about their needs. A customer might say to the salesperson, "I'd like to buy a new car and I want a Cadillac, loaded with accessories. What can you show me?"

At the second level, the **preconscious need level,** buyers may not be fully aware of their needs. Needs may not be fully developed in the conscious mind. They know what general type of product they want, but may not wish to discuss it with you fully. For example, a buyer may want to buy a certain product because of a strong ego need, yet be hesitant about telling you so. If you don't make a sale, and ask why, this buyer may present false reasons (such as saying your price is too high), rather than revealing the real motivation. Falsification is much easier than stating the true reasons for not buying your product, thus getting into a long conversation with you, arguing with you, or telling you that your product is unsatisfactory. You must avoid this brush-off and determine a buyer's real needs first, and then relate your product's benefits to these needs.

At the third level, the **unconscious need level,** people do not know why they buy a product, only that they do buy. When people say, "I really don't know what I want to buy," it may be true. Their buying motives might have developed in early childhood and may have been repressed. In this case, the salesperson needs to determine which needs are influential. Often this is accomplished by skillful questioning to draw out prospective buyers' unconscious needs. An awareness of the types of needs that buyers may have will allow you to present your product as a vehicle for the satisfaction of those needs. Several methods of presenting a product's benefits are available.

A *FAB*ULOUS APPROACH TO BUYER NEED SATISFACTION

Possibly the most powerful selling technique used by successful salespeople today is **benefit selling.** In benefit selling, the salesperson relates a product's benefits to the customer's needs, using the product's features and advantages as support. This technique is often referred to as the *FAB*

selling technique (*Feature*, *Advantage*, and *Benefit*).★ These key terms are defined as follows:

- A product **feature** is any *physical characteristic* of a product.
- A product **advantage** is the *performance characteristic* of a product that describes how it can be used or will help the buyer.
- A product **benefit** is a favorable *result* the buyer receives from the product because of a particular advantage that has the ability to satisfy a buyer's need.[4]

The Product's Features: So What?

All products have features or "physical characteristics." The following are examples:

- Size
- Terms
- Packaging
- Color
- Quantity
- Flavor
- Taste
- Price
- Service
- Quality
- Shape
- Uses
- Delivery
- Ingredients
- Technology

Descriptions of a product's features answer the question, "What is it?" Typically, when used by themselves in the sales presentation, features have little persuasive power since buyers are interested in specific benefits rather than features.

When discussing a product's features *alone,* imagine the customer is thinking, "So what? So your product has this shape or quality; how does it perform and how will it benefit me?" This situation warrants discussion of the product's advantages as they relate directly to the buyer's needs.

The Product's Advantages: Prove It!

Once a product feature is presented to the customer, the salesperson normally begins to discuss the advantages provided by that product's physical characteristics. This is much better than discussing only its features. Chances of making a sale are increased by describing the product's advantages, how a product can be used, or how it will help the buyer. Examples of product advantages (performance characteristics) follow:

★Some companies train their salespeople using only features and benefits. They would see an advantage and benefit as one and the same. Most companies use FAB.

- It is the fastest-selling soap on the market.
- You can store more information and retrieve it more rapidly with our computer.
- This machine will copy on both sides of the page instead of only one.

How does the prospective customer know that your claims for a product are true? Imagine a prospect thinking, "Prove it!" You have to be prepared to substantiate any claims you make.

Companies typically train their salespeople thoroughly on the product's physical and performance characteristics. A salesperson may have excellent knowledge of the product, yet be unable to describe it in terms that allow the prospect to visualize the benefits of purchasing it. This is because many salespeople present only a product's features and advantages, leaving the buyer to imagine its benefits.

While your chances of making a sale increase when you discuss both the features and the advantages of your product, you must learn how to stress product benefits that are important to the prospect in your presentation. Once you have mastered this selling technique, your sales will increase.

The Product's Benefits: What's in It for Me?

People are interested in what the product will do for them. Benefit selling appeals to the customer's personal motives by answering the question, "What's in it for me?" In your presentation, stress how the prospect will benefit from the purchase rather than the features and advantages of your product.

To illustrate this idea of buying benefits instead of only features or advantages, consider four items: (1) a diamond ring, (2) camera film, (3) STP motor oil, and (4) movie tickets. Do people buy these products or services for their features or advantages? No, people buy the product's benefits such as:

- Two-carat diamond ring—image of success, investment, or to please spouse.
- Camera film—memories of places, friends, and family.
- STP motor oil—engine protection, car investment, or peace of mind.
- Movie tickets—entertainment, escape from reality, or relaxation.

As you can see, people are buying benefits, not a product's features or advantages. These benefits can be both practical, such as an investment, and psychological, such as an image of success. The salesperson needs to discuss benefits to answer the prospect's question, "What's in it for me?"

EXAMPLE:

Vacuum cleaner salesperson to householder: "This vacuum cleaner's high speed motor (feature) works twice as fast (advantage) with less effort (advantage), saving you 15 to 30 minutes in cleaning time (benefit) and the aches and pains of pushing a heavy machine (benefit)."

Notice that the benefit specifically states favorable results of buying the vacuum cleaner, answering the buyer's question, "What's in it for *me*?" You can see the benefits are specific statements, not generalizations. Instead of just saying, "This vacuum cleaner will save you time," you also say, "you will save 15 to 30 minutes."

Notice that a benefit can result in a further benefit to the prospect. For example, by saving cleaning time (a benefit) you reduce the aches and pains of pushing a heavier machine (a benefit of a benefit). Examples of product benefits include:

- Greater profit
- Time savings
- Increased sales
- Cost reductions
- More customers drawn into retail store
- Elimination of out–of–stock merchandise

Not only are benefits important, but the order in which you introduce product benefits during your presentation, along with its features and advantages, is also necessary to plan.

Order Can Be Important

Some salespeople prefer to state the benefit first and then state that the feature or advantage makes that benefit possible, such as, "The king-size Tide will bring you *additional profits* (benefits) because it is the *fastest-selling size* (advantage)." In this example, the advantage supports the statement of derived customer benefits.

While stating the benefit first is the preferable method, you do not always have to discuss the three parts of the FAB formula in any particular order.

EXAMPLE:

Air conditioning salesperson to customer: "This air conditioner has a high energy-efficiency rating (feature) *that will save you 10 percent on your energy costs* (benefit) because it uses less electricity (advantage)."

EXAMPLE:

Sporting goods salesperson to customer: "With this ball, you'll get an extra 10 to 20 yards on your drives (advantage) *helping to reduce your score* (benefit) because of its new solid core (feature)."

EXAMPLE:

Salesperson to buyer of grocery store health and beauty aids: "Prell's economy size (feature) sells the best of all brands (advantage) in

TABLE 3.1 Examples of features, advantages, and benefits

Features	Advantages	Benefits
1. Nationally advertised consumer product	1. Will sell more product	1. Will make you high profit
2. Air conditioner with high energy rating efficiency	2. Uses less electricity	2. Saves 10 percent energy costs
3. Product made of stainless steel	3. Will not rust	3. Reduces your replacement costs
4. Supermarket computer system with the IBM 3651 Store Controller	4. Can store more information and retrieve it rapidly by supervising up to 24 grocery check-out scanners and terminals and look up prices on up to 22,000 items	4. Provides greater accuracy, register balancing, store ordering, inventory management
5. Five percent interest on money in bank checking NOW account	5. Earns interest which would not normally be received	5. Gives you one extra bag of groceries each month

stores like yours. You can increase store traffic 10 to 20 percent (benefit) and build your sales volume by at least 5 percent (benefit) by advertising and reducing its normal price (feature) in next Wednesday's ad."

New salespeople frequently are not accustomed to using feature, advantage, and benefit phrases. To aid in using them as a regular part of your sales conversation, a standardized *FAB sequence* can be used as follows:

The . . . (feature) . . . means you . . . (advantage) . . . with the real benefit to you being . . . (benefit). . . .

This FAB sequence allows you to easily remember to state the product's benefit in a natural, conversational manner. For example, "*The* new solid core center of the Gunshot Golf Ball *means you* will have an extra 10 to 20 yards on your drives, *with the real benefit to you being* a lower score." You can substitute virtually any features, advantages, and benefits between these transition phrases to develop FAB sequences. Several sequences can be used one after another to emphasize your product's benefits.

Table 3.1 presents five examples of features, advantages, and benefits of products. The first column lists features or product characteristics such as size, shape, performance and maintenance data. The second column shows advantages that arise from respective features. These are the performance characteristics, or what the product will do. The third column contains benefits to the customer of these features and advantages. For each major product feature, you should develop the resulting advantage and benefit and incorporate these into your sales presentation, as discussed more fully in Chapter 8.

Why should you emphasize benefits? There are two reasons (illustrated in Figure 3.1). First, they fulfill a person's needs or solve a problem. That

FIGURE 3.1   Discuss benefits to fulfill people's needs and to increase sales

· *Industrial salespeople, like this Wallace salesperson, work closely with customers to design products and systems that fit their needs. In the health care industry, Wallace salespeople service several departments in a hospital, including selling to physicians in this clinical laboratory.*

· *Consumer goods salespeople, like Todd Kephart and Becky Roy of General Mills, stress that a display of their nationally advertised product will result in increased sales and higher profits for this Kroger store.*

is what buyers want to know about. Second, your sales will increase. Stressing benefits in your presentation, rather than features or advantages, will bring you success.

Given that people make a buying decision based on whether they believe a product's benefits will satisfy their needs, how can you uncover a buyer's needs?

HOW TO DETERMINE IMPORTANT BUYING NEEDS—A KEY TO SUCCESS

Your initial task when first meeting the customer is to differentiate between important buying needs and those of lesser or no importance. Figure 3.2 illustrates the concept that buyers have both important needs and needs that are not major reasons for buying a product (relatively unimportant buying needs).

You should determine buyers' important needs and concentrate on emphasizing product benefits that will satisfy these needs. Benefits that

FIGURE 3.2   Match buyer's needs to product's benefits and emphasize in sales presentation

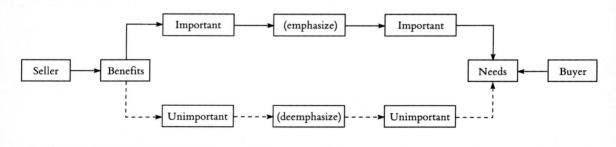

would satisfy buyers' unimportant needs should be deemphasized in the sales presentation. Suppose your product had benefits involving service, delivery, time savings, and cost reductions. Is the buyer interested in all four benefits? Maybe not. If you determine that delivery is not important, concentrate on discussing service, time savings, and cost reductions.

This selling strategy is important to your success in selling. One of the things low-performance salespeople do that loses more sales is discussing benefits of little or no interest to the prospect.

Elmer Wheeler, a famous sales speaker, said "Sell the sizzle, not the steak!" Wheeler is saying that people buy for reasons other than what the product will actually do or its price. They have both practical (rational) and psychological (emotional) reasons for buying. Customers may not buy the product to solve the rational need that the salesperson perceives as important.[5] They may buy to satisfy an emotional need not so easily recognized. It is important to understand this sales concept and learn to determine the buyer's important buying needs. A list of some of the most common psychological buying needs includes:

- Fear
- Vanity (keep up with the Joneses)
- Desire for gain or prevention of loss
- Security
- Love of family

- Personal pleasure
- Desire to succeed
- Comfort or luxury
- Self-preservation

It is up to you to determine which buying needs are most important to the customer. How can you do this? Several methods are frequently used to uncover important needs. These methods create the acronym **L-O-C-A-T-E**.[6]

Listen: Prospects may drop leading remarks like, "I wish I had a television like this one."

Observe:	Look at prospects; study their surroundings. Experienced salespeople can determine a great deal about people by observing such things as the way they dress, or where they live and work.
Combination:	A skillful salesperson may talk to others, listen to a prospect, probe with questions, make careful observations, and empathize—all in an effort to uncover the prospect's needs.
Ask questions:	Questions can often bring out needs that the prospect would not reveal or does not know exist. The salesperson asks, "Is a quiet ceiling fan important to you?" "Yes, it is," says the buyer. "If I could provide you with the quietest ceiling fan on the market, would you be interested?"
Talk to others:	Ask others about a prospect's needs. For instance, ask an office manager's secretary about the manager's satisfaction with a copy machine.
Empathize:	Look at the situation from the customer's point of view.

Once the major buying need is determined, you are ready to relate the person's needs to your product's benefits. Like the television camera that transmits images to the television receiver, buyers picture desired products in their minds. Before the picture is focused clearly, buyers often need to be "turned on and tuned in." Once you find their real reasons for wanting to buy a particular type of product, or identify major problems that they want to solve, you have uncovered the key to selling to them.

Uncovering these important buying needs is like pushing a button that turns on a machine. You have just pushed the customer's "hot button." You have awakened a need, and customers realize that you understand their problems. *Basically, this is what selling is all about—determining needs and skillfully relating your product's benefits to show how its purchase will fulfill customers' needs.*

This is not always an easy task. As we have seen, people have a multitude of different needs, and may not truly understand or see their unconscious needs or problems. In this situation, your challenge is to convert customers' apparently unconscious needs into recognized and understood needs. Several of the later chapters in this book are devoted to selling techniques aimed at uncovering or "smoking out" buyer needs. Getting buyers to realize their needs enables them to focus on your sales presentation to determine if your product will meet these needs. Once buyers experience a need, their perceptions of your product become important.

YOUR BUYER'S PERCEPTION

Why would two people have the same need but buy different products? Likewise, why might the same individual at different times view your product in diverse ways? The answers to both of these questions involves how the person perceives your product.

Perception is the process by which a person selects, organizes, and interprets information. The buyer receives the salesperson's product information through the senses: sight, hearing, touch, taste, and smell. These senses act as filtering devices through which information must pass before it can be used.

As the definition indicates, perception has three components. Each plays a part in determining buyers' responses to you and to your sales presentation. Buyers often receive large amounts of information in a short period of time, and typically perceive and use only a small amount of it. Some information is ignored or quickly forgotten because of the difficulty of retaining large amounts of information. This process is known as **selective exposure,** because only a portion of the information an individual is exposed to is selected to be organized and interpreted, and allowed to be exposed to our awareness.

Why does some information reach a buyer's consciousness while other information does not? First, the salesperson may not present the information in a manner that assures its proper reception. For example, there may be too much information given at one time. This causes confusion, and the buyer tunes you out. In some cases, information may be haphazardly presented, causing the buyer to receive it in an unorganized manner.

A sales presentation that appeals to the buyer's five senses helps to penetrate perceptual barriers. It also enhances understanding and reception of the information as you present it. Selling techniques such as asking questions, using visual aids, and demonstrating a product can force buyers to participate in the presentation. This helps determine if they understand your information.

Second, buyers tend to allow information to reach consciousness if it relates to needs they recognize and wish to fulfill. If, for example, someone is giving you reasons for purchasing life insurance, and you do not perceive a need for it, there is a good chance that your mind will allow little of this information to be perceived. However, if you need life insurance, chances are you will listen carefully to the salesperson. If you are uncertain about something, you will ask questions to increase your understanding.

A buyer's perceptual process also may result in **selective distortion,** or the altering of information. It frequently occurs when information is received that is inconsistent with a person's beliefs and attitudes. When buyers listen to a sales presentation on a product that they perceive as low quality, they may mentally alter the information to coincide with present beliefs and attitudes, thereby reinforcing themselves. Should buyers believe that the product is of high quality, even when it is not, they may change any negative information about the product into positive information. This distortion can substantially lessen the intended *effect* of a salesperson attempting to compare a product to the product currently used by the individual.

Selective retention also can influence perception. Here, buyers may remember only information that supports their attitudes and beliefs, forgetting whatever does not. After a salesperson leaves, buyers may forget the product's advantages as stressed by the salesperson, because they are not consistent with their beliefs and attitudes.

These perceptions help explain why a buyer may or may not buy. The buyer's perceptional process acts as a filter by determining what part of the sales message is heard, how it is interpreted, and what product information is retained. Therefore, two different sales messages given by two different salespeople, even though they concern very similar products, can be received differently. A buyer can tune out one of the sales presentations, tune in to the other presentation, and purchase the perceived product.

While you cannot control a buyer's perceptions, you can often influence and change them. To be successful, you must understand that perceptual barriers can arise during your presentation. You must learn to recognize when they occur and overcome them.

BUYER PERCEPTIONS, ATTITUDES, AND BELIEFS ARE LEARNED

You make a sales presentation concerning a product's features, advantages, and benefits. Your goal is to provide information that makes the buyer knowledgeable enough to make an educated purchase decision. However, a person's perceptual process may prevent your information from being fully utilized by the buyer. Understanding how people develop their perceptions can help you be more successful in selling.

Perceptions are learned. People develop their perceptions through experience. This is why **learning** is defined as acquiring knowledge or a behavior based on past experiences.

Successful salespeople must help buyers learn about them and their products. If buyers have learned to trust you, they will listen and have faith in what you say, therefore increasing your chance of making sales. If your products perform as you claim they will, buyers will repurchase them more readily. If your presentation provides the information necessary to making a decision, your probability of making the sale increases. Product knowledge influences the buyer's attitude and beliefs about your product.

A person's **attitudes** are learned predispositions toward something. These feelings can be favorable or unfavorable. If a person is neutral toward the product or has no knowledge of the product, no attitude exists. A buyer's attitude is shaped by past and present experience.

Creating a positive attitude is important, but it alone will not result in your making the sale. To sell to someone, you also must convert a buyer's belief into a positive attitude. A **belief** is a state of mind in which trust or confidence is placed in something or someone. The buyer must believe your product will fulfill a need or solve a problem. A favorable attitude toward one product rather than another comes from a belief that one of them is better.

Also, a buyer must believe you are the best person from whom to buy. If you are not trusted as the best source, people will not buy from you. Assume, for example, that someone decides to buy a 19-inch, portable, XL-100 RCA color television. Three RCA dealers are in the trading area and each dealer offers to sell an XL-100 at approximately the same price. Chances are that the purchaser will buy from the salesperson believed to be the best, even though there is no reason not to trust the other two dealers.

If buyers' perceptions create favorable attitudes leading them to believe that your product is best for them and that they should buy from you—you make sales. Often, however, people may not know you or your product. Your job is to provide information about your product that allows buyers to form positive attitudes and beliefs. Should their perception, attitudes, and beliefs be negative, distorted, or incorrect, you must change them. As a salesperson, you spend much time creating or changing people's learned attitudes and beliefs about your product. This is the most difficult challenge a salesperson faces.

Example of a Buyer's Misperceptions

Assume, as an example, that a woman is shopping for a ceiling fan for her home. The three main features of the product she is interested in are price, quality, and style. While shopping around, she had seen two brands, the Hunter and the Economy brand. The information she received on these two brands has caused her to conclude that all ceiling fans are basically alike. Each brand seems to offer the same features and advantages. Because of this attitude, she has formed the belief that she should purchase a low-price fan, in this case the Economy ceiling fan. Cost is the key factor influencing this purchase decision.

She decides to stop at one more store that sells Casa Blanca fans. She asks the salesperson to see some lower-priced fans. These fans turn out to be more expensive than either the Hunter or Economy models. Noting their prices, she says to the salesperson, "That's not what I had in mind." She walks away as the salesperson says, "Thanks for coming by."

What should the salesperson have done? When the customer walked into the store, the salesperson knew her general need was for a ceiling fan. However, the customer had wrongly assumed that all brands are alike. It was the salesperson's job to first ask the customer fact-finding questions such as, "Where will you use the fan?" "What color do you have in mind?"

"Is there a particular style you are interested in?" "What features are you looking for?" "What price range would you like to see?" These questions allow the salesperson to determine the customer's specific needs, her attitudes and beliefs about ceiling fans.

Learning the answers to these questions enables the salesperson to explain the benefits of the Casa Blanca fan as compared to the Hunter and Economy brands. The salesperson can show that fans have different features, advantages, and benefits, and why there are price differences among the three fans. The buyer then can make a decision as to which ceiling fan best suits her specific needs. Knowledge of a buyer's learned attitudes and beliefs can make sales; with this information, a salesperson can alter the buyer's perceptions or reinforce them when presenting the benefits of his product.

THE BUYER'S PERSONALITY SHOULD BE CONSIDERED

People's personalities can also affect buying behavior by influencing the types of products that fulfill their particular needs. **Personality** can be viewed as the individual's distinguishing character traits, attitudes, or habits. While it is difficult to know exactly how personality affects buying behavior, it is generally believed that personality does have some influence on a person's perceptions, attitudes, and beliefs, and thus on buying behavior.

Self-Concept

One of the best ways to examine personality is to consider a buyer's **self-concept,** the view of the self.[7] Internal or personal self evaluation may influence a buyer's attitude toward the products desired or not desired. Some theorists believe that people buy products that match their self-concept.

According to the self-concept theory, buyers possess four images:

1. The **real self**—people as they actually are.
2. The **self-image**—how people see themselves.
3. The **ideal self**—what people would like to be.
4. The **looking-glass self**—how people think others regard them.

As a salesperson, you should attempt to understand the buyer's self-concept, for it may be the key to understanding the buyer's attitudes and beliefs. For example, if a man is apparently unsatisfied with his self-image, he might be sold through appeals to his ideal self-image. You might compliment him by saying, "Mr. Buyer, it is obvious that the people in your community think very highly of you. They know you as an ideal family man and good provider for your family [looking-glass self]. Your purchase of this life insurance policy will provide your family the security you want for them [ideal self]." This appeal is targeted at the looking-glass self and the ideal self. Success in sales is often closely linked to the salesperson's knowledge of the buyer's self-concept rather than the buyer's real self.

Selling Based on Personality

While it is important to know a buyer's self-concept, you should also attempt to uncover any additional aspects of the prospect's personality that might influence a decision to buy so that you can further adjust your sales approach. One way to do this is through "personality typing."

Personality Typing. Carl Gustav Jung (1875–1961), with Sigmund Freud, laid the basis of modern psychiatry. Jung divided human awareness into four functions: (1) feeling, (2) sensing, (3) thinking, and (4) intuiting.★ He argued most people can be placed into one of these four groups. Each group, or personality, has certain characteristics formed by their past experiences.

Table 3.2 shows numerous guidelines you can use to identify a personality style that someone possesses. You can diagnose styles by: (1) identifying the key trait, (2) focusing on time orientation, (3) identifying the environment, and (4) what people say. Imagine that four of your buyers say the following things to you:

- "I'm not interested in all of those details. What's the bottom line?"
- "How did you arrive at your projected sales figure?"
- "I don't think you see how this purchase fits in with our whole operation here."
- "I'm not sure how our people will react to this."

How would you classify their personality styles?†

Adapt Your Presentation to the Buyer's Style

The major challenge is to adapt your personal style to best relate to the people you deal with. For example, if you consider the customer (or person) that you best relate to, the one that you find it easiest to call on, the odds are that his or her primary style is similar to yours. The other side of the coin states that the person that is the hardest for you to call on usually has a primary style that differs from yours.

★There are numerous methods of personality typing. Each is due to the conceptual theory used by the method. Currently, personality typing is a popular sales training technique. I use Jung's classification because of his scientific reputation.

†(A) Senser, (B) Thinker, (C) Intuitor, and (D) Feeler.

TABLE 3.2 Guidelines to identify personality style

Guideline	Thinker	Intuitor	Feeler	Senser
How to describe this person	A direct, detail-oriented person. Likes to deal in sequence on *his/her time.* Very precise, sometimes seen as a nit-picker. Fact-oriented.	A knowledgeable, future-oriented person. An innovator who likes to abstract principles from a mass of material. Active in community affairs by assisting in policy making, program development, etc.	People-oriented. Very sensitive to people's needs. An emotional person rooted in the past. Enjoys contact with people. Able to read people very well.	Action-oriented person. Deals with the world through his/her senses. Very decisive and has a high energy level.
The person's strengths	Effective communicator, deliberative, prudent, weighs alternatives, stabilizing, objective, rational, analytical, asks questions for more facts.	Original, imaginative, creative, broad-gauged, charismatic, idealist, intellectual, tenacious, ideological, conceptual, involved.	Spontaneous, persuasive, empathetic, grasps traditional values, probing, introspective, draws out feelings of others, loyal, actions based on what has worked in the past.	Pragmatic, assertive, directional, results-oriented, technically skillful, objective—bases opinions on what he/she actually sees, perfection seeking, decisive, direct and down to earth, action-oriented.
The person's drawbacks	Verbose, indecisive, over-cautious, over-analyzes, unemotional, nondynamic, controlled and controlling, over-serious, rigid, nit-picking.	Unrealistic, "far-out," fantasy-bound, scattered, devious, out-of-touch, dogmatic, impractical, poor listener.	Impulsive, manipulative, over-personalizes, sentimental, postponing, guilt-ridden, stirs up conflict, subjective.	Impatient, doesn't see long-range, status seeking, self-involved, acts first then thinks, lacks trust in others, nit-picking, impulsive, does not delegate to others.
Time orientation	Past, present, future	Future	Past	Present
Environment:				
Desk	Usually neat	Reference books, theory books, etc.	Personal plaques and mementos, family pictures.	Chaos
Room	Usually has a calculator and IBM runs, etc.	Abstract art, book cases, trend charts, etc.	Decorated warmly with pictures of scenes or people. Antiques.	Usually a mess with piles of papers, etc. Action pictures or pictures of the manufacturing plant or products on the wall.
Dress	Neat and conservative.	Mod or rumpled.	Current styles or informal.	No jackets; loose tie or functional work clothes.

The objective is to increase your skill at recognizing the style of the people you deal with. Once the basic style of a buyer is recognized, for example, it is possible to modify and adapt your presentation to the buyer's style to achieve the best possible results. While this method is not 100-percent foolproof, it does offer an alternative way of presenting material if you are not succeeding. Let's examine a suggested tailored selling method based on the prospect's style preferences.

The Thinker Style. This person places high value on logic, ideas, and systematic inquiry. Completely pre-plan your presentation with ample facts and supporting data and be precise. Present your material in an orderly and logical manner. When closing the sale, be sure to say, "Think it over, Joe, and I'll get back to you tomorrow," whenever the order does not close on the spot.

The Intuitor Style. This person places high value on ideas, innovation, concepts, theory, and long-range thinking. The main point is to tie your presentation into the buyer's "big picture" or overview of this person's objectives. Strive to build the buyer's concepts and objectives into your presentation whenever possible. In presenting your material, be sure you have ample time.

In closing the sale, stress time limitations on acting. A good suggestion is to say, "I know you have a lot to do—I'll go to Sam to get the nitty-gritty handled and get this off the ground."

The Feeler Style. This person places high value on being people-oriented and sensitive to people's needs. The main point to include in your presentation is the impact on people that your idea will have. The feeler likes to small talk with you, so engage in conversation and wait for this person's cue to begin your presentation. The buyer will usually ask, "What's on your mind today?" or something similar. Use emotional terms and words, such as, "We're *excited* about this!"

In your presentation, start with something carried over from your last call or contact. Keep the presentation on a personal note. Whenever possible, get the buyer away from the office (lunch, snack, etc.) on an informal basis; this is how this person prefers to do business. Force the close by saying something such as, "OK, Joe, if there are no objections, let's set it up for the next week." Even if the buyer says "No," you are not dead. The key with a feeler is to push the decision.

The Senser Style. This person places high value on action. The key point with a senser is to be brief and to the point. Graphs, models, samples, etc., help as the senser can visualize your presentation. With a senser, verbal communication is more effective than written communication.

In presenting, start with conclusions and results and have supporting data to use when needed. Suggest an action plan—"Let's move *now*"—the buyer has to feel you know what to do.

In closing, give one best way. Have options, but do not present them unless you have to. An effective senser close is, "I know you're busy; let's set this up right now."

Each of the four styles is present, in some degree, in all of us. However, one style (the "primary" style), is usually dominant, and another style (the "complementary" style) is used as a back-up style. The primary style employed by an individual remains the same in both normal and stress situations, while the secondary style could change.

For some reason, some individuals do not have a primary or secondary style but have a personal style comprising all four. Dealing with this type of individual requires strong rapport to isolate this prospect's strong personal likes and dislikes.

YOU CAN CLASSIFY BUYING SITUATIONS

Some people may appear to make up their minds quickly and easily either to buy or not to buy. This is not always the case. The quickness and ease of deciding which product to buy typically depends on the type of buying situation. Purchasing a gallon of milk is quite different from buying an automobile. People have more difficulty in selecting, organizing, and interpreting information in purchasing an automobile. Also, their attitudes and beliefs toward the automobile may not be well formed.

True, a few people have the type of personality (and resources) that allows them to purchase quickly an expensive product like an automobile, but this is unusual. When purchasing some types of products, most people carefully compare competing brands. They talk to salespeople. As information is collected, attitudes and beliefs are formed toward each product. People must decide which product has the most desirable features, advantages, and benefits. When considering several brands, people may seek information on each. The more information collected, the greater difficulty they may have in deciding which product to buy.

Purchase decisions can usually be classified as to the difficulty involved in deciding which product to buy. The purchase decision can be viewed as a problem-solving activity falling into one of the three classifications shown in Figure 3.3. These situations are routine decision making, limited decision making, and extensive decision making.

Some Decisions Are Routine

Many products are repeatedly purchased. People are in the habit of buying a particular product. They give little thought or time to the routine purchase; they fully realize the product's benefits. These are called low-involvement goods because they involve a routine buying decision. People's attitudes and beliefs toward the product are already formed and are usually positive. Cigarettes, cold drinks, beer, and many grocery items are often purchased through **routine decision making.**

FIGURE 3.3   The three classes of buying situations

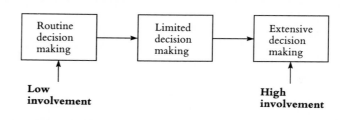

For a customer currently making a routine purchase decision, you should reinforce the point that this is a correct buying decision. It is important to have the product in stock. If you do not have it, the customer may go to another supplier.

For someone not currently using your product, the challenge is to change this person's product loyalty or normal buying habits. The features, advantages, and benefits of your product should be directly compared to the buyer's preferred brand. Of course, not all purchase decisions are routine.

Some Decisions Are Limited

When buyers are unfamiliar with a particular product brand, they seek more information in making a purchase decision. In this case, there is **limited decision making**—a moderate level of actual buyer involvement in the decision. The general qualities of goods in the product class are known to the buyer. However, buyers are not familiar with each brand's features, advantages, and benefits. For example, they may perceive that Xerox, 3M, and Canon copiers are the same in performance.

These buyers have more involvement in buying decisions in terms of shopping time, money, and potential dissatisfaction with the purchase than in the routine purchase decision. They seek information to aid them in making the correct decision. A sales presentation should be developed that provides buyers with the necessary knowledge to make brand comparisons and to increase their confidence that the purchase of your product is the correct decision. Occasionally, the purchase of some products requires prospective buyers to go one step further and apply extensive decision making.

Some Decisions Are Extensive

Buyers seeking to purchase products such as insurance, a home, or an automobile are highly involved in making the buying decision. They may be unfamiliar with a specific brand or type of a product and have difficulty in making the purchase decision. This kind of purchase requires more of an investment in time and money than the limited decision. This situation demands **extensive decision making** and problem-solving activities.

In making extensive decisions, buyers believe that much more is at stake relative to other buying decisions. They may become frustrated during the decision-making process, especially if a large amount of information is available. They may become confused, not knowing what product features they are interested in because of unfamiliarity with the products. Buying an automobile or a life insurance policy, for example, entail potentially confusing purchase decisions.

You should determine all possible reasons why buyers are interested in a product. Then, in a simple, straightforward manner, present only enough information to allow the buyer to make a decision. At this time, product comparisons can be made, if necessary. You can also help the buyer evaluate alternative products.

In summary, it becomes your job to *provide buyers with product knowledge that allows them to develop positive beliefs that your products fulfill their needs.* Determining the type of decision process a buyer is engaged in is critical to you as a salesperson.

VIEW BUYERS AS DECISION MAKERS

Buyers, whether private consumers or industrial purchasing agents, are constantly exposed to information about various products. Manufacturers use newspaper, radio, and television advertising, direct-mail offers, and salespeople to stimulate people to buy their products. What steps do people go through in making a purchase decision?

Typically, the buying decision involves the five basic steps shown in Figure 3.4. Buyers recognize a need, collect information provided by the salesperson, evaluate that information, decide to buy, and after the purchase determine whether they are satisfied with the purchase. This sequence reveals that several things occur before and after the purchase, all of which should be considered by the salesperson.

FIGURE 3.4 Five-step model of buying process

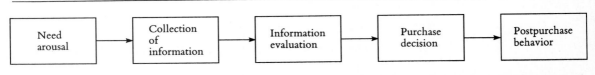

Need Arousal

Remember from the first part of this chapter that buyers may experience a need, or the need can be triggered by the salesperson **(need arousal)**. It could be psychological, social, or economic; it could be a need for safety, self-actualization, or ego fulfillment. It is important to determine a person's needs to know what product information to provide. This information should relate the product's benefits to the person's needs.[8]

Collection of Information

If buyers know which product will satisfy a need, they will buy quickly. The salesperson may need only to approach them; they already want to buy the product.

However, when buyers are faced with limited or extensive problem solving, they may want to **collect information** about the product. They might visit several retail stores, contact several potential suppliers. They may talk with a number of salespeople about a product's price, advantage, size, and warranty before making a decision.

Information Evaluation

A person's product **information evaluation** determines what will be purchased. After mentally processing all the information about products that will satisfy a need—and this may or may not include your product—a buyer matches this information with needs, attitudes, and beliefs, as discussed earlier, in making a decision. Only then will a **purchase decision** be made.

This evaluation process includes rating preferences on factors such as price, quality, and brand reputation. Attitudes on different products are based on either psychological or rational reasons.

At this stage, a salesperson can be very effective. Providing information that matches product features, advantages, and benefits with a buyer's needs, attitudes, and beliefs will increase the chances of a favorable product evaluation. So, the salesperson is charged with the responsibility of uncovering the person's needs, attitudes, and beliefs early in the discussion so as to match the product with the person's needs.

One way to get such information is to determine not only needs, beliefs, and attitudes, but also the type of information a person needs before making a decision. Here are examples of questions you need to know how to answer:

- What product attributes are important in this decision—price, quality, service?
- Of these attributes, what are *most* important?

- What are the prospect's attitudes toward your products?
- What are the prospect's attitudes toward your competitor's products?
- What level of satisfaction is expected from buying the product?

This type of questioning not only tells you about the customer's needs but also involves the customer in the presentation and may convey the idea that you are truly interested in his or her needs. The attitude toward you is enough to create positive attitudes about your product.

Armed with this knowledge about the customer, the salesperson is in a better position to provide the information necessary for a decision and also to help the customer evaluate that information in favor of your product. The information should be provided simply, clearly, and straightforwardly. It should seek to correct any negative information or impressions about your product. Matching information with a customer's needs may enable you to:

- Alter the person's beliefs about your product, for example, by convincing the customer that your product is priced higher than the competition because it is a quality product.
- Alter the person's beliefs about your competitor's products.
- Change the amount of importance a person attaches to a particular product attribute, for example, by getting the customer to consider quality and service rather than price alone.
- Bring out unnoticed attributes of your product.
- Change the search for the "ideal" product into a more realistic pursuit, such as by substituting a $100,000 home for a $200,000 home, or showing a man whose height is six feet ten inches a mid-sized car rather than a compact.

A company has no better promotional device than having its sales force help their prospects and customers to evaluate products on the market—and not merely their own. The two-way communication between buyer and seller is exceptionally effective in providing the information needed to make the sale on the one hand, and to evaluate the product on the other. Salespeople provide knowledge to aid people in their decision-making process. In many respects, salespeople can be viewed as teachers (professors, if you will) who provide helpful information.

Purchase Decision

Is the sale made, once the prospect states an intention to buy? No. You should not consider the sale final until the contract is signed, or you have the buyer's money, because there is still a chance for a change of mind. Even after a customer has selected a product, purchase intentions can be changed by four basic factors. These are:

1. The attitude of others, such as a spouse, friend, or boss. Consideration should be given to both the intensity of another person's attitude and the level of motivation the buyer has to comply with or to resist this other person's attitude.
2. The perceived risk of buying the product—will it give a return on the money?
3. Uncontrollable circumstances, such as not being able to finance the purchase of a house or to pass the physical examination for a large life insurance policy.
4. The salesperson's actions after the decision has been reached; sometimes it is unwise to continue to talk about a product after this point; something could change the customer's mind.

The third factor, uncontrollable circumstances, is self-explanatory. However, how can attitudes of others influence a sale? A man may want to buy a dark, conservative business suit, whereas his wife wants him to buy a sport coat and slacks. The buyer's original favorable attitude toward the business suit may have been changed by his wife. In industrial selling, others in the buyer's firm can influence the sale. Be sure and tell your story.

Since buyers may not always be sure that they will be satisfied with a purchase, they may perceive a risk; they may experience tension and anxiety after buying your product. Haven't we all asked ourselves, "Have I made the correct decision?" The levels of tension and anxiety people experience are related to their perceptions of and attitudes about the products they had to choose from. Uncertainty about differences between your product and those of your competitors can create anxiety, especially if both products' benefits appear similar, or if your product is more expensive yet promises better benefits. This is especially true for products involving limited or extensive decisions. Prospects might see little difference between products, or may like them all—and thus can fairly easily change their minds several times before buying.

Finally, many sales have been lost when, after a buyer has said, "I will buy," the salesperson continues to talk. Additional information sometimes causes buyers to change their minds. It is important to finalize the sale as quickly as possible after the buyer makes a decision. Once the prospect decides, stop talking, pack up your bag, and leave.

Postpurchase

No, the decision process does *not* end with the purchase—not for the buyer at least! A product, once purchased, yields certain levels of satisfaction and dissatisfaction. **Purchase satisfaction** comes from receiving benefits expected, or greater than expected, from a product. If buyers' experiences from the use of a product exceed expectations, they are satisfied, but if experiences are below expectations, customers are dissatisfied.

The buyer can experience **purchase dissonance** after the product's purchase. Dissonance causes tension over whether the right decision was made in buying the product. Some people refer to this as buyer's remorse. Dissonance increases with the importance of the decision and the difficulty of choosing between products. Should dissonance occur, buyers may get rid of a product by returning it, or by selling it to someone else. Alternatively, they may seek assurance from the salesperson or friends that the product is a good one and that they made the correct purchase decision (positively reinforcing themselves).

You can help the buyer to be satisfied with the product and lower the level of dissonance in several ways. First, if necessary, show the buyer how to use the product properly. Second, be realistic in your claims made for the product. Exaggerated claims may create dissatisfaction. Third, continually reinforce buyers' decisions by reminding them how well the product actually performs and fulfills their needs. Remember, in some situations buyers can return the product to the seller after purchase. This cancels your sale and hurts your chances of making future sales to this customer. Fourth, follow up after the sale to determine if a problem exists. If so, help correct it. This is a great way to increase the likelihood of repeat business.

In summary, seek to sell a product that satisfies the buyer's needs. In doing so, remember the sale is made only when the actual purchase is complete, and that you should continue to reinforce the buyer's attitudes about the product at all times, even after the sale. This practice reduces the perceived risk of making a bad buy, which allows buyers to listen to and trust your sales message even though some of your proposals may be out of line with their purchase plans. It also can reduce the buyers' postpurchase dissonance. Buyers who have developed a trust in your product claims believe that you will help them properly use the product.

SUMMARY OF MAJOR SELLING ISSUES

As a salesperson, be knowledgeable about factors that influence your buyer's purchase decision. This knowledge, which helps to increase the salesperson's self-confidence and the buyer's confidence in the salesperson, is obtained through training and practice.

A firm's marketing effort involves various efforts to create exchanges to satisfy the buyer's needs and wants. The salesperson should understand the characteristics of their target market (consumer or industrial), and how these characteristics relate to the buyer's behavior in order to better serve and sell to customers.

The individual goes through various steps or stages in the three buying situations of routine decision making, limited problem solving, and extensive problem solving. Uncover who is involved in the buying decision and the main factors that influence the decision. These factors include various psychological and practical buying influences.

Psychological factors include the buyer's motives, perceptions, learning, attitudes, beliefs, and personality—all of which influence the individual's needs and result in a search for information on what products to buy to satisfy them. The information is evaluated, resulting in the decision to buy or not to buy. These same factors influence whether the buyer is satisfied or dissatisfied with the product.

Salespeople should realize that all prospects will not buy their products, at least not all of the time, due to the many factors influencing their buying decisions. You need to be able to uncover buyers' needs and provide the knowledge that allows them to develop personal attitudes toward the product that result in positive beliefs that your products fulfill their needs. Uncovering prospects' needs is often difficult, since they may be reluctant to tell you their true needs or may not really know what and why they want to buy. You can usually feel confident that people buy for reasons such as to satisfy a need, fulfill a desire, and obtain a value. To determine these important buying needs, you can ask questions, observe prospects, listen to them, and talk to their associates about their needs.

4

Communication and Persuasion
It's Not All Talk

C. Edward Tucker is senior vice president and director of marketing for Cannon Financial Institute, Athens, Georgia. In his job, Ed is involved in administration, sales training, and acts as a consultant when selling his firm's services.

C. Edward Tucker
Cannon Financial Institute

Cannon operates trusts schools for bankers held annually at Pepperdine University, the University of North Carolina, and Notre Dame. Cannon also sells numerous services to financial institutions.

Prior to joining Cannon as a consultant to the financial industry, he spent 18 years with the Citizens and Southern National Bank of South Carolina, serving as vice president of sales training and regional marketing. Ed graduated from the University of South Carolina with a B.S. degree in banking and finance.

"Sales communication involves exchange of thoughts," says Ed. "Whenever you are communicating to a prospective buyer, there has to be an even flow of information. It is a give and take proposition. I believe many salespeople are still a little overbearing and do not really understand the customer's actual needs. They try to sell the product or service, and when the customer does not buy it, the salesperson cannot believe the customer did not want it. This is a situation where communication was only flowing one way.

"A reverse of this is where the customer knows what he wants (or thinks he does) and walks into the store or bank and places the order. The salesperson takes the order, takes the check for the goods or services purchased, thanks the customer, and the sales process is over. Once again, one-way communication has occurred.

"The most effective sales approach is to let the customer communicate his specific needs. After effective communications from the salesperson (probing, asking specific questions) it can be determined what product or service is best for the customer. Then you are ready to sell the benefits to the customer. That is what is going to make the sale." •

"An example of effective and ineffective communication occurred on a flight from Atlanta to Los Angeles, a four-hour trip," said Ed Tucker. "There were two flight attendants serving my cabin. When it was time for the movie, the attendant on my aisle used the following sales pitch: 'Would you like to rent a headset?' I asked 'How much?' and with that, she responded '$3.' I said 'No' and thanked her. She went on to her next prospective customer, who also said 'No.' What went wrong here? She never told me what the headset was for; she only asked if I wanted one. One would look a little foolish sitting for the remainder of the flight with a headset on without anything to listen to, plus it costs $3 to wear it.

"Now, the other attendant used a different approach. She sold the benefits of the movie, which was her core product. She named the movie, the two leading actors, length of time of the movie, and said 'You will be in L.A. before you know it.' 'Sounds good to me,' were most of her responses. 'That will be *just* $3.' And after the exchange of currency took place, the eagerly waiting moviegoer was handed a headset. The difference between the two approaches was the way in which the product was presented." •

While there may be many other factors that are crucial to sales success, the ability to communicate effectively, as discussed by Ed Tucker, is of prime importance. In order to convincingly convey this important sales skill, this chapter directly applies a basic communication model to the buyer-seller interaction. Afterward, several factors influencing communication, along with possible barriers to effective communication, are described. The often ignored—though always critical—topic of nonverbal communication is also examined in depth. The balance of this chapter relates some techniques used to improve sales communication.

COMMUNICATION: IT TAKES TWO

Communication, in a sales context, is the act of transmitting verbal and nonverbal information and understanding between seller and buyer. This definition presents communication as an exchange process of sending and receiving messages with some type of response expected between seller and buyer.

Communication during the sales presentation takes many forms. Ideas and attitudes can be effectively communicated by media other than just language. Actually, in a normal two-person conversation, less than 35 percent of the social meaning utilizes verbal components. Said another way, much of the social meaning in a conversation is conveyed nonverbally.

Research has found that face-to-face communication is composed of *verbal, vocal,* and *facial* communication messages. One equation presents the

FIGURE 4.1   The basic communication model has eight elements

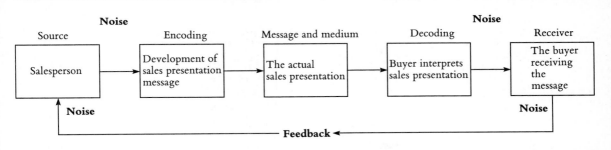

total impact of communicated messages as equal to 7 percent verbal plus 38 percent tone of voice plus 55 percent nonverbal expressions.[1] If one recognizes these findings as a reasonable approximation of the total communicative process, then uninformed salespeople actually ignore a major part of the communication process that occurs during buyer-seller interaction. How the sales message is given can be as important to making the sale as what is said. Thus, nonverbal communications are important in communication between buyer and seller. An awareness of nonverbal communication is a valuable tool in successfully making a sale.

Vocal communication includes such factors as voice quality, pitch, inflection, and pauses. Radio newscaster Paul Harvey is famous for "how" he broadcasts the news. His vocal pauses and inflections are masterfully used to obtain and hold the attention of his radio audience. A salesperson's use of vocal factors can aid in sales presentation, too. Along with verbal, vocal, and facial communication, a number of other elements are also involved in sales communications.

Salesperson-Buyer Communication Process Requires Feedback

A basic communication model that depicts how the salesperson-buyer communication process works is shown in Figure 4.1. Basically, communication takes place when a "sender" transmits a "message" through some type of "medium" to a "receiver" who responds to that message. Figure 4.1 presents a model that contains eight major communications elements. Each of these elements is defined below:

- **Source.** The source of communication (also called the communicator); in our case, the salesperson.
- **Encoding Process.** The conversion by the salesperson of ideas and concepts into the language and materials used in the sales presentation.
- **Message.** The information conveyed in the sales presentation.

SELLING TIPS

Say What You Mean

There are at least six messages involved in the communication process:

1. What you mean to say.
2. What you really say.
3. What the other person hears.
4. What the other person thinks is heard.
5. What the other person says about what you said.
6. What you think the other person said about what you said.

Gets a bit complicated, doesn't it? Sue and I were looking at a gorgeous moon together under romantic circumstances. As we shared the moment, how was I actually feeling? I was feeling romantic. If we followed the six messages, that incident would have looked something like this:

1. What you mean to say.	("The moon puts me in a romantic mood.")
2. What you really say.	("Isn't that a brilliant moon?")
3. What the other person hears.	("The moon is bright.")
4. What the other person thinks she hears.	("Yes, it's bright enough for a walk.")
5. What the other person says about what you said.	("Yes, it's bright enough to shoot a golf ball by.")
6. What you think the other person said about what you said.	("I don't feel romantic.")

We can miss each other's wavelengths completed by the time the six messages are completed without even realizing what has happened. All of us are constantly in the process of encoding and decoding messages.

We need to learn to ask questions, or restate the point for clarification of meaning. To say what we mean, and say it straight, must be our constant goal in order for those around us to discard all decoding devices.

- **Medium.** The form of communication used in the sales presentation and discussion; most frequently words, visual materials, and body language.
- **Decoding Process.** Receipt and translation (interpretation) of the information by the receiver (prospective buyer).
- **Receiver.** The person the communication is intended for; in our case, the prospect or buyer.
- **Feedback.** Reaction to the communication as transmitted to the sender. This reaction may be verbal or nonverbal.
- **Noise.** Factors that distort communication between buyer and seller. Noise includes barriers to communication, which will be discussed later.

This model portrays the communication process. A salesperson should know how to develop a sales presentation (encoding) so that the buyer obtains maximum understanding of the message (decoding). Communication media that most effectively communicate a specific sales message should be used. Clear verbal discussion, employment of visual aids such as pictures or diagrams, and development of models or samples of the product are several types of media a salesperson might use in communicating a sales message.

One-way communication occurs when the salesperson talks and the buyer only listens. The salesperson needs a response or feedback from the buyer to know if communication occurs. Does the buyer understand the message? Once feedback or interaction and understanding between buyer and seller exists in a communication process, two-way communication has been established.

Two-way communication is essential to make the sale. The buyer must understand your message's information to make a buying decision. Two-way communication gives the salesperson the ability to present a product's benefits, instantly receive buyer reactions, and answer questions. Buyers usually react both verbally and nonverbally to your presentation.

NONVERBAL COMMUNICATION: WATCH FOR IT

Amos Skaggs, purchasing agent, stands as a salesperson enters his office. "Hi, Mr. Skaggs," he says, offering his hand. Mr. Skaggs returns a limp, one-second handshake and sits down behind his desk. He begins to open his afternoon mail, almost as though no one else was in the room.

The salesperson sits down and begins his canned sales talk by saying, "Mr. Skaggs, I'm here to show you how your company can lower manufacturing costs by 10 percent." Mr. Skaggs lays his mail down on his desk, leans back in his chair, crosses his arms, and with a growl says: "I'm glad to hear that. You know something, young fellow, pretty soon it won't cost us anything to manufacture our products." "Why is that?" the salesman mumbles, meekly looking down to the floor. "Well, you are the ninth person I've seen today who has offered to save us 10 percent on our costs."

Mr. Skaggs stands up, leans over the table and while peering over his glasses says slowly, "I believe I've heard enough sale pitches for one day." The initially enthusiastic salesperson now apologetically says, "If this is not a good time for you, sir, I can come back at a later date."

In this imaginary sales call, buyer and seller communicated both verbal and nonverbal messages. Here, nonverbal messages conveyed both parties' attitudes better than the actual verbal exchange. The salesperson's negative reactions served to increase Mr. Skaggs's hostile attitude. He could sense the salesperson did not understand his problem and was there to sell him something, not solve his problem. This impression caused a rapid breakdown in communication. The end result, as in this case, is usually NO SALE.

Recognition and analysis of nonverbal communication in sales transactions is relatively new. Only in the past 10 to 15 years has the subject been formally examined in detail. The presence and use of nonverbal communication, however, has been acknowledged for years. In the early 1900s, Sigmund Freud noted that people cannot keep a secret, even if they do not speak. A person's gestures and actions reveal hidden feelings about something.

People communicate nonverbally in several ways. Four major **nonverbal communication** channels are: the physical space between buyer and seller, appearance, handshake, and body movements.

Concept of Space

The concept of **territorial space** refers to the area around the self a person will not allow another person to enter without consent. Early experiments in territorial space dealt with animals. These experiments determined that higher-status members of a group are often afforded a freedom of movement that is less available to those of lower status. This idea has been applied to socially acceptable distances of space that human beings keep between themselves in certain situations. Territorial space can easily be related to the selling situation.

Space considerations are important to salespeople because violations of territorial space without customer consent may set off the customer's defense mechanisms and create a barrier to communications. A person (buyer) has four main types of distances to consider—intimate (up to two feet); personal (two to four feet); social (four to twelve feet); and public (greater than twelve feet).

Intimate space of up to two feet, or about arm's length, is the most sensitive zone, since it is reserved for very close friends and loved ones. To enter intimate space in the buyer-seller relationship, for some prospects, could be socially unacceptable—possibly offensive.

During the presentation, a salesperson should carefully listen and look for signs that indicate the buyer feels uncomfortable, perhaps that the salesperson is too close. A buyer may deduce from such closeness that the salesperson is attempting to dominate or overpower the buyer. This feeling can result in resistance to the salesperson. If such uneasiness is detected, the salesperson should move back, which reassures the customer.

Personal space is the closest zone a stranger or business acquaintance is normally allowed to enter. Even in this zone, a prospect may be uncomfortable. Barriers, such as a desk, are often used to reduce the threat implied when someone enters this zone.

Social space is the area normally used for a sales presentation. Again, the buyer often uses a desk to maintain a distance of four feet or more between buyer and seller. Standing while facing a seated prospect may communicate to the buyer that the salesperson seems too dominating.

Thus, the salesperson should normally stay seated to convey a relaxed manner.

A salesperson should consider beginning a presentation in the middle of the social distance zone, six to eight feet, to avoid the prospect's erecting negative mental barriers. This is especially true if the salesperson is not a friend of the prospect.

Public space is often used by the salesperson making a presentation to a group of people. It is similar to the distance between teacher and student in a classroom. People are at ease and thus easy to communicate with at this distance, since they do not feel threatened by the salesperson.

Space Threats. The "territorial imperative" causes people to feel that they should defend their space or territory. The salesperson who pulls up a chair too close, takes over all or part of the prospect's desk, leans on or over the desk, or touches the objects on the desk runs the risk of invading a prospect's territory. Be careful not to create defensive barriers. However, should you sense a friendliness between yourself and the prospect, use territorial space to your benefit.

Space Invasion. The prospect who allows you to enter or invade personal and intimate space is saying, "Come on into my space, let's be friends." Now you can use space to your advantage.

In most offices, the salesperson sits directly across the desk from the prospect. The prospect controls the space arrangement. This is one kind of defensive barrier, allowing the prospect to control much of the conversation. Often, seating is prearranged and it could be a space threat if you moved your chair when calling on a prospect for the first time.

However, if you have a choice between a chair across the desk or beside the desk, take the latter seat, as shown in Figure 4.2. Sitting at the side lowers the desk communication barrier. If you are friends with the buyer, move your chair to the side of the desk yourself. This helps create a friendly, cooperative environment between you and the buyer.

Communication through Appearance and the Handshake

Other common methods of nonverbal communication are signals conveyed by a person's physical appearance and the handshake. Once territorial space has been established, general appearance is the next medium of nonverbal communication conveyed to a customer by a salesperson. Appearance not only conveys information such as age, sex, height, weight, race, and physical characteristics, but provides a great deal of data on personality. Hairstyle is one of the first things a buyer notices about a salesperson.

Style Hair Carefully. Hairstyle traditionally has been an important factor in evaluating personal appearance. Although the longer hairstyles for men that emerged in the late 1960s have gained increased acceptance, longer hair has traditionally been associated with a liberal outlook on life and thus could

FIGURE 4.2 Office arrangements and territorial space

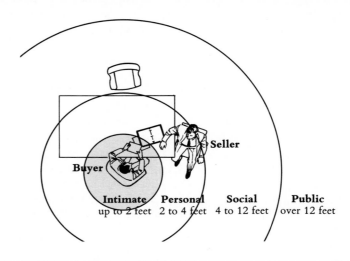

affect the customer's attitude toward a salesperson. Today's salespeople must consider what type of customer they will call on and adjust their hairstyles accordingly.

Though recently decreasing somewhat in popularity, male facial hair is still worn by some male salespeople. For several decades, American males did not sport beards and moustaches to any great extent, but that trend reversed in the 1960s and 70s. A research study in the early 1970s asked people their opinion of facial hair and came up with two very different opinions. One group felt that bearded men are perceived as more sensitive, more masculine, more intelligent, and warmer than clean-shaven men. The other group felt that men with beards are perceived as more deviant, radical, independent, and introverted![2]

Salespeople should carefully consider their grooming and its impact on customer's perceptions. Some companies ask male salespersons to be clean shaven and wear conservative haircuts. Their female salespersons are asked to choose a simple, businesslike, shoulder-length hair style. Other companies leave grooming up to each individual. Your grooming objective is to eliminate communication barriers. Your grooming can convey a favorable first impression. Should your company not have a policy on grooming, examine your customer's grooming before deciding on your style.

Dress as a Professional.   Wardrobe has always been a major determinant of sales success, and today it is emphasized as never before. A variety of books and articles have appeared on proper dress for business people. These books espouse the doctrine that male and female sales representatives should wear conservative, "serious" clothing that projects professionalism, just the right amount of authority, and a desire to please the customer. Sporty clothing is believed to accentuate sales aggressiveness, placing a purchasing agent on the defensive, and resulting in lost sales.

Many companies believe that decision rules exist for every major clothing item and accessory, but these are derivatives of one basic commandment—dress in a simple, elegant style. Xerox, IBM, and other large companies have incorporated these ideas into their sales training and daily policies. These firms encourage sales personnel to wear dark, conservative clothing. This practice is designed to project a conservative, stable corporate image to both customers and the general public.

Figure 4.3 illustrates several key considerations for appropriate dress and grooming. If you are uncertain about what to do, visit several retailers. Make sure at least one retailer is a specialty store. They will have the latest styles and will spend time with you. Tell the salespeople what you are looking for and see what they say. Think of this as an investment in yourself, because it is expensive to build a wardrobe. However, you are worth it!

Clothes, accessories, and shoes are very important, but do not forget personal grooming, such as skin care and hairstyle. Women and men should visit a hairstylist. Learn to recognize "image" symbols in business dress and use them to your advantage. Be cautious in becoming too individualistic— the unspoken message in most companies is that freedom in dress may be a privilege of rank. Remember, too, that these guides for dress, including the remainder of the chapter, apply to selling *yourself* in job interviews.

The nonverbal messages that salespeople emit through appearance should be positive in all sales situations. Characteristics of the buyer, cultural aspects of a sales territory, and the type of product being sold all determine a mode of dress. In considering these aspects, create a business wardrobe that will send positive, nonverbal messages in every sales situation. Once you have determined appropriate dress and hairstyle, the next nonverbal communication channel to consider is your contact with a prospect through the handshake.

Shake Hands Firmly and Look 'em in the Eye. The handshake is said to have evolved from a gesture of peace between warriors. By joining hands, two warriors were unable to bear arms against one another (assuming that a shield—not a weapon—was held in the other hand).

Today, a handshake is the most common way for two people to touch one another in a business situation, and some people feel that it is a revealing gesture. A firm handshake is more intense and is indicative of greater liking and warmer feelings. A prolonged handshake is more intimate than a brief one, and it could cause the customer discomfort, especially in a sales call on a new prospect. A loosely clasped, cold, or limp handshake is usually

FIGURE 4.3   The correct clothes, grooming, attitude, and physical conditioning all contribute to success. This applies to your career as well as interviewing and life.

• *Choose a suit that means business.*

• *Natural fibers, a proper fit, and current styling are important.*

• *A navy pinstripe is a must in anyone's wardrobe.*

• *Keep sports clothes conservative. Find special career lines that retailers offer.*

• *Men and women should consider the looks of their hairstyles and eyewear.*

interpreted as aloof and unwilling to become involved. This "cold fish" handshake is also perceived as unaffectionate and unfriendly.

General rules for a successful handshake include extending your hand first—if appropriate. Remember, however, a few people may be uncomfortable shaking hands with a stranger. At times, you may want to allow your customer to initiate the gesture. Maintain eye contact with the customer during the handshake, gripping the hand firmly. These actions allow you to initially establish an atmosphere of honesty and mutual respect—starting the presentation in a positive manner.

FIGURE 4.3 *(concluded)*

• *Some companies do not allow facial hair.*

• *A navy or gray suit, a tailored blouse, jewelry, and a briefcase project a professional image.*

• *Physical fitness produces the stamina and positive mental attitude needed to win in your career and life.*

• *Attention to personal grooming is a must for both men and women.*

• *Correct outerwear is important, too.*

Body Languages Gives You Clues

From birth, people learn to communicate their needs, likes, and dislikes through nonverbal means. The salesperson can learn much from a prospect's raised eyebrow, a smile, a touch, a scowl, or reluctance to make eye contact during a sales presentation. The prospect can communicate with you literally without uttering a word. An ability to interpret these signals is an invaluable tool to the successful sales professional. In conjunction with interpretation of body language, the salesperson's skillful use and control of physical actions, gestures, and overall body position is also helpful.

FIGURE 4.4 Five main nonverbal body movement communication channels

· *Body angle*   · *Face*   · *Hands*

· *Arms*   · *Legs*

The buyer can send nonverbal signals via five communication modes, as shown in Figure 4.4. They are: the body angle, facial expression, arm movement or position, hand movements or position, and leg position. Likewise these modes can generally send three basic types of messages: (1) acceptance, (2) caution, and (3) disagreement.

Acceptance signals indicate that your buyer is favorably inclined toward you and your presentation. These signals give you the green light to proceed. While this may not end in a sale, at the least the prospect is saying, "I am willing to listen." What you are saying is both acceptable and interesting. Some common acceptance signals are:

· **Body angle**—leaning forward or upright at attention
· **Face**—smiling, pleasant expression, relaxed, eyes examining visual aids, direct eye contact, positive voice tones.
· **Hands**—relaxed and generally open, perhaps performing business calculations on paper, holding on as you attempt to withdraw a product sample or sales materials, firm handshake.
· **Arms**—relaxed and generally open.
· **Legs**—crossed and pointed toward you or uncrossed.

Salespeople frequently rely only on facial expressions as indicators of acceptance. This practice may be misleading, since buyers may consciously control their facial expressions. Scan each of the five key body areas to verify your interpretation of facial signals. A buyer who increases eye contact, maintains a relaxed position, and exhibits positive facial expressions gives excellent acceptance signals.

Acceptance signals indicate that buyers perceive that they may have a need that your product might meet. You have obtained their attention and interest. You are free to continue with your planned sales presentation.

Caution signals should alert you that buyers are either neutral or skeptical toward what you say. Caution signals are indicated by:

- **Body angle**—leaning away from you.
- **Face**—puzzled, little or no expression, averted eyes or little eye contact, neutral or questioning voice tone, saying little, and then only asking a few questions.
- **Arms**—crossed, tense.
- **Hands**—moving, fidgeting with something, clasped, weak handshake.
- **Legs**—moving, crossed away from you.

Caution signals are important for you to recognize and adjust to for two main reasons. First, they indicate blocked communications. Buyers' perceptions, attitudes, and beliefs regarding your presentation may cause them to be skeptical, judgmental, or uninterested in your product. They may not recognize that they need your product or that it can benefit them. Even though you may have their attention, they show little interest in or desire for your product.

Second, if caution signals are not properly handled, they may evolve into disagreement signals, creating a breakdown in communication and making a sale difficult. Proper handling of caution signals requires that you:

- Adjust to the situation by slowing up or departing from your planned presentation.
- Use open-ended questions to encourage your buyers to talk and express their attitudes and beliefs. "Have you ever been interested in improving efficiency of your workers?" or "What do you think about this benefit?" are examples of open-ended questions.
- Carefully listen to what buyers say and respond directly.
- Project acceptance signals. Be positive, enthusiastic, and smile. Remember, you are glad to be there to help buyers satisfy their needs. Refrain from projecting caution signals even if a buyer does so. If you project a positive image in this situation, there is greater probability that you will change a caution light to a green one and make the sale.

Your objective in using these techniques is to change the caution signal to the green, go-ahead signal. If you continue to receive caution signals, proceed carefully with your presentation. Be realistic, alert to the possibility that the buyer may begin to believe your product is not beneficial and begin sending disagreement or red-light signals.

Disagreement signals tell you immediately to stop the planned presentation and quickly adjust to the situation. Disagreement, or red-light signals, indicate that you are dealing with a person becoming uninterested in your product. Anger or hostility may develop if you continue the presentation. Your continuation can cause a buyer to feel an unacceptable level of sales pressure resulting in a complete communication breakdown. Disagreement signals may be indicated by:

- **Body angle**—retracted shoulders, leaning away from you, moving the entire body back from you or wanting to move away.
- **Face**—tense, showing anger, wrinkled face and brow, little eye contact, negative voice tones, may become suddenly silent.
- **Arms**—tense, crossed over chest.
- **Hands**—motions of rejection or disapproval, tense and clenched, weak handshake.
- **Legs**—crossed and away from you.

You should handle disagreement signals, as you do caution signals, by using open-ended questions, and by projecting acceptance signals. There are four additional techniques to use. First, stop your planned presentation. There is no use in continuing until you have changed disagreement signals into caution or acceptance signals. Second, temporarily reduce or eliminate any pressure on the person to buy or to participate in the conversation. Let the buyer relax as you slowly move back to selling. Third, let your buyer know you are aware that something upsetting has occurred. Show that you are there to help, not to sell at any cost. Finally, you may wish to use direct questions to determine a buyer's attitudes and beliefs such as, "What do you think of . . . ?" or "Have I said something you do not agree with?"

Body Guidelines. Over time, you should know customers well enough to understand the meaning of their body movements. Although a prospect may say "no" to making a purchase, body movements may indicate uncertainty. As Richard Dreyfuss says in the movie *The Goodbye Girl,* "Your lips say *no, no, no,* but your eyes say *yes, yes, yes!*" This phrase sometimes hold true for selling.

Figure 4.5 relates some common nonverbal signals that buyers may give off.[3] The interpretation of most body language is obvious. However, be cautious in interpreting an isolated gesture, such as assuming that little eye contact means the prospect is displeased with what you are saying. Instead, concentrate on nonverbal cues that are part of a cluster or pattern. Let's say your prospect begins staring at the wall. That is a clue that may mean nothing. You continue to talk. Now, the prospect leans back in the

FIGURE 4.5   What nonverbal signals are these buyers giving to you?

 1. When you mention your price, this purchasing agent tilts her head back, raises her hands and assumes a rigid body posture. What nonverbal signals is she communicating and how would you move on with the sale?

 2. As you explain your sales features, this buyer looks away, clasps his hands, and crosses his legs away from you. What nonverbal signals is he communicating and how would you move on with the sale?

 3. As you explain the quality of your product, this company president opens his arms and leans toward you. What nonverbal signals is he communicating and how would you move on with the sale?

Answers to Figure 4.5

1. Your buyer is sending red signals. That means you are facing nearly insurmountable barriers. You've got to stop what you are doing, express understanding, and redirect your approach.
2. This buyer is sending yellow signals that warn you to exercise caution. Your own words and gestures must be aimed at relaxing the buyer or he may soon communicate red signals.
3. This buyer is sending green signals that say: everything is "go." With no obstacles to your selling strategy, simply move on to the close.

chair. That is another clue. By itself, it may be meaningless, but in conjunction with the first clue, it begins to take on meaning. Now, you see the prospect turn away, legs crossed, brow wrinkled. You now have a cluster of clues, all forming a pattern. It is time to adjust or change your presentation.

In summary, remember that nonverbal communication is well worth considering in selling. A salesperson ought to:

- Be able to recognize nonverbal signals.
- Be able to interpret them correctly.
- Be prepared to alter a selling strategy by slowing, changing, or stopping a planned presentation.
- Respond nonverbally and verbally to a buyer's nonverbal signals.

Effective communication is essential in making a sale. Nonverbal communication signals are an important part of the total communication process between buyer and seller. Professional salespeople seek to learn and understand nonverbal communication as a way of increasing their sales success.[4]

BARRIERS TO COMMUNICATION

Like the high hurdler, a salesperson often must overcome a multitude of obstacles. These obstacles are more aptly called "barriers to communication." Consider this example:

Salesperson Joe Jones heard that the XYZ Company buyer, Jake Jackson, was displeased with the company's present supplier. Joe had analyzed XYZ's operation and knew that his product could save the company thousands of dollars a year. Imagine Joe's surprise when Jackson terminated the visit quickly with no sale and no mention of a future appointment.

Joe told his boss about the interview. "Jackson kept asking me where I went to school, whether I wanted coffee, and how I liked selling, while I was trying to explain to him the features, advantages, and benefits of our product. Suddenly, Jackson stopped the interview." Joe asked the boss, "What did I do wrong? I know he needed our product."

The buyer was sending Joe signals that he likes doing business with people he knows. He did not want to get down to business immediately. He wanted to visit for a while. There was never any true communication established between Jackson and Jones, causing Jones to misread the customer and incorrectly handle the situation.

Salespeople, as illustrated in this example, often lose a sale after failing to recognize communication barriers between buyer and seller. The main reasons communication breaks down in the sales situation are:

1. **Differences in Perception.** If the buyer and seller do not share a common understanding of information contained in the presentation, communication will break down. The closer a buyer's and seller's perceptions, attitudes, and beliefs, the stronger communication will be between them.

2. **Buyer Does Not Recognize a Need for Product.** Communication barriers exist if the salesperson is unable to convince the buyer of a need, and/or that the salesperson represents the best supplier to buy from.

3. **Selling Pressure.** There is a fine line between what is acceptable sales pressure or enthusiasm and what the buyer perceives as a high-pressure sales technique. A pushy, arrogant selling style can quickly cause the prospect to erect a communication barrier.

4. **Information Overload.** You may present the buyer with an excess of information. This overload may cause confusion, perhaps offense, and the buyer will stop listening. The engineer making a presentation to a buyer who is not an engineer may concentrate on the technical aspects of a product, while the buyer only wants a small amount of information.

5. **Disorganized Sales Presentation.** Sales presentations that seem unorganized to the buyer tend to cause frustration, even anger. Buyers commonly expect you to understand their needs or problems and to customize your sales presentation to their individual situation. If you fail to do this, communication can break down.

6. **Distractions.** When a buyer receives a telephone call or someone walks into the office, distractions occur. A buyer's thoughts may become sidetracked, and it may be difficult to regain attention and interest.

7. **Poor Listening.** At times, the buyer may not be listening to you. This often occurs if you do all or most of the talking, not allowing the buyer to participate in the conversation.

The seven barriers to communication listed above are not the only ones that may occur. Mainly, it is important to understand that communication barriers can exist. As in the example of Joe Jones, the buyer may actually need the product and the salesperson may have excellent product knowledge and believe that a good sales presentation was made, yet because of communication barriers, the buyer rejects the salesperson and the product. As a salesperson, constantly seek ways of recognizing and overcoming communication barriers, and identify and satisfy buyer needs through persuasive communication.

MASTER PERSUASIVE COMMUNICATION AND YOU MAINTAIN CONTROL

To become a better communicator, you need to consider two major elements of communication. First, always strive to improve the message delivered in the sales presentation. You need to be a capable encoder. Second, improve your ability to determine what the buyer is communicating to you. Therefore, you need to be a good listener or decoder. A good sales communicator knows how to effectively encode *and* decode during a presentation.

Salespeople want to be good communicators to persuade people to purchase their products. **Persuasion** means the ability to change a person's belief, position, or course of action. The more effective you are at communicating, the greater your chances of being successful at persuasion.

The chapters on the selling process go into greater detail on specific persuasion techniques. For now, let's review several general factors to consider in developing persuasive communications. These factors relate to several components of the communication model shown in Figure 4.1: feedback, empathy, simplicity, listening, attitude, and proof statements.

Feedback Guides Your Presentation

Learn how to generate feedback to determine whether your listener has received your intended message. Feedback does not refer to just any type of listening behavior by the buyer, but to a recognizable response from the buyer. A shake of the head, a frown, or an effort to say something are all signals to the salesperson. If the salesperson fails to notice or respond to these signals, no feedback can occur, which means faulty or incomplete communication. A salesperson's observation of feedback is akin to an auto racer's glances at the tachometer. Both aid in ascertaining a receiver's response.

Often, feedback must be sought openly because the prospect will not always give it voluntarily. By interjecting into the presentation questions that require the customer to give a particular response, you can stimulate feedback. Questioning, sometimes called probing, allows the salesperson to determine the buyer's attitude toward the sales presentation.

Fisk Telephone Systems, Inc., included this type of feedback in their sales training sessions. Fisk sales trainers suggested to their salespeople that they use questions in their presentations. Some of the questions were:

- Do you think you are paying too much for telecommunications equipment?
- Are you happy with the service now being provided?
- Are you happy with the equipment your present supplier has installed for your company?

These questions were intended to draw negative responses from the customers concerning the relationship with their present supplier. They provided the Fisk salespeople with a method of determining how the prospect felt about the competitor. These responses allow the salesperson to discuss the specific features, advantages, and benefits of Fisk products relative to the products presently used by the prospect. Thus, in planning your presentation, it is important to predetermine when and what feedback-producing questions to ask. One way of creating positive feedback is through empathy.

Empathy Puts You in Your Customer's Shoes

Empathy is the ability to identify and understand the other person's feelings, ideas, and situation. As a salesperson, you need to be interested in what the buyer is saying, not just in giving your sales presentation. Many

SELLING   TIPS

Don't Complicate Things

How Can You Simplify the Following Statements?

1. A mass of concentrated earthly material perennially rotating in its axis will not accumulate an accretion of bryophytic vegetation.

2. Individuals who are perforce constrained to be domiciled in vitreous structures of patent frangibility should on no account employ petrous formations as projectiles.

3. A superabundance of talent skilled in the preparation of gastronomic concoctions will impair the quality of a certain potable solution made by immersing a gallinaceous bird in embullient Adam's ale.

Answers:
1. A rolling stone gathers no moss. 2. People who live in glass houses shouldn't throw stones. 3. Too many cooks spoil the broth.

of the barriers to communication mentioned earlier can be overcome when you place yourself in the buyer's shoes. Empathy is saying to a prospect, "I'm here to help you," or asking, "Tell me your problems and needs so I can help *you.*" Empathy is also evidenced by a salesperson's display of sincerity and interest in the buyer's situation.

This may mean acknowledging from time to time that a prospect may not truly need your product. Take, for example, the Scott Paper Company salesperson who finds that the customer still has 90 percent of the paper towels purchased three months ago. There is no reason to sell this customer more paper towels. It is time to help the customer sell the paper towels now on hand by suggesting displays, price reductions, and formats for newspaper advertisements. It is wise always to adopt your customer's point of view to meet the customer's needs best.

Keep It Simple, You Silver-Tongued Devil

The new salesperson was sitting in a customer's office waiting for the buyer. Her boss was with her. As they heard the buyer come into the office, the sales manager said, "Remember, a **KISS** for him." No, he was not saying to give the buyer a kiss, but to use the old selling philosophy of **K**eep **i**t **s**imple, **s**alesperson.

The story is told of a little old lady who went into a hardware store. The clerk greeted her and offered her some help. She replied that she was looking for a heater. So the clerk said, "Gee, are you lucky! We have a big sale on these heaters, and a tremendous selection. Let me show you." So, after maybe 30 or 45 minutes of discussing duothermic controls, heat induction, and all the factors involved with how a heater operates, including the features and advantages of each of the 12 models, he turned to the little old lady and said, "Now, do you have any questions?" To which she replied, "Yes, just one, Sonny. Which one of these things will keep a little old lady warm?"

An overly complex, technical presentation should be avoided when it is unnecessary. Use words and materials that are understood easily by the buyer. The skilled salesperson can make a prospect feel comfortable with a new product or complex technology through the subtle use of nontechnical information and a respectful attitude.

Creating Mutual Trust Develops Friendship

Salespeople who develop a mutual trust relationship with their customers cannot help being successful. This type of relationship eventually results in high "source credibility" and even friendship.

The buyer realized that in the past she was sold products that performed to expectations; the products were worth their price; and the salesperson did everything promised. Building mutual trust is important to effective long-run communication.

Listening Clues You In

Hearing refers to being able to detect sounds. **Listening** means getting meaning from sounds that are heard. Everything you hear is not worth your undivided attention; for the salesperson, however, listening is a communication skill critical to success.

Salespeople often believe that their job is to talk rather than listen. If they both talk *and* listen, their persuasive powers will increase. Since people can listen (about 400 words per minute) roughly twice as fast as the average rate of speech, it is understandable that a person's mind may wander while listening to a salesperson's presentation or that the salesperson may tune out a prospect. To keep the buyer listening to you, ask questions, get the buyer involved in the conversation, show visual aids. Once you ask a question, carefully listen to what is said.

Listen to Words and Thoughts. This may seem obvious, but when someone speaks to you, the person is expressing thoughts and feelings. Despite the logic of this statement, most of us listen only to the words being said. Spoken language is an inexact form of communication, but it is the best we have in this stage of evolution. If you come back 2,000 years from now, perhaps you will communicate with your prospects via mental telepathy. For now, given the limitations of words, look beyond them to hear the entire story.

Listen *behind* the words for the emotional content of the message. This is conveyed in the nuances of voice and body language. Some people, such as sensors (discussed in Chapter 3) on the one hand, will give you very little emotional information. That's all right, because you will deal with them in

MAKING THE SALE

Do You Have Any of These Listening Habits?

No one is perfect. We all have some bad listening habits that we get away with when we talk to our family and friends. In a business context, however, leave these bad habits behind and practice active listening. To gain insight into your listening habits, read through this list of common irritating listening habits and be honest with yourself; mark those that you are guilty of and use this awareness to begin eliminating them:

1. You do all the talking.
2. You interrupt when people talk.
3. You never look at the person talking or indicate that you are listening.
4. You start to argue before the other person has a chance to finish.

5. Everything that is said reminds you of an experience you've had, and you feel obligated to digress with a story.
6. You finish sentences for people if they pause too long.
7. You wait impatiently for people to finish so that you can interject something.
8. You work too hard at maintaining eye contact and make people uncomfortable.
9. You look as if you are appraising the person talking to you, looking him or her up and down as if considering the person for a job as a model.
10. You overdo the feedback you give—too many nods of your head or "uh-huh's."

a factual, business-only style. Feelers, on the other hand, will reveal their emotions, and in turn, they will appreciate your acknowledgement of their feelings. It will be appropriate to discuss their feelings and treat them more as friends than as strict business associates.

There are several ways to hear the emotions behind the words. First, look for changes in eye contact. After establishing a comfortable and natural level of eye contact, any sudden deviations from the norm will tip you off to emotional content in the message. People tend to look away from you when they talk about something embarrassing. When this happens, make a quick mental note of what it pertained to and treat that subject delicately. Also give a person the courtesy of looking away momentarily yourself, as if you are saying, "I respect your privacy."

Listen *between* the words for what is not said. Some people reveal more in what they don't say. Part of this is due to the emotional content of the message and part is due to the information they give you. A story will illustrate this point.

A salesperson was talking to the president of a large paper mill. "I simply asked him what kind of training he had for his salespeople. He went into a long discourse on all the seminars, training films, videotapes, and cassettes they had from the parent company, suppliers, industry associations, and in-house programs. I sat, listened, and took notes. At the end of his speech, I said to him, 'I noticed you didn't mention anything about time management for salespeople.' He raised his voice and emphatically said, 'You know, just this morning I was talking to a guy and I told him we have to have some time-management training for our salespeople.'''

The lesson here is to get the prospect talking and listen actively. Take notes, look for clues to emotions, and don't interrupt or start thinking about your next question. Concentrate.

The Three Levels of Listening. Whenever people listen, they are at one of the three basic levels of listening. These levels require various degrees of concentration by the listener. As you move from the first to the third level, the potential for understanding and clear communication increases dramatically.

Marginal Listening. Marginal listening, the first and lowest level, involves the least concentration, and typically the listener is easily distracted by her own thoughts. During periods of marginal listening, a listener will exhibit blank stares, nervous mannerisms, and gestures that tend to annoy the prospect and cause communication barriers. The salesperson hears the message, but it doesn't sink in. There is enormous room for misunderstanding when a salesperson is not concentrating on what is said. Moreover, the prospect cannot help but feel the lack of attention, which insults him and diminishes trust. It may be funny in comedy when family members continually patronize each other with, "Yes dear," regardless of what is said. In real life, however, it is not funny:

PROSPECT: What I need, really, is a way to reduce the time lost due to equipment breakdowns.

SALESPERSON: Yeah, OK. Let's see, uh, the third feature of our product is the convenient sizes you can get.

Salespeople of all experience levels are guilty of marginal listening. Beginners who lack confidence and experience may concentrate so intensely on what they are supposed to say next that they stop listening. Old pros, by contrast, have heard it all before. They have their presentations memorized and want the prospect to hurry up and finish so the "important" business can continue. These traditional salespeople forget that the truly important information lies in what the prospect is saying.

Evaluative Listening. Evaluative listening, the second level of listening, requires more concentration and attention to the speaker's words. At this level, the listener is actively trying to hear what the prospect is saying but isn't making an effort to understand the intent. Instead of accepting and trying to understand a prospect's message, the evaluative listener categorizes the statement and concentrates on preparing a response.

The evaluative listening phenomenon is a result of the tremendous speed at which a human can listen and think. It is no surprise that evaluative

SELLING TIPS

Listening Guidelines

Here are several things to do for improving your listening skills:

- Stop talking.
- Show the prospect you want to listen.
- Watch for nonverbal messages and project positive signals.

- Recognize feelings and emotions.
- Ask questions to clarify meaning.
- If appropriate, restate the prospect's position for clarification.
- Listen to the full story.

listening is the level of listening we use most of the time. Unfortunately, it is a difficult habit to break, but it can be done with practice:

> PROSPECT: What I need, really, is a way to reduce the time lost due to equipment breakdowns.
>
> SALESPERSON: (defensively) We have tested our machines in the field, and they don't break down often.

In this example, the salesperson reacted to one aspect of the prospect's statement. Had the salesperson withheld judgment until the end of the statement, he could have responded more objectively and informatively.

In evaluative listening, it is easy to be distracted by emotion-laden words. At that point, you aren't listening to the prospect. Instead, you are obsessed with the offensive word and wondering what to do about it. This is a waste of time for both you and the prospect. It increases personal and relationship tension and throws your communication off course. To avoid the problems of marginal and evaluative listening, practice active listening.

Active Listening. Active listening is the third and most effective level of listening. The active listener refrains from evaluating the message and tries to see the other person's point of view. Attention is not only on the words spoken but on the thoughts and feelings they convey. Listening in this way means the listener puts herself into someone else's shoes. It requires the listener to give the other person verbal and nonverbal feedback.

> PROSPECT: What I need is a way to reduce the time lost due to equipment breakdowns.
>
> SALESPERSON: Could you tell me what kind of breakdowns you have experienced?

In the example above, the salesperson spoke directly to the prospect's concerns, not around them. Her desire to make a presentation was deferred so she could accomplish a more important task: effectively communicate with the prospect.[5]

Active listening is a skill that takes practice in the beginning, but after a while, it becomes second nature. The logic behind active listening is based on courtesy and concentration, as noted in the listening guidelines.

Active listening is sometimes difficult to do, especially for the novice salesperson. The novice may continue to talk about a particular situation or problem. However, the salesperson must *learn to listen*. It is a key to sales success. People like and appreciate a listener as this unknown author says so well:

> *His thoughts were slow,*
> *His words were few,*
> *And never made to glisten.*
> *But he was a joy*
> *Wherever he went.*
> *You should have heard him listen.*
> —*Author Unknown*

Record What Went On.   A distinction must be drawn between listening and remembering. Listening is the process of receiving the message the way the speaker intended to send it. **Memory** is simply recall over time. Listening and time have profound effects on memory. An untrained listener is likely to understand and retain only about 50 percent of a conversation. After 48 hours, this relatively poor retention rate drops 25 percent. Think of the implications. Memory of a conversation that occurred more than two days ago may be incomplete and inaccurate.

After you leave the prospect's office, take a few minutes to write down, or put in a computer, what occurred during the sales call (see Figure 4.6). This is valuable information for doing what you promised and planning the next sales call.

Your Attitude Makes the Difference

While a variety of methods and techniques exist in selling, truly effective sales persuasion is based on the salesperson's attitude toward the sales job and customers. The most important element of this attitude is the salesperson's degree of interest and enthusiasm in helping people to fulfill their needs. This is the foundation for building effective communication techniques. **Enthusiasm** is a condition in which an individual is filled with excitement toward something. "Excitement" does not mean an aggressive attitude, but rather a positive view toward solving the customers' problems.

You need to sell yourself *on* yourself and *on* being a salesperson. The highly successful salesperson goes all out in helping customers. You should strive to make the buyer feel important. Show the buyer that you are there

FIGURE 4.6   Tom Dwyer finds that the lap top computer helps record what occurred in his sales calls.

solely as a problem-solver. Do this by developing methods of expressing true interest such as asking questions, instead of talking at the buyer. This type of attitude will in turn benefit you by allowing you to look at the sales situation from the buyer's viewpoint (empathy).

Salespeople who have established **credibility** with their customers through continued empathy, willingness to listen to specific needs, and continual enthusiasm toward their work and customers' business can make claims that their customers treat as "gospel" in some cases. Enthusiasm combined with proof statements greatly improve a salesperson's persuasive ability.

Proof Statements Make You Believable

Salespeople have known for years that the use of highly credible sources can improve persuasiveness of the sales presentation message. **Proof statements** are statements that substantiate claims made by the salesperson. Pharmaceutical companies often quote research studies done by outstanding physicians at prestigious medical schools to validate claims of product benefits. These proof statements add high credibility to a sales message.

Salespeople sometimes quote acknowledged experts in a field on the use of products. By demonstrating that other customers or respected individuals use the products, they encourage customer belief in the validity of information presented in a sales presentation. People place greater confidence in a trustworthy, objective source (particularly one not associated with the salesperson's firm) and are therefore more receptive to what is said by the salesperson.

SUMMARY OF MAJOR SELLING ISSUES

Communication is defined as transmission of verbal and nonverbal information and understanding between salesperson and prospect. Modes of communication commonly used in a sales presentation are: words, gestures, visual aids, and nonverbal communication.

A model of the communication process is composed of a sender (encoder) who transmits a specific message via some media to a receiver (decoder) who responds to that message. The effectiveness of this communication process can be hampered by noise that distorts the message as it travels to the receiver. A sender (encoder) can judge the effectiveness of a message and media choice by monitoring the feedback from the receiver.

Barriers, which hinder or prevent constructive communication during a sales presentation, may develop or already exist. These barriers may relate to the perceptional differences between the sender and receiver, outside distractions, or how sales information is conveyed. Regardless of their source, these barriers must be recognized and either overcome or eliminated if communication is to succeed.

Nonverbal communication has emerged as a critical component of the overall communication process within the past 10 or 15 years. Recognition of nonverbal communication is essential for sales success in today's business environment. Awareness of the prospect's territorial space, a firm and confident handshake, and accurate interpretation of the language of body and limb positioning is a tremendous aid to a salesperson's success.

A salesperson's overall persuasive power is enhanced through the development of several key characteristics. The salesperson who creates a relationship based on mutual trust with a customer by displaying true empathy (desire to understand customer's situation and environment), a willing ear (more listening, less talking), and a positive attitude of enthusiastic pursuit of lasting solutions to that customer's needs and problems, greatly increases the likelihood of making that sale—not just in the short run, but over the long haul.

5

So, What Do I Need to Know?

My name is Michael Bevan, and I'm 31 years old. I went to the University of Toronto for one year. I chose to go into business in 1975, and from then until December 1984, I held a variety of positions with Coronet Carpets, Ltd., Ivac Canada, and Milliken Contract Carpets. In December 1984, I began my current position as executive vice president of Parbron International in Canada. In the time I've been with Parbron, sales have risen from $85,000 to $5 million.

We are currently in the commercial carpet and floor systems business. We install raised marketplace computer floors and commercial carpet to many of the Fortune 500 companies in Canada. We represent every major brand in Canada.

I think a college degree gives more discipline to a person, but I prove that you don't need it if you have the innate ability to sell. I think that a four-year program at a university helps develop the discipline required to do a job properly. If I had an option, I would have preferred to finish my degree.

One reason students should choose a career in sales is that, without the sale, nothing goes. If you don't sell something, nothing gets manufactured or bought, and the whole cycle stops. To be a sales representative for any company is exciting, because you are the reason that company will become successful, and you're only held back by your abilities. The career path is endless.

Long hours are a part of sales. When I put in long hours to build something, it's very fulfilling. I don't have difficulty with long hours; I probably work from 6:30 in the morning until 6:30 or 7:00 at night. That's a full 12-hour day; and it's not with a two-hour executive lunch. It means being on hand all the time. If a customer wants to see me on a weekend, I'm there because I have to be there; the customer needs me. I don't like to do it; I don't want to compromise my family—but they recognize that I have to build a business, and that takes commitment. •

Michael Bevan
Parbron International

"We'll do things like design carpets and work on the colorations with the interior design firms," says Michael Bevan. "We develop specifications, and design custom products and logos. We're capable of doing virtually anything that can go on floors. We'll work very closely with someone like Crosby-Couristan Carpets. We'll bring them into it and develop a pricing scheme and product deliveries, and work directly for the end user.

"In our business, being successful takes a lot of knowledge. The key is understanding every aspect of the business. This involves working with the design concept (developing a color, texture, and style for the interior design) and working with the architectural company (meeting the architect's requirements). It also involves working with the end user and assuring him that the other two steps are correct because he's the one who has to live with that whole scenario.

"Finally, we are involved in installing the product. We have on our staff 65 installers who will complete the job for the end user. We must understand every single stage from the beginning right through to the end much better than our competition.

"Since I have a background in manufacturing, I think I have a lead against my competitors in the marketplace, because I understand how a manufacturer works. That alone, encompassed with a lot of knowledge, will allow us to have an edge against competition." •

Successful salespeople, such as Michael Bevan, keep current on information concerning the company, product, distribution, promotion, pricing, competition, industry trends, and the economy. This chapter examines areas of information that are essential to the success of all salespeople.

WHERE'D YOU LEARN THAT? SOURCES OF SALES KNOWLEDGE

Knowledge for selling is obtained in two ways. First, most companies provide some form of formal sales training. This information is taught through preliminary training programs and sales meetings. Second, the salesperson learns by being on the job. Experience is the best teacher for the beginning salesperson.

Sales training is the effort put forth by an employer to provide the opportunity for the salesperson to receive job-related culture, skills, knowledge, and attitudes that result in improved performance in the selling environment.

John H. Patterson, founder of the National Cash Register Company and know as the "father of sales training," used to say, "At NCR our salesmen never stop learning."[1] This philosophy is the reason that successful companies thoroughly train new salespeople and maintain ongoing training programs for their experienced sales personnel. Companies are interested in training primarily to increase sales volume, salesperson productivity, and profitability.

Like many professional careers, selling is a skill that is truly developed only through *experience*. Sales knowledge obtained through education, reading, formalized sales training, and word-of-mouth is helpful in enhancing overall sales ability, but actual experience is the critical source of sales knowledge. Some sales managers will hire only experienced people to fill entry-level selling slots. Indeed, some corporations will not allow people to fill marketing staff positions unless they have had field sales experience with the company or a major competitor.

Sales experience makes for a better salesperson by: showing how buyers perceive a product or product line; revealing unrecognized or undervalued product benefits or shortcomings; voicing a multitude of unanticipated protests and objections; showing a great number of prospect moods and attitudes over a short period; and generally providing a challenge that makes selling a skill that is never truly mastered, only improved. No author or sales trainer can stimulate the almost infinite variety of situations that a salesperson confronts over the span of a career. Authors and trainers can provide only general guidelines as a framework for action. Actual selling experience alone gives a person direct feedback on how to function in a specific selling situation.

The sales knowledge gained through periodic sales training and actual experience benefits not only the salesperson but also the firm and its customers.

WHY SALESPEOPLE REQUIRE KNOWLEDGE

A knowledgeable salesperson provides better service to customers.[2] Knowledge based on experience should result in increased sales. However, there are two other important reasons for the salesperson to have selling knowledge. These are (1) to increase the salesperson's self-confidence and (2) to build the buyer's confidence in the salesperson. These reasons are, for the salesperson, the major need for acquiring sales knowledge.

Knowledge Increases Confidence in Salespeople . . .

Salespeople who call on, for example, computer systems engineers, university professors, or aerospace experts may be at a disadvantage. In many cases, they will have less education and experience than prospects in their fields of expertise.

Imagine making a sales call on Dr. Michael DeBakey, the distinguished heart surgeon. Can you educate him in the use of your company's synthetic heart valves? Not really, but you can offer help in supplying product information from your firm's medical department. This personal service, your product knowledge, and his specific needs are what will make the sale. Knowledge about your company, its market, and your buyer enables you to acquire confidence in yourself, ultimately resulting in increased sales.

. . . and in Buyers

Furthermore, prospects and customers want to do business with salespeople who know their business and the products they sell. When a prospect has confidence in the salesperson's expertise, a sales presentation becomes more acceptable and believable to the prospect.

Strive to be "the" expert on all aspects of your product. Knowledge of your product and its uses also allows you to confidently answer questions and field objections raised by prospects. You can explain better how a product suits a customer's needs. But product knowledge alone may not be enough to convince every buyer.

Know Your Firm

Knowledge of your firm sometimes aids you in projecting an "expert" image to the prospect. Company knowledge includes information of the history, policies, procedures, distribution systems, promotional activities, and pricing practices that have guided the firm to its present status.

The type and extent of company knowledge to be used depends on the company, its product lines, and the industry. (See Figure 5.1.) In general, consumer goods salespeople require little information about the technical nature of their products; however, selling high-technology products (computers, rocket engine components, complex machinery, etc.) to highly knowledgeable industrial buyers requires extensive knowledge.

General Company Information

All salespeople need to know the background and present operating policies of their company. These policies are your guidelines, and you must understand them to do your job effectively. Information on company growth, policies, procedures, production, and service facilities may often be used in sales presentations. Here are four examples:

Company Growth and Accomplishment. Knowledge of your firm's development since its origin provides you with promotional material and builds your confidence in the company. An IBM office products salesperson might say to a buyer:

> In 1952, IBM placed its first commercial electronic computer on the market. That year, our sales were $342 million. Currently, our sales are projected to be over $54 billion. IBM has reached these high sales figures because our

FIGURE 5.1   What would you need to know for selling. . . .

• . . . *Fragrances to retail customers?*   • . . . *Engine components to rocket scientists?*

advanced, technological office equipment and information processors are the best available at any price. This IBM "Star Trek I" system I am showing you is the most advanced piece of equipment on the market today. It is five years ahead of any other computer!

Policies and Procedures. To give good service, be able to tell a customer about policies: how an order is processed; how long it takes for orders to be filled; your firm's returned goods policy; how to open a new account; and what to do in the event of a shipping error. If you handle these situations quickly and fairly, your buyer will gain confidence in your and the firm.

Production Facilities. Many companies require their new salespeople to tour their production facilities to give them a first-hand look at the company's operations. This is a good opportunity to gain product knowledge. For example, the Bigelow-Sanford Carpet Company salesperson can say, "When I was visiting our production plant, I viewed each step of the carpet production process. The research and development department allowed us to watch comparison tests between our carpets and competitor's carpets. Our carpets did everything but fly . . . but they are working on that!"

Service Facilities. Many companies have both service facilities and service representatives to help customers. Being able to say, "We can have a service representative here the same day you call our service center," strengthens a sales presentation, especially if service is important for the customer (as it is in the office copier and computer industries).

KNOW YOUR PRODUCT

Knowledge about your company's product and your competitor is a major component of sales knowledge. Become an expert on your company's products. Understand how they are produced, and their level of quality. This type of product knowledge is important to the buyer.

Product knowledge may include such technical details as:

- Performance data.
- Physical size and characteristics.
- How the product operates.
- Specific features, advantages, and benefits of the product.
- How well the product is selling in the marketplace.

Many companies have their new salespeople work in the manufacturing plant (for example, on the assembly line), or in the warehouse (filling orders and receiving stock). This hands–on experience may cost the salesperson a lot of sweat and sore muscles for a couple of weeks or months, but the payoff is a world of product knowledge and help in future selling that could not be earned in any other way. U.S. Steel, for example, has its new salespeople spend several weeks in a production plant. Often, new salespeople in the oil and gas industry find themselves roughnecking and driving trucks during the first few months on the job. Also, a sales representative for McKesson Chemical is apt to spend the first two or three weeks on the job in a warehouse unloading freight cars and flatbed trucks and filling 55-gallon drums with various liquid chemicals.

Much is learned at periodic company sales meetings. At sales meetings, a consumer goods manufacturer may concentrate on developing sales presentations for the products to receive special emphasis during the company sales period. Company advertising programs, price discounts, and promotional allowances for these products are discussed. Although little time is spent on the technical aspects of consumer products, much time is devoted to discussing the marketing mix for these products (product type, promotion, distribution, and price).

Sales managers for technical products might spend as much as 75 percent of a sales meeting discussing product information. The remaining time might be allotted to sales techniques.

In many cases, distributors of low-priced, high-volume products (food retailers, for instance) or users of high-priced "critical components" (tires for autos) are equally or more concerned with how quickly and by what means they will receive a product. This involves an important kind of information: knowledge of your firm's channels of distribution.

A LITTLE KNOWLEDGE OF DISTRIBUTION CAN GO A LONG WAY

It is essential to understand the channel of distribution used by your company to move its products to the final consumer. Knowledge of each channel member (also called middleman) is also vital. Wholesalers and retailers often stock thousands of products, and each may have hundreds of salespeople, like you, from a multitude of companies calling on its buyers. Know as much about each channel member as possible. Some important information you will need includes:

- Likes and dislikes of each channel member's customers.
- Product lines and the assortment each one carries.
- When each member sees salespeople.
- Distribution, promotion, and pricing policies.
- What quantity of which product each channel member has purchased in the past.

While most channel members will have similar policies concerning salespeople, keep abreast of the differences between them.

Conflict and Cooperation in Distribution Channels

A **trade channel** is ideally a group of firms acting together to move goods from the manufacturer to users. Yet, power struggles exist in distribution channels. Wholesalers may resist buying a new product until it is actually demanded by their retail customers. Supermarket retailers may already have 12 different brands of hand soap, toothpaste, or cookies. Why should they buy another brand that comes in three sizes? If they were to buy this new product, would a present product need to be dropped?

What about the large retailer, such as Sears or Safeway, that typically demands special favors such as products built to specifications, lower prices, and special delivery from the manufacturer? The manufacturer selling to mass merchandisers who discount their products may find it difficult to convince nondiscounters, like Sears, to help sell these products.

These are just a few examples of the type of channel conflicts you may have to face. If the problem turns into a stalemate, the channel member affected by the problem may be forced to take an alternative course of action. If wholesalers will not cooperate as the manufacturer wishes, the manufacturer may sell only to retailers. If a manufacturer will not cooperate with a wholesaler or retailer, that wholesaler or retailer may begin manufacturing its own "house brand" products.

These alternative solutions can be costly to both parties involved in terms of lost sales, or the additional costs incurred. Both manufacturers and their channel members can promote a spirit of cooperation by establishing policies and taking actions to benefit their channel counterparts.

Cooperation from the Manufacturer. The manufacturer should enable its salespeople to offer their wholesalers and retailers:

- A reasonable assortment of products that are properly designed, reasonably priced, and available in the quantities requested.
- Deletion of individual products from the product line when needed.
- A fair or proportionate amount of advertising for new products (when applicable) to build product demand.
- A pledge to honor service guarantees and to refund or replace damaged merchandise.
- Regular sales call schedule on wholesalers and retailers.
- Reasonable estimates of product quantities to stock or order.
- Useful market information.

By treating each channel member as a partner rather than an adversary, and considering their viewpoints, you can reduce channel conflicts for the manufacturer.

Cooperation from the Channel Member. Likewise, wholesalers and retailers should consider the manufacturer's point of view. Often, a manufacturer has spent years developing a product, and is prepared to spend millions of promotional dollars to introduce the product to the market. Failure by a channel member to stock a new product, or in some cases to carry adequate quantities of a new product, can jeopardize the tremendous investment in time, capital, and human resources that the manufacturer has made.

What can channel members do to cooperate with the manufacturer?

- Give careful consideration to the sale proposal of a manufacturer's salesperson, especially those representing large suppliers.
- Provide their employees with essential product information.
- Carry an adequate product supply.
- Properly display and price products to avoid consumer confusion.
- Advertise and promote as agreed to by manufacturer's salesperson.
- Honor manufacturer's warranties and coupons.
- Pay bills on time.

While periodic channel conflicts are almost unavoidable, cooperation between channel members is important for efficient movement of goods from manufacturer to end user. Although they may seem fairly obvious, the actions and policies suggested here are important to stress. They can aid channel members in avoiding costly conflicts, thereby furthering the efficient diffusion of industrial and consumer goods.

In many cases, the manufacturer or channel member's sales representative is the medium through which channel-smoothing policies are administered. In this important function, effective salespeople can benefit employers, customers, and themselves. Channel cooperation aids salespeople by increasing sales revenue and maintaining long-run supplier relationships. Another help comes from advertising.

ADVERTISING AIDS SALESPEOPLE

Personal selling, advertising, publicity, and sales promotion are the main ingredients of a firm's promotional effort. Companies sometimes coordinate these three promotional tools in a promotional campaign. A sales force may be asked by the corporate marketing manager to concentrate on selling product A for the months of April and May. Meanwhile, product A is simultaneously promoted on television and in magazines, and direct mail samples or cents-off coupons for product A are sent to consumers.

Keeping abreast of your company's advertising and sales promotion activities is a must. By incorporating this data into your sales presentation, you can provide customers with a world of information that they probably knew little about, and that could secure the sale. Table 5.1 illustrates the type of advertising and sales promotion you would use when making a sales presentation for a mouthwash called Fresh Mouth. Suppose Fresh Mouth was a new product and had just emerged from the test market. As a lead-in to the information in Table 5.1, you might say:

> Ms. Buyer, Fresh Mouth was a proven success in our Eastern test markets. Fresh Mouth had a 9.8 percent market share only nine months after the start of advertising. Laboratory tests proved that the Fresh Mouth formula is superior to that of the leading competition. Consumer panels significantly preferred Fresh Mouth to leading competing brands. There was a repurchase rate of 50 percent after sampling. The trade (retailers) gave enthusiastic support in the test market areas.

Now you would discuss the information contained in Table 5.1.

Types of Advertising Differ

The development and timing of an advertising campaign for a product or service is handled by a firm's advertising department or by an outside advertising agency. The result of this effort is the television commercial, radio spot, print media (newspaper or magazine), or other form of advertisement (billboard, transit placard, etc.). Following development of the ad, the firm must establish and coordinate a plan for tying in sales force

TABLE 5.1   Example of advertising and sales promotion information
salesperson tells buyer

1. **Massive sampling and couponing:**
   - There will be a blanketing of the top 300 markets with 4.4-oz. samples plus eight-cents-off coupons. Your market is included.
   - There will be a 75 percent coverage of homes in the top 100 markets. Your market is included.
2. **Heavy advertising:**
   - Nighttime network TV.
   - Daytime network TV.
   - Saturation spot TV.
   - Newspapers.
   - The total network and spot advertising will reach 85 percent of all homes in the United States five times each week, based on a four-week average. This means that, in four weeks, Fresh Mouth will have attained 150 million home impressions—130 million of these will be women.
   - There will be half-page, two-color inserts in local newspapers in 50 markets, including yours. This is more than 20 million circulation. Scheduled to tie in with saturation sampling is a couponing program.
   - $15 million will be spent on promotion to ensure consumer acceptance.
3. **TV advertising theme**—the salesperson would show pictures or drawings of the advertisement:
   - The commercial with POWER to sell!
   - "POWER to kill mouth odor—POWER to kill germs—POWER to give FRESH MOUTH."
   - The commercial shows a young male, about 20 years of age, walking up to a young girl, saying, "Hi, Susan!" They kiss and she says, "My, you have a fresh mouth, Bill!" He looks at the camera with a smile and says, "It works!" The announcer closes the commercial by saying, "FRESH MOUTH—it has the POWER!"
4. **Display materials:**
   - Shelf display tag.
   - Small floor stand for end-of-aisle display—holds two dozen 12-oz. bottles.
   - Large floor stand—holds four dozen 12-oz. bottles.

efforts with the new ad campaign. There are six basic types of advertising programs that a company can use: national, retail, cooperative, trade, industrial, and direct-mail advertising.

National advertising: Designed to reach all users of the product, whether consumers or industrial buyers. These ads are shown across the country. In some cases, national advertisers may restrict their expenditures to the top 100 markets. "Top 100" refers to the 100 largest major metropolitan areas where most of the U.S. population is concentrated. Therefore, the advertiser gets more punch per ad dollar. Giant marketing

TABLE 5.2   A typical advertising aggrement

BACTERIA FIGHTERS INCORPORATED
Advertising Agreement
between
Bacteria Fighters Inc.
and
the Undersigned Account

1. APPLICABILITY: This agreement provides for special advertising services on **Fresh Mouth.**

2. AVAILABILITY: This agreement is available on proportionally equal terms to all competing accounts who purchase **Fresh Mouth** during the period of December 1', 1990, to January 31, 1991, on one order with split shipments acceptable. Straight stock purchases of the 6 Fl. Oz., 12 Fl. Oz., 15 Fl. Oz., 24 Fl. Oz. (1 Pt. 4 Fl. Oz. Marked Weight) sizes may be applied to the total advertising fund.

3. AMOUNT OF EARNINGS AVAILABLE:

	No. of Dozens Purchased		Adv. Allowance Rate per Dozen		Total Fund
Fresh Mouth 24 Fl. Oz. Size	_____	×	40¢	=	_____
Fresh Mouth 18 Fl. Oz. Size	_____	×	30¢	=	_____
Fresh Mouth 12 Fl. Oz. Size	_____	×	20¢	=	_____
Fresh Mouth 6 Fl. Oz. Size	_____	×	10¢	=	_____
			TOTAL FUND	=	_____

4. ADVERTISING SERVICES REQUIRED: Account agrees to advertise **Fresh Mouth** in print and/or radio and/or television at least once during the period January 31, 1991, to April 30, 1991, subject to the following terms and conditions:

    a. For the purpose of this agreement the term "print" means newspapers and/or other print media having a circulation or not less than 3,000.

    b. Radio and/or television advertising is also acceptable under this agreement.

    c. Advertising must include retail price, and/or number of Bonus Trading Stamps, and/or other special consumer incentive.

    d. Any advertising furnished under this agreement shall not be considered as advertising furnished under any other agreement.

5. RATES OF PAYMENT: Subject to the maximum fund available. **B.F. Inc.** will pay to accounts the allowances as set forth in #3 above for Account's print and/or radio and/or television advertising of any size(s) of **Fresh Mouth.**

6. CERTIFICATION AND PAYMENT:

    a. Print Media—Payment for newspaper and other print media features will be made after receipt by **Fresh Mouth** of a properly executed certificate of performance accompanied by newspaper advertising tear sheets or copies of other print media used, together with an affidavit indicating the date, method, and extent of circulation.

    b. Radio and/or Television—Payment for radio and/or television features will be made after receipt by **B.F. Inc.** of a properly executed certificate of performance and Account's statement certifying the number, date, time, and type of radio and/or television features run, accompanied by affidavits from an authorized representative of the station(s), or other satisfactory proof, that such announcements were so broadcast over said station(s).

7. CANCELLATION: Any funds for which payment has not been applied by June 30, 1991, shall be cancelled and **B.F. Inc.** shall have no further liability to account with respect thereto. No amount claimed to be due hereunder is to be deducted from any invoice.

8. TERMINATION: This agreement may be terminated at any time by either party on fifteen (15) days' written notice.

9. MODIFICATION: **B.F. Inc.** representatives are not authorized to modify or waive any provisions of this agreement.

TABLE 5.2 *(concluded)*

Bacteria Fighters Inc.

_____	_____
B.F. Inc. Representative's Signature	Print Account's Name
_____	_____
Region Unit No.	Account's Signature
Date _____ , 199___	_____
	Advertising As
	_____
	Street Address
	_____
	City State

CERTIFICATE OF PERFORMANCE

This is to certify that we have accepted delivery of the goods and have performed the services required under the **B.F. Inc.** agreement dated _____ and are entitled to $_____ Total.

	_____
	Dealer's Name IBM No.
_____	_____
B.F. Inc. Representative's Signature	Dealer's Signature
Date_____ , 199___	

companies like Procter & Gamble, IBM, Ford, Holiday Inn, and Coca-Cola commonly use national advertising.

Retail advertising: Used by a retailer to reach customers within its geographic trading area. Local supermarkets and department stores regularly advertise nationally distributed brand products. National-brand advertising may be totally paid for by the retailer, or partially paid by the manufacturer.

Cooperative or **"co-op" advertising:** Refers to advertising conducted by the retailer with cost paid for by the manufacturer or shared by the manufacturer and retailer.[3] It is an attractive selling aid for the salesperson to give the buyer an "advertising allowance" to promote a firm's goods.

Table 5.2 shows an advertising agreement between a retailer and a manufacturer. The agreement provides for:

- The duration (time period) of the advertisement.
- The product(s) to be advertised.
- The amount of money paid to the retailer for advertising purposes (based on amount and sizes of product purchased).

- The type of advertising.
- Proof by the retailer that the product has been advertised as agreed (a copy of the advertisement).

Cooperative advertising follows a simple cycle. After agreeing on the size of the order, you (the salesperson) and the buyer complete the advertising agreement and both sign it. You then give the buyer a copy of the signed agreement. On your next sales visit, the retailer gives you a copy of the advertisement. Again, both of you sign the agreement, and you send the signed agreement and the advertisement to the appropriate company personnel. In response, your office sends you the reimbursement check, and on your next sales call you give the check to the buyer. The cycle ends.

An advertising agreement, skillfully employed, is an effective selling tool. The salesperson with a positive attitude toward making the sale will already have an advertising agreement filled out before seeing a retail buyer. Based on past sales and future sales potential, and using this advertising money, the salesperson can present a "suggested order" for the buyer. After discussing the information in Table 5.2, the salesperson might close the sale by saying:

> Considering the size of your store, your past purchases, and the promotional campaign my company has suggested for Fresh Mouth, I suggest you buy 12 dozen of the 24 oz. size, 14 dozen of the 18 oz. size, and 24 dozen of the 12 oz. size, and 12 dozen of the 6 oz. size. Let's reduce the price of the 18 oz. size and advertise it. I will build you a display over on that wall and pay $54 of your advertising cost. (The salesperson hands the filled-out contract to the buyer.)

Generally, national and retail advertising is aimed at the final consumers. Trade and industrial advertising are aimed at other members in the channel of distribution and other manufacturers.

Trade advertising: Undertaken by the manufacturer and directed toward the wholesaler or retailer. Such an advertisement appears in trade magazines serving only the wholesaler or retailer. (Figure 5.6 on page 150 is an example of a manufacturer advertising to retail pharmacies in the popular trade magazine *American Druggist*.)

Industrial advertising: Aimed at individuals and organizations who purchase products for manufacturing other products. General Electric may advertise small electric motors in magazines read by buyers employed by firms such as Whirlpool or Sears.

Direct-mail advertising: Mailed directly to the consumer or industrial user; an effective method of exposing these users to a product, or a reminder that the product is available to meet a specific need. Often, trial samples or coupons accompany the direct-mail piece.

Direct-mail advertising can solicit a response from a current user of a product. For example, the user may be asked to fill out and mail in a

TABLE 5.3   Top 10 U.S. advertisers

Rank			Total U.S. Ad Spending ($000)		
1987	1986	Advertiser/Headquarters	1987	1986	Percent Change
1	2	**Philip Morris Inc.,** New York	$1,557,846	$1,451,170	7.4
2	1	**Procter & Gamble Co.,** Cincinnati	1,386,710	1,500,268	−7.6
3	5	**General Motors Corp.,** Detroit	1,024,852	838,912	22.2
4	3	**Sears, Roebuck & Co.,** Chicago	886,529	1,105,398	−19.8
5	4	**RJR Nabisco,** Atlanta	839,589	894,237	−6.1
6	10	**PepsiCo, Inc.** Somers, N.Y.	703,973	641,538	9.7
7	34	**Eastman Kodak Co.,** Rochester, N.Y.★	658,221	610,192	7.9
8	8	**McDonald's Corp.,** Oak Brook, Ill.	649,493	591,808	9.7
9	6	**Ford Motor Co.,** Dearborn, Mich.	639,510	650,875	−1.7
10	7	**Anheuser-Busch Cos., Inc.** St. Louis	635,067	643,893	−1.4

★Reflects acquisition of Sterling Drug.

questionnaire. In return, the manufacturer sends the user a sample of the product, or information about the product.

Why Spend Money on Advertising?

Table 5.3 lists the 10 U.S. companies that spent the most money on advertising in 1985. Why would a company spend so many millions on advertising? Companies advertise because they hope to:

• Increase overall sales and sales of a specific product.
• Pave the way for their salespeople by building product and/or company recognition. (See Figure 5.2.)
• Give salespeople additional selling information for sales presentations.
• Develop leads for salespeople (through mail-ins, ad response, etc.).
• Increase cooperation from channel members (through co-op advertising and promotional campaigns).
• Help educate the customer about the company's products.
• Inform prospects that a product is on the market and where to buy it.
• Aid in reducing cognitive dissonance over the purchase.
• Create sales or presell customers between a salesperson's calls.

Advertising serves a variety of purposes, depending on the nature of a product or industry. The majority of the 10 top advertisers listed in Table 5.3 are well-known manufacturers of consumer goods.[4] This indicates that advertising dollars are lavished on consumer items. However, as industrial advertising has more specified channels of communication (such as trade periodicals and trade shows) and a smaller number of potential customers, advertising costs tend to be lower. In either case, carefully employed advertising benefits both a firm and its sales force. Sales promotion is another potential aid to a company and its sales force.

FIGURE 5.2   Advertising can pave the way for salespeople

"*I don't know who you are.*
I don't know your company.
I don't know your company's product.
I don't know what your company stands for.
I don't know your company's customers.
I don't know your company's record.
I don't know your company's reputation.
Now—what was it you wanted to sell me?"

MORAL: Sales start **before** your salesman calls—with **business** publication advertising.

McGRAW-HILL MAGAZINES
BUSINESS • PROFESSIONAL • TECHNICAL

SALES PROMOTION GENERATES SALES

Sales promotion involves activities or materials other than personal selling, advertising, and publicity used to create sales for goods or services. Sales promotion can be divided into consumer and trade sales promotion. **Consumer sales promotion** includes free samples, coupons, contests, and demonstrations to consumers. **Trade sales promotion** encourages resellers to purchase and aggressively sell a manufacturer's products by offering incentives like sales contests, displays, special purchase prices, and free merchandise (for example, buy 10 cases of a product and get 1 case free).

The company's promotional efforts can be a useful sales tool for an enterprising salesperson. Sales promotion offers may prove to the retailer or wholesaler that the selling firm will assist actively in creating consumer

FIGURE 5.3   Examples of point-of-purchase displays

  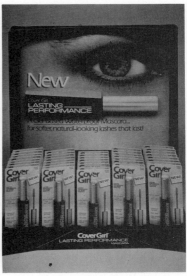

• *General Mills' Mark Failor made two sales. He sold this Kroger grocery store a promotional-size order of Cheerios, and he had to sell the store manager on allowing him to build this giant display.*

• *This Noxell salesperson's Cover Girl floor stand draws shoppers to it.*

• *Counter displays are effective because a product is easily seen and purchased.*

demand. This in turn improves the salesperson's probability of making the sale. Some of the more popular sales promotion items, which we will briefly discuss, are: point-of-purchase displays, shelf positioning, and consumer and dealer premiums, including contests and sweepstakes.

Point-of-Purchase Displays: Get 'em Out There

Point-of-purchase (POP) displays allow a product to be easily seen and purchased. A product POP display may include photographs, banners, drawings, coupons, a giant-sized product carton, aisle dumps, counter displays, or floor stands. POP displays greatly increase product sales. It is up to the salesperson to obtain the retailer's cooperation to allow the POP display in the store.

Figure 5.3 shows Mark Failor of General Mills making a giant display

MAKING THE SALE

Get the Buyer Interested!

Kathyleen Paynter of Campbell Soup believes that a large part of her job involves getting retailers to promote her products in their stores. Kathyleen says:

"Aside from basic selling skills, I think two very important selling aids are enthusiasm and imagination to get the buyer interested in the sale. Using imaginative selling ideas will get the buyer's attention and make him interested in the sale. Dare to do something different or 'crazy' to get attention. If applicable, sampling your product—in my case, out of a thermos—is a great way to get even the busiest buyer to talk with you.

"Here are some unusual selling ideas I've had success with:

- I once made a cookie shaped like a V8 trademark to sell a 50-case display, advertisement, and feature of V8 products.
- I made a 6½-foot Chunky Soup Robot out of excess point-of-sale material to sell a large Chunky Soup display.
- I helped a product manager win a Caribbean cruise by designing a Soup'n'Celery tie-in display, and dressing up as a can of soup and getting his wife to dress as a stalk of celery."

The use of unusual display pieces and costumes gets the store personnel and customers interested in a display and, therefore, increases sales—and that helps everyone.

of Cheerios. People are attracted to displays. They catch the customer's attention and make products easy to purchase, which results in increased product sales.

Shelf Positioning Is Important to Your Success

Another important sales stimulator is the shelf positioning of products. **Shelf positioning** refers to the physical placement of the product within the retailer's store. **Shelf facings** are the number of individual products placed beside each other on the shelf. Determine where a store's customers can easily find and examine your company's products, and place products in that space or position with as many shelf facings as the store will allow. Figure 5.4 shows how a General Mills' salesperson effectively obtained excellent shelf positioning and multiple shelf facings in a retail grocery outlet.

The major obstacle faced when attempting to obtain shelf space for products is limited space. A retail store has a fixed amount of display space—and thousands of products to stock. You compete for shelf space with other salespeople and with the retailer's brands.

FIGURE 5.4   Shelf positioning and shelf facings will stimulate sales

• *Mark Failor of General Mills obtained excellent shelf positioning and shelf facings. He knows this will boost sales. Mark also places a 79-cent shelf-talker by the product to help attract shoppers' attention.*

It is often up to the salesperson to sell the store manager on purchasing different sizes of a particular product. Also, the salesperson may want a product displayed at several locations in the store. A Johnson & Johnson salesperson may want J&J baby powder and baby shampoo displayed with baby products and adult toiletries.

SAMI Data Helps Get Shelf Space.   **SAMI (Selling Areas—Marketing, Inc.)** is a company that supplies sales data (**SAMI data**) to manufacturers who sell through retail food stores. This data shows manufacturers the movement of products to retail food stores from wholesale warehouses in 54 major television market areas that contain about 88 percent of national food sales. These warehouses contract to provide SAMI with this information every four weeks on computer cards or tapes. This service provides manufacturers who sell to warehouses with sales data both for their brands and for competitors.

Manufacturers, in turn, relay this information to salespeople as an aid in promoting certain products to retail buyers and to improve shelf positioning for products. The Quaker Oats Company is one of many food companies that provide salespeople with SAMI information.

Suppose a Quaker salesperson finds that a supermarket has 100 feet of shelf space allocated to dog food, and that Quaker Ken-L-Ration Kibbles-'n'Bits has five feet of shelf space. In checking SAMI data, the salesperson finds that Kibbles'n'Bits has a 10 percent market share in the retailer's trading area. Given this discrepancy, the Quaker salesperson now has a logical reason as to why the store buyer should allow an increase in shelf space for this product from 5 to 10 feet. Such a move could increase Kibbles'n'Bits sales in that store, benefiting both the retailer and Quaker.

Premiums

The premium has come a long way from being just a trinket in a Cracker Jack box. Today, it is a major marketing tool. American businesses spend billions of dollars on consumer and trade premiums and incentives.[5] Premiums create sales.

A **premium** is an article of merchandise offered as an incentive to the user to take some action. The premium may act as an incentive to buy, to sample the product, to come into the retail store, or to stir interest so the user will request further information. Premiums serve a number of purposes: to promote consumer sampling of a new product; to introduce a new product; to encourage point-of-purchase displays; and to boost sales of slow products. Figure 5.5 presents the three major categories of premiums: (1) contests and sweepstakes, (2) consumer premiums, and (3) dealer premiums.

Contests and Sweepstakes Are Fun. **Contests and sweepstakes** are popular premium offers. Coca-Cola, for example, offered consumers the chance to win up to $1,000 by completing the phrase "Coke, The Real Thing" with words found under Coke, Tab, and Sprite bottle caps marked with a number "1." General Mills once offered a one-week family vacation to Nashville, Tennessee, plus $5,000 to consumers who redeemed 10-cents-off coupons on the back of boxes of Golden Grahams cereal.

Consumer Premiums Get Cooperation. The widest variety of premiums are directed at consumers. When a company has offered a premium for a product, its salespeople can use that premium in sales presentations for two

FIGURE 5.5   Examples of premiums

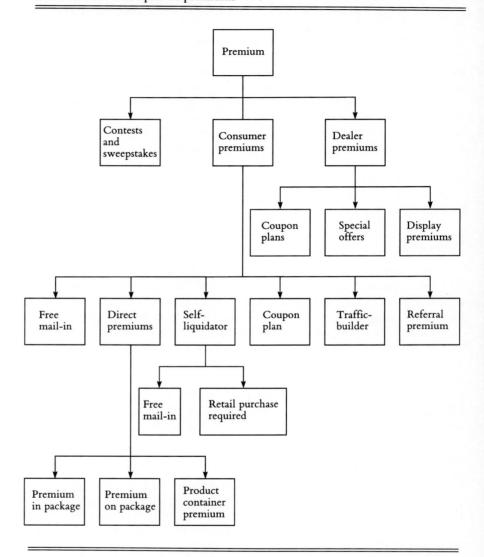

reasons. First, the premium can be used to help make a sale. Second, the premium can be used to urge the customer to buy a larger than normal quantity of the product. Six types of **consumer premiums** commonly used by companies are shown in Figure 5.5.

The consumer can "mail in" for a premium, or receive the premium (a direct premium) when the product is purchased. The third type of consumer premiums are called self-liquidators. These are an offer to sell a second product, usually at a reduced cost, when the consumer sends in proof of purchase of buying a first product. The salesperson says to the buyer, "This month we have a self-liquidator with Gillette Foamy Shave Cream. Your customer buys Foamy and sends in your sales receipt and for $1 they will receive a Gillette Trac II shaver and blades. This should increase your normal sales 10 percent." In another instance, Gillette has attached razors to cans of Foamy, making it a direct premium.

Coupon plans, the fourth type of consumer premium, require the buyer to save each coupon received from the purchase of a product and trade in accumulated coupons for merchandise. For example, the Betty Crocker coupon program promotes Gold Medal flour, Wheaties, and Bisquick. Coupons taken from packages of these goods can be exchanged for silver-plated flatware.

Free products offered to customers who come in to see a product demonstration are called traffic-builders. For example, an appliance dealer might offer a plastic laundry basket to homeowners who come into the store to examine a line of washers and dryers. An auto dealership may give a free U.S. road map to individuals who test-drive a new automobile.

Many people believe that the best form of advertising is a satisfied customer. This type of customer can positively influence someone else's attitude toward a product. The referral premium plan works this way: You have sold your product to Ms. Young. She liked it. You ask her for the names of one or more friends who have seen the product and might be prospective buyers. You offer her an attractive premium if any of her friends or neighbors buys your product.

If carefully designed and administered, consumer premiums can benefit all parties involved—consumer, wholesaler, retailer, sponsoring firm, and salesperson. Premiums also work when directed at distributors.

Dealer Premiums. Premiums are usually consumer-oriented. Yet, many companies also offer premiums to middlemen, as channel members. There are three principal types of **dealer premiums:**

1. The *coupon plan* offers the dealer a choice of items from a catalog in return for coupons included with purchases of the manufacturer's product.
2. The *special deal* is a "one-shot" premium tied to the purchase of products.
3. The *display premium* allows the retailer who buys a product to get and keep a store display. The salesperson tells the buyer, "With your purchase of 20 dozen assorted toothbrushes, you will receive free this beautiful, high-quality display rack worth $50. You can place it on this shelf and it will hold all of your various brands of toothbrushes."

The grocery, drug and toiletries, and automotive supply industries are several major users of dealer premiums. Although promotional devices are often extremely effective selling aids, customers are still concerned with unit price, quantity discounts, and credit terms. Therefore, these are key areas of selling knowledge.

WHAT'S IT WORTH? PRICING YOUR PRODUCT

An important part of a comprehensive marketing strategy for a product is establishing its price. **Price** refers to the value or worth of a product that attracts the buyer to exchange money or something of value for the product or service. A product has some want-satisfying attributes for which the prospect is willing to exchange something of value. The person's wants assign a value to the item offered for sale. For instance, a golfer who wants to purchase a dozen golf balls has already conceived some estimated measure of the product's value. Of course, the sporting goods store may have set a price higher than estimated. This could diminish want somewhat, depending on the difference between the two. Should the golfer then find the same brand of golf balls on sale at a discount store, at a price more in line with a preconceived idea of the product's value, the want may be strong enough to stimulate purchase of the product.

Many companies offer customers various types of discounts from normal prices to entice them to buy. These discounts become an important part of the firm's marketing effort. They are usually developed at the corporate level by the firm's marketing managers. Immediately before the sales period when the product's promotion begins, the sales force is informed of special discounts that they may offer to customers. This discount information becomes an important part of the sales presentation. It is important for salespeople to familiarize themselves with the company's price, discount, and credit policies so that they can use them to competitive advantage, as well as enhance their professional image with the buyer.

Types of Prices

While a firm may engage in many pricing practices, all companies have a list price, net price, and prices based on transportation terms. Five of the most common types of prices are defined as follows:

- **List price**—the standard price charged to customers.
- **Net price**—price after allowance for all discounts.
- **Zone price**—price based on geographical location or zone of customers.

- **FOB shipping point**—FOB (free on board) means the buyer pays transportation charges on the goods—the title to goods passes to the customer when they are loaded on shipping vehicles.
- **FOB destination**—seller pays all shipping costs.

These prices are established by the company. The salesperson is not normally involved in pricing the product. This type of pricing allows the salesperson to quote prices according to company guidelines.

Selling the same quantity of like products at different prices to two different industrial users or resellers is illegal. Laws such as the Robinson-Patman Act of 1936 forbid price discrimination in *interstate* commerce that will injure competition. While the law does not apply to sales within a state (intrastate sales), a majority of states have similar laws.

A company can justify different prices if it can prove to the courts that its price differentials do not substantially reduce competition. Often, companies justify price differentials by showing the courts one of two things. First, take the case of one customer buying more of a product than another. For the customer purchasing larger quantities, a firm can manufacture and market the products at a lower cost. These lower costs are passed on to the customer in reduced prices. Second, price differentials can be justified when a company must lower prices to meet competition. Thus, if justified, companies can offer customers different prices. They typically do this through discounts.

Discounts Lower the Price

Discounts are a reduction in price from the list price.[6] In developing a program to sell a product line over a specified period, marketing managers consider discounts along with the advertising and personal selling efforts engaged in by the firm. The main types of discounts allowed to buyers are quantity, cash, trade, and consumer discounts.

Quantity Discounts: Buy More, Pay Less. Quantity discounts result from the manufacturer's saving in production costs because it can produce large quantities of the product. As shown in Figure 5.6, these savings are passed on to customers who buy in large quantities using discounts. Quantity discounts are either noncumulative or cumulative.

One-time reduction in prices are **noncumulative quantity discounts,** which are commonly used in the sale of both consumer and industrial goods. The Schering salesperson might offer the buyer of Coricidin "D" a 16⅔ percent price reduction. The Colgate salesperson may offer the retailer 2 dozen of the king-size Colgate toothpaste free for every 10 dozen purchased.

FIGURE 5.6   Various types of promotional allowances available to resellers

GREAT NEW DEAL!
Four double-strength sizes to strengthen your profits!

Promotional Allowances					Promotional Support
Free-goods allowance*	Plus advertising allowance†		Plus merchandising allowance		Direct to consumer national TV promotion... 1.705 GRPs 88% reach 1.7 billion impressions Year-round physician detailing and sampling Major trade and medical journal advertising support
	Option A	Option B‡	Reduced price feature	Display	
12 oz liquid 8⅓% off invoice	Up to $1.25 per dozen	$1.00 per dozen	$.75 per dozen reduced price feature	$.75 per dozen floor or end cap display	
5 oz. liquid 8⅓% off invoice	Up to $.75 per dozen	$.50 per dozen	$.50 per dozen reduced price feature	$.50 per dozen floor or end cap display	
60s tablets 8⅓% off invoice	Up to $1.25 per dozen	$1.00 per dozen	$.75 per dozen reduced price feature	$.75 per dozen floor or end cap display	
24s tablets 8⅓% off invoice	Up to $.75 per dozen	$.50 per dozen	$.50 per dozen reduced price feature	$.50 per dozen floor or end cap display	

Also available—up to 2% billback allowance for four-color roto advertising or consumer coupon programs.
Unlimited purchases allowed for claiming billback allowances.
Retail buy-in period: July 15 through August 30, 1990.
Advertising performance period: July 15 through November 8, 1990.
Claim deadline: 45 days following appearance of ad.
Contact your Representative for complete details.

*Through participating wholesaler.
†All ads should feature both liquid and tablets.
‡Provided advertising coverage is in at least 75% of the applicant's trading area.

The salesperson is expected to use these discounts as inducements for the retailer to buy in large quantities. The sales goal is to get the customer to display and locally advertise the product at a price lower than normal. Ideally, the retailer's selling price should reflect the price reduction allowed because of the quantity discount.

Cumulative quantity discounts are discounts received for buying a certain amount of a product over a stated period, such as one year. Again, these discounts reflect savings in manufacturing and marketing costs.

To receive a 10 percent discount, a buyer may have to purchase 12,000 units of the product. Under the cumulative discount, the buyer would not be required to purchase the 12,000 units at the same time, say 1,000 units each month, for example. As long as the agreed-on amount is purchased within the specified time, the 10 percent discount on each purchase applies. A cumulative discount allows the buyer to purchase the products as needed rather than in a single order.

Cash Discounts: Get the Customer to Pay on Time. **Cash discounts** are earned by buyers who pay bills within a stated period. For example, if the customer purchases $10,000 worth of goods on June 1 and the cash discount is "2/10 net 30," the customer pays $9,800 instead of $10,000. "2/10 net 30" can be translated into a 2 percent discount if the bill is completely paid within 10 days of the sale. If the payment is not made within 10 days, the full $10,000 is due in 30 days. The salesperson might ask the buyer to reduce the price of the product to its net invoice costs and advertise it. The buyer's gross margin (profit) would be the 2 percent cash discount.

Trade Discounts Get Middlemen's Attention. The manufacturer may reduce prices to middlemen (channel members) to compensate them for the services they perform. These are **trade discounts.** The trade discount is usually stated as a percentage off of the list retail price. A wholesaler may be offered a 50 percent discount and the retailer offered a 40 percent discount off the list price. The wholesaler's price to its retail customers is 10 percent above its cost or 40 percent off the list price. The wholesaler earns a 10 percent gross margin on sales to retail customers. Middlemen are still eligible to earn the quantity and cash discounts.

Consumer Discounts Increase Sales. **Consumer discounts** are one-time price reductions passed on from the manufacturer to the middlemen or directly to the consumer. "Cents-off" product labels are price reductions passed directly to the consumer. A package marked 15 cents off each product or $1.80 a dozen uses a consumer discount.

The manufacturer expects middlemen to reduce the price from their normal price. A mass merchandiser might normally sell a product with a list price of $2.50 for $1.98. The manufacturer would want their salespeople to persuade the retailer to price the product 15 cents lower than the $1.98, or at a price of $1.83.

Cents-off coupons that the consumer brings to the retail store are another example of a temporary price discount. In both the cents-off and coupon examples, the manufacturer ensures that the price reduction is passed on to the consumer. This is done because the middlemen may not have promoted the product or reduced the price, keeping the quantity or off-invoice savings for themselves. An offer of a cents-off product label and coupons are used by the salesperson to sell larger quantities to customers. A summary of discounts, and examples of each, is provided in Table 5.4.

TABLE 5.4   Types and examples of discounts

Types of Discounts	Discount Examples
Quantity discount Noncumulative (one-time):	• Buy 11 dozen, get 1 dozen free. • 20 percent off on all purchases. • $5 off-invoice for each floor-stand purchase.
Cumulative (yearly purchases):	• 5 percent discount with purchase of 8,000 units. • 8 percent discount with purchase of 10,000 units. • 10 percent discount with purchase of 12,000 units.
Cash discounts:	• 2/10 end-of-month. • 2/10 net 30.
Trade discounts:	• 40 percent off to retailers. • 50 percent off to wholesalers.
Consumer discounts:	• 15 cents off regular price marked on product's package. • 10 cents-off coupon.

MARKUP REPRESENTS GROSS PROFIT

Markup refers to the dollar amount added to the cost of the product to get its selling price. Markup is often expressed as a percentage and represents gross profit, not net profit. **Gross profit** is the money available to cover the costs of marketing the product, operating the business, and profit. **Net profit** is the money remaining after the costs of marketing and operating the business are paid.

Figure 5.7 presents an example of markup based on a product's selling price for each channel-of-distribution member. Each channel member has a different percentage markup. The product that costs the manufacturer $3 to produce eventually costs the consumer $12. The manufacturer's selling price represents the wholesaler's cost. Price markups enable the wholesaler to pay business operating costs, to cover the product's cost, and to make a profit. The wholesaler's selling price of $6 becomes the retailer's cost. In turn, the retailer marks the product up to cover its cost, and the associated costs of doing business (such as stocking the product and allocation of "fixed costs" per square foot), and to maintain a desired level of profit.

The percentage markup is based on either the product's selling price or its cost. It is important to know which method of determining markup is used. Using manufacturer's cost of $3, markup of $2, and selling price of $5 shown in Figure 5.7, the methods of determining percentage markup can have different results, as shown below:

$$\text{Percentage markup on selling price} = \frac{\text{Amount added to cost}}{\text{Selling price}} = \frac{\$2.00}{\$5.00} = 40 \text{ percent}$$

FIGURE 5.7   Example of markup on selling price in channel of distribution

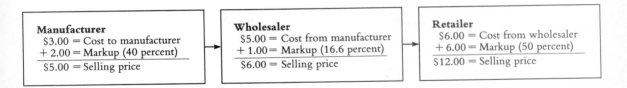

$$\text{Percentage markup on cost} = \frac{\text{Amount added to cost}}{\text{Cost}} = \frac{\$2.00}{\$3.00} = 66.6 \text{ percent}$$

In general, middlemen want to buy goods at low prices and establish selling prices at a competitive level that allows for a reasonable profit. Such objectives result in retailers having different markups on different goods. For example, a retailer may have markups of 10 percent on groceries, 30 percent on cameras, and 50 percent on houseware items. Based on the type of store (discount—high volume; specialty—low volume; department—high service), markups may vary greatly depending on the volume of sales and degree of service rendered.

In preparing the sales presentation for an individual customer, the salesperson should consider all the discounts available to suggest a promotional plan for the retailer. For example, the advertisement shown in Figure 5.6 illustrates several of the discounts a retailer can receive with the purchase of three decongestants. The salesperson can use these discounts in the sales presentation by suggesting that the retailer advertise the products at a reduced price and place the promotional displays by each of the store's cash registers.

Be Creative in Pricing

Salespeople often use creative pricing techniques when selling to retailers and helping them to resell products they have purchased. Take, for example, the RCA salesperson who presented a $100 promotional discount to a retailer and suggested that the retailer purchase 30 units and sell an $800 color television for $599. The salesperson pointed out that the retailer would still make the normal 50 percent markup as shown in Figure 5.8. The retailer said no, since even though the percentage gross profit (markup) would be the same, the actual dollar return would be too low. (Compare "Normal cost and profit" box with "Salesperson's first suggestion" in Figure 5.8.)

FIGURE 5.8   Examples of creative pricing

Normal cost and profit
$800 = Television retail price
− 400 = Normal cost
$400 = Markup (400/800 = 50 percent of retail price)

Deal cost and profit
$400 = Normal cost
− 100 = Promotional allowance
$300 = Deal Cost

Salesperson's first suggestion:
$599 = Promotional selling price
− 300 = Deal cost
$299 = Markup (299/599 = 50 percent of selling price)

Salesperson's second suggestion:
$799 = advertised price
− 350 = total cost ($300 deal cost plus $50 fan)
$450 = markup (450/800 = 56 percent of selling price)

The salesperson wasn't finished yet, however. After leaving the store briefly to visit a local appliance retailer who agreed to sell 30 ceiling fans (at a retail price of $99) for $50 each, the salesperson returned with a second suggestion: Advertise the televisions for $799 and offer a "free" ceiling fan with each purchase. As shown in Figure 5.8, the retailer would make a higher percentage markup of 56 percent and receive more actual cash— $450. The retailer agreed and purchased the fans. All 30 TV sets were sold in a single weekend! The salesperson used this same creative pricing technique for six other customers in different cities. The moral of this story is to look for new, creative ways to sell your product. If you combine a little extra effort with a little ingenuity, any sale is possible.

Customer Credit: Get 'em to Pay on Time

It is often the salesperson's responsibility to open up new accounts, see that customers pay on time, and collect overdue bills. Table 5.5 shows an example of a salesperson's customer accounts receivable and aged trial balance. Five customers are 30 days or more past due on paying their account balances.

The next time the salesperson calls, Jones Lumber and Hardware Unlimited may be required to pay at least their 90-day balance before any more products are ordered. Otherwise, friction could develop. The salesperson's credit department may prohibit further sales to overdue customers.

The salesperson should know the company's credit policies and receive a statement of the customer's accounts receivable. Given this information, this salesperson is prepared when the buyer from Jones Lumber appears:

TABLE 5.5 Example of a salesperson's customer accounts receivable and aged trial balance

Territory Number	Customer Number	Customer Name	Total Balance	Current Balance	30 Days	60 Days	90 Days	Sales to Date
043	00035	Ace Hardware	$ 943.65	$ 943.65				$ 5,628.11
043	00605	Jones Lumber	584.54	247.78	$ 85.55	$ 154.30	$ 96.91	626.76
043	01426	ABC Fix-it	1,103.69	377.04	435.14	291.51		1,434.17
043	39782	Hardware Unlimited	2,932.59	743.04	846.50	773.44	569.61	3,387.99
043	04568	McNeal Supplies	72.02		72.02			952.81
043	04569	Building Supplies	400.41	392.37	8.04			1,422.82
		Territory total or grand total	6,036.90	2,703.88	1,447.25	1,219.25	666.52	13,452.66

BUYER: Jill, send me $300 worth of your product.

SALESPERSON: Mr. Jones, you will have it next Friday. Would you have your bookkeeper make out a check for $336.76? I'll send it in with your order.

The $336.76 is the total past due amount owed by Jones Lumber to the salesperson's company, as shown in Table 5.5. The salesperson can get in a tough spot between serving her customer and her company. However, she must avoid bad-debt losses, and should politely get straight to the point with customers who are not paying their bills.

The sale is not complete until the product is paid for. If it is not paid for, both the salesperson and the company lose. The salesperson must know the customer's past and future ability to pay. Credit and payment cooperation between salesperson and customer results in better service to the customer and profitable sales for the salesperson.

KNOW YOUR COMPETITION, INDUSTRY, AND ECONOMY

What would the bank salesperson shown in Figure 5.9 need to know about competition, industry, and economic conditions important to selling her services? She needs to be knowledgable about such things as the economy's impact on interest rates; will interest rates increase or decrease; what interest rates are paid by other financial organizations; how do my services compare to competition; and what are people's attitudes toward banks in general and her bank.

Today's successful salespeople understand their *competitors'* products, policies, and practices just as well as their own. It is common for a buyer to ask a salesperson, "How does your product compare to the one I'm presently using?" If unable to confidently answer such a question, a salesperson will lose ground in the selling race. A salesperson needs to be prepared to discuss product features, advantages, and benefits in compari-

FIGURE 5.9   What does this salesperson need to know about competition, industry, and the economy?

son to other products, and confidently show why the salesperson's product will fulfill the buyer's needs better than competitive products.

One method to obtain information on competitors is through advertisements. From a competitor's advertising, Joe Mitchell, a salesperson representing a large business machines firm, developed a chart for comparing the sales points of his machines against the competition. Joe does not do this for fun, nor does he name the competitive equipment on the chart. Instead, he just calls them "Machine A, Machine B, Machine C, etc." When he finds a claimed benefit in one of the other machines, which his product does not have, he works to find a better benefit to balance it.

"Maybe the chart isn't always useful," Joe says, "but it certainly has prepared me to face a customer. I know just what other machines have— and what they do not have—that my prospect might be interested in. I know the principal sales arguments used in selling these machines and the benefits I must bring up to offset and surpass competition. Many times a prospect will mention an advertisement of another company and ask about some statement or other," Joe says. "Because I've studied those ads and taken the time to find out what's behind the claims, I can give an honest answer and also can point out how my machine has the same feature or quality, and then offer additional benefits. Of course, I never run down a competitor's product. I just try to run ahead of it."

TABLE 5.6   Top 10 PC applications

PC applications are focused on the customer. Here are the top 10 applications in order of use:

1. Customer/prospect profile.
2. Lead tracking.
3. Call reports.
4. Sales forecasts.
5. Sales data analysis.

6. Sales presentation.
7. Time/territory management.
8. Order entry.
9. Travel and expense reports.
10. Checking inventory/shipping status.

The salesperson selling industrial goods and the industrial buyer work for different companies but are both in the same industry. The industrial buyer often seeks information from salespeople on the *industry* itself, and how economic trends might influence the industry *and* both of their companies. Thus, the salesperson should be well informed on the industry and the economy. The salesperson can get this type of information from the company, newspapers, television, radio, *The Wall Street Journal,* industrial and trade periodicals, and magazines such as *Business Week* and *U.S. News & World Report.* The salesperson who is well informed will generally be more successful than the poorly informed salesperson.

PERSONAL COMPUTERS AND SELLING

The growing use of personal computers (PCs) by sales personnel indicates the need to learn about computers and how to use them. To the nontechnical person—and that includes many of us—the PC may cause an uncomfortable feeling at first. There is often apprehension about being able to use the PC and its software properly. However, computer manufacturers, software suppliers, and company training programs are quickly and effectively training people and providing easier-to-use computer software.

Sales personnel are finding PCs a valuable tool for increasing productivity within the sales force. The 10 most widely used applications of PCs are shown in Table 5.6.[7] Here are several major reasons for salespeople to use the PC:

- More effective management of sales leads and better follow-through on customer contacts. Computerization provides a permanent lead file.
- Improves customer relations due to more effective follow-ups. This leads to further productivity gains.
- Improves organization of selling time. PCs help reps keep track of everything.
- Provides more efficient account control and better time and territory management. There is a better awareness of each account's status. This provides more time for customer contacts.

FIGURE 5.10   The PC has numerous uses. This salesperson finds that the PC can develop professional-looking proposals and presentations.

- There is a definite increase in the number and quality of sale calls.
- Faster speed and improved accuracy in getting reports and orders to the company.
- Helps develop more effect proposals and persuasive presentations (see Figure 5.10).

If you have little or no knowledge about the computer—start learning! In your readings, look for how the computer is or can be used in your industry. Take a beginning computer course at a college or through your local public school's continuing education program. Computers are here to stay. It is never to late to learn.

SUMMARY OF MAJOR SELLING ISSUES

Company knowledge includes information on a firm's history, development policies, procedures, products, distribution, promotion, and pricing. A salesperson must also know the competition, the firm's industry, and the economy. This type of knowledge can even be used as an aid in improving one's self-concept. A high degree of such knowledge helps the salesperson build a positive self-image and feel thoroughly prepared to interact with customers.

Wholesalers and retailers stock thousands of products, often making it difficult for them to support any one manufacturer's products as wanted by the manufacturer. This situation may result in conflicts between members of the channel of distribution. To reduce these conflicts and aid middlemen in selling its products, manufacturers offer assistance in advertising, sales promotion aids, and pricing allowances. In addition, many manufacturers spend millions of dollars to compel consumers and industrial buyers to purchase from the middlemen and the manufacturer.

National, retail, trade, industrial, and direct-mail advertising are used to create demand for products and as a powerful selling tool for the salesperson in sales presentations. Sales promotion activities and materials are another potential selling tool for the salesperson to use in selling to consumer and industrial buyers. Samples, coupons, contests, premiums, demonstrations, and displays are effective sales promotion techniques that can be employed to help sell merchandise.

Price, discounts, and credit policies are additional facts the salesperson should be able to discuss confidently with customers. Each day the salesperson is involved in informing or answering questions posed by customers in these three areas. Customers always want to know the salesperson's list and net price, and if there are any transportation charges. Discounts (quantity, cash, trade, or consumer) represent important buying incentives offered by the manufacturer to the buyer. The buyer will want to know the terms of payment. The salesperson will need to understand company credit policies to open new accounts, see that customers pay on time, and collect overdue bills.

PART

The Dynamics of Selling

6

Find Your Prospect
Then Plan Your Sales Call

Vikki's company has four offices in Orange County, California, which are currently closing escrow on between $70 and $80 million a month in volume. Her office is in Huntington Beach, California. FirstTeam has over 200 agents and Vikki is their top producer. Her sales have topped $90 million, making Vikki the top salesperson in the United States and Canada.

Vikki Morrison
FirstTeam Walk-In Realty

Vikki strongly believes in effective sales prospecting. "Prospecting for business is the only way you can obtain clientele," says Vikki. "Each person you meet is a potential client; everyone, from your dry cleaner and your grocer, to local gas station owners, as well as my individual geographical residential areas I call a 'farm.' In my field, I contact a household on a once-a-month basis in hopes of establishing face-to-face contact, and a chance to chat with the homeowner." Vikki often knocks on doors of some 400 homes each month.

"After four or five contacts with the same individuals, and hopefully a positive response, I actually build a relationship with these people, based on friendship. I don't discuss selling real estate with them unless they bring up the subject. We are friends. We discuss everything else and I especially enjoy learning about their different talents and hobbies. There are some very unique people in the world if you take the time to find out about them.

"I plan each day in advance. I have a Day-Timer (appointment book) that I follow religiously. I go into my farm with 3x5 cards containing each person's name, address and any other pertinent information about them. I have been doing it for so long that if someone from my farm telephones and says, 'Hi, this is Sally Jones,' I can immediately picture her house and the street on which she lives. I can usually recall the names of her children and sometimes even that of her dog. I provide a number of services for these people throughout the year, and when they decide to sell their homes, they many times call me.

"Selling, to me, is the lifeblood of our economy. Salespeople lead the way for all forms of business. I love selling real estate, but I could sell anything I believe in." •

"Planned sales calls are a must," says IBM's Matt Suffoletto. "I begin my planning by carefully examining the account's situation and what product they will probably need. Then I review the latest trade journals for that industry's current trends. With this information, I develop several sales presentation scenarios with potential questions and answers that the consumer may wish me to discuss.

"While it is important to plan the presentation, you must be prepared to be flexible and anticipate the need to change your plan. A sales call must be fluid and dynamic based on your customer's actual situation and needs at the time of the call which is difficult to plan." •

The first two parts of this book give much of the background a salesperson needs for making an actual presentation. You can be the most knowledge-able person on topics such as buyer behavior, competitors, and product information, yet still have difficulty being a successful salesperson unless you are thoroughly prepared for each part of the sales call. Part III of this book examines the various elements of the sales process and sales presentation.

Vikki Morrison has introduced the importance of prospects and methods to obtain an appointment with the prospect. Later in this chapter, Matt Suffoletto's remarks on planning the sales call will be closely examined in a discussion of the four steps in planning. Let's begin by explaining what is meant by the sales process.

THE SALES PROCESS HAS 10 STEPS

As discussed in Chapter 1, the **sales process** refers to a sequential series of actions by the salesperson that leads toward the customer taking a desired action and ends with a follow-up to ensure purchase satisfaction. Although many factors may influence how a salesperson makes a presentation in any one situation, there does exist a logical, sequential series of actions that, if followed, can greatly increase the chances of making a sale. This selling process involves 10 basic steps as briefly listed in Figure 6.1. Steps one and two will be discussed in this chapter, and all steps will be discussed in greater detail in the following chapters. Steps three through nine compose the sales presentation itself. Before a sales presentation can be attempted, several important preparatory activities should be carried out.

FIGURE 6.1 The selling process has 10 important steps

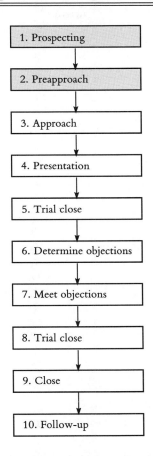

STEPS BEFORE THE SALES PRESENTATION

As indicated in Figure 6.2, a successful salesperson is involved in prospecting, obtaining an appointment with the prospect, and planning the sales interview prior to ever actually meeting with the prospect. Like a successful lawyer, the salesperson does a great amount of background work before meeting the judge—the prospect. One rule of thumb states that a good sales process involves 20 percent presentation, 40 percent preparation, and 40 percent follow-up, especially when selling large accounts. As in most professions, success in selling often requires as much or more

FIGURE 6.2 Before the sales presentation

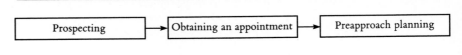

preparation before and between calls than is involved in actually making the calls themselves.

PROSPECTING—LIFEBLOOD OF SELLING

Prospecting is the first step in the selling process. A **prospect** is a qualified person or business that has the potential to buy your product or service. **Prospecting** is the lifeblood of sales because it identifies potential customers. There are two reasons that a salesperson must look constantly for new prospects: (1) to increase sales, and (2) to replace customers that will be lost over time.

A prospect should not be confused with a "lead." The name of a person or business who might be a prospect is referred to as a **lead.** A lead can also be referred to as a "suspect," indicating the person or business is suspected of being a prospect. Once the lead has been "qualified," the lead becomes a prospect.[1] You can ask yourself seven questions to determine if an individual or business is a **qualified prospect:**

1. Does this individual or business *need* my services or products?
2. Does this individual or business *perceive* a *need* or *problem* that may be satisfied by my product or *service?*
3. Does the individual or business have a sincere *desire* to fulfill this need or solve this problem?
4. Can this person's desire to fulfill needs or solve problems be converted into a *belief* that my product is needed?
5. Does this individual or business have the *financial resources* to pay?
6. Does the individual have the *authority* to buy?
7. Is this potential prospect's purchase large enough to be *profitable?*

The majority of salespeople operate in single sales territories containing customers, prospects, and leads. Although locating leads and qualifying prospects are important activities for all salespeople, those selling products directly to the consumer, such as life insurance, automobiles, or real estate rely more heavily on prospecting than their industrial and retail store counterparts. Yet, prospecting is also important to the latter. Take, for example, Matt Suffoletto's (IBM) comments on prospecting:

Prospecting is the process of acquiring basic demographic knowledge of potential customers for your product. Lists are available from many vendors that break down businesses in a given geography by industry, revenue, and number of employees. These lists can provide an approach to mass marketing, via either mailings or telephone canvassing. That canvassing is either done by the salesperson or through an administrative sales support person. No matter who performs the canvass or how it is done, it is an important element in increasing sales productivity. The next step of qualifying the potential customer is often included in the prospecting process. Qualification is a means of quickly determining two facts. First, is there a potential need for your product? Second, is the prospect capable of making a purchase decision? Specifically, does he or she have the decision authority and the financial ability to acquire your product?

Where to Find Prospects

Sources of prospects can be many and varied or few and similar, depending on the service or product provided by the salesperson. Basically, these sources are categorized as follows:

- Personal acquaintances.
- "Bird dogs," who are people knowledgeable about area residents, such as a real estate salesperson, banker, gas station attendant, or lawyer.
- Newspaper leads.
- Lists and directories such as the telephone directory.
- Old accounts.
- Observation.

Naturally, persons selling different services and products might not use the same sources for prospects. A salesperson of oil-field pipe supplies would make extensive use of various industry directories in a search for names of drilling companies. A life insurance salesperson could use personal acquaintances, "bird dogs," and old accounts as sources of prospects. A pharmaceutical salesperson would scan the local newspaper looking for announcements of new physicians and hospital, medical office, and clinical laboratory openings, whereas a sales representative for a company such as General Mills or Quaker Oats would watch announcements of construction for new grocery stores and shopping centers.

Top real estate salesperson Vikki Morrison feels that prospecting, which for her means knowing people in her neighborhood, has greatly aided her in becoming a successful salesperson. She strives to become her prospect's friend.

"In my area, most of the people I see are wives—and any woman who tried to farm in this tract in high heels and a dress, dripping with jewelry, would never make it," she believes. "I'm not trying to impress anybody. These people either know me or they know about me from the neighbors. I'm no threat—especially in my tennies, polyester pants, and T-shirt!"

"Usually, I never meet the husband until the actual listing—then he wants to meet me to find out if I really know what I'm doing in real estate. As far as he's concerned, I'm just a friend of his wife's. These are the people I care about," she explains. "If someone needs a plumber or babysitter or a dentist, they call me. If I need a closing gift and someone on the block does creative things, I call them. We're all in this together!"

Planning a Prospective Strategy

Prospecting, like other sales activities, is a skill that can be constantly improved by a dedicated salesperson. Some salespeople charge themselves with finding X number of prospects per week. Indeed, Burroughs Corp. (a large manufacturer of computers and other types of business equipment) asks its sales force to allocate a portion of each working day to finding and contacting several new prospects. A successful salesperson continually evaluates prospecting methods, comparing results and records with the mode of prospecting used in pursuit of a prospecting strategy that will result in the most effective contact rate.[2]

Prospecting Methods

The actual method by which a salesperson obtains prospects may vary. Several of the more popular prospecting methods, as shown in Figure 6.3, are the cold canvas method, the endless chain method, public exhibitions and demonstrations, finding and getting help of centers of influence, direct mail, telephone prospecting telemarketing, and observation.

The **cold canvas prospecting method** is based on the law of averages. For example, if past experience reveals that one person out of ten will buy a product, then 50 sales calls could result in 5 sales. Thus, the salesperson contacts as many leads as possible, recognizing that a certain percentage of people approached will buy. There is normally no knowledge about the individual or business called on. This form of prospecting relies solely on the volume of "cold" calls made.

The door-to-door and the telephone salesperson both employ cold canvas prospectors. For example, each summer the South-Western Publishing Company hires college students to sell their medical books, children's books, and Bibles. These salespeople go into a town and knock on the door of every person living on each block they work, often contacting up to 50 people each day. They frequently ask people if they know of others who might like to purchase their products.

FIGURE 6.3 Methods of prospecting for customers

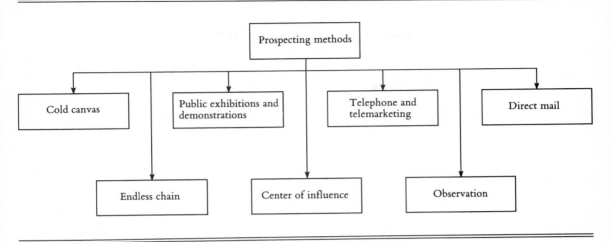

Another popular method of obtaining prospects is the **endless chain referral method.** After every sale (or contact with a person), the salesperson asks the customer for a list of several friends who might also be interested in the product. The salesperson then approaches these prospects, attempts to sell to them, and also asks them for the names of potential prospects. The salesperson says, "Ms. Jones, who of your friends can you recommend for me to contact?" Ideally, this procedure provides the salesperson with a constant supply of prospects. The endless chain is widely used in the sale of such services as insurance and products such as Tupperware and Avon cosmetics.

Exhibitions and demonstrations frequently take place at trade shows and other types of special interest gatherings. Many times, related firms will sponsor a booth at such shows and staff it with one or more salespeople. As people walk up to the booth to examine the products, a salesperson has only a few minutes to qualify leads and get names and addresses so as to later contact them at their homes or offices for demonstrations. Although salesperson-buyer contact is usually brief, this type of gathering gives a salesperson extensive contact with a large number of potential buyers over a brief period of time.[3]

For example, Figure 6.4 shows a Richard D. Irwin, Inc. trade exhibit. Irwin exhibits all of their college textbooks at meetings attended by college professors. The professors interested in a particular textbook are mailed a complimentary copy of the text, and the local salesperson then contacts the professor in his or her office.

FIGURE 6.4   Irwin salespeople staff their booth at a trade show aimed at selling textbooks to college professors

Prospecting via the **center of influence method** involves finding and cultivating people in a community or territory who are willing to cooperate in helping to find prospects. They typically have a particular position that includes some form of influence over other people, as well as information that allows the salesperson to identify good prospects. For example, a person who graduates from a college and begins work for a local real estate firm might contact professors and administrators at his alma mater to obtain the names of teachers who have taken a job at another university and are moving out of town. He wants to help them sell their homes.

Clergy, salespeople who are selling noncompeting products, officers of community organizations like the Chamber of Commerce, and members of organizations such as the Lions Club or a country club are other individuals who may function as a center of influence. Be sure to show your appreciation for this person's assistance. Keeping such influential persons informed on the outcome of your contact with the prospect helps to secure future aid.

In cases where there are a large number of prospects for a product, **direct mail prospecting** is sometimes used effectively to contact individuals and businesses. Direct-mail advertisements have the advantage of contacting large numbers of people, who may be spread across an extended geographical area, at a relatively low cost compared to using salespeople. People who request more information from the company subsequently are contacted by a salesperson.

Like direct mailing, use of **telephone prospecting** to contact a large number of prospects across a vast area is far less costly than use of a canvassing sales force, though usually more costly than mailouts.[4]

This person-to-person contact afforded by the telephone allows for interaction between the lead and the caller—enabling a lead to be quickly qualified or rejected. Salespeople can even contact their local telephone company for aid in incorporating the telephone into the sales program.

One example of telephone prospecting is the aluminum siding salesperson who telephones a lead and asks two questions that quickly determine if that person is a prospect. The questions are:

TELEPHONE SALESPERSON: Sir, how old is your home?

LEAD: One year old.

TELEPHONE SALESPERSON: Is your home brick or wood?

LEAD: Brick!

TELEPHONE SALESPERSON: Since you do not need siding, would you recommend we contact any of your neighbors or friends who can use a high-quality siding at a competitive price? [Endless chain technique]

The biggest sales buzzword of the 1990s is **telemarketing.** Telemarketing is a marketing communication system using telecommunication technology and trained personnel to conduct planned, measurable marketing activities directed at targeted groups of consumers.

The internal processes of a telemarketing center are shown in Figure 6.5. Many firms initiate telemarketing ventures by featuring an 800 number in some advertisement. In prints ads, a coupon may be made available for the reader. When the coupon response or a telephone call comes in to the center, a trained specialist calls the respondent (in the case of coupons) or answers the incoming call. The telemarketing center specialist fulfills the request and, in many cases, determines whether the customer has sufficient potential to warrant a face-to-face sales call.

From thousands of such contacts with the public, a firm can develop a valuable database that produces many informational reports. Many Fortune 500 companies, a few of which are discussed below, use telemarketing centers in this way. Table 6.1 describes some of their informational reports.

Examples of Firms Using Telemarketing. The B. F. Goodrich Chemical Group uses a telemarketing center for order taking, customer service, and information dissemination. When customers call, a center specialist brings up the customer's file on a data terminal screen, records the order, checks

FIGURE 6.5   The processing system within a telemarketing center

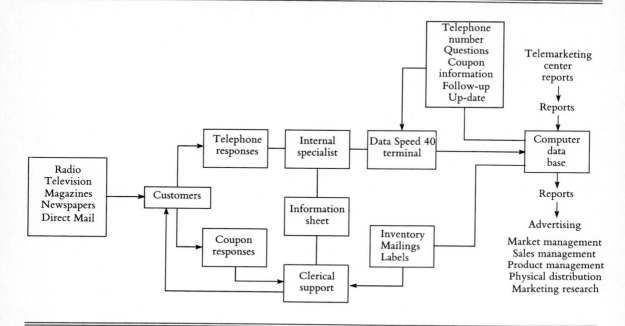

inventory and, when necessary, talks with production and shipping to schedule the shipment. Field sales personnel are also given current inventory data and estimated arrival times. High-volume accounts are scheduled for field visits—thereby increasing the number and quality of contacts between B. F. Goodrich and its best customers.

The Fotomat Company is another successful adopter of telemarketing. They introduced a new product—videotape sales and rentals—through media advertising, which features an 800 number to encourage call-in orders. They closely coordinated distribution activities with the telemarketing system and have realized cost savings and improved customer service.

The 3M Company relies on a telemarketing center to assist customers with equipment trouble. After calling 3M's 800 number, the customer describes the problem to a skilled technician with access to an on-line computer system. On more than 30 percent of the calls, 3M has found, the equipment difficulty can be solved in minutes without having to dispatch a service technician. This has improved customer service activities and provided a valuable service at a reasonable cost to 3M.

Westinghouse Credit Corporation uses telemarketing to qualify leads and develop good prospects for field salespeople. Calls are made from the

TABLE 6.1   Reports from a telemarketing center to other marketing groups within the firm

Advertising	Physical Distribution
Inquiries per advertisement	Consumers' orders
Profiles of respondents	Distributors' orders
Sales conversion rates per advertisement	Tracing and dispatching
	Shipment requirements
	Inventory requirements
	Product return needs
	Customer service needs
Market Management	**Product Management**
Segment analyses	Sales per product
Marginal account identification	Questions and complaints
	Consumer profiles
Marketing Research	**Sales Management**
Demographic data	Lead qualification
Image and attitude	Marginal account status
Forecasting data	

telemarketing center to determine interest, verify mailing information, and transmit leads to branch offices. Results are used for planning future distribution needs such as volume and locations.

The publication of an 800 number on packages, information sheets, and sale displays invites a two-way information exchange between customers and the telemarketing centers for Proctor & Gamble and Johnson & Johnson. This exchange not only facilitates effective distribution activities, but encourages the use of a familiar channel for future or repeat sales. Clairol and Scott's also offer follow-up services for their hair-tinting products and lawn products, respectively.

Telemarketing is not only for prospecting. It is also great for maintaining contact with regular customers and providing salespeople with up-to-date information.

A salesperson can often find prospects by constantly watching what is happening in the sales area—the **observation method.** Office furniture, computer, and copier salespeople look for new business construction in their territories. New families moving into town are excellent leads for real estate and insurance salespeople. No matter what prospecting method is used, it is always important to keep your eyes and ears open for information on who needs your product.

MAKING THE SALE

Successful Selling Secrets: Vikki Morrison

"There are no secrets to successful selling. There is only hard work from 7:00 in the morning to 10:00 at night. The biggest secret is total honesty at all times with all parties. You should act with integrity and treat clients with the same respect you want from them.

"Never call clients with anything but calm assurance in your voice, because if they feel you are panicked, they will become panicked. Your walk, speech, mannerisms, and eye-to-eye contact say more about you than you'll ever know, so practice all forms of your presentation every day in every way. I suppose a secret is to save the best house for last. I just try to do the best job for the client, even when it means turning them over to another agent who would have a more suitable property in a different area."

Vikki does not work alone; she uses her available resources in selling. A computer terminal in Vikki's office gives her up-to-date information on listing and analysis of proposed transactions. She personally employs three assistants to help her keep up with the listings and shoppers. Vikki knows the value of the real estate in her area and can give free market analysis with less than one hour's notice.

"An important part of my job is providing customers personal service via constant follow-up, before the appointment, during, and after the sale. I have periodic follow-ups to see how they like their new home or investments. Anniversary flowers and cards on their birthday are a specialty of mine. I try to eliminate any and all of their buying fears when I can, and be available to reassure them.

"I sell on emotional appeal. No matter what the facts, most people still buy based on emotion. The triggers for someone's emotional side can be quite varied. For example, for some men, their families are their hot button; for others, the greed appeal of a good deal is more important. Every person is different and should be handled as the very important individual that they are.

"Another factor in my selling is that I care about my clients. They know it, I know it, and they feel it when I'm working with them and long after the escrow is closed. These people are my good friends and we have fun together."

WHAT IS THE BEST PROSPECTING METHOD?

Like many other components of the selling process, prospecting methods should be chosen in light of the major factors defining a particular selling situation. As in most other optional situations discussed in this text, there is *no* one optimal mode of prospecting to fit all situations. Generalizations can be made, however, regarding the criteria used in choosing an optimal prospecting method for a particular selling situation. Three criteria that should be used in developing the "best" prospecting method should have you:

1. *Customize* or choose a prospecting method that fits the specific needs of your individual firm. Do not copy another company's method.
2. Concentrate on *high potential* customers first, leaving for later prospects of lower potential.

3. Always *call back* on prospects who did not buy. With new products, do not restrict yourself to present customers only. A business may not have purchased your present products because they did not fit their present needs; however, your new product may be exactly what they need.

Always keep knocking on your customer's door to help them solve problems through the purchase of your product.

OBTAINING THE SALES INTERVIEW

Given a satisfactory method of sales prospecting and an understanding of the psychology of buying, a key factor in the selling process that has yet to be addressed is obtaining a sales interview. Although cold calling (approaching a prospect without prior notice) is suitable in a number of selling situations, industrial buyers and some other types of individuals may have neither the time nor the desire to consult with a sales representative who has not first secured an appointment.

The Benefits of Appointment Making

The practice of making an appointment before calling on a prospect can save a salesperson hours in time wasted in traveling and waiting to see someone who is busy or even absent, as seen in Figure 6.6. When an appointment is made, a buyer knows you are coming. People are normally in a more receptive mood when they expect someone than when an unfamiliar salesperson "pops in." Appointment making is often associated with a serious, professional image and is sometimes taken as an outward gesture of respect toward a prospect.

From the salesperson's point of view, an appointment provides a time set aside for the buyer to listen to a sales presentation. This is important, since adequate time to explain a proposition improves the chance of making the sale. In addition, a list of appointments aids a salesperson in optimally allocating each day's selling time. Appointments can be arranged by telephone or by contacting the prospect's office personally.

Telephone Appointment. For obvious reasons of time and cost, the telephone is often used to make sales appointments. Though seemingly a simple task, obtaining an appointment over the telephone is frequently difficult. Business executives are generally busy and their time is scarce. However, there are a number of practices that can aid in successfully making an appointment over the telephone:

- Plan and write down what you will say. This will help organize and concisely present your message.
- Clearly identify you and your company.

FIGURE 6.6   Steve Ellis of General Mills finds that scheduling appointments by telephone is a time saver

- State the purpose of your call and briefly outline how the prospect may benefit from the interview.
- Prepare a brief sales message, stressing product benefits over features. Present only enough information to stimulate interest.
- Do not take "no" for an answer. You should be persistent even if there is a negative reaction to the call.
- Ask for an interview so that you can further explain product benefits.
- Phrase your appointment request as a question. Your prospect should be given a choice, such as: "Would nine or one o'clock Tuesday be better for you?"

Successful use of the telephone in the appointment scheduling requires an organized, clear message that will capture interest quickly. Before you dial a prospect's number, mentally or physically sketch out exactly what you plan to say. While on the telephone get to the point quickly (as you may have only a minute), disclosing just enough information to stimulate the prospect's interest. For example:

> Mr. West, this is Sally Irwin of On-Line Computer Company calling you from Birmingham, Alabama. Businessmen such as yourself are saving the costs of rental or purchase of computer systems, while receiving the same

MAKING THE SALE

Getting an Appointment Is Not Always Easy

The owner of an oil field supply house in Kansas City was Jack Cooper's toughest customer. He was always on the run, and Jack had trouble just getting to see him, much less getting him to listen to a sales presentation. Jack would have liked to take him to lunch so he could talk to him, but the owner never had time. Every day he called a local hamburger stand and had a hamburger sent to this office so he wouldn't have to waste time sitting down to eat.

Jack wanted to get the owner interested in a power crimp machine that would enable him to make his own hose assemblies. By making them himself, the owner could save about 45 percent of his assembly costs—and Jack would make a nice commission.

The morning Jack was going to make his next call, his wife was making sandwiches for their children to take to school. Jack had a sudden inspiration. He asked his wife to make two deluxe bag lunches for him to take with him.

Jack arrived at the supply house just before lunchtime. "I know you're too busy to go out for lunch," he told the owner, "so I brought it with me. I thought you might like something different for a change."

The owner was delighted. He even took time to sit down and talk while they ate. After lunch, Jack left with an order for the crimper—plus a standing order for hose and fittings to go with it!

benefits they get from the computer they presently have. May I explain how they are doing this on Tuesday at nine o'clock in the morning or would one o'clock in the afternoon be preferable?

One method for obtaining an appointment with anyone in the world is for you to have someone else make it for you. Now, that sounds simple enough, doesn't it? However, do not just have anyone make the appointment. It should be a satisfied customer. Say, "Listen, you must have a couple of people who could use my product. Would you mind telling me who they are? I'd like you to call them up and say I'm on my way over." Or, "Would you just call them up and ask them if they would meet with me?" This simple technique frequently works. In some situations, an opportunity to make an appointment personally arises or is necessitated by circumstances.

Personally Making the Appointment. Many business executives are constantly bombarded with an unending procession of interorganizational memos, correspondence, reports, forms, and *salespeople*. In order to use their time optimally, many executives establish policies to aid in determining whom to see, what to read, and so on. They maintain gatekeepers (secretaries or receptionists) who execute established time-use policies by acting as filters for all correspondence, telephone messages, and people seeking entry to the executive suite. Successful navigation of this filtration system often requires a professional salesperson who: (1) is determined to see the executive and believes it can be done; (2) develops friends within the firm (many times including the gatekeepers); and (3) optimizes time by calling only on individuals who make or participate in the purchase decision.

Believe in Yourself. As a salesperson believe that you can obtain interviews because you have a good offer for prospects. Develop confidence by knowing your products and by knowing prospects—their business and needs. Speak and carry yourself as though you expect to get in to see the prospect. Instead of saying, "May I see Ms. Vickery," you say, while handing the secretary your card, "Could you please tell Ms. Vickery that Mr. Baker from XYZ Corporation is here?"

Develop Friends in the Prospect's Firm. Successful salespeople know that people within the prospect's firm often indirectly help in arranging an interview and influence buyers to purchase a product. A successful Cadillac salesperson states.

> To do business with the boss, you must sell yourself to everyone on his staff. I sincerely like people—so it came naturally to me. I treat secretaries and chauffeurs as equals and friends. Ditto for switchboard operators and maids. I regularly sent small gifts to them all. An outstanding investment.
> The little people are great allies. They can't buy the product. But they can kill the sale. Who needs influential enemies? The champ doesn't want anyone standing behind him throwing rocks. In many cases, all you do is treat people decently—an act that sets you apart from 70 percent of your competitors.

Matt Suffoletto, the IBM sales representative profiled in Chapter 1, says it another way:

> I have observed one common distinction of successful salespeople. They not only call on the normal chain of people within the customer's organization, but they have periodic contact with higher level decision-makers to communicate the added value which their products and services have provided. This concept, when exercised judiciously, can have a tremendous impact on your effectiveness.

Respect, trust, and friendship are three key elements in any salesperson's success. Timing is also important.

Call at the Right Time on the Right Person. Both gatekeepers and busy executives appreciate salespeople who do not waste their time. Using past sales call records or by calling the prospect's receptionist, a salesperson can determine when the prospect prefers to receive visitors. Direct questions, such as asking the receptionist, "Does Mr. Smith purchase your firm's office supplies?" or "Who should I see concerning the purchase of office supplies?" can be used in determining whom to see.

Do Not Waste Time Waiting. Once you have asked the receptionist if the prospect can see you today, you should: (1) determine how long you will have to wait, and if you can afford to wait that length of time; (2) be productive while waiting by reviewing how you will make the sales presentation to the prospect; and (3) once an acceptable amount of waiting time has passed, tell the receptionist, "I have another appointment and must leave in a moment." When politely approached, the receptionist will usually attempt to get you in. If still unable to enter the office, you can ask for an appointment as follows: "Will you please see if I can get an appointment for 10 on Tuesday?" If this request does not result in an immediate interview, it implies the establishment of another interview time. If you establish a positive relationship with a prospect and with gatekeepers, waiting time normally decreases while productivity increases.

CUSTOMER SALES PLANNING— THE PREAPPROACH

Once the prospect has been located and qualified, the salesperson is ready to plan the sales interview.[5] To illustrate why planning is important, let's first review an actual sales call using disguised names.

Dan Roberts was a salesperson for University Press, a publisher of college textbooks. He called on professors at colleges and universities to show his firm's new books, and to remind them of the backlist of older books. Dan entered the office of Elizabeth Johnston, a professor at a school in his territory. The conversation went like this:

SALESPERSON: Hello, Professor Johnson? [Pronouncing the name incorrectly.]

BUYER: Yes, I am Professor Johnston. Can I help you?

SALESPERSON: I'm Dan Roberts, with University Press.

BUYER: I'm off to class. I can see you during my office hours.

SALESPERSON: Office hours. Oh, well, I wanted to talk to you about our new salesmanship book. Do you teach a course on selling?

BUYER: [abruptly] That's my favorite subject. Who is the author?

SALESPERSON: Oh, I'm not sure, let me check my catalog. Yes, here it is, it's . . . Johnston. Say, that is you!

Dan Roberts certainly was unprepared for the call. He did not know how to pronounce Professor Johnston's name; he did not find out the professor's office hours; he was not aware that the professor taught the course in selling; and he did not know his product. He was embarrassed to find out that the professor had written the book he was promoting. The one

SELLING TIPS

Matt Suffoletto of IBM: Planning the Sales Call

"The sales call is still the key to most sales efforts, and planning a sales call is the foundation of a successful sale. You would never consider going on a long distance trip without looking at a roadmap. Similarly, you should plan what you want to accomplish on a sales call, and later measure yourself against that plan.

"If I were to ask you to describe the best salesperson you have ever encountered, you would probably respond that he or she was convincing and impressive. You can prepare yourself to be both convincing and impressive. First, you must know your product and more importantly, the product's application for your customer. Second, you must know your customer. You can gain a wealth of background knowledge about your customer's business from such sources as corporate annual reports, *Dun & Bradstreet* directories, and the local Chamber of Commerce. Overall, planning shows up and pays off in increased sales when you do your homework."

thing Dan did do correctly was to have an objective for the call—to visit with professors who teach good sales procedure. However, he should have looked at the school's class schedule to determine who was teaching the course and at what time. Dan's lack of preparation implied to Professor Johnston that he was not a good salesperson, and that he did not regard the call as worthy of preparation. These shortcomings got Dan off to a bad start with Professor Johnston.

Reasons for Planning the Sales Call

While salespeople say there are numerous reasons for planning the sales call, four of the most frequently mentioned reasons are: planning aids in building confidence; it develops an atmosphere of goodwill between the buyer and seller; it reflects professionalism; and it generally increases sales. Each of these claims is worthy of consideration.

Builds Self-Confidence. In giving a speech before a large group of people, most people are nervous. This nervousness can be greatly reduced and self-confidence increased by planning what to say and practicing your talk. The same is true in making a sales presentation. By carefully planning your presentation, you increase confidence in yourself and your ability as a salesperson. This is why planning the sales call is especially important.

Develops an Atmosphere of Goodwill. The salesperson who understands a customer's needs and is prepared to discuss how a product will benefit the

MAKING THE SALE

Computer Information with Your Bacon and Eggs

Tomorrow's traveling salesperson will start the day by hooking a portable computer-printer-plotter combination to the motel room telephone. While dressing for work or having breakfast in bed, the computer will receive from the home office the newest sales leads that came in the day before, along with special messages put on the system by the sales manager such as price changes, advice on how to counter a new competitive product that will debut that week, and improvements made in the delivery schedule that would be a strong selling point.

The printer will also churn out the leads the salesperson is scheduled to call on that day, including a profile of the prospect's product application, interfaces with the company, and buying potential. A recap of the salesperson's last visit and comments, along with any problems the prospect may have, will also be printed. The plotter will provide a map of the territory to cover, with information on the location of each call, travel time, and an estimate of the time needed based on each account's buying potential.

The computer will also remind the salesperson that tomorrow is the manager's birthday.

---

prospect is appreciated and respected by the buyer. Knowledge of a prospect and concern for the prospect's needs demonstrates a sincere interest in a prospect that is generally awarded with an attitude of goodwill from the prospect. This goodwill gradually aids in building the buyer's confidence and results in a belief that the salesperson can be trusted to fulfill obligations.

Creates Professionalism. Good business relationships are built on your knowledge of your company, industry, and customers' needs. Show prospects that you are calling on them to help solve their problems or satisfy their needs. These factors are the mark of a professional salesperson who uses specialized knowledge in an ethical manner to aid customers.

Increases Sales. A confident salesperson who is well prepared to discuss how products will solve particular needs will always be more successful than the unprepared salesperson. Careful planning ensures that you have diagnosed a situation and have a remedy for a customer's problem. Planning assures that a sales presentation is well thought out and appropriately presented.

Like other beneficial presales call activities, planning is most effective (and time efficient) when done logically and methodically. Some salespeople try what they consider "planning," later discarding the process because "it took too much time." In many cases, these individuals were not aware of the basic elements of sales planning.

FIGURE 6.7   Steps in planning the sales call

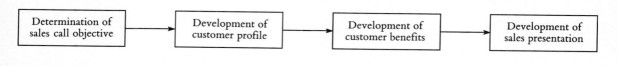

Elements of Sales Call Planning

Figure 6.7 depicts the four facets considered in **sales planning.** These facets are: (1) determining the sales call objective; (2) developing or reviewing the customer profile; (3) development of a customer benefit plan; and (4) development of the individual sales presentation based on the sales call objective, customer profile, and customer benefit plan.

Always Have a Sales Call Objective. A salesperson must meet with a prospect or customer with an objective in mind. The **sales call objective** should be: (1) specific, (2) measurable, and (3) directly beneficial to the customer. For example, the Colgate salesperson might have objectives of checking all merchandise, having the customer make a routine reorder on merchandise, and selling promotional quantities of Colgate toothpaste.

The Colgate salesperson might call on a chain store manager with the multiple objectives of: making sure that Colgate products are placed where they will sell most rapidly; replenishing the store's stock of Colgate products so that customers will not leave the store disgruntled due to stockouts; and aiding the manager in deciding how much "promotional" Colgate toothpaste and Rapid Shave shaving cream should be displayed.

Industrial salespeople develop similar objectives to determine if customers need to reorder or to sell new products. A customer profile sheet, such as shown in Table 6.2, can be a guide for determining the appropriate strategy to use in contacting each customer.

Customer Profile Provides Insight. As much relevant information as possible should be reviewed regarding the firm, the buyer, and the individuals who influence the buying decision—before a sales call is made—to properly develop a customized presentation, as seen in Figure 6.8. The material discussed in Chapters 3 and 13 concerning factors of why the buyer buys need to be considered by the salesperson at this time. A **customer profile** should tell you:

• Who makes the buying decisions in the organization—an individual or committee?

• What is the buyer's background? The background of the buyer's company? The buyer's expectations of you?

• What are the desired business terms and needs of the account, such as delivery, credit, technical service?

TABLE 6.2 Example of information used in a profile and for planning

Customer Profile and Planning Sheet

1. Name: _____
    Address: _____
2. Type of business: _____
    Name of buyer: _____
3. People who influence buying decision or aid in using or selling our
    product: _____
4. Buying hours and best time to see buyer: _____
5. Receptionist's name: _____
6. Buyer's profile: _____
7. Sales call objectives: _____
8. What are customer's important buying needs: _____
9. Sales presentation
    a. Sales approach: _____
    b. Features, advantages, benefits: _____
    c. Method of demonstrating FAB: _____
    d. How to relate benefits to customer's needs: _____
    e. Trial close to use: _____
    f. Anticipated objections: _____
    g. Trial close to use: _____
    h. How to close this customer: _____
    i. Hard or soft close: _____
10. Sales made—product use/promotional plan agreed on: _____

11. Post sales call comments (reason did–did not buy; what to do on next call;
    follow-up promised): _____

- What competitors successfully do business with the account? Why?
- What are the purchasing policies and practices of the account? For example, does the customer buy special price offer promotions, or only see salespeople on Tuesday and Thursday?
- What is the history of the account? For example, past purchases of our products, inventory turnover, profit per shelf foot, our brand's volume sales growth, payment practices, and attitude toward resale prices.

Determine this information from a review of records on the company or through personal contact with the company.

Customer Benefit Plan: What It's All About! Beginning with your sales call objectives and what you know about your prospect, you are ready to develop a **customer benefit plan.** The customer benefit plan contains the nucleus of the information used in your sales presentation; thus, it should be developed to the best of your ability. Creating a customer benefit plan can be approached as a four-step process:

FIGURE 6.8   The telephone and computer aid in planning sales calls

• *This Xerox salesperson uses the telephone and computer to make appointments and plan sales calls. By examining an account's past sales, sales potential, and the buyer's profile information stored on the computer, customer sales call planning is improved.*

Step 1:

   Select the "features, advantages, and *benefits*" of your product to present to your prospect. This addresses the issue of "why" your product should be purchased. The main reason your product should be purchased by your prospect is that its benefits fulfill certain needs or solve certain problems. Carefully determine the benefits you wish to present.

Step 2:

   Develop your "marketing plan." If selling to a wholesaler or retailer, your marketing plan should include how, once they buy, they will sell your product to their customers. An effective marketing plan includes suggestions on how a retailer, for example, should promote the product through displays, advertising, proper shelf-space and positioning, and pricing. For an end-user of the product, such as the company who buys your manufacturing equipment, computer, or photocopier, develop a program showing how your product is most effectively used or coordinated with existing equipment.

Step 3:

Develop your "business proposition," which includes items such as price, percent markup, forecasted profit per square foot of shelf-space, return-on-investment, and payment plan. Value analysis (see Chapter 13) is an example of a business proposition for an industrial product.

Step 4:

Develop a "suggested purchase order" based on a customer benefit plan. A proper presentation of your customer needs analysis and your product's ability to fulfill these needs, along with a satisfactory business proposition and marketing plan, allows you to justify to the prospect what product and/or how much to purchase. This suggestion may include, depending on your product, such things as what to buy, how much to buy, what assortment to buy, and when to ship the product to the customer.

Visual aids should be developed to effectively communicate the information developed in these four steps. The visuals should be organized in the order you will discuss them. Your next step is to plan all aspects of the sales presentation.

The Sales Presentation Is Where It All Comes Together. It is now time to plan your **sales presentation** from beginning to end. This process involves developing the seven steps of the sales presentation described earlier in Figure 6.1: the approach, presentation, and trial close method to uncover objections; ways to overcome objections; additional trial closes; and the close of the sales presentation. Each step is discussed in the following chapters.

Figure 6.9 summarizes the procedures and steps relevant to planning a sales presentation. First, develop your sales call objective by determining which products to present for a prospect. Based on your call objective and what you know about the prospect (customer profile), determine product benefits to present, a market plan for your prospect, the business proposition you will discuss with the prospect, and your suggestion of what and how much the prospect should buy. This information is sequenced as you wish to present it. Visual aids and demonstrations can be developed to help create an informative and persuasive sales presentation. As mentioned earlier, the *last step* in planning your sales call is the development and rehearsal of the sales presentation.

In developing the sales presentation, think of leading the prospect through the five steps or phases that salespeople believe constitute a purchase decision. These phases are referred to as the prospect's mental steps.

FIGURE 6.9   A sequence of events to complete in developing a sales presentation

```
┌─────────────────────────────┐
│      Sales call objective   │────────┐
└──────────────┬──────────────┘        │
               ↓                       │
┌─────────────────────────────┐        │
│        Product to sell      │        │
└──────────────┬──────────────┘        │
               ↓                       │
┌─────────────────────────────┐        │
│       Customer profile      │        │
└──────────────┬──────────────┘        │
               ↓                       │                  ┌────────────────────────┐
┌─────────────────────────────────┐    │                 │                        │
│ Product's features, advantages, │────┼────────────────▶│   Sales presentation   │
│            benefits             │    │                 │                        │
└──────────────┬──────────────────┘    │                 └────────────────────────┘
               ↓                       │
┌─────────────────────────────┐        │
│       Marketing plan        │        │
└──────────────┬──────────────┘        │
               ↓                       │
┌─────────────────────────────┐        │
│ Develop business proposition │       │
└──────────────┬──────────────┘        │
               ↓                       │
┌─────────────────────────────┐        │
│  Suggested purchase order   │        │
└─────────────────────────────┘        
```

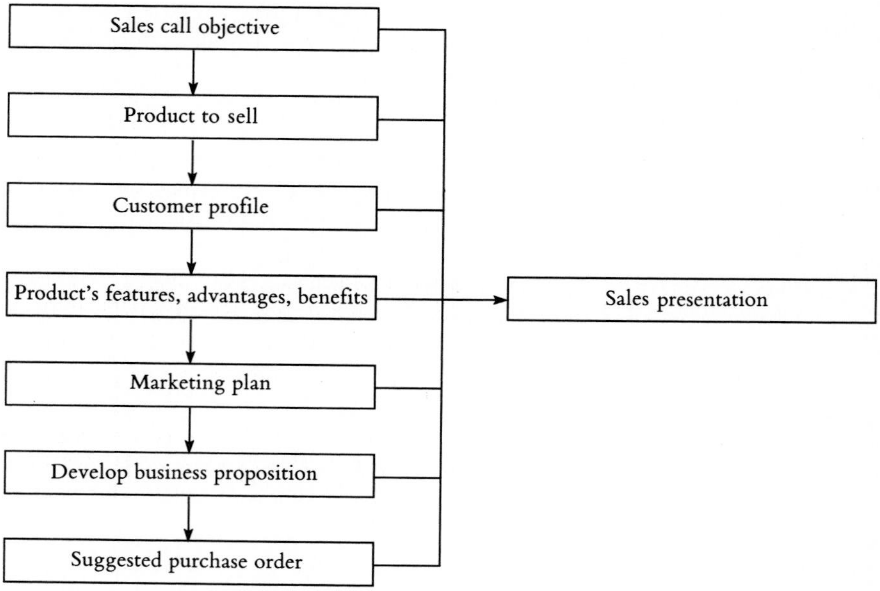

THE PROSPECT'S MENTAL STEPS

In making a sales presentation, quickly obtain the prospect's full attention, develop interest in your product, create a desire to fulfill a need, establish the prospect's conviction that the product fills a need, and finally, promote action by having the prospect purchase the product. As in Figure 6.10, these steps occur in the following order:

Attention

From the moment you begin to talk, quickly capture and maintain the prospect's attention. This may be difficult at times because of distractions, pressing demands on the prospect's time, or lack of interest. Carefully plan what to say and how to say it. Since attention-getters have only a temporary effect, be ready to quickly move to Step 2, sustaining the prospect's interest.

Interest

Before meeting with prospects, determine their important buying motives. These can be used in capturing interest. If not, you may have to determine them at the beginning of your presentation by asking questions. Prospects enter the interest stage if they listen to and enter into a discussion with you.

FIGURE 6.10   The prospect's five mental steps in buying

Quickly strive to link your product's benefits to prospects' needs. If this link is completed, prospects usually express a desire for the product.

Desire

Using the FAB formula (Chapter 3), strive to bring prospects from lukewarm interest to a boiling desire for your product. Desire is created when prospects express a wish or wanting for a product like yours.

To better determine if the product should be purchased, prospects may have questions for you and may present objections to your product. Anticipate prospects' objections and provide information to maintain their desire.

Conviction

While prospects may desire a product, they still have to be convinced that your product is best for their needs and that you are the best supplier of the product. In the conviction step, strive to develop a strong *belief* that the product is best suited to prospects' specific needs. Conviction is established when no doubts remain about purchasing the product from you.

Purchase or Action

Once the prospect is convinced, plan the most appropriate method of asking the prospect to buy or act. If each of the preceding steps have been implemented correctly, closing the sale is the easiest step in the sales presentation.

OVERVIEW OF THE SALES PROCESS

We have briefly discussed the various steps in the selling process, reviewed the sales presentation, and examined the five mental steps a prospect moves through toward purchasing a product. Each step will be examined in more depth later, along with methods and techniques that successful salespeople use to lead the prospect to make the correct purchase decision. Table 6.3 presents an overview of the selling process and gives corresponding examples of the prospect's mental stages and questions that may be posed at various points during the presentation.

TABLE 6.3 The selling process and examples of prospect's mental thoughts and questions

Steps in the Selling Process	Prospect's Mental Steps	Prospect's Potential Verbal and Mental Questions
1. Prospecting Salesperson located and qualifies prospects.		
2. Preapproach Salesperson obtains interview, determines sales call objective, develops customer profile, customer benefit program, and selling strategies. Customer's needs are determined.		
3. Approach Salesperson meets prospect and begins individualized sales presentation. Needs are further uncovered.	*Attention* due to arousal of potential need or problem. *Interest* due to recognized need or problem and the desire to fulfill the need or solve the problem.	Should I see salesperson? Should I continue to listen, interact, devote much time to a salesperson? What's in it for me?
4. Presentation Salesperson relates product benefits to needs, using demonstration, dramatizations, visuals, and proof statements.	*Interest* in information that provides knowledge and influences perceptions and attitude. *Desire* begins to develop based on information evaluation of product features, advantages, and benefits. This is due to forming positive attitudes that product may fulfill need or solve problem. Positive attitudes brought about by knowledge obtained from presentation.	Is the salesperson prepared? Are my needs understood? Is the seller interested in my needs? Should I continue to listen and interact? So what? (to statements about features) Prove it! (to statements about advantages) Are the benefits of this product the best to fulfill my needs?
5. Trial Close Salesperson asks prospect's opinion on benefits during and after presentation.	*Desire* continues based on information evaluation.	
6. Objections Salesperson uncovers objections.	*Desire* continues based on information evaluation.	Do I understand the salesperson's marketing plan and business position? I need more information to make a decision. Can you meet my conditions?
7. Meet Objects Salesperson satisfactorily answers objections.	*Desire* begins to be transformed into belief. *Conviction* established due to belief the product and salesperson can solve needs or problems better than competitive products. Appears ready to buy.	Let me see the reaction when I give the salesperson a hard time. I have a minor/major objection to what you are saying. Is something nonverbal being communicated? Did I get a reasonable answer to my objection?

TABLE 6.3 *(concluded)*

8. Trial Close Salesperson uses another trial close to see if objections have been overcome; or if presentation went smoothly before the close, to determine if the prospect is ready to buy.	*Conviction* becomes stronger.	Can I believe and trust this person? Should I reveal my real concerns?
9. Close Salesperson has determined prospect is ready to buy and now asks for the order.	*Action* (purchase) occurs based on positive beliefs that the product will fulfill needs or solve problems.	I am asked to make a buying decision now. If I buy and I am dissatisfied, what can I do? Will I receive after-the-sale service as promised? What are my expectations toward this purchase? Why don't you ask me to buy? Ask one more time and I'll buy.
10. Follow-Up Salesperson provides customer service after the sale.	*Satisfaction—Dissatisfaction*	Did the product meet my expectations? Am I experiencing dissonance? How is the service associated with this product? Should I buy again from this salesperson?

The approach used is to get the prospect's attention and interest by having the prospect recognize a need or problem, and stating a wish to fulfill the need or solve the problem. The presentation constantly maintains interest in the information you present and generates desire for the product.

Uncovering and answering the prospect's questions and revealing and meeting or overcoming objections results in more intense desire. This desire is transformed into the conviction that your product can fulfill the prospect's needs or solve problems. Once you have determined the prospect is in the conviction stage, you are ready for the close.

SUMMARY OF MAJOR SELLING ISSUES

The sales process involves a series of actions beginning with prospecting for customers. The sales presentation is the major element of this process. Before making the presentation, the salesperson must find prospects to contact, obtain appointments, and plan the entire sales presentation.

Prospecting involves locating and qualifying the individuals or businesses that have the potential to buy a product. A person or business who might be a prospect is a *lead*. Questions that are used to determine if someone is qualified are: "Is there a real need?" "Is the prospect aware of that need?" "Is there a desire to fulfill the need?" "Does the prospect believe a certain product can be beneficial?" "Does the prospect have the finances and authority to buy?" and "Are potential sales large enough to be profitable to me?"

Several of the more popular prospecting methods are cold canvas and endless chain methods, public exhibitions and demonstrations, locating centers of influence, direct mailouts, and telephone and observation prospecting. To obtain a continual supply of prospects, the salesperson should develop a prospecting method suitable for each situation.

Once a lead has been located and qualified as a prospect, the salesperson can make an appointment with that prospect by telephone or in person. At times, it is difficult to arrange an appointment, so the salesperson must develop ways of getting to see the prospect. One of the best ways to see the prospect is to develop friends within the prospect's firm who can help arrange for an interview. Believing in yourself and feeling that you have a product needed by the prospect are important.

The importance of careful planning of the sales call cannot be overemphasized. Plan your sales call to build self-confidence, to develop goodwill between you the prospect, to create an image of professionalism in the prospect's mind, and to increase your sales. In planning the sales call, the salesperson should determine the objective for contacting the prospect, develop or review the customer's profile, develop a customer benefit plan, and create an individualized sales presentation. Once these steps are accomplished, you are ready to meet the prospect.

7

Select Your Presentation Method, Then Open It Strategically

Emmett Reagan is a senior training analyst at the Xerox International Center for Training and Management Development at Leesburg, Virginia. He joined Xerox Corporation in 1963 after graduating from the University of Alabama. Following basic sales training, he was assigned to a geographic sales territory in Southeast Virginia. Emmett was subsequently promoted to the position of sales manager in Richmond, Virginia, where he remained until the summer of 1971. He was then transferred to Rochester, N.Y., where he became school manager for advanced sales training. In 1973, he moved to Northern Virginia as part of a group responsible for planning and developing the Xerox International Training Center.

With respect to the sales presentation, Emmett feels that "at the outset it's important to understand that the most productive behavior in which we can engage is that which uncovers, refines, and develops needs. This is what the professional salesperson does best. It is also what the professional does first.

"Unless we are able to gather sufficient information, there is little likelihood that we will be able to uncover problems for which our product could become the solution. Obviously, the best way to do this is by asking questions.

"The most basic questions we would ask early in the presentation would be those that would provide general information about the customer as an individual and the company in general. To develop a need further we must then make a transition from the gathering of general information to the point where the information is specific. Often a great deal of mutual trust is required before the prospect will open up.

"You should make sure you understand the prospect's concern. Clarify it. Restate it several times if necessary. Also, help the customer resolve the issue. Ask how it should be handled. Once the prospect identifies an appropriate solution, build on it and extend or expand the benefit of what you are selling. After all of the above steps have been completed, we should now be in a position to ask for the order. We will probably be successful." •

Emmett Reagan
Xerox Corporation

"Once a strong need has been clearly identified," says Xerox's Emmett Reagan, "there is often a tendency to become smug. The new or inexperienced salesperson is often guilty of this particular sin. Needs development is often the most difficult period of the entire cycle. It is, as often as not, also the most productive. Many times the seller, feeling good because of knowing that a good job was done of needs development, simply goes back to the office and waits for the telephone to ring or for the big order to come in the mail.

"Often this conduct is encouraged by the buyer who makes statements like, 'This looks good. I'll be in touch.' What the buyer neglects to tell our enterprising seller is that he'll also be in touch with everybody else in town who might have a solution for this need that we have worked so diligently to uncover. The salesperson is often critical of buyers who take such steps. We often forget that in addition to finding solutions to problems our customer is also charged with the responsibility for protecting the corporate assets. To do this he must explore all the options at his disposal.

"It is this point that establishes the criteria for making the decision. So rather than skipping blithely back to the office and waiting for the order to fall, we would do well to spend some time influencing these criteria in our own behalf. Some call it 'writing the specs,' others refer to it as 'guidelines for decision,' but regardless of what we call it we must understand that our prospect goes through this agonizing exercise in every big-ticket transaction.

"The agony is in direct proportion to the dollar amount of the sale. The main point here is not to quit after the need has been developed. Begin working to assist the buyer in developing criteria for the decision-making process. Remember, too, that it is at this point in the cycle that competition is likely to be most active." •

Salespeople, sales trainers, and sales managers agree that the most challenging, rewarding, and enjoyable aspect of the buyer-seller interaction is the sales presentation. An effective presentation completely and clearly explains all aspects of a salesperson's proposition as it relates to a buyer's needs. Surprisingly, or perhaps not so surprisingly, attaining this objective is not as easy as you might think. Few successful salespeople will claim that they had little trouble developing a good presentation, or mastering the art of giving the sales presentation. How then can you, as a novice, develop a sales presentation that will improve your chances of making the sale?

You must select a sales presentation method according to your prior knowledge of the customer, your sales call objective, and your customer benefit plan. You are now ready to develop your sales presentation. The particular sales presentation method selected will make an excellent framework for building your specific presentation. The sales opener, or

FIGURE 7.1   The third step in the sales process is the first step in the sales presentation. *The sales presentation method determines how you open your presentation.*

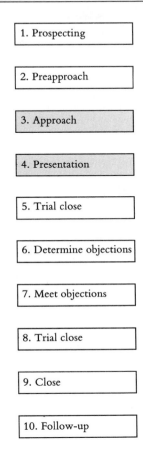

1. Prospecting

2. Preapproach

3. Approach

4. Presentation

5. Trial close

6. Determine objections

7. Meet objections

8. Trial close

9. Close

10. Follow-up

approach, as shown in Figure 7.1, is the first major part of the sales presentation.

This chapter discusses four sales presentation methods. The reasons successful salespeople develop special approaches for the sales interview are examined with objectives of the approach, several types of approaches, and applied examples of each approach. Matching the proper approach to the situation, and how to handle a prospect who shows little or no interest, are then reviewed. The chapter begins by examining a question frequently pondered by new salespeople—"Do I have the right to present my product to a prospect?"

THE RIGHT TO APPROACH

You have the right (or duty) to present your product if you can show that it will definitely benefit the prospect. In essence, you have to prove *you* are worthy of the prospect's time and serious attention. You may earn the right to this attention in a number of ways:

- By exhibiting specific product or business knowledge.
- By expressing a sincere desire to solve a buyer's problem and satisfy a need.
- By stating or implying that your product will save money or increase the firm's profit margin.
- By displaying a service attitude.

Basically, prospects want to know how you and your product will benefit *them* and *the companies* they represent. Your sales approach should initially establish and thereafter concentrate on your product's key benefits for each prospect.

This strategy is especially important during the approach stage of a presentation because it aids in securing the prospect's interest in you and your product. At this point you, at the very least, want this unspoken reaction from the prospect: "Well, I'd better hear this salesperson out. I may hear something that will be of use to me." Now that you have justified the right to sell to a prospect, you must determine how to present your product.

SALES PRESENTATION METHODS—SELECT ONE CAREFULLY

The sales presentation involves a persuasive vocal and visual explanation of a business proposition. While there are many ways of making a presentation, only four are discussed here. These four methods are presented to highlight the alternatives available to help sell your products.

As shown on the continuum in Figure 7.2, the four sales presentation methods are: (1) memorized, (2) formula, (3) need-satisfaction, and (4) problem-solution selling methods. The basic difference in the four methods concerns what percentage of the conversation is controlled by the salesperson. In the more structured memorized and formula selling techniques, the salesperson normally requires a monopoly on the conversation, while the less structured methods allow for greater buyer-seller interaction; both parties participate equally in the conversation.

The Memorized Sales Presentation

The **memorized presentation** is based on either of two assumptions: that a prospect's needs can be stimulated by direct exposure to the product, via the sales presentation, or that these needs have already been stimulated

FIGURE 7.2   The structure of sales presentations

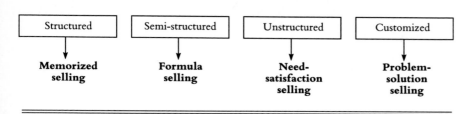

because the prospect has made the effort to seek out the product. In either case, the salesperson's role is to develop this initial stimulus into an affirmative response to an eventual purchase request.

The salesperson does 80 to 90 percent of the talking during a memorized sales presentation, only occasionally allowing the prospect to respond to predetermined questions, as shown in Figure 7.3.[1] Notably, the salesperson does not attempt to determine the prospect's needs during the interview, but gives the same canned sales talk to all prospects. Since no attempt is made at this point to learn what goes on in the consumer's mind, the salesperson concentrates on discussing the product and its benefits, concluding the pitch with a purchase request. It is hoped that a convincing presentation of product benefits will cause the prospect to buy.

National Cash Register Co. (now NCR Corp.) pioneered the use of canned sales presentations. An analysis of the sales approaches of some of its top salespeople done during the 1920s revealed to NCR that they were saying the same things. The firm proceeded to prepare a series of standardized sales presentations based on the findings of their sales approach analysis, ultimately requiring its sales force to memorize these approaches during sales calls. The method worked quite well for NCR, and was later adopted by other firms. Canned sales presentations are still used today, mainly in telephone and door-to-door selling.

However, parts of any presentation may be canned, yet linked with freeform conversation. Over time, most salespeople develop proven selling sentences, phrases, and sequences in which to discuss information. They tend to use these in all presentations.

Despite its impersonal aura, the canned or memorized sales presentation has distinct advantages, as seen in Table 7.1:

- It ensures that the salesperson gives a well-planned presentation and that the same information is discussed by all of the company's salespeople.
- It both aids and lends confidence to the inexperienced salesperson.
- It is effective when selling time is short, as in door-to-door or telephone selling.

FIGURE 7.3   Example of a memorized sales presentation and participation time
by customer and salesperson

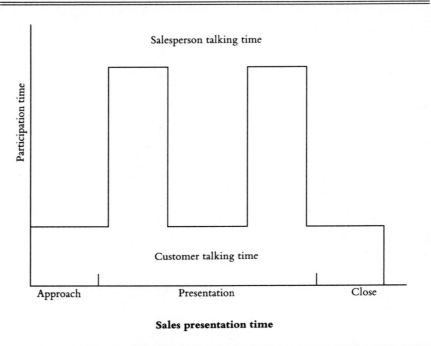

Sales presentation time

• It is effective when the product is nontechnical—such as books, cooking utensils, and cosmetics.

As may be apparent, the memorized method has several major drawbacks:

• It presents features, advantages and benefits that may not be important to the buyer.
• It allows for little prospect participation.
• It is impractical to use when selling technical products that require prospect input and discussion.
• It proceeds quickly through the sales presentation to the close, requiring the salesperson to close or ask for the order several times, which may be interpreted by the prospect as high-pressure selling.

The story is told of the new salesperson who was halfway through a canned presentation when the prospect had to answer the telephone. When the prospect finished the telephone conversation, the salesperson had

TABLE 7.1 Dyno Electric Cart memorized presentation

Situation: You call on a purchasing manager to elicit an order for some electric cars (like a golf cart) to be used at a plant for transportation around the buildings and grounds. The major benefit to emphasize in your presentation is that the carts save time; you incorporate this concept in your approach. For this product, you use the memorized stimulus-response presentation.[2]

SALESPERSON: Hello, Mr. Pride, my name is Karen Nordstrom and I'd like to talk with you about how to save your company executives time. By the way, thanks for taking time to talk with me.

BUYER: What's on your mind?

SALESPERSON: As a busy executive, you know time is a valuable commodity. Nearly everyone would like to have a few extra minutes each day and that is the business I'm in, selling time. While I can't actually sell you time, I do have a product that is the next best thing . . . a Dyno Electric Cart—a real time-saver for your executives.

BUYER: Yeah, well, everyone would like to have extra time. However, I don't think we need any golf carts. [First objection.]

SALESPERSON: Dyno Electric Cart is more than a golf cart. It is an electric car designed for use in industrial plants. It has been engineered to give comfortable, rapid transportation in warehouses, plants and across open areas.

BUYER: They probably cost too much for us to use. [Positive buying signal phrased as an objection.]

SALESPERSON: First of all, they only cost $2,200 each. With a five-year normal life, that is only $400 per year plus a few cents electricity and a few dollars for maintenance. Under normal use and care, these carts only require about $100 of service in their five-year life. Thus, for about $50 a month, you can save key people a lot of time. [Creative pricing—show photographs of carts in use.]

BUYER: It would be nice to save time, but I don't think management would go for the idea. [Third objection, but still showing interest.]

SALESPERSON: That is exactly why I am here. Your executives will appreciate what you have done for them. You will look good in their eyes if you give them an opportunity to look at a product that will save time and energy. Saving time is only part of our story. Dyno carts also save energy and thus keep you sharper toward the end of the day. Would you want a demonstration today or Tuesday? [Alternative close.]

BUYER: How long would your demonstration take? [Positive buying signal.]

SALESPERSON: I only need one hour. When would it be convenient for me to bring the cart in for your executives to try out?

BUYER: There really isn't any good time. [Objection.]

SALESPERSON: That's true. Therefore, the sooner we get to show you a Dyno cart, the sooner your management group can see its benefits. How about next Tuesday? I could be here at 8:00 and we could go over this item just before your weekly management group meeting. I know you usually have a meeting Tuesdays at 9:00 because I tried to call on you a few weeks ago and your secretary told me you were in the weekly management meeting. [Close of the sale.]

BUYER: Well, we could do it then.

SALESPERSON: Fine, I'll be here. Your executives will really be happy! [Positive reinforcement.]

---

forgotten the stopping point and started over again. The prospect naturally became angry.

In telling of his early selling experiences, salesperson John Anderson remembers that he was once so intent on presenting his memorized presentation that halfway through it the prospect yelled, "Enough, John, I've been waiting for you to see me. I'm ready to buy. I know all about your products." John was so intent on giving his canned presentation, and listening to himself talk, that he did not recognize the prospect's buying signals.

For some selling situations, a highly structured presentation can be used successfully. Its advantages and disadvantages should be examined to determine if it is appropriate for your prospects and products.

Some situations may seem partially appropriate for the memorized approach but require a more personal touch. Such circumstances warrant the examination of formula selling.

The Formula Presentation

The **formula presentation,** often referred to as the "persuasive selling presentation," is akin to the memorized method: it is based on the assumption that similar prospects in similar situations can be approached with similar presentations. However, for the formula method to apply the salesperson must first know something about the prospective buyer. The salesperson follows a less structured, general outline in making a presentation, allowing more flexibility and less direction.

The salesperson generally controls the conversation during the sales talk, especially at the beginning. Figure 7.4 illustrates how a salesperson should take charge during a formula selling situation.[3] For example, the salesperson might make a sales opener (approach), discuss the product's features, advantages, and benefits, and then start to solicit comments from the buyer using trial closes, answering questions, and handling objections. At the end of the participation curve, the salesperson regains control over the discussion, and moves in to close the sale.

The formula selling approach obtains its name from the salesperson using the attention, interest, desire, and action (AIDA) procedure of developing and giving the sales presentation. We earlier added "conviction" to the procedure because the prospect may want or desire the product, yet not be convinced this is the best product or the best salesperson from which to buy.

Straight rebuy and modified rebuy situations, especially with consumer goods, lend themselves to this method. Many prospects or customers will buy because they are familiar with the salesperson's company. The question is, "How can a salesperson for Quaker Oats, Revlon, Gillette, Procter & Gamble, or any other well-known manufacturer develop a presentation that will convince a customer to purchase promotional quantities of a product, participate in a local advertising campaign, or stock a new untried product?"

Beecham Products, a consumer goods manufacturer, has developed a sequence, or formula, for their salespeople to follow. They refer to it as the "10-step productive retail sales call." The Beecham salesperson shown in Figure 7.5 is headed into the grocery store to find his buyer for products such as Cling Free Sheets, Aqua-Fresh toothpaste, Aqua Velva, and Sucrets. The 10 steps and their major components are:

FIGURE 7.4   Example of a formula sales presentation and participation time by customer and salesperson

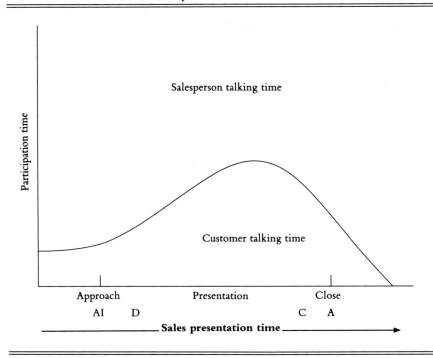

Step 1:
> Plan the call.
> - Review the situation.
> - Analyze problems and appointments.
> - Set objectives.
> - Plan the presentation.
> - Check your sales materials.

Step 2:
> Review plans.
> - Before you leave your car to enter the store, review your plans, call objectives, suggested order forms, etc.

Step 3:
> Greet personnel.
> - Give a friendly greeting to store personnel.
> - Alert the store manager for sales action.

FIGURE 7.5   This Beecham salesperson will use the formula sales presentation
to sell the buyer

Step 4:

Check store conditions.
- Note appearance of stock on shelf.
- Check distribution and pricing.
- Note out-of-stocks.
- Perform "quick fix" by straightening shelf stock.
- Report competitive activity.
- Check back room (storeroom):
  Locate product to correct out-of-stocks.
  Use reserve stock for special display.
- Update sales plan if needed.

Step 5:

Approach.
- Keep it short.

FIGURE 7.6   Example of need-satisfaction and problem-solution sales
presentations and participation time by customer and salesperson

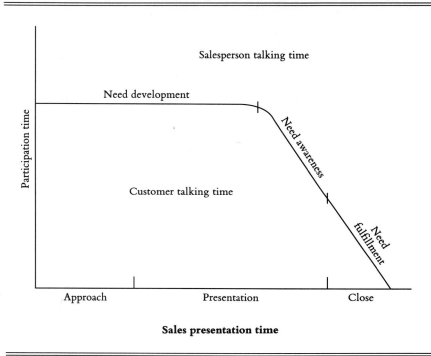

"What type of computer needs does your company have?" This opening
starts a discussion of the prospect's needs, and also gives the salesperson an
opportunity to determine whether any of the products being offered might
be beneficial. When something the prospect has said is not understood by
the salesperson, it can be clarified by a question or by restating what the
buyer has said. The need-satisfaction format is especially suited to the sale
of industrial and technical goods with stringent specifications and high price
tags.

Often, as shown in Figure 7.6, the first 50 to 60 percent of conversation
time (referred to as the *need-development* phase) is devoted to a discussion of
the buyer's needs.[4] Once aware of the prospect's needs (the *need-awareness*
phase), the salesperson begins to take control of the conversation by
restating the prospect's needs to clarify the situation. During the last stage
of the presentation, the *need-fulfillment* (or need-satisfaction) phase, the salesperson shows how the product will satisfy mutual needs. As seen in Table
7.3, the salesperson selling the Dyno Electric Cart begins the interview with
the prospect by using the planned series of questions to uncover problems
and to determine whether the prospect is interested in solving them.[5]

TABLE 7.3   Example of a need-satisfaction presentation

SALESPERSON: Mr. Pride, you really have a large manufacturing facility. How large is it?

BUYER: We have approximately 50 acres under roof, with our main production building almost 25 acres under one roof. There are six buildings used for production.

SALESPERSON: How far is it from your executives' offices to your plant area? It looks like it must be two miles over to there.

BUYER: Well, it does, but it's only one mile.

SALESPERSON: How do your executives get to the plant area?

BUYER: They walk through our underground tunnel. Some walk on the road when we have good weather.

SALESPERSON: When they get to the plant area, how do they get around in the plant?

BUYER: Well, they walk or catch a ride on one of the small tractors the workers use in the plant.

SALESPERSON: Have your executives ever complained about having to do all that walking?

BUYER: All the time!

SALESPERSON: What don't they like about the long walk?

BUYER: Well, I hear everything from "It wears out my shoe leather," to "It's hard on my pacemaker." The main complaints are the time it takes them and that some older executives are exhausted by the time they get back to their offices. Many people need to go to the plant but don't.

SALESPERSON: It sounds as if your executives are interested in reducing their travel time and not having to exert so much energy. By doing so, doesn't it seem they would get to the plant as they need to, saving them time and energy and saving the company money?

BUYER: I guess so.

SALESPERSON: Mr. Pride, on the average, how much money do your executives make an hour?

BUYER: Maybe $20 an hour.

SALESPERSON: If I could show you how to save your executives time in getting to and from the plant, would you be interested?

BUYER: Yes, I would. [Now the salesperson moves into the presentation.]

Should you have to come back a second time to see the prospect, as is often the case in selling industrial products, you would use the formula sales presentation method in calling on the same prospect. You might begin with a benefit statement such as:

Mr. Pride, when we talked last week you were interested in saving your executives time and energy in getting to and from your plant, and you felt the Dyno Electric Cart could do this for you. (You could pause and let him answer or say, "Is that correct?")

From the buyer's response to your question, you can quickly determine what to do. If an objection is raised, you can respond to it. If more information is asked for, you can provide it. If what you have said about your product has pleased the buyer, you simply ask for the order.

Be cautious when uncovering a prospect's needs. Too many questions can alienate the prospect. Remember, many prospects do not want to initially open up to salespeople. Actually, some salespeople are uncomfortable with the need-satisfaction approach because they feel less in control of the selling situation than with a canned or formula presentation. A good point to remember is that you are not a performer on a stage, but that rather, your job is to meet your prospect's needs—not your own. Eventually, you can learn to anticipate customer reactions to this presentation method and learn to welcome the challenge of the interaction between you and the buyer.

The Problem-Solution Presentation

In selling highly complex or technical products such as insurance, industrial equipment, accounting systems, office equipment, and computers, salespeople are often required to make several sales calls to develop a detailed analysis of a prospect's needs. After completing this analysis, the salesperson arrives at a solution to the prospect's problems and usually uses both a written analysis and an oral presentation. The **problem-solution presentation** usually consists of six steps:

1. Convincing the prospect to allow the salesperson to conduct the analysis.
2. Making the actual analysis.
3. Buyer and seller agreeing on the problems and determining that the buyer wants to solve them.
4. Preparing the proposal for a solution to the prospect's needs.
5. Preparing the sales presentation based on the analysis and proposal.
6. Making the sales presentation.

The problem-solution presentation is a flexible, customized approach involving an in-depth study of a prospect's needs, and requires a well-planned presentation. Often, the need-satisfaction and problem-solution presentations are used when it is necessary to present the proposal to a group of individuals.

The Group Presentation

There are times when you will meet with more than one decision maker in a group presentation.[6] Many group presentation elements are similar to other types of presentations. The primary difference is that either you or your team present the proposal to a group of decision makers.

The group presentation, depending on size, may be less flexible than a one-on-one meeting. The larger the group, the more structured your presentation. It would not work if everyone jumped in with feedback and ideas simultaneously, so a semblance of order has to be arranged. As the salesperson in charge, you can structure the presentation and provide a question-and-answer period at the end of or during the presentation.

The ideal situation is to talk with most or all of the decision makers involved during the analysis phase. That way, they will have contributed to determining what is needed. The points you discuss will hit on thoughts they have expressed regarding the problems at hand. In the first part of the presentation, you should accomplish the following:

Give a Proper Introduction. State your name, company, and explain in a clear, concise sentence the premise of your proposal. For example, your statement might sound like this: "Good morning. I'm Jeff Baxter from International Hospitality Consultants. I'm here to share my findings, based on research of your company and discussions with Mary Farley, that suggest my company can help increase your convention bookings by 15 to 30 percent."

Establish Credibility. Give a brief history of your company that includes the reason the business was started, the company philosophy, its development, and its success rate. Mention a few companies that you have worked with in the past, especially if they are big names. This "grounds" the client and lets the group know who you are and the extent of your experience and credibility.

Provide an Account List. Have copies of an account list available for everyone in attendance. It would be monotonous to say each company that you've worked with. Instead, hand out copies either in advance or while you talk. This list shows the various sizes, locations, and types of companies you've helped in the past.

State Your Competitive Advantages. Right up front you can succinctly tell the group where your company stands relative to the competition. Don't get into a detailed analysis of comparative strengths and weaknesses; make it clear that you can do better than the competition.

Give Quality Assurances and Qualifications. Get the group on your side by stating guarantees in the beginning. This shows pride in your product and that you don't skirt the issue of guarantees. Also, give your company's qualifications and credentials. For example, "We are certified by the United States government and licensed in forty-eight states to treat or move toxic waste," or "I have copies of the test reports from an independent lab. . ." If your company has an impressive money-back guarantee or an extended warranty, mention it.

Cater to the Group's Behavioral Style. Every group is comprised of individuals with personal styles. However, a group also exhibits an overall or dominant style; that is, it has a decision-making mode that characterizes one of the four behavioral styles. (See Chapter 3.) If you can quickly determine the group style, you will hold their attention and give them what

FIGURE 7.7   Selling to a group requires planning and a skilled presentation to be successful

they want more effectively. Some people are more impatient than others. If you don't address their needs, you will lose their attention. (See Figure 7.7.)

After establishing the credibility of your company, involve the group in the presentation. The first thing to do is go around the room asking for everyone's input into the success criteria and decision-making criteria. Preface this with, "I spoke to Fred, Sally, and Sue and learned their views on what your company would like to see changed in this area. In my research, I discovered it would also benefit you to have X, Y, and Z improved. I'd like to hear all of your thoughts on this matter." Ask each person to add to the list of benefits and the decision-making criteria. Take notes, perhaps on a flip chart, of what everyone says to help shape your presentation.

After everyone has had a chance to speak, go through your presentation exactly as in a one-on-one presentation. The primary difference is that you want to answer all the questions, fears, and concerns in the group. Meet each person's specific needs with a specific proposal.

When using this method, it is essential during your preparation to brainstorm all possible concerns and questions the decision makers may have. This information comes from talking to people within the company, other salespeople, and people in the industry. Be so well prepared that there is nothing they could come up with as a decision-making criteria that you haven't already thought of and answered.

When you prepare for a group, write a proposal document that ranges from one page to an entire notebook with data, specifications, reports, and solutions to specific problems. The proposal document is a reference source that tells your customer what she bought if she said yes and what she didn't buy if the answer was no. This document addresses everything you and your prospect discussed in the analysis phase: problems, success criteria, decision-making criteria, and how your product or service answers each. At the end, include relevant documents and copies of testimonial letters from satisfied customers.

During your presentation, do not read from the document. It is not the presentation; it is strictly a resource of facts to give your prospect after a decision is made. In addition, when making your presentation, do not expect to cover every point in the proposal unless you are brief. Your presentation will focus on the issues that relate to the customer's specific need gap; tangential information should be left in the document. Remember that proposal documents don't sell products; people sell products. The document is no substitute for a first-rate presentation.

The best way to present a proposal document is without prices. There are several reasons for this. First, some people will go directly to the prices without reading through the document. Second, prices tend to prejudice nondecision makers—who should not be concerned with prices. If the decision maker asks why the prices are missing, tell him, "I thought you would prefer the flexibility of showing the document to other people without their knowing prices. It's a matter of confidentiality." The third reason is politics. Imagine a board of directors who have not had a raise in two years looking at a document that proposes a $2 million computer for the company. This may stir up problems.

Make it clear that you are not trying to hide the prices and that you would be more than happy to talk about them with the appropriate people, the decision makers. It is important to present prices in the proper perspective and context.

When you share the proposal, address each problem and give specific information about your solutions. Make sure you discuss features, advantages, and benefits—and get feedback from the group. Ask trial closes like:

- "Can you see any other advantages to this?"
- "How do you feel about that; do you think that would solve the problem?"

At the end, summarize your proposal by giving a benefits summary. "Here is what you will get if you accept my proposal. . . ." Talk about how the benefits will address their specific problems.

Before your presentation, find out from your primary contact in the company if the group will make a decision while you are there or if they will discuss it and inform you later. You should also know if they are responsible for dealing with the financial aspects of the purchase. If so, you will have to talk about the costs and the benefits they will receive in relation to the costs. If they will not be concerned with prices, don't discuss them.

When you have completed the benefits summary, solicit impressions from the group. Ask if they agree that the solution you proposed would solve their problem or meet their needs. Without asking for it, get a feeling for the disposition of the group. If you are working with one person, it is easier to ask for an impression.

At the end of your summary, ask if there are any questions. At this point, you are close to the end of your allotted time. When someone asks a question that is answered in your proposal document, refer him to the appropriate section of the document and assure him that a complete answer is provided.

Negotiating So Everyone Wins

No matter what type of presentation method used, or whether you talk to one person or a group of people, be prepared to negotiate. Many salespeople negotiate during the confirming phase of the sale. Their products or services are big-ticket items with many negotiable details. The negotiating process during the sale confirmation becomes a critical point that can affect the business relationship.

There are many negotiating styles with various names. For example, there are cooperative, competitive, attitudinal, organizational, and personal modes of negotiating. Most inexperienced negotiators operate in the competitive mode because they mistakenly think the shrewd businessperson is one who wins at the other's expense. With a win–lose attitude in mind, they "don't show all their cards" and use other strategies to gain the upper hand. This is often done at the expense of the business relationship.

If you see prospects as adversaries rather than business partners, you will have short-term, adversarial relationships. The tension, mistrust, and buyer's remorse created are not worth the small gains you may win using this negotiating style. There is a better way.

Professional salespeople negotiate in a way that achieves satisfaction for both parties. They rely on trust, openness, credibility, integrity, and fairness. Their attitude is not, "How can I get what I want out of this person" but, "There are many options to explore that will make both of us happy. If two people want to do business, the details will not stand in the way." It is important *not* to negotiate the details before your customer has made a commitment to your solution.

Phases of Negotiation. If your product or service requires negotiating on a regular basis, set the stage for negotiation early in the sales process. There are things you can do to prepare for negotiation from the beginning.

Planning. The number one asset of a strong negotiator is preparation. During the planning phase, after completing a competition analysis, you know how your company compares to the competition for price, service, quality, reputation, and so on. This knowledge is important at negotiation time. You may be able to offer things the competition cannot. It is advantageous to point these advantages out to your prospect when the time is right.

Before you make a proposal to a client, search your company's sales records to find any reports of previous sales to your prospect or similar businesses. If these records documented the successes and failures of negotiating, you will learn from other salespeople's experience. For this reason, your call reports should include details of what transpired during any negotiation. The knowledge gained from these records is not a strategy per se but insight into the priorities of this market segment. For example, businesses in a certain industry segment may value service more than price, or they may care more about help in training and implementation than a discount.

During your preparation, review the various bargaining chips available to you. Some of the questions to answer are:

- What extra services can you offer?
- How flexible is the price or the payment plan?
- Are deposits and cancellation fees negotiable?
- Is there optional equipment you can throw in for free?
- Can you provide free training?
- What items in the negotiation will be inflexible for you?
- How can you compensate for these items?

Meeting. When you meet a prospect, you start building the relationship by proving you are someone who is credible, trustworthy, and hopefully the type of person your prospect likes to do business with. If you are all of these things, you will eliminate tension from the relationship and thereby ease the negotiation process.

As proof of this concept, imagine selling your car to a friend. Now imagine selling it to a stranger. Who would be easier to negotiate with? The friend, of course. For both of you, the top priority is the relationship; the secondary priority is the car deal. (See Figure 7.8.)

Studying. When you study a prospect's business, look at the big picture. As mentioned earlier in the book, don't focus on features; look for benefits you can provide. Look behind a prospect's demands for reasons. You can ask, "What are you trying to accomplish by asking for this?" After you are told, you may be able to say, "We can accomplish that another way. Consider

FIGURE 7.8   This packaging salesperson says she typically uses the problem-
             solution presentation. However, she must be prepared to negotiate
             no matter what presentation method is used.

this alternative. . . ." The more options for providing benefits, the more
flexible the negotiation.

It is important, during this phase, to find out what other company's
products or services your prospect is considering. This gives insight into
what they are looking for and willing to pay. If you are selling a half-million
dollar CAT Scanner and your prospect is also considering a three-quarter-
million-dollar CAT Scanner, you know your product is not priced too
high. If, however, your prospect is looking at a lot of lower-priced units, it
may be an uphill struggle to get the prospect to spend what you're asking.
Knowing who your competitors are will help you assess bargaining
strengths and weaknesses.

Every purchase is made with decision-making criteria in mind, either
consciously or unconsciously. Find out what they are for your prospect and
the prospect's company. Within those criteria, there are usually three levels
of desire: "must have," "should have," and "would be nice to have." Be
clear about these levels and how they create limits for negotiations.

SELLING TIPS

Negotiating

- When you give something up, try to gain something in return. When you give something for nothing, there is a tendency for people to want more. In all fairness to you and your prospect, therefore, balance what you give and receive. For example, "I'll lower the price if you pay in full within thirty days," or "I'll give you 10 percent off, but you will be charged for additional services such as training."

- Look for items other than price to negotiate. For example, gain some flexibility by offering: better terms, payment plans, return policies, and delivery schedules; lower deposits or cancellation fees;

or implementation and training programs. Often these items are provided for less than your company would lose if you lowered the price.

- Do not attack your prospect's demand; look for the motive behind it. Never tell a prospect his demand is ridiculous or unreasonable. Remain calm and ask for the reason behind the desire.

- Do not defend your position; ask for feedback and advice from the prospect. If you meet resistance to an offer, don't be defensive. Say something like, "This is my thinking. What would you do if you were in my position?"

Obviously, "must haves" are much less flexible than "would be nice to haves."

Proposing. Proposing is another phase that indirectly affects subsequent negotiations. What you do in the presentation sets the stage for what may come later. During your presentation, tie features and advantages to benefits and emphasize unique benefits. In this way, your product or service and company are positioned above the rest. It is important to position yourself as well. Don't be afraid to let your prospect know she is getting you and everything you have promised to do after the sale.

The successful resolution of a negotiation starts with a commitment to do business together. It is then necessary for both parties to maintain common interests and resolve any conflicts cooperatively. The key to selling and negotiating is to always seek a win-win solution in which both buyer and seller are happy.[7]

What Is the Best Presentation Method?

Each of these sales presentation methods is the best one when the method is properly matched with the *situation*. For example, the stimulus-response method can be used where time is short and the product is simple. Formula selling is effective in repeat purchases or when you know or have already determined the needs of the prospect.

MAKING THE SALE

Matt Suffoletto of IBM Uses the Problem-Solution Presentation Method

"A successful salesperson has expertise in the products he or she sells, as well as an in-depth knowledge of the customer's business. The salesperson often makes recommendations which alter the mainstream of the customer's business process. Recognizing the requirement for business skills, IBM provides training in both the technical aspects of our products, as well as their industrial application.

"My territory consists of manufacturing customers; hence, I pride myself in understanding concepts such as inventory control, time phased requirements planning, and shop floor control. Typically, I work with customer user department and data processing people to do application surveys and detailed justification analysis. After the background work is completed, I make proposals and presentations to educate the chain of decision makers on the IBM recommendations.

"Selling involves the transformation of the features of your product into benefits for the customer. The principal vehicles for that communication are the sales call, formal presentations, and proposals. The larger the magnitude of the sale, the more time and effort is spent on presentations and proposals. A proposal may range from a simple one-page letter and attachment with prices, terms, and conditions, to multi-volume binders with detailed information on the product, including its use, detailed justification, implementation schedules, and contracts. The wide range of comprehensiveness implies an equal range in time commitment of the salesperson.

"Very few sales are made in a single call. At the first sales call the salesperson generally searches for additional information that needs to be brought back, analysis that needs to be done, or questions to be answered. These are opportunities to demonstrate responsiveness to the customer. Getting back to the customer in a very timely and professional manner is a way to build trust and confidence into a business relationship."

The need-satisfaction method is most appropriate where information needs to be first gathered from the prospect as is often the case in selling industrial products. Finally, the problem-solving presentation is excellent for selling high-cost technical products or services, and especially for system selling involving several sales calls and a business proposition. To help improve sales, the salesperson should understand and be able to use each method based on each situation.

Select the Presentation Method, Then the Approach

Before developing the presentation, you must know which presentation method you will use. Once you determine which presentation method is best for your situation, then plan what you will do when talking with your prospect. The first consideration should be how to begin your sales presentation.

THE APPROACH—OPENING THE SALES PRESENTATION

Raleigh Johnson spent days qualifying the prospect, arranging for an appointment, and planning every aspect of the sales presentation; and in the first 60 seconds of the sales presentation, he realized his chance of selling was excellent. He quickly determined the prospect's needs and evoked attention and interest in his product because of the technique he used to begin the sales interview.

A buyer's reactions to the salesperson in the early minutes of the sales presentation are critical to a successful sale. This short period is so important that it is treated as an individual step in selling referred to as the approach. Part of any approach is the prospect's first impression of you.

Your Attitude during the Approach

As shown in Figure 7.9, it is common for a salesperson to experience tension in various forms when contacting a prospect. Often this is brought on when the salesperson has preconceived ideas that things may go wrong during the sale. Prospects may be viewed as having negative characteristics that will make the sales call difficult.

All salespeople experience some degree of stress at times. Yet successful salespeople have learned a relaxation and concentration technique called *creative imagery,* which allows them to cope with stress. The salesperson envisions, "What is the worst that can happen?" Then preparation is made to react to it and even accept it if need be. The best that can happen is also envisioned, as seen in Figure 7.10. Furthermore, contingency plans are mentally prepared should the planned sales talk need to be abandoned.

The last question the salesperson should ask is, "What are the chances that things will go wrong?" Chances are the answer involves a low probability. Usually, there is less than a 1 percent chance that things will go wrong, especially when careful planning has taken place before the sales call. A greater than 99 percent probability that things will go as planned should dim fears of the most worrisome of salespeople.

The First Impression You Make Is Critical to Success

When you first meet your prospect, the initial impression you make is based on appearances. If this impression is favorable, your prospect is more likely to listen to you, but if it is not favorable, your prospect may erect communication barriers that are difficult to overcome.

The first impression is centered on the image projected by your (1) appearance, and (2) attitude. Here are some suggestions for making a favorable first impression:

FIGURE 7.9 Make sure your attitude is positive

Tiny brain

Small ears making
hearing difficult

Mouth
programmed
to say "No" and
"Price too high"

Leather windbags
for lungs

Small heart

Big stomach to
hold free meals

Cold fish hands

Dizziness

Fear of
memory lapse and
brain disconnecting
from mouth

Dryness in mouth

Adam's apple
that won't work

Rapid heartbeat

Upset stomach

Sweating palms

Trembling hands

Weakness in knees

- Wear business clothes that are suitable and fairly conservative.
- Be neat in dress and grooming.
- Refrain from smoking, chewing gum, or drinking when in your prospect's office.
- Keep an erect posture to project confidence.
- Leave all unneccessary materials outside the office (overcoat, umbrella, or newspaper).
- If possible, sit down. Should the prospect not offer a chair, ask, "May I sit here?"
- Be enthusiastic and positive toward the interview.
- Smile, always smile! (Try to be sincere with your smile; it will aid you in being enthusiastic and positive toward your prospect.)
- Do not apologize for taking the prospect's time.
- Do not imply that you were just passing by and that the sales call was not planned.
- Maintain eye contact with the prospect.
- If the prospect offers to shake hands, do so with a firm, positive grip while maintaining eye contact.
- If possible, before the interview, learn how to pronounce your prospect's name correctly and use it throughout the interview. Should

FIGURE 7.10   Creative imagery is a great way to relax while psyching yourself up before seeing your prospect

the prospect introduce you to other people, remember their names by using the five ways to remember names shown in Table 7.4.

Like an actor, the salesperson must learn how to project and maintain a positive, confident, and enthusiastic first impression no matter what mood the prospect is in when first encountered by the salesperson.

The Situational Approach

The situation you face will determine what approach technique you should use to begin your sales presentation. The situation is dictated by a number of variables, which only you can identify. Some of the more common situational variables are:

- The type of *product* you are selling.
- Whether this is a *repeat call* on the same person.
- Your degree of knowledge about the *customer's needs*.
- The *time* you have for making the sales presentation.
- Whether the customer *is aware of a problem*.

TABLE 7.4 Five ways to remember prospect's name

1. Be sure to hear the person's name and use it, "It's good to meet you, Mr. Firestone."
2. Spell it out in your mind, or if it is an unusual name, ask the person to spell the name.
3. Relate the name to something you are familiar with, such as relating the name Firestone to Firestone automobile tires.
4. Use the name in the conversation.
5. Repeat the name at the end of the conversation, such as "Goodbye, Mr. Firestone."

- Your sales call *objective*.
- The *type of approach* that will be well received by the customer.
- Your *customer benefit plan*.

These factors must be examined and assigned a degree of importance before entering your customer's office. This approach selection process can greatly aid in making a satisfactory impression.

Approach Techniques and Objectives. Approach techniques are grouped into three general categories: (1) opening with a statement; (2) opening with a demonstration; and (3) opening with a question or questions.

Your choice of approach technique depends on which of the four sales presentations methods you have selected based on your situation and sales presentation plan. Table 7.5 presents one way of determining the approach technique to use. Using questions in a sales approach is feasible with any of the four presentation methods, whereas statements and demonstrations typically are reserved for either the memorized or formula sales presentation methods. Because of their customer-oriented nature, the need-satisfaction and problem-solving sales presentation methods always employ questions at the outset. The next three sections of this chapter review each of the approach techniques with examples of their uses and benefits.

Both the "statement" and "demonstration" approach techniques have three basic objectives:

1. To capture the *attention* of the prospect.
2. To stimulate the prospect's *interest*.
3. To provide a *transition* into the sales presentation.

Imagine the prospect silently asking three questions: (1) "Shall I see this person?" (2) "Shall I listen, talk with, and devote more time to this person?" and (3) "What's in it for me?" The answers to these questions will help determine the outcome of the sale. If you choose to use either of these two approaches, create a statement or demonstration approach that will cause the prospect to say yes to each of these three questions.

TABLE 7.5 The approach technique to use for each of the four sales presentation methods

Sales Presentation Methods	Approach Techniques		
	Statement	Demonstration	Questions
Memorized ("canned")	✓	✓	✓
Formula (persuasive selling)	✓	✓	✓
Need-satisfaction			✓
Problem-solving			✓

The sales approach can be a frightening, lonely, heart-stopping experience. It can easily lead to ego-bruising rejection. Your challenge is to move the prospect from an often cold, indifferent, or sometimes even hostile frame of mind to an aroused excitement about the product. By quickly obtaining the prospect's attention and interest, the conversation can make a smooth transition into the presentation that greatly improves the probability of making the sale by allowing you to quickly lead into the sales presentation, shown in Figure 7.11.

In addition to creating attention, stimulating interest, and providing for transition, using questions in your approach includes the following objectives:

1. To *uncover* the needs or problems *important* to the prospect.
2. To determine if the prospect wishes to *fulfill* these needs or *solve* these problems.
3. To have the prospect *tell you* about these needs or problems, and the intention to do something about them.

Since people buy to fulfill needs or solve problems, the use of questions in your approach is preferable to statements or demonstrations. Questions allow you to uncover needs, whereas statements and demonstrations are used when you assume knowledge of the prospect's needs. However, all three approach techniques can be used by the salesperson in the proper situation.

Opening with Statements

Opening statements are effective if properly planned, especially if the salesperson has uncovered the prospect's needs before entering the office. Four statement approaches frequently used are: (1) the introductory approach; (2) the complimentary approach; (3) the referral approach; and (4) the premium approach.

The **introductory approach** is the most common and the least powerful because it does little to capture the prospect's attention and

FIGURE 7.11   The approach leads quickly into the sales presentation

interest. It opens with the salesperson's name and business: "Hello, Ms. Crompton, my name is John Gladstone, representing the Pierce Chemical Company."

The introductory approach is needed when meeting a prospect for the first time. In most cases, though, the introductory approach should be used in conjunction with another approach. This additional approach could be the complimentary approach.

Everyone likes a compliment. If the **complimentary approach** is sincere, it is an effective beginning to a sales interview:

- "Ms. Rosenburg, you certainly have a thriving restaurant business. I have enjoyed many lunches here. While doing so, I have thought of several products that could make your business even better and make things easier for you and your employees."
- "Mr. Davidson, I was just visiting with your boss who commented that you were doing a good job in keeping the company's printing costs down. I have a couple of ideas which may help you further reduce your costs!"

Sometimes a suitable compliment is not in order or cannot be generated. Another way to get the buyer's attention is to mention a mutual acquaintance as a reference.

The use of another person's name, the **referral approach,** is effective if the prospect respects that person; it is important to remember, however, that the referral approach can have a negative effect if the prospect does not like the person:

- "Ms. Rosenburg, my name is Carlos Ramirez, with the Restaurant Supply Corporation. When I talked to your brother last week, he wanted me to give you the opportunity to see Restaurant Supply's line of paper products for your restaurant."
- "Hello, Mr. Gillespie—Linda Crawford with the Ramada Inn suggested that I contact you concerning our new Xerox table copier."

One salesperson tells of asking the customer to tape-record a brief introduction to a friend. When calling on the friend, the salesperson placed the recorder on the desk and said, "Amos McDonald has a message for you, Ms. James . . . let's listen."

Few people can obtain a reference for every prospect they intend to contact (this may be especially true for a beginning salesperson). Even if you don't know "all the right people," you can still get on track by offering the buyer something for nothing—a premium.

A **premium approach** is effective because everyone likes to receive something free. When appropriate, use free samples and novelty items in a premium approach:

- Early in the morning of her first day on a new campus, one textbook salesperson makes a practice of leaving a dozen doughnuts in the faculty lounge with her card stapled to the box. She claims that prospects actually come looking for her!
- "Mr. Jones, here is a beautiful desk calendar with your name engraved on it. Each month I will place a new calendar in the holder which, by the way, will feature one of our products. This month's calendar, for example, features our lubricating oil."
- "Ms. Rogers, this high-quality Fuller hair brush is yours, free, for just giving me five minutes of your time."
- "Ms. McCall [handing her the product to examine], I want to leave samples for you, your cosmetic representative, and your best customers of Revlon's newest addition to our perfume line."

Creative use of premiums is an effective sales approach. Demonstrations also leave a favorable impression with a prospect.

Demonstration Openings

Openings using demonstrations and dramatics are effective because of their ability to force the prospect into participating in the interview. Of the two methods discussed here, the product approach is more frequently used by itself or in combination with statements and questions.

In the **product approach,** the salesperson places the product on the counter or hands it to the customer, saying nothing. The salesperson waits for the prospect to begin the conversation. The product approach is useful if the product is new, unique, colorful, or if it is an existing product that has changed noticeably.

If, for example, Pepsi-Cola completely changed the shape of its bottle and label, the salesperson simply hands the new product to the retail buyer and waits for a reaction. In marketing a new pocket calculator for college students, the Texas Instruments salesperson might simply lay the product on the buyer's desk and wait. It is possible to effectively combine the product approach with the showmanship approach.

The **showmanship approach** involves doing something unusual to catch the prospect's attention and interest; this should be done carefully so that the approach does not backfire, which can happen if the demonstration does not work or is so flamboyant that it is inappropriate for the situation:

MAKING THE SALE

A Successful Salesperson's Approach

Sheila Fisher, a middle-aged widow, lived in California for 25 years before returning to her native England three years ago. She wanted to move back to California and wanted a home of her own. She had some cash available for a down payment, but her income was fixed and she was not sure what she could make if she went back to work as a hair stylist. However, she knew what she did not want. "I don't want exotic financing," Sheila told Vikki Morrison. "I want to keep my life simple. I don't want to get in a situation where, in three years, I'll have to sell."

This encounter was their first face-to-face meeting. Vikki has a formula for such situations. In a previous telephone conversation, she had a rough idea of what Ms. Fisher wanted: A three-bedroom home with a formal dining room and assumable financing that would keep her monthly payments at or below $600 after a $50,000 down payment.

Before the meeting, Vikki had combed the multiple listing book for condominiums that matched Ms. Fisher's needs and compiled a list of addresses. If she had viewed the home before, she simply called the owners to warn them she would be dropping in. If she hadn't visited the home, Vikki put it on the list of homes to screen before Ms. Fisher's arrival.

By the time the two women met, Vikki had mapped out a tour of five homes, building up to a spacious condominium with a $144,000 price tag that the realtor thought was the best of the lot. But she didn't really expect to sell any of them that day.

"This is our getting-acquainted day," Vikki told Sheila as she turned into traffic on busy Golden West Avenue. "So be very blunt, very up-front. That's the only way I can learn your tastes. Okay?"

Ms. Fisher agreed. She had already decided that she liked Vikki Morrison, the fourth real estate agent whom she had consulted.

"I think she's listening to me," she confided in Vikki's absence. "I think she understands."

- "Ms. Rosenburg, our paper plates are the strongest on the market, making them drip-free, a quality your customers will appreciate." [The salesperson places a paper plate on her lap and pours cooking grease or motor oil onto it while speaking to the prospect.]

- As she hands the buyer a plate from a new line of china, she lets it drop to the floor. It does not break. While picking it up, she says, "Our new breakthrough in treating quality china will revolutionize the industry. Your customers, especially newlyweds, will love this feature. Don't you think so?"

- The salesperson selling Super Glue would repeat the television advertisement for the prospect. In the prospect's office, the salesperson glues two objects together, such as a broken handle back onto a coffee cup, waits one minute, hands the cup to the buyer for a test, and then begins the sales presentation. The mended cup can be left with the buyer as a gift and a reminder.

- The life insurance salesperson hands the prospect a bunch of daisies saying, "Steve, when you're pushing daisies, what will your family be doing?" [This might be too tactless to use on anyone except a close friend, but you get the picture.]

Opening with Questions

Questions are the most common openers because they allow the salesperson to better determine the prospect's needs, and force the prospect to participate in the sales interview. Only questions that the salesperson knows from experience and preplanning will receive a positive reaction from the buyer should be used, since a negative reaction is hard to overcome.

Like opening statements, opening questions can be synthesized to suit a number of selling situations. In the following sections, several basic questioning approaches are introduced. This listing is by no means exclusive, but serves to introduce the reader to a smattering of questioning frameworks. With experience, a salesperson develops a knack for determining what question to ask what prospect.

Customer Benefit Approach. Using this approach, the salesperson asks a question that implies the product will benefit the prospect; if it is their initial meeting, the salesperson can include both his(her) and the company's name:

- "Hi, I'm Charles Foster of ABC Shipping and Storage Company! Mr. McDaniel, would you be interested in a new storage and shipping container that will reduce your transfer costs by 10 to 20 percent?"
- "Would you be interested in saving 20 percent on the purchase of our IBM typewriters?"
- "Ms. Johnson, did you know that several thousand companies—like yours—have saved 10 to 20 percent of their manufacturing cost as described in the *Newsweek* article? [Continue, not waiting for a response.] They did it by installing our computerized assembly system! Is that of interest to you?"

Your **customer benefit approach** statement should carefully be constructed to anticipate the buyer's response. However, always be prepared for the unexpected, as when the salesperson said, "This office machine will pay for itself in no time at all." "Fine," the buyer said. "As soon as it does, send it to us."

A customer benefit approach is also implemented through the use of a direct statement of product benefits. While the customer benefit approach begins with a question, it can be used with a statement showing how the product can benefit the prospect. The three customer benefit questions shown earlier can be converted into benefit statements:

- "Mr. McDaniel, I want to talk with you about our new storage and shipping container, which will reduce your costs by 10 to 20 percent."
- "I'm here to show you how to save 20 percent on the purchase of our IBM typewriters."
- "Ms. Johnson, several thousand companies—like yours—have saved 10 to 20 percent on their manufacturing cost by installing our computerized assembly system! I'd like 15 minutes of your time to show how we can reduce your manufacturing costs."

Benefit statements are useful in situations where you know the prospect's or customer's critical needs and have a short time to make your presentation. However, to assure a positive atmosphere, statements can be followed by a short question—"Is that of interest to you?"—to help ensure that the benefits are important to the buyer. Even if you know of the buyer's interest, a positive response—"Yes"—to your question is a commitment; the buyer will listen to your presentation because of the possible benefits offered by your product.

Furthermore, you can use the buyer's response to this question as a reference point throughout your presentation. A continuation of an earlier example illustrates the use of a reference point:

- "Mr. McDaniel, earlier you mentioned interest in reducing your shipping costs. The [now mention your product's feature] eanbles you to [now discuss your product's advantages]. And the benefit to you is reduced manufacturing costs."

Sometimes, salespeople have to prepare an approach that temporarily baffles a prospect. One common method of baffling entails the exploitation of human curiosity.

Curiosity Approach. The salesperson asks a question or does something to make the prospect curious about the product or service. For example, a salesperson for Richard D. Irwin, Inc., the company that publishes this text, might use the **curiosity approach** by saying:

- "Do you know why college professors such as yourself have made this [as she hands the book to the prospect] the best-selling book about how to sell on the market?"
- "Do you know why a recent *Newsweek* article described our new computerized assembly system as revolutionary?" [The salesperson briefly displays the *Newsweek* issue, then puts it away before the customer can request to look at the article. Interrupting a sales presentation by urging a prospect to review an article would lose the prospect's attention for the rest of the interview.]

One manufacturer's salesperson sent a telegram to a customer saying, "Tomorrow is the big day for you and your company." When the salesperson arrived for the interview, the prospect could not wait to find out what the salesperson's message meant.

In calling on a male buyer who liked to smoke cigars, a saleswoman set a cigar box on the buyer's desk. After some chatting, the buyer said, "What's in the box?" The salesperson handed the box to the buyer and said, "Open it." Inside was a product she wanted to sell. After he bought, she gave him the cigars. Selling can be fun, especially if the salesperson enjoys being creative.

Opinion Approach. People are usually flattered when asked their opinion on a subject. Most prospects are happy to discuss their needs if asked correctly. Here are some examples:

- "I'm new at this business, so I wonder if you could help me? My company says our Model 100 copier is the best on the market for the money. What do you think?"
- "Mr. Jackson, I've been trying to sell you for months on using our products. What is your honest opinion about our line of electric motors?"

The **opinion approach** is especially good for the new salesperson because it shows that you value the buyer's opinion. Opinion questioning also shows that you will not challenge a potential buyer's expertise by spouting a memorized pitch.

Shock Approach. As its title implies, the **shock approach** uses a question designed to make the prospect think seriously about a subject related to the salesperson's product. For example:

- "Did you know that you have a 20 percent chance of having a heart attack this year?" (Life insurance.)
- "Did you know that home burglary, according to the FBI, has increased this year by 15 percent over last year?" (Alarm system.)
- "Shoplifting costs store owners millions of dollars each year! Did you know that there is a good chance you have a shoplifter in your store right now?" (Store cameras and mirrors.)

This type of question must be used carefully, as some prospects may feel you are merely trying to pressure them into a purchase by making alarming remarks.

Multiple Question Approach (SPIN). In many selling situations it is wise to use questions to determine the prospect's needs. A series of questions is an effective sales interview opener. Multiple questions force the prospect to immediately participate in the sales interview, and quickly develop two-way communication. Carefully listening to the prospect's needs will aid in determining what features, advantages, and benefits to use in the sales presentation.

A relatively new method of using multiple questions to the **multiple question approach (SPIN),** which involves using a series of four types of questions in a specific sequence.[8] SPIN stands for: (1) *Situation*, (2) *Problem*, (3) *Implication*, and (4) *Need–payoff* questions. Since SPIN requires questions asked in their proper sequence, its parts are carefully described in the following four steps:

Step 1:

Situation questions. Ask about the prospect's general situation as it relates to your product.

Industrial examples: Dyno Electric Cart salesperson to purchasing agent: "How large are your manufacturing plant facilities?"

IBM typewriter salesperson to purchasing agent: "How many secretaries do you have in your company?"

Consumer examples: Real estate salesperson to prospect: "How many people do you have in your family?"

Appliance salesperson selling a microwave oven to prospect: "Do you like to cook?" "Do you and your family eat out much?"

As the name of this question implies, the salesperson first asks a "situation" question that helps provide a general understanding of the buyer's needs. Situation questioning allows the salesperson to move smoothly into questions on specific problem areas. Also, beginning an approach using specific questions may make the prospect uncomfortable and unwilling to talk to you about problems, and may even deny them. These are warm-up questions enabling you to get a better understanding of the prospect's business.

Step 2:

Problem questions. Ask about specific problems, dissatisfactions, or difficulties perceived by the prospect relative to your situation question.

Industrial examples: Dyno Electric Cart salesperson to purchasing agent: "Have your executives ever complained about having to do so much walking in and around the plant?"

IBM typewriter salesperson to purchasing agent: "Do your Royal typewriters do all that your secretaries want them to do?" (You may have previously asked the secretaries this question and know that they are dissatisfied.)

Consumer examples: Real estate salesperson to prospect: "Has your family grown so that you need more space?"

Appliance salesperson selling microwave oven to prospect: "Are you happy with your present oven?" "Are there time when you must quickly prepare meals?"

Problem questions are asked early in the presentation to bring out the needs or problems of the prospect. Your goal is to have the prospect admit, "Yes, I do have a problem."

To maximize your chance of making the sale, determine which of the prospect's needs or problems are important (explicit needs) and which are unimportant. The more explicit needs you can discover, the more vividly you can relate your products' benefits to areas the prospect is actually interested in, and thus, the higher your probability of making the sale.

An important or explicit need or problem is recognized as such by the prospect. There is a desire to fulfill the need or solve the problem. Problem questions are useful in developing explicit needs.

If the prospect should state a specific need after your situation or problem questions, do not move directly into your sales presentation. Continue with the next two steps to increase your chance of making the sale. A prospect may sometimes not appreciate all the ramifications of a problem.

Step 3:

Implication questions. Ask about the implications of the prospect's problems or how a problem affects various related operational aspects of a home, life, or business.

Industrial examples: Dyno Electric Cart salesperson to purchasing agent: "It sounds as if your executives would have an interest in reducing their travel time and not having to exert so much energy in transit. Doesn't it seem that if they could do so, they would get to the plant as quickly as they need to, saving themselves time and energy, and saving the company money?"

IBM typewriter salesperson to purchasing agent: "Does this problem mean your secretaries are not as efficient as they should be, thus increasing your costs per page typed?"

Consumer examples: Real estate salesperson to prospect: "So with the new baby and your needing a room as an office in

> your home, what problems does your present residence create for you?"
>
> Appliance salesperson to prospect: "With both of you working, does your present kitchen oven mean . . . inconvenience for you? . . . that you have to eat out more than you want to? . . . that you have to eat junk foods instead of well-balanced meals?"

Implication questions seek to help the prospect realize the true dimensions of a problem. The phrasing of the question is important in getting the prospect to discuss problems or areas for improvement, and it fixes them in the prospect's mind. In this situation, the prospect is motivated to fulfill this need or solve this problem.

If possible, attach a "bottom line" figure to the implication question. You want the prospect to state, or agree with you, that the implications of the problem are causing such things as: production slowdowns of one percent resulting in increased cost of 25 cents per unit; increased reproduction costs of 1 cent per copy; loss of customers; or hiring added personnel to make service calls costing an extra $500 per week.

Use this hard data later in your discussion of the business proposition. Using the prospect's data, you can show how your product can influence the prospect's costs, productivity, or customers.

S-P-I questions do not have to be asked in order, and you can ask more than one of each type. You will generally begin with a situation question and follow with a problem question. However, you could ask a situation question, a problem question, and another situation question, for example. The need-payoff question is always last.

Step 4:

> Need-payoff questions. Ask if the prospect has an important, explicit need.
>
> *Industrial examples:*   Dyno Electric Cart salesperson to purchasing agent: "If I could show you how you can solve your executives' problems in getting to and from your plant, and at the same time save your company money, would you have an interest?"
>
> IBM office products salesperson to purchasing agent: "Would you be interested in a method to improve your secretaries' efficiency at a lower cost than you now incur?"
>
> *Consumer examples:*   Real estate salesperson to prospect: "If I could show you how to cover your space problems at the same cost per square foot, would you be interested?"

Appliance salesperson to prospect: "Do you need a convenient way to prepare well-balanced, nutritious meals at home?"

Phrasing the need-payoff question is the same as opening with a benefit statement. However, in using the SPIN approach, the prospect defines the need. If the prospect responds positively to the need-payoff questions, you know this is an important (explicit) need. You may have to repeat the P-I-N questions to fully develop all of the prospect's important needs.

The Procter & Gamble and Tide sales presentation shown in Table 7.2 is an example of using the P-I-N approach for a customer with whom you are familiar. Let's say your customer says yes to the need-payoff question: "If we could determine how much volume you're missing, I think you'd be willing to make space for the larger size, wouldn't you?" Then, you move directly into a brief sales presentation.

If the answer is no, this is not an important need. Start over again by asking *P*roblem, *I*mplication, and *N*eed-payoff questions to determine important needs.

Product Not Mentioned in SPIN Approach. As you see from SPIN examples, the product is not mentioned in the approach. This allows you to develop the prospect's need without revealing exactly what you are selling.

When a salesperson first walks into the buyer's office and says, "I want to talk about Product X," the chances of a negative response greatly increase because the buyer does not perceive a need for the product. SPIN questions allow you to better determine the buyer's needs before starting the presentation.

USING QUESTIONS RESULTS IN SALES SUCCESS

Since this chapter introduces questioning techniques, and since properly questioning a prospect or customer is important to sales success, you are ready for the many uses and types of questions.

Asking questions, sometimes called probes, is an excellent technique for: (1) obtaining information from the prospect, (2) developing two-way communication, and (3) increasing prospect participation.

When using questions in selling, you need to know or anticipate the answer you want for a question. Once you know the answer wanted, you can develop the question. This procedure can be used to request information you do not have, and to confirm information you already know.

An ideal question is one a prospect is willing and able to answer. Only questions that help make the sale should be asked, so use questions sparingly and wisely.

Why would asking a question get the prospect's attention? To give an answer, a prospect must think about the topic. There are four basic categories of questions that can be used at any point during the presentation. These categories are: (1) direct, (2) nondirective, (3) rephrasing, and (4) redirect questions.

The Direct Question

The **direct question** or closed-ended question is answered with very few words. A simple yes or no answers most direct questions. They are especially useful in moving a customer toward a specific topic. Examples the salesperson might use are: "Mr. Berger, are you interested in saving 20 percent on your manufacturing costs?" or, "Reducing manufacturing costs are important, aren't they?" You can anticipate a yes response from these questions.

Never phrase the direct question as a direct negative-no question. A *direct negative-no question* is any question that can be answered in a manner that cuts you off completely. The retail salesperson says, "May I help you?" and the reply usually is "No, I'm just looking." It's like hanging up the telephone on you. You are completely cut off.

Other types of direct questions ask "what kind?" or "how many?" The questions also ask for a limited, short answer from the prospect. The implication and need-payoff questions used in SPIN are examples of direct questions used for the approach.

However, the answer to a direct question does not really tell you much, because there is little feedback involved. You may need more information to determine the buyer's needs and problems, especially if you could not determine them before the sales call. Nondirective questioning aids you in the quest for information.

The Nondirective Question

To open up two-way communication, the salesperson can use an open-ended or **nondirective question** by beginning the question with one of six words: Who, what, where, then, how, and why. Examples include:

- Who will use this product?
- What features are you looking for in a product like this?
- Where will you use this product?
- When will you need the product?
- How often will you use the product?
- Why do you need or want to buy this type of product?

One word questions such as "Oh?" or "Really?" can also be useful in some situations. One-word questions should be said so that the tone increases or is emphasized: "Oh?!" This prompts the customer to continue talking. Try it—it works.

To practice using the open-ended questioning technique, ask a friend a question—any question—beginning with one of these six words, or use a one-word question, and see what answer you get. Chances are, the response will consist of several sentences. In a selling situation, this type of response allows the salesperson to better determine the prospect's needs.

The purpose of using a nondirective question is to obtain unknown or additional information, to draw out clues to hidden or future needs and problems, and to leave the situation open for free discussion of what is on the customer's mind. Situation and implication questions are examples of the nondirective question.

The Rephrasing Question

The third type of question is called the **rephrasing question.** At times, the prospect's meaning is not clearly stated. In this situation, if appropriate, the salesperson might say:

- Are you saying that price is the most important thing you are interested in? (sincerely, not too aggressively)
- Then what you are saying is, if I can improve the delivery time you would be interested in buying?

This form of restatement allows for clarifying meaning and determining the prospect's needs. If the prospect answers yes to the second question, you would find a way to improve delivery. If no is the answer to the delivery question, you know delivery time is not an important buying motive; continue to probe for the true problem.

The Redirect Question

The fourth type of question is the **redirect question.** This is used to "redirect" the prospect to selling points that both parties agree on. There are always areas of agreement between buyer and seller even if the prospect is opposed to purchasing the product. The redirect question is an excellent alternative or backup opener. An example will clarify the concept of redirective questioning.

Imagine you walk into a prospect's office, introduce yourself, and get this response, "I'm sorry, but there is no use in us talking. We are satisfied with our present suppliers. Thanks for coming by." Respond by replacing your planned opener with a redirecting question. You might say:

- We agree that having a supplier who can reduce your costs is important.
- You would agree that manufacturers must use the most cost efficient equipment to stay competitive these days, wouldn't you?
- Wouldn't you agree that you continually need to find new ways to increase your company's sales?

MAKING THE SALE

Keep Quiet and Get the Order

Dennis DeMaria, Branch Manager, Westvaco, Folcroft (Penn.), says, "One of the biggest single weapons you as a salesperson can use in getting an order from a customer or prospect is keeping quiet and patiently waiting for the buyer to answer your questions. A general rule in the selling profession is that the person who asks the questions is the person who has control of the interview. The information obtained from asking questions is the necessary ammunition you use to find the buyer's likes, dislikes, hot buttons, and areas to avoid.

This valuable information also informs the salesperson whether the customer is ready to buy or whether he or she should continue selling.

"Experience has shown that salespeople *do* ask questions but they forget the most important part of this sales principle: *After you ask a question you must be patient, don't talk, and let the buyer answer.* It does not matter how long it takes for the buyer to respond; keep quiet and wait for the answer. Remember, the first person to speak after a question has been asked, loses."[9]

Using a redirect question moves the conversation from a negative position to a positive or neutral one while reestablishing communications between two people. The ability to redirect a seemingly terminated conversation through a well-placed question may impress the prospect simply by showing that you are not a run-of-the-mill order taker, but a professional salesperson who sincerely believes in the beneficial qualities of your product.

Three Rules for Using Questions

The first rule is to use only questions that you can anticipate the answer to or that will not lead you into a situation from which you cannot escape. While questions are a powerful selling technique, they can easily backfire.

The second rule in using a question is to pause or wait after submitting a question to allow the prospect time to respond to it. Waiting for an answer to a well-planned question is sometimes an excruciating process—seconds may seem like minutes. A salesperson must allow the prospect time to consider the question, and hope for a response. Failing to allow a prospect enough time defeats the major purpose of questioning, which is to establish two-way communication between the prospect and the salesperson.

The third rule is to listen. Many salespeople are so intent on talking that they forget to listen to what the prospect says (or disregard nonverbal signals). Salespeople need to listen consciously to prospects so that they can ask intelligent, meaningful questions that will aid both themselves and their prospects in determining what needs and problems exist and how to solve them. Prospects appreciate a good listener and view a willingness to listen as an indication that the salesperson is truly interested in their situation.

IS THE PROSPECT STILL NOT LISTENING?

What happens when, using your best opening approach, you realize that the prospect is not listening? What about prospects who open mail, who fold their arms while looking at the wall or seem to be looking beyond you into the hallway, who make telephone calls in your presence, or who may even doze off, as shown in Figure 7.12.

This is the time to use one of your alternative openers, which will tune the prospect into your message. The prospect must be forced to participate in the talk by using either the question or demonstration approach. By handing the person something, showing something, or asking a question, attention can be briefly recaptured, no matter how indifferent a prospect is to your presence.

If you can overcome such preoccupation or indifference in the early minutes of your interview by quickly capturing the prospect's attention and interest, the probability of your making a sale will greatly improve. This is why the approach is so important to the success of a sales call.

It is crucial to never become flustered or confused when a communication problem arises during your approach. As mentioned earlier, the salesperson who can deftly capture another person's imagination earns the right to a prospect's full attention and interest. Your prospect should not be handled as an adversary, for in that type of situation you will seldom gain the sale.

BE FLEXIBLE IN YOUR APPROACH

Picture yourself as a salesperson getting ready to come face-to-face with an important prospect, Ellen Myerson. You have planned exactly what to say in the sales presentation; but how can you be sure Ms. Myerson will listen to your sales presentation? You realize she is busy and may be indifferent to your being in the office; she probably is preoccupied with her own business-related situation and several of your competitors may already have seen her today.

You have planned to open your presentation with a statement on how successful your memory typewriter has been in helping secretaries save time and eliminate errors in their typing. When you enter the office, Ms. Myerson comments on how efficient her secretaries are and how they produce error-free work. From her remarks, you quickly determine that your planned statement approach is inappropriate. What do you do now?

You might begin by remarking how lucky she is the have such conscientious secretaries, and then proceed into the SPIN question approach, first asking questions to determine general problems that she may have, and then using further questions to uncover specific problem areas she might like to solve. Once you have determined specific problems, you could ascertain whether they are important enough for her to want to solve

FIGURE 7.12 What does it take to get your prospect's attention?

them in the near future. If so, you can make a statement that summarizes how your product's benefits will solve her critical needs, and test for a positive response. A positive response allows you to conditionally move into the sales presentation.

SUMMARY OF MAJOR SELLING ISSUES

Prospects want to talk to you when they believe you will directly benefit them. Your product knowledge and an appreciation of your prospects and their individual situations should aid you in developing a presentation keyed to your prospects and their needs and problems.

Depending on your product type, the number of sales calls that you have to make each day, the type of prospects that you are calling on, and whether you talk with one person or a group of people, you can develop a sales presentation. Simpler products that may be applicable to a number of prospects can be presented using a memorized or formula type of presentation, while more complex, customer-specific items require a need-satisfaction or problem-solution type of presentation. Having decided on a basic mode of sales presentation, you are ready to concentrate on developing a sales approach.

As the first real step in your sales presentation, your approach is an extremely critical factor. To assure your prospect's attention and interest during a memorized or formula mode of presentation, you may want to use a statement or demonstration approach. In more technically oriented situations where you and the prospect must agree on needs and problems, a questioning approach (SPIN, for instance) is in order. Generally, in developing your approach, imagine prospects asking themselves: "Do I have time to listen, talk with, or devote to this person?" "What's in it for me?"

Words alone will not assure a hearing. The first impression made on a prospect can negate an otherwise positive and sincere opening. To assure a favorable impression in most selling situations, generally dress conservatively, be well groomed, and act as though you are truly glad to meet this person.

Your approach statement should be especially designed for each prospect. You can choose to open with a statement, question, or demonstration by using one of many techniques. Several alternative approaches should be held in readiness if you need to alter plans for a specific situation.

Carefully phrased questions are extremely useful at any point in a sales presentation. Questions must display a sincere interest in prospects and their situations. Skillfully handled questions employed in a sales approach can wrest a prospect's attention from distractions—centering it on you and the presentation. Questions are useful in determining prospect wants and needs, thereby increasing prospect participation in the sales presentation. Four basic types of questions discussed in this chapter are direct, nondirective, rephrasing, and redirect questions.

In using questions, ask the type of questions that you can anticipate the answer to. Also, remember to allow prospects time to completely answer the question, and be sure to listen carefully to their answers for a guide as to how well you are progressing toward selling to them. If you determine that your prospect is not listening, do something to recapture attention. Techniques such as offering something or asking questions can refocus the prospect's attention long enough for you to move back into your presentation.

8

Elements of Making a Great Presentation

My career in the food industry began during my sophomore year in college. I decided the best way to learn the industry was to start at the "grass roots" level. I deduced that by my senior year, I should know which career in the industry was best suited for me. During my college years, I worked as a dietary supervisor at Hermann Hospital, as a food intern for the catering department of the Brasewood Marriott Hotel, and as an order clerk for the product buying office of Fleming Foods. These jobs taught me valuable human relations skills, and a good appreciation for people at *all* levels of an operation. The experience also paved the way for my first career opportunity with the Quaker Oats Company.

I began my career with the Quaker Oats Company in February 1980 as an account representative. This position required servicing 50 to 60 independent grocery operations. In the grocery industry, selling time is a valuable commodity. The typical grocery manager gives you 5 to 10 minutes to sell new items, book promotional cases, or suggest space management improvements. Needless to say, your presentation must be short, persuasive, concise, and organized.

My presentation experience was a key factor in determining the success of my next two positions: account supervisor and account manager. These two positions entailed calling on divisional or independent direct accounts. The presentations were given to one or more buyers for 30 or more retail stores. My presentation time of 5 to 10 minutes was increased to 15 to 60 minutes; but, ironically, the same presentation principles applied. My buyer was constantly interrupted by the phone or his/her secretary. My biggest problem was bringing the buyer back into the presentation. During the presentation, I needed to immediately catch the buyer's attention, meet his/her needs, and close the sale. These were the essentials to a successful presentation. •

Linda M. Slaby-Baker
Quaker Oats

"Your presentation," says Linda Slaby-Baker, "should be a give-and-take of mutually beneficial information between you and your buyer. Probe the buyer with questions and then let the buyer talk. Asking questions invites the buyer into your presentation and you quickly learn what the buyer wants to hear. Buyers are human; they love to give their viewpoints. Ask the buyer for input into the structuring of trade deals, the spending of advertising dollars, or how to increase the sales on a slow product.

"Visual aids bring life to your presentations. Visuals take the buyer's mind off you and on a graph, a chart, an advertisement, or a sample. Samples of the product are a must in consumer product presentation. Always leave a sample for the buyer to try.

"In my presentations, I use a number of bar graphs to illustrate the sales growth of products and indexing charts to illustrate shares of the market. Since I am in a business where the products are edible, I bring samples for my buyers to taste. To sell a new syrup, I brought in a small toaster and heated up some frozen waffles. I poured the syrup over the warm waffles and the buyer sampled the product in his office. The result was that I sold all three sizes of the syrup." •

This chapter discusses the elements of the presentation—the fourth step in the sales process (see Figure 8.1). We begin by examining the purpose and essential steps in the presentation. Next, we review and expand on presentation techniques used by salespeople such as Linda Slaby-Baker of the Quaker Oats Company. We end the chapter discussing the importance of the proper use of trial closes and difficulties that may arise in the presentation, along with the need to design your presentation around an individual situation and buyer.

THE PURPOSE OF THE PRESENTATION

The main goal of *your* presentation is to sell *your* product to *your* customer. However, we know that a prospective buyer considers many things before making a decision on which product to buy. As we have seen, the approach or first few minutes of the interview should be constructed to determine the prospect's need, capture attention and interest, and allow for a smooth transition into the presentation.

The presentation is a continuation of the approach. What is the purpose of the presentation? The purpose is to provide *knowledge* via the features, advantages, and benefits of your product, marketing plan, and business proposal. This allows the buyer to develop positive personal *beliefs* toward your product. The beliefs result in *desire* (or *need*) for the type of product you sell. Your job, as a salesperson, is to convert that need into a want, and into the *attitude* that your specific product is the best product to fulfill a

FIGURE 8.1   The presentation is the heart of the sale. An effective approach
             allows you to move smoothly into the discussion of your
             product's features, advantages and benefits.

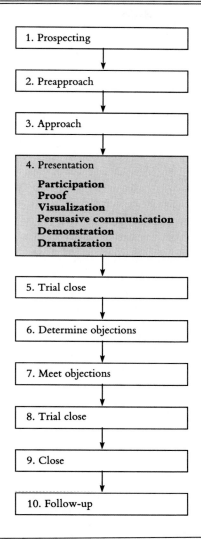

1. Prospecting

2. Preapproach

3. Approach

4. Presentation

   **Participation
   Proof
   Visualization
   Persuasive communication
   Demonstration
   Dramatization**

5. Trial close

6. Determine objections

7. Meet objections

8. Trial close

9. Close

10. Follow-up

certain need. Furthermore, you must convince the buyer that not only is
your product the best but that you are the best source to buy from. When
this occurs, your prospect has moved into the *conviction* stage of the mental
buying process.

A real need is established, the buyer wants to fulfill that need, and there
is a high probability your product is best for the purpose. This results in

FIGURE 8.2   The five purposes of the presentation

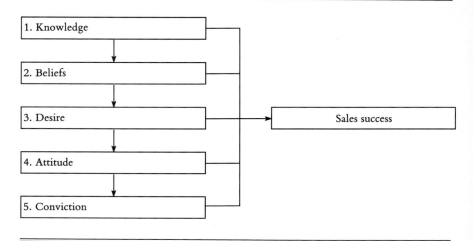

your making a sale, as shown in Figure 8.2. Whether to buy or not is a "choice decision," and you have provided the necessary information so that the customer chooses to buy from you.

Assume, for example, you are a salesperson for IBM and you wish to sell a company 10 of your new memory electric typewriters costing $5,000 each. The prospect's company is presently using your competitor's electric typewriters, which cost $3,000 each. How should you conceptualize the prospect's thought processes regarding whether to buy or not buy from you (as shown in Figure 8.1) in order to develop your presentation?

First, realize that the prospect has certain attitudes toward present equipment (typewriters). The prospect's job performance is judged according to the management of certain responsibilities. Thus, improving the performance of company employees is important. However, the prospect knows nothing about you, your product, or your product's benefits. The prospect may feel that IBM products are good, high-quality, expensive products. However, you cannot be sure about the buyer's present attitudes.

Develop a SPIN approach to determine the buyer's attitudes toward typewriters in general and the memory typewriter specifically. Once you have gone through each of the four SPIN questions, and you feel more information about your product is in order, you begin the presentation.

Present the product information that allows the buyer to develop a positive attitude toward your product. Next, possibly using a value analysis type of proposal, show how a memory typewriter can increase a secretary's efficiency, reduce costs per item typed, and pay for itself in one year, using a return–on–investment (ROI) technique. A positive reaction from your prospect indicates that the desire stage of the mental buying process has been reached. There is a need for some brand of memory typewriter.

Now, show why your IBM memory typewriter is the best solution to the buyer's need and show that you will provide service after the sale. A positive response on these two items indicates that the prospect believes your product is best and that the "conviction" stage has been reached. The prospect wants to buy the IBM memory typewriter.

Up to this point, you have discussed your product's features, advantages, and benefits, your marketing plan, and your business proposition. You have *not* asked the prospect to buy. Rather, you have developed a presentation to lead the prospect through four of the five mental buying steps: the attention, interest, desire, and conviction steps. It may take you five minutes, two hours, or several weeks of repeat calls to move the prospect into the conviction stage.

You should realize that you must move the prospect into the conviction stage before a sale is made. So hold off asking the prospect to buy until the conviction stage. Otherwise, this usually results in objections and failure to listen to your whole story and fewer sales. The sales presentation has seven major steps. Each step is taken in order to logically and sequentially move the prospect into the conviction stage of the buying process.

When a person buys something, did you ever stop to think what is actually purchased? Is the customer really buying your product? No. What is actually bought is a mental picture of the future in which your product helps to fulfill some expectation. The buyer has mentally conceived certain needs. Your presentation must create mental images that move your prospect into the conviction stage.

THREE ESSENTIAL STEPS
WITHIN THE PRESENTATION

No matter which of the four sales presentation methods used, your presentation must follow the three essential steps shown in Figure 8.3.★ They are:

Step 1:

Fully discuss the features, advantages, and *benefits* of your product. Tell the whole story.

Step 2:

Present your marketing plan. For wholesalers and retailers, this is your suggestion on how they should *resell* the product. For end users, it is your suggestion on how they can *use* the product.

★The three steps are discussed in Chapter 6 under the topic "Customer Benefit Plan."

FIGURE 8.3   Three essential steps within the presentation

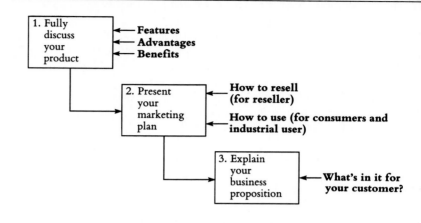

Step 3:

Explain your business proposition. This step relates the *value* of your product to its *cost*. It should be discussed last, since you always want to present your product's benefits and marketing plan relative to your product's price.

Ideally, information in each of these steps should be presented in such a manner as to create a visual picture in the prospect's mind of the benefits of the purchase. To do this, use persuasive communication and participation techniques, proof statements, visual aids, dramatization, and demonstrations as you move through each of the three steps during the presentation.

THE SALES PRESENTATION MIX

Salespeople sell different products in many different ways, but all use six broad classes of presentation elements to some degree in their presentations to provide information in a meaningful way to the prospect or customer. For this reason, I refer to these elements as the *presentation mix.*

The **sales presentation mix** refers to the elements the salesperson assembles to sell to prospects and customers. While all elements should be part of the presentation, it is up to the individual to determine the extent to which each element is emphasized. This determination is primarily based on the sales call objective, customer profile, and customer benefit plan. Let's examine each of the six elements, as shown in Figure 8.4.

FIGURE 8.4 The salesperson's presentation mix

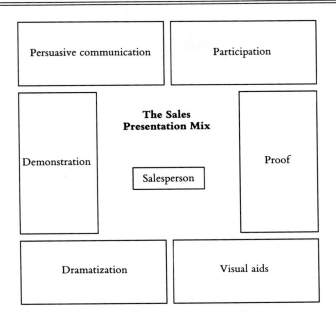

Persuasive Communication

To be a successful salesperson, do you need to be a smooth talker? No, but you need to consider and use factors that aid in clearly communicating your message. As shown in Table 8.1, sales managers in 44 major manufacturing firms ranked three factors (enthusiasm, persuasiveness, and verbal skills) as important attributes for salespeople.[1] Enthusiasm was ranked most important, with high persuasiveness and high verbal skill ranking fourth and sixth, respectively.[2]

In Chapter 4, we discussed seven factors which, if used, help you to be a better communicator. The factors are:

1. Using questions.
2. Having empathy.
3. Keeping the message simple.
4. Creating mutual trust.
5. Listening.
6. Having a positive attitude and enthusiasm.
7. Being believable.

TABLE 8.1   Sales manager's ranking of characteristics for salespeople

| Attribute | Rank Assigned by Respondents★ | | | | | | | | | | Total Points |
	1 (10)	2 (9)	3 (8)	4 (7)	5 (6)	6 (5)	7 (4)	8 (3)	9 (2)	10 (1)	
1. Enthusiasm	16	5	85		1	5	–	1	–	–	388
2. Well organized	6	8	11	3	5	5	1	2	–	–	304
3. Obvious ambition	8	6	5	7	4	3	2	3	3	–	285
4. High persuasiveness	2	10	3	1	10	4	5	3	1	2	254
5. General sales experience	3	2	4	6	6	2	8	8	5	4	226
6. High verbal skill	2	3	3	6	2	7	7	6	4	1	215
7. Specific sales experience	2	4	2	8	6	1	5	4	4	5	214
8. Highly recommended	1	–	1	4	3	3	7	2	7	2	149
9. Follows instructions	–	2	–	3	4	4	2	9	9	8	142
10. Sociability	–	1	1	2	–	7	6	6	8	10	134

★The top numeral in each column is the ranking given by executives, with 1 most important and 10 least important. Numbers in parentheses are point ratings assigned to each rank. Numbers in the table show the number of respondents who assigned each rank to each attribute.

Additional persuasive factors to consider in the presentation are logical reasoning, persuasive suggestions, a sense of fun, personalized relationships, trust, body language, a controlled presentation, diplomacy, the "Paul Harvey dialogue" or conversation style, and using words as selling tools.

Logical Reasoning. The application of logic through reasoning is an effective persuasive technique that appeals to prospects' common sense by requiring them to think about the proposition and to compare alternative solutions to problems. It can have excellent results when applied to selling computers, heavy equipment, and communication systems. This is especially so when selling complicated proposals involving comparative cost data, when price versus benefits must be judged, and when the product is a radically new concept.

Logical reasoning involves a presentation constructed around three parts: a major premise, a minor premise, and a conclusion. Here is an example:

1. Major premise: All manufacturers wish to reduce costs and increase efficiency.
2. Minor premise: My equipment will reduce your costs and increase your efficiency.
3. Conclusion: Therefore, you should buy my equipment.

If presented exactly in the straightforward manner as above, the logical formula may be too blunt; the prospect may raise defenses. However, you can develop the framework or outline of the presentation to first determine if the prospect is interested in reducing costs and increasing manufacturing efficiency. If so, then a value analysis can be presented showing the benefits of your product over other alternatives. Information such as performance data, costs, service, and delivery information can be presented in a persuasive manner using various elements of the presentation mix.

Persuasion through Suggestion. Suggestion, like logical reasoning, is used effectively to persuade prospects. The skilled use of suggestions can arouse attention, interest, desire, conviction, and action. Types of suggestions that may be considered for incorporation into the presentation are:

1. **Suggestive propositions** imply that the prospect should act now, such as, "Shouldn't you go ahead and buy now before the price goes up next month?" Prospects often like to postpone their buying decisions, so the suggestive approach can help overcome this problem.

2. **Prestige suggestions** are used to get the prospect to visualize using products that famous people, companies, or someone the prospect might trust uses, such as, "The National Professional Engineers Association has endorsed our equipment. That's the reason several hundred of the Fortune 500 manufacturers are using our products. This elite group of manufacturers are finding the equipment helps them to increase their profits, sales, and market share. Is this of interest to you?"

3. **Autosuggestion** attempts to have prospects imagine themselves using the product. Television advertisements frequently use this form of suggestion. The salesperson visualizes the product, saying, "Just imagine how this equipment will look and operate in your store. Your employees will perform much better and will thank you."

4. The **direct suggestion** is widely used by professional salespeople in all industries because it does not "tell," but suggests they buy, which does not offend the buyer. Such a suggestion might state: "Based on our survey of your needs, I suggest you purchase. . . ." or, "Let's consider this: we ship you three train carloads of Whirlpool washers and dryers of the following colors and models. . . ."

5. The **indirect suggestion** is used at times for some prospects when it is better not to be direct in suggesting a recommended course of action. Indirect suggestions help instill in prospects' minds factors such as doubt about a competitor's products or desire for your product, which makes it seem as if it is their idea: "Should you buy 50 or 75 dozen 12-oz. cans of Revlon hairspray for your promotion?" or, "Have you talked with anyone who has used that product?"

6. The **counter suggestion** is used to get an opposite response from the prospect: "Do you really want such a high-quality product?" Often the

buyer will begin expanding on why a high-quality product is needed. This is an especially effective technique to include in the presentation if you have already determined the prospect wants a high-quality product.

Make the Presentation Fun. Selling is fun, not a battle between the prospect and salesperson, so loosen up and enjoy the presentation. This is easy to do, once you believe in yourself and what you are selling — so sound like it! Have the *right mental attitude* and you can be successful.

Personalize Your Relationship. When I worked for a large national industrial manufacturer, my sales manager taught me to personalize the presentation. He would say, "Charles, you are enthusiastic, you believe in yourself, your products, your company, and you give a very good presentation. To improve, however, you need to personalize your relationship with each of your customers. In some manner let them know during your presentation that you have their best interests at heart." He would always say, "Show 'em that you love 'em."

   I came up with the short phrase, "You have me." Once I incorporated this into my presentation at the appropriate time, I saw a significant increase in my total sales and sales to customer call ratio by saying something like: "You are not only buying my products but also me. You have me on call 24 hours a day to help you in any way I can."

   Yes, it does sound somewhat corny, but it helped show my customers that I cared for them and they could believe in me. This helped to build trust between us. You might choose a different way, yet it is important to demonstrate that you look out for their interests.

Build Trust. Two of the best and easiest ways to build your persuasive powers with prospects are *being honest* and *doing what you say* you will. This results in building trust, which increases sales. Most professional buyers have elephant-like memories that can be used to your advantage if you follow through after the sale and do what you said you would when presenting the proposal.

   Honesty is always the best policy, and it is an effective way to build trust. The salesperson should never claim more than the product can accomplish. If the product does not live up to expectations, then apologize, return the product for credit, or trade for another product. This is extremely important in obtaining repeat sales. This builds trust; the next time the prospect is reluctant to buy, then you say, "Haven't I always taken care of you? Trust me, this product is what you need. I guarantee it!"

Use Body Language. Just as you watch for buying signals from a prospect, the prospect watches your facial expressions and body movements. The salesperson's nonverbal communication must project a positive image to the prospect, one that shows you know what you are talking about and understand the buyer's needs. Your customer will think, "I can trust this person."

The best nonverbal selling technique to use is the smile. As my sales manager said, "It's often not what you say but how you say it and you can say almost anything to anyone if you do it with a smile. So practice your facial expressions and smile—always smile."

Control the Presentation.   In making the presentation, you need to direct the conversation as planned to lead the prospect through the presentation and proposal. The salesperson is often faced with how to maintain control and what to do if the prospect takes control of the conversation. For example, what do you do if the prospect likes to talk about hobbies, attacks your company or products for poor service or credit mix-ups, or is a kidder and likes to poke fun at your products?

When this happens, the salesperson should stay with a planned presentation if possible. If there is some complaint, this should be addressed first. If the prospect likes to talk about other things, then do so briefly. When the prospect's attention and interest are hard to maintain, questions or some manner of getting participation in the presentation are the two best methods to rechannel the conversation.

Be sure to control the visual aids and any materials you use in the presentation. New salespeople often make the mistake of handing propsects their catalog, price list, or brochures showing several products. When buyers are looking through these items, chances are they are not listening. Too much information can cause frustration and they will not buy. So hold on to your product materials with one hand and discuss the points of information you wish to present while prospects look and listen to you.

Be a Diplomat.   All salespeople face the situation where the prospects feel they are right, or know it all, and the salesperson has different opinions. For example, the salesperson may have previously sold the prospect's company a machine that is always breaking down due to its operator, not the piece of equipment, yet the salesperson's company gets the blame. What to do?

The salesperson has to be a diplomat in cases where tempers rise and prospects are wrong but feel they are correct and will not change their opinions. Retreat may be the best option; otherwise, you run the risk of destroying the relationship. If you challenge the prospect, you could win the battle only to lose the war. This is a decision the salesperson must make based on the individual situation.

Use the Paul Harvey Dialogue.   Paul Harvey has the most listened-to radio news broadcast in America because of what he says and how he says it. Listen to him yourself. (His broadcast is syndicated; you may have to search to find it.) Then use the **Paul Harvey dialogue.** Construct your presentation to incorporate his excellent methods of speech, delivery, and particularly how he "builds" suspense into his stories. With these techniques, your talk comes alive rather than sounding like a dull, memorized presentation, spoken in a monotone.

Simile, Metaphor, and Analogy. Words are selling tools. Similes, metaphors, analogies, pauses, silence, and changes in the rate of speaking, tone, and pitch are effective methods of gaining prospects' attention and capturing their interest in a proposal.

A **simile** is a direct comparison statement using the words "like" or "as": A poorly manicured lawn *is like* a bad haircut. Our Sylvania Safeline bulbs *are like* a car's shatterproof windshield. Shaklee diet drinks *are like* a chocolate milkshake. The carton folds *as flat as* a pancake for storage.

A **metaphor** is an *implied* comparison that uses a contrasting word or phrase to evoke a vivid image: Our power mowers *sculpt* your lawn. Our cabin cruiser *plows* the waves smoothly. The computer's *memory* stores your data. The components *telescope* into a two-inch-thick disk.

The **analogy** compares two different situations that have something in common such as, "Our 'Sun Screen' for your home will stop the sun's heat and glare before it hits your window. It's like having a shade tree in front of your window without blocking the view." Remember to talk the prospect's language by using familiar terminology and buzzwords in a conversational tone.

Participation Is Essential to Success

The second major part of the presentation involves techniques for getting the prospect to participate in the presentation. Four ways to induce participation are:

1. Questions.
2. Product use.
3. Visuals.
4. Demonstrations.

We have already discussed the use of questions and will discuss the use of visuals and demonstrations later, so let's briefly consider having prospects use the product:

• If you sell stereos, let them see, hear, and feel them!
• If you sell food, let them see, smell, and taste it!
• If you sell clothes, let them feel and wear them!

By letting prospects use the product, you can appeal to their sense of sight, sound, touch, smell, and taste. The presentation shoud be developed with appeal to the senses, since people often buy because of emotional needs and the senses are keys to developing emotional appeals.

Proof Statements Build Believability

Prospects often say to themselves, before I buy, you must *prove it!* "Prove it" is a thought everyone has at times. Salespeople must therefore prove they will do what they promise to do, such as helping to make product displays when the merchandise arrives. Usually, prove it means proving to a prospect during a presentation that the product's benefits and the salesperson's proposal are legitimate.

Because salespeople often have a reputation for exaggeration, prospects are at times skeptical of the salesperson's claims. By incorporating **proof statements** into the presentation, the salesperson can increase the prospect's confidence and trust that product claims are accurate. Several useful proof techniques are customer's past sales figures, the guarantee, testimonials, company proof results, and independent research results (see Figure 8.5).[3]

Past Sales Help Predict the Future. Customers' past sales proof statements are frequently used by the salesperson when contacting present customers. Customers keep records of their past purchases from each of their suppliers that can be used by the salesperson to suggest what quantities of each product to purchase. For example, the Colgate salesperson checks a customer's present inventory of all products carried; determines the number of products sold in a month; subtracts inventory from forecasted sales and suggests the customer purchase that amount. It is difficult for buyers to refuse when presentations are based on their own sales records. If they are offered a price discount and promotional allowances, they might purchase three to ten times the normal amount (a promotional purchase).

Assume, for example, that a food store normally carries 10 dozen of the king-size Colgate toothpaste in inventory with 3 dozen on the shelf, and sells approximately 20 dozen a month. The salesperson produces the buyer's past sales record and says, "You should buy 7 to 10 dozen king-size Colgate toothpaste." If offering promotional allowances, the salesperson might say:

> The Colgate king size is your most profitable and best-selling item. You normally sell 20 dozen Colgate king size each month with a 30 percent gross profit. With our 15 percent price reduction this month only, and our advertising allowances, I suggest, based on your normal sales, that you buy 80 to 100 dozen, reduce the price 15 percent, display it, and advertise the discount in your newspaper specials. This will attract people to your store and help increase store sales and allow you to make your normal profit.

The salesperson stops talking to see the buyer's reaction. A suggested order plus an alternative on the quantity to purchase have been proposed. Does the quantity seem high? It may be high, just right, or low, but it is the buyer's decision. The salesperson is saying that, given your past sales and with my customer benefit plan, I believe you can sell X amount.

FIGURE 8.5   Researching proof statements before a sales presentation

· *Quaker Oats' Eli Jones uses his personal computer to keep track of customer information such as past sales and customer profile data. This helps him develop the suggested purchase order.*

Be realistic about your suggested increase in order size. Some salespeople double the size of the order expecting the prospect to cut it in half. Your honesty builds credibility with the buyer.

The Colgate salesperson (like comparable consumer goods salespeople such as Quaker Oats' Linda Slaby-Baker) might suggest purchases not only of toothpaste but of all Colgate products. That same sales call could involve multiple presentations of several products that have promotional allowances, plus the recommended purchase of 10 or more items based on present inventories and the previous month's sales.

The Guarantee. The guarantee is a powerful proof technique. It assures prospects that if they are dissatisfied with their purchase, the salesperson or the company will stand behind a product. The manufacturer has certain product warranties the retail salesperson can use in a presentation.

Furthermore, the consumer goods salesperson selling to retailers may say, "I'll guarantee this product will sell for you. If not, we can return what you do not sell." The industrial salesperson may explain the equipment's warranties and service policies and state, "This is the best equipment for your situation that you can buy. If after you have used it for three months and you are not 100 percent satisfied, I will return it for you."

Testimonials. Use of testimonials in the presentation as proof of the product's features, advantages, and benefits is an excellent method to build trust and confidence. Today we see manufacturers effectively advertising their consumer products using testimonials, such as Roger Staubach, the ex–Dallas Cowboys football star, asking people, "How do you spell relief?" Professional buyers are impressed by testimonials from prominent people, experts, and satisfied customers as to a product's features, advantages, and benefits.

Company Proof Results. Companies routinely furnish data concerning their products. Consumer goods salespeople can use sales data such as test market information and current sales data. Industrial salespeople use performance data and facts based on company research as proof of their products' performance.

A consumer goods manufacturer gave its salespeople test market sales information to use in their presentation on a new product that was being introduced nationally. Using this information, a salesperson might say:

> Our new product will begin to sell as soon as you put it on your shelf. The product was a success in our eastern test market. It had 9.8 percent market share only nine months after the start of advertising. Laboratory tests proved our formula superior to that of the leading competition in our consumer product tests. There was a high repurchase rate of 50 percent after sampling. This means increased sales and profits for you.

Independent Research Results. Proof furnished by reputable sources outside the company usually have more credibility than company-generated data. Pharmaceutical salespeople frequently tell physicians about medical research findings on their products that are published in leading medical journals by medical research authorities.

"On a typical day," says Sandra Snow of The Upjohn Company, "I see as many physicians as possible and initiate a discussion with them about one of our products that will have importance to them in their fields of medicine. I attempt to point out advantages that our drugs have in various states by using third-party documentation published in current medical journals and texts. The information has much more meaning to a physician who knows that it is not me or The Upjohn Company that has shown our drug to have an advantage, but rather a group of researchers who have conducted a scientific study. All of the material that we give to the physician has previously been approved for our use by the Food and Drug Administration."

Publications such as *Road Test Magazine, Consumer Reports,* newspaper stories, and government reports, such as Environmental Protection Agency publications, may contain information the salesperson can use in the presentation. For a proof statement referring to independent research results to be most effective, it should contain: (1) a restatement of the benefit before proving it, (2) the proof source and relevant facts or figures about the product, and (3) expansion of the benefit. Consider the following example of a salesperson's proof statement:

> I'm sure that you want a radio that's really going to sell and be profitable for you (benefit restatement). Figures in *Consumer Guide* and *Consumer Sales* magazine indicate that the Sony XL-100 radios, although the newest on the market, are the third largest in sales (source and facts). Therefore, when you handle the Sony XL line, you'll find that your radio sales and profits will increase, and you will see more customers coming into your store (benefit expansion).

Proof statements must be incorporated into the presentation. They provide a logical answer to the buyer's challenge to "prove it!" Often, proof statements are presented through visual aids.

The Visual Presentation — Show and Tell

In giving a sales presentation, the salesperson does two things. You *show* and *tell* the prospect about a proposal. You *tell* using persuasive communications, participation techniques, and proof statements. You *show* by using visual aids.

People retain approximately 10 percent of what they hear, but 50 percent of what they see. Consequently, you have five times the chance of making a lasting impression with an illustrated sales presentation rather than with words alone.

Visuals are most effective when you believe in them and have woven them into your sales presentation message. Use them to:

- Increase retention.
- Reinforce the message.
- Reduce misunderstanding.
- Create a unique and lasting impression.
- Show the buyer that you are a professional.

The visual presentation ("showing") incorporates the three remaining elements of the presentation mix: visual aids, dramatization, and demonstration. Certainly there is some overlap between the three, for a demonstration uses visuals and has some dramatics. Let's examine each of the elements to consider how they can be used separately or together in a sales presentation.

VISUAL AIDS HELP TELL THE STORY

Visuals, or visual aids, refer to devices that appeal chiefly to the prospect's vision with the intent of producing mental images of the product's features, advantages, and benefits. Many companies routinely supply salespeople with visuals for their products. Some common visuals are:

FIGURE 8.6   A salesperson makes a slide presentation for Uarco Business Forms

- The product.
- Charts and graphics illustrating product features and advantages such as performance and sales data.
- Photographs of the product and its uses.
- Models of products, especially for large, bulky products.
- Audiovisual equipment such as videos, slides, and audiocassettes.
- Sales manuals and product catalogs.
- Order forms.
- Letters of testimony.
- Copy of guarantee.
- Flip-boards and posters.
- Sample advertisements.

Figure 8.6 illustrates an Uarco Business Forms salesperson making a slide presentation to company exercises. Many sales organizations supply their salespeople with video equipment to show things such as examples of their advertisements or products in operation.

FIGURE 8.7   Salesperson Linda Slaby-Baker illustrates the use of visual aids

• 1. Linda reviews call plan before seeing buyer.

• 2. Products and sales aids are placed in and arranged in her sales bag.

• 3. She enters the buyer's office.

• 4. She greets buyer with a firm handshake, a smile, and eye contact.

Most visual aids are carried in the salesperson's bag. The sales bag should be checked before each sales call to ensure that all visuals necessary for the presentation are organized in a manner that allows the salesperson to easily access needed visuals. Only new, top quality, professionally developed visuals should be used. Tattered, torn, or smudged visuals should be routinely discarded. The best visual aid is showing the actual product.

Quaker Oats salesperson Linda Slaby-Baker illustrates in Figure 8.7 the use of visual aids when calling on customers. After planning her sales call, she packs her sales bag, enthusiastically greets her buyer, and begins her sales presentation. Her visual aids consist of the product, visuals she has created tailored to this buyer, and visuals furnished to her by Quaker Oats. The use of visuals allows Linda to give her sales presentation in a persuasive manner. As you see in Figure 8.7, Linda uses different visuals, different body positions, and different conversational techniques to actively bring her

FIGURE 8.7 *(concluded)*

• *5. Linda begins the presentation using products and sales aids in her bag.*

• *6. She uses personally developed sales aids customized to her buyer.*

• *7. She shows facts, figures, and reasons to buy.*

• *8. Linda uses company sales aids to get the buyer involved in presentations.*

buyer into their conversation. This provides her sales presentation with a dramatic element that improves her probability of making the sale.

DRAMATIZATION IMPROVES YOUR CHANCES

Dramatics refers to talking or presenting the product in a striking, showy, or extravagant manner. Thus, sales expertise can involve **dramatization** or theatrical presentation of products. However, dramatics should be incorporated into the presentation only when you are 100 percent sure that the dramatics will work effectively. This was not considered by the salesperson who set the buyer's trash can on fire. The salesperson had difficulty extinguishing the fire with a new fire extinguisher and ran the buyer out of the room because of extensive smoke. However, if carried out correctly, dramatics are effective. One of the best methods of developing ideas for the dramatization of a product is to watch television commercials. Products are presented using visuals, many are demonstrated, and most are dramatized. Take, for example, the following television advertisements:

- "We challenged the competition . . . and they ran!" says the Heinz tomato ketchup advertisement. Two national brands of ketchup and Heinz Ketchup are poured into a paper coffee filter held up by a tea strainer. The competition's ketchup begins to drip, then runs through the filter. The Heinz ketchup does not drip or run, indicating the high quality of the Heinz ketchup relative to the competition.
- Bounty paper towel advertisements show coffee spilled and how quickly the product absorbs the coffee relative to the competitive paper towel.
- The STP motor oil additive advertisement shows a person dipping one screwdriver into STP motor oil additive and another screwdriver into a plain motor oil. The person can pick up and hold with two fingers the end of the screwdriver covered with plain motor oil. The screwdriver covered with STP motor oil additive slips out of the fingers—indicating STP provides better lubrication for an automobile engine.

Use a dramatic demonstration to set you apart from the many salespeople that buyers see each day. Buyers, such as industrial purchasing agents, like to see you as they know you will have an informative and often entertaining sales presentation. One salesperson known for his effective presentations was George Wynn. George was an industrial salesperson for Exxon U.S.A. and responsible for the sales of machine lubricating oils and greases in Dayton, Cincinnati, and Columbus, Ohio.

One group of products sold by George consisted of oils and greases sold to the food processing industry. These lubricants had to be approved by the Federal Food and Drug Administration for "incidental food contact." One of the products sold was a lubricating grease, Carum 280. George ordered a number of one-pound cans for customer samples. As George started his sales presentation of these FDA-approved products, he would take one of the cans from his sample case, open it, and spread this grease on a slice of bread he had also removed from his sample case. After taking a bite of the bread spread with the grease, he then offered a bite to the buyer. The buyer generally refused the offer. However, in the mind of the buyer, this dramatic demonstration set George's presentation apart from others. It helped prove to the buyer the product was safe to use in a food processing plant.

Another dramatic demonstration used by George involved lubricating greases used by the steel industry. Greases that are resistant to high temperatures are desirable for most applications in the steel industry. Exxon developed a line of temperature-resistant greases that used a new thickener that held the oil in suspension better than competitive products. In order to demonstrate this product attribute, George used a pie tin held at a 45° angle centered over a small lighted alcohol lamp. A small glob of the Exxon grease as well as globs of several better-known competitors were placed on the pie tin. As the pie tin was heated, the oil separated from each of the competitive greases and ran down the pie tin. The oil did not separate from the Exxon product, thus dramatically demonstrating the high temperature resistance of this steel mill grease when compared to the leading competitive products.

DEMONSTRATIONS PROVE IT!

One of the best ways to convince a prospect that a product is needed is to show the merits of the product through a **demonstration,** as did George Wynn. If a picture is worth a thousand words, then a demonstration is worth a thousand pictures. Therefore, it is best to show the product, if possible, and to actually have the prospect use it. If this is not feasible, then pictures, models, videotapes, films, or slides are the next best alternative. Whatever the salesperson is attempting to sell, the prospect should be able to see it.

Psychological studies have shown that people receive 87 percent of their information on the outside world through their eyes and only 13 percent through the other four senses. What this says to the salesperson is to make a product visible. Also let the prospect feel, see, hear, smell, and use the product. The dynamic demonstration appeals to human senses by telling, showing, and creating buyer–seller interaction.

Demonstrations are part of the dramatization and fun of your presentation. Do not underestimate their ability to make sales for you, no matter how simple they may appear. For example, a glass company some years ago came out with a shatterproof glass. This was not standard equipment in automobiles then, as it is now. They had their salespeople going around the country trying to sell shatterproof glass. One of the salespeople completely outsold the rest of the sales force. When they had their convention, they said, "Joe, how come you sell so much glass?" He replied, "Well, what I've been doing is taking little chunks of glass and a ball peen hammer along with me on my sales calls. I take the little chunk of glass and I hit it with the hammer. This shows that it's shatterproof. It splinters, but doesn't shatter and fall all over the ground. This has been helping me to sell a lot of glass."

So the next year they equipped every one of their salespeople with a little ball peen hammer and little chunks of glass. But an interesting thing happened. Joe still far outsold the rest of the sales force in his sales. So, when the convention came around again the next year, they asked, "Joe, how is

TABLE 8.2

Sales Demonstration Checklist

☑ Is the demonstration *needed* and *appropriate?*
☑ Have I developed a specific demonstration *objective?*
☑ Have I properly *planned* and *organized* the demonstration?
☑ Have I rehearsed to the point that the demonstration *flows smoothly* and appears to be *natural?*
☑ What is the probability the demonstration will *go as planned?*
☑ What is the probability the demonstration will *backfire?*
☑ Does my demonstration present my product in an *ethical* and *professional* manner?

it you're selling so much? You told us what you did last year. What are you doing different?" He replied, "Well, this year, I gave the glass *and* the hammer to the customer and let *him* hit it." You see, the first year he had dramatization in his demonstration. The second year Joe had dramatization and participation in his demonstration. Again, it's often not what you say but how you say it that makes the sale for you.

A Demonstration Checklist.   There are seven points to keep in mind as you prepare your demonstration. These points are shown in Table 8.2. First, is the demonstration really needed and appropriate for your prospects? Every sale does not need a demonstration nor will all products lend themselves to a demonstration.

If the demonstration is appropriate, what is its objective? What should the demonstration accomplish? Next, be sure you have properly planned and organized the demonstration. It is important to rehearse it so that the demonstration flows smoothly and appears natural. Take your time in talking and going through your demonstration; make it look easy. Remember, if you, the expert, cannot operate the machine, for example, imagine how difficult it will be for the prospect.

The only way to ensure a smooth demonstration is to practice. Yet, there is always the possibility that the demonstration will not go as planned or will backfire no matter how simple it may be. Be prepared for this. An example was a former student who was demonstrating his new Kodak slide projector. Two bulbs in a row burned out as he demonstrated the product to a buyer for a large discount chain. He anticipated what could go wrong and always carried extra parts in his sales bag. When the first bulb went out, he began talking of how easy it was to change bulbs, and when the second one blew, he said "I want to show you that again," with a smile. He always carried two spare bulbs, but now he carries three.

Finally, make sure your demonstration presents the product in an ethical and professional manner. You do not want to misrepresent the product or proposal. A complex product, such as a large computer system, can be presented as simple to install with few start-up problems, yet the buyer may find the computer system difficult to operate.

Get Participation in Your Demonstration. By having the prospect participate in the demonstration, you can be assured that you obtain a buyer's attention and direct it where you want it. It also helps the prospect visualize owning and operating the product. The successful demonstration aids in reducing buying uncertainties and resistance to its purchase. The salesperson has the prospect do four things in a successful demonstration:

1. Let the prospect do something simple.
2. Let the prospect work an important feature.
3. Let the prospect do something routine, frequently repeated.
4. Have the prospect answer questions throughout the demonstration.

First, get the prospect to do something simple with a low probability of foul-up. Second, in planning the demonstration, select the main features you will stress in the interview and allow the prospect to participate on the feature that relates most to an important buying motive. Again, keep it simple.

A third way to have a successful demonstration is having the prospect do something with the product that is frequently done. Finally, receive feedback from the prospect throughout the demonstration by asking questions or pausing in your conversation. This is extremely important, as it will:

• Determine the prospect's attitude toward the product.
• Allow you to progress in the demonstration or wait and answer any questions or address any objections.
• Aid in getting the prospect into the positive "yes" mood.
• Set the stage for closing the sale.

Little agreements lead to the big agreement and saying yes. Phrase questions in a positive manner, such as, "That is really easy to operate, isn't it?" instead of, "This isn't hard to operate, is it?" They ask the same thing, yet the response to the first question is positive instead of negative. The best questions force the prospect to mentally place the product in use, such as the question phrased, "Do you feel this feature could increase your employee's production?" The answer yes commits the buyer to the idea that the feature will increase employee production. Remember, it is often not what you say, but how you say it.

Reasons for Using Visual Aids, Dramatics, and Demonstrations

As we have seen, visual aids, dramatics, and demonstrations are important to the salesperson's success in selling a prospect. The reasons to use them include:

- Capture attention and interest.
- Create two-way communication.
- Involve the prospect through participation.
- Afford a more complete, clear explanation of products.
- Increase a salesperson's persuasive powers by obtaining positive commitments on a product's single feature, advantage, or benefit.

Guidelines for Using Visual Aids, Dramatics, and Demonstrations

While visual aids, dramatics, and demonstrations are important, their proper use is critical if they will be effective. When using them, consider:

- Rehearsing by practicing in front of a mirror, on a tape recorder, and to a friend. Figure 8.8 shows Santo Laquatra, the national sales training manager for Beecham Products, videotaping two salespeople role-playing their sales presentation. He plays it back so everyone can critique the presentation. Once you are ready to make the presentation, first see your less important prospects. This allows you to refine the presentation further before contacting large accounts.
- Customizing them to the sales call objective, prospect's customer profile, and customer benefit plan, concentrating on the prospect's important buying motives and using appropriate multiple appeals to sight, touch, hearing, smell, and taste.
- Making them *simple, clear* and *straightforward*.
- Being sure to *control* the demonstration by not letting the prospect take you away from selling. It can be disastrous to have the prospect not listen or pass up major selling points you wished to present.
- Making them *true to life*.
- Encouraging *prospect participation*.
- Incorporating *trial closes* (questions) after showing or demonstrating a major feature, advantage, or benefit to determine if it is believed and important to the prospect.

FIGURE 8.8   Beecham's Santo Laquatra uses videotaping to prepare his
salespeople to sell

THE TRIAL CLOSE—A MAJOR STEP IN THE SALES PRESENTATION

The **trial close** is one of the best selling techniques to use in your sales
presentation. It is used to check the "pulse" or attitude of your prospect
toward the sales presentation. The trial close should be used at the following
four important times:

1. After making a *strong selling point* in the presentation.
2. After the *presentation*.
3. After answering an *objection*.
4. *Immediately before* you move to *close* the sale.

    The trial close allows you to determine: (1) whether the prospect likes
your product's feature, advantage, or benefit (the strong selling point); (2)
whether you have successfully answered the objection; (3) whether any
objections remain; and (4) whether the prospect is ready for you to close the
sale. It is a powerful technique to induce two-way communication
(feedback) and participation from the prospect.

SELLING TIPS

Using Trial Closes

The trial close is an important part of the sales presentation. It asks for the prospect's opinion concerning what you have just said. The trial close does not directly ask the person to buy. Here are examples:

- "How does that sound to you?"
- "What do you think?"
- "Are these the features you are looking for?"
- "That's great—isn't it?"
- "Is this important to you?"
- "Does that answer your concern?"

- "I have a hunch that you like the money-saving features of this product. Did I guess right?"
- "It appears you have a preference for this model. Is this what you had in mind?"
- "I can see that you are excited about this product. On a scale from one to ten, how do you feel it will fit your needs?"
- "I notice your smile. What do you think about . . . ?"
- "Am I on the right track with this proposal?"

If, for example, the prospect says little while you make your presentation, and if you get a "no" when you come to the close, you may find it difficult to change the prospect's mind. You have not learned the real reasons why the prospect says no. To help avoid this, salespeople use the trial close to determine the prospect's attitude toward the product throughout the presentation.

The trial close asks for the prospect's *opinion,* not a decision to buy. It is a direct question that can be answered with few words.★ Take a look at the trial close examples shown in Selling Tips.

Remember the prospect's positive reactions. Use them later to help overcome objections and in closing of the sale. Also, remember the negative comments. You may need to offset the negatives with the positives later in the presentation. Generally, however, you will not bring up the negative again.

Here is an example of using the prospect's positive comments to ask for the order. Assume that during the presentation you have learned from the prospect that she likes the product's profit margin, fast delivery, and credit policy. You can summarize these benefits in a positive manner such as:

SALESPERSON: Ms. Stevenson, you say you like our profit margin, fast delivery, and credit policy. Is that right? [Summary and trial close.]

PROSPECT: Yes, I do.

★See Chapter 7 for other uses and examples of direct questions.

SALESPERSON: With the number of customers coming into your store and our expected sales of the products due to normal turnover, along with our marketing plan, I *suggest you buy.* . . . [State the products and their quantities.] This will provide you sufficient quantities to meet customer demand for the next two months, plus provide you with the profit you expect from your products. I can have the order to you early next week. [Now wait for her response.]

Note that the prospect has said there are three things she likes about what you are selling. She has committed herself. It will be hard for her to say no.

If the prospect responds favorably to your trial close, then you are in agreement or you have satisfactorily answered an objection. Thus, the prospect may be ready to buy. However, if you get a negative response, do not close. Either you have not answered some objection or the prospect is not interested in the feature, advantage, or benefit you are discussing. This type of feedback allows you to better uncover what your prospect thinks about your product's potential for satisfying needs.

SELL Sequence

One way to remember to incorporate a trial close into your presentation is the use of the **SELL sequence.** Figure 8.9 shows how each letter of the word "sell" stands for a sequence of things to do and say to stress benefits important to the customer. By remembering the word sell, you remember to *show the feature, explain the advantage, lead into the benefit, and then let the customer talk by asking a question about the benefit (trial close).*

EXAMPLE:

Industrial salesperson to industrial purchasing agent: "This equipment is made of stainless steel [feature], which means it won't rust [advantage]. The real benefit is that it reduces your replacement costs, thus saving you money! [benefit] That's what you're interested in—right? [trial close]

EXAMPLE:

Beecham salesperson to consumer goods buyer: "Beecham will spend an extra $1 million in the next two months advertising Cling Free fabric softener [feature]. Plus, you can take advantage of this month's $1.20 per dozen price reduction [feature]. This means you will sell 15 to 20 percent more Cling Free in the next two months [advantage], thus making higher profits and pulling more customers into your store [benefits]. How does that sound? [trial close]

Once you use a trial close, carefully listen to what the customer says and

FIGURE 8.9   SELL Sequence

S	E	L	L
Show feature	Explain advantage	Lead into benefit	Let customer talk

watch for nonverbal signals to determine if what you have said has made an impact. If you get a positive response to your trial close, you are on the right track.

Remember, the trial close does not ask the customer to buy or make any type of purchase decision. It asks only for an "opinion." The trial close is a trial question to determine the customer's opinion towards the salesperson's proposition to know if it is time to close the sale. Thus, its main purpose is to induce feedback from the buyer.

THE IDEAL PRESENTATION

In the ideal presentation, your approach technique quickly captures your prospect's interest and immediately gets signals that the prospect has a need for your product and is ready to listen. The ideal prospect is friendly, polite, relaxed, will not allow anyone to interrupt you, asks questions, and participates in your demonstration as planned. This allows you to move skillfully through the presentation.

The ideal customer cheerfully and positively answers each of your questions, allowing you to anticipate the correct moment to ask for the order. You are completely relaxed and sure of yourself when you come to the close. The customer says "Yes," and enthusiastically thanks you for your valuable time. Several weeks later, you receive a copy of the letter your customer wrote your company's president glowing with praise for your professionalism and sincere concern for the customer.

BE PREPARED FOR PRESENTATION DIFFICULTIES

Yes, a few sales presentations go somewhat like that, yet most have one or more hurdles you should be prepared for. Refer back to Linda Slaby-Baker's profile for her example of interruptions. While all of the difficulties you might face cannot be discussed here, three main problems that are encountered during sales presentations are interruptions; how to handle the discussion of competition; and the necessity of making the presentation in a less–than–ideal situation.

How to Handle Interruptions

It is quite common for **interruptions** to occur during the presentation. The secretary comes into the office or the telephone rings, distracting the prospect. What should you do?

First, determine if the discussion that interrupted your presentation is personal or confidential. If so, by gesture or voice you can offer to leave the room—which is always appreciated by the prospect. Then, while waiting, regroup your thoughts and mentally review how to move back into the presentation. Once the discussion is over, you can:

1. Wait quietly and patiently until you have completely regained the prospect's attention.
2. Briefly restate the selling points that had interested the prospect, for example, "We were discussing your needs for a product such as ours and you seemed especially interested in knowing about our service, delivery, and installation. Is that right?"
3. Do something to increase the prospect's participation, such as showing the product, using other visuals, or asking questions. Watch closely to determine if you have regained the prospect's interest.
4. If interest is regained, move deeper into the presentation.

Should You Discuss the Competition?

Competition is something all salespeople must contend with every day. If you sell a product, you must compete with others selling comparable products. How should you handle competition? Basically, keep in mind three considerations: (1) do not refer to a competitor unless absolutely necessary; (2) acknowledge your competitor only briefly; and (3) make a detailed comparison of your product and that of the competitor.[4]

1. Do Not Refer to Competition. First of all, lessen any surprises the buyer may present by properly planning for the sales call. In developing your customer profile, chances are you will find out what competing products are used, and your prospect's attitude toward your products and those of competitors. Based on your findings, the presentation can be developed without specifically referring to competition.

2. Acknowledge Competition and Drop It. Many salespeople feel their competition should not be discussed unless the prospect brings it up. Then acknowledge competition only briefly and return to your product. "Yes, I am familiar with that product's features. In fact, the last three of my customers were using that product and have switched over to ours. May I tell you why?"

Here you do not knock competition, but acknowledge it and in a positive manner move the prospect's attention back to your products. If the prospect continues to bring up a competing product, you should determine the prospect's attitude toward it. You might ask, "What do you think about the Burroughs B1900 computer system?" The answer will help you mentally determine how you can prove that your product offers the prospect more benefits than your competitor's product.

3. Make a Detailed Comparison. At times, it is appropriate to make a **detailed comparison** of your product to a competing one, especially for industrial products. If products are similar, then emphasize your company's service, guarantees, and what you personally do for customers.

If your product has features that are lacking in a competitor's product, refer to these advantages, possibly indirectly. "Our product is the only one on the market with this feature! Is this important to you?" Ask the question and wait for the response. A "yes" answer is one step closer to the sale.

Often the prospect can use both your product and that of a competitor. For example, a pharmaceutical salesperson is selling an antibiotic that functions like penicillin, as well as killing bacteria resistant to penicillin. However, it costs 20 times more than penicillin. This salesperson would say, "Yes, Dr. Jones, penicillin is the drug of choice for . . . disease. But do you have patients for whom penicillin is not effective?" "Yes, I do," says the doctor. "Then for those patients I want you to consider my product because. . . ."

Competition Discussion Based on the Situation. Whether or not you discuss competition depends on the individual prospect. Based on your selling philosophy and your knowledge of the prospect, you can choose how to deal with competition. If you are in doubt due to insufficient prospect knowledge, it is best not to discuss competition.

Be Professional

No matter how you discuss competition with your prospect, always act as a professional. If you discuss competition, talk only about information you know is accurate and be straightforward and honest, not belittling and discourteous.

Your prospect may like both the competitor's products and yours. A loyalty to the competitor may have been built over the years; by knocking competition, you may insult and alienate your prospect. However, the advantages and disadvantages of a competitive product can be pointed out acceptably if done in a professional manner. One salesperson relates this story:

Several customers I called on were very loyal to my competitors; however, just as many were loyal to my company. I will always remember the president of a chain of retail stores who flew 500 miles to be at one of our salesmen's retirement dinners. In his talk, he noted how some 30 years ago, when he opened his first store, this salesperson extended him company credit and made him a personal loan which helped him get started.

It would be difficult for a competing salesperson to sell to this loyal customer. When contacting customers, especially those buying competitive products, it is important to uncover why they use competitive products before discussing competition in the presentation.

Where the Presentation Takes Place

The ideal presentation takes place in a quiet room with only the salesperson and the prospect and no interruptions. However, at times the salesperson may meet the prospect somewhere other than a private office and feel the need to make the presentation under less than ideal conditions.

Figure 8.10 shows an Atlantic Richfield salesperson talking with the customer in front of his filling station, and a Wallace Business Forms salesperson making a presentation somewhere in the prospect's business.[3] For short presentations, a stand-up situation may be adequate; however, when making a longer presentation you may want to ask the prospect, "Could we go back to your office?" or make another appointment.

FIGURE 8.10 Examples of less than ideal presentation situations

Diagnose the Prospect to Determine Your Sales Presentation

You have seen that in contacting prospects you must prepare for various situations. That is why selling is so challenging and why companies reward their salespeople so well. A major challenge is adapting your sales presentation to each potential buyer. In Chapter 3, you read about "selling based on personality." Reexamine that discussion to better understand "how" and "why" you should be prepared to adapt your presentation.

SUMMARY OF MAJOR SELLING ISSUES

The sales presentation is a persuasive vocal and visual explanation of a proposition. While there are numerous methods for making a sales presentation, the four common ones are the memorized, formula, need-satisfaction, and problem-solution selling methods. Each method is effective if used for the proper situation.

In developing your presentation, consider which elements of the sales presentation mix you will use for each prospect. The proper use of persuasive communication techniques, methods to develop prospect participation, proof statements, visual aids, dramatization, and demonstrations greatly increases your chance of illustrating to your prospect how your products will satisfy needs.

As we know, it is often not what we say but how we say it that results in making the sale. Persuasive communication techniques (questioning, listening, logical reasoning, suggestion, and the use of trial closes) help to uncover needs, to communicate effectively, and to pull the prospect into the conversation.

Proof statements are especially useful in showing your prospect that what you are saying is true and that you can be trusted. When challenged, "Prove it" by incorporating in your presentation facts on a customer's past sales, guaranteeing the product will work or sell, testimonials, and company and independent research results.

To both show and tell, visuals need to be properly designed to illustrate features, advantages, and benefits of your products through graphics, dramatization, and demonstration. This allows you to capture the prospect's attention and interest, create two-way communication and participation, express your proposition in a clearer, more complete manner, and make more sales. Careful attention to the development and rehearsal of the presentation is needed to ensure it occurs smoothly and naturally.

At any time, be prepared for the unexpected, such as a demonstration that breaks down, interruptions, the prospect's questions about the competition, or the necessity to make your presentation in a less than ideal place, such as the aisle of a retail store or in the warehouse.

The presentation part of the overall sales presentation is the heart of the sale. It is where you develop the desire, conviction, and action. By giving an effective presentation, you will have fewer objections to your proposition, which makes for an easier close of the sale.

If you want to be a real professional in selling, acquire or create materials that will help convey your message and get others to believe it. If you try to sell without using the components of the sales presentation mix, you are losing sales not because of what you say but how you say it. Exhibits, facts, statistics, examples, analogies, testimonials, and samples should be part of your repertoire. Without them you are not equipped to do a professional job of selling.

9

Welcome Your Prospect's Objections

After Bruce Scagel graduated from Washington and Jefferson College, he went to work with Scott Paper in 1976 as a consumer products sales representative in Jacksonville, Florida. Bruce's promotions have been to the positions of assistant marketing personnel manager, territory sales manager, in-house consultant on organization development, and training and development manager of Scott's consumer sales and marketing division. Now, he is the national sales trainer for M&M—Mars. Bruce says, "I began my career in a sales position because it offered opportunities for rapid advancement as well as a variety of interesting and challenging activities.

Bruce Scagel
M&M—Mars

"My philosophy of selling incorporates traditional sales techniques with personal approaches. I believe it's initially necessary to learn as much as possible about each customer, the objectives, challenges, and the particular problems he or she faces. By addressing these objectives and challenges with specific products and services, the salesperson enhances opportunity for success."

Ask Bruce what he believes are the key factors for sales success, and he will stress four points. "First, know your customers and their operations. I believe it's necessary to know as much about my customers as possible, including their needs and objectives—how they operate and who their key people are before attempting the sale. Consistency and follow-through make up the second key selling point. Generally, the most respected and successful salesperson is the one who is consistent in dealing with the customer, and who follows through on commitment and promises. Third, you must lose your fear of failure. One of the greatest impediments to successful selling is fearing that the buyer will not buy. In my career, I've been most successful when I've been well prepared and confident. However, I am also aware that I will not make every sale. Accept the results and move on to the next project. Fourth, to be successful you must ask questions. Through questioning, the salesperson can identify the buyer's needs, objectives, and primary challenges. Timely questioning can keep a sale alive when the buyer appears to be losing interest in the product or service being offered. My observations have been that many inexperienced salespeople find this aspect of the sale the most difficult to master because they fear that they will lose control of the presentation. In fact, conversation is one of the most appropriate means to lead the buyer to the desired conclusions." •

Bruce Scagel of M&M—Mars has a positive philosophy regarding sales objections: "During the sale, objections are often raised, and the manner in which the salesperson responds often constitutes the difference between success and failure. The salesperson should resist being defensive or put off by objections; rather he or she should address them confidently, keeping in mind that they're fundamental to the sale. It's been said that the selling process doesn't begin until the buyer raises an objection. For the most part I would agree.

"Objections are often raised for the following reasons: the buyers want to avoid a decision; they are operating with misinformation; they want or need more information; or they simply want reassurance. In each case, the salesperson who listens closely and attempts to understand the buyer's needs and objectives can respond appropriately." •

This chapter expands on Bruce's comments, and discusses how to meet objections, techniques to use in overcoming objections, and how to proceed after an objection has been addressed.

WELCOME OBJECTIONS!

When a prospect first gives an objection, *smile,* because that's when you start earning your salary. You want to receive personal satisfaction from your job and at the same time increase your salary—right? Well, both will occur when you learn to accept objections as a challenge that, handled correctly, will benefit both your prospect and you. The more effectively you meet customers' needs and solve their problems, the more successful you will be in sales. If you *fear* objections, you will *fumble* your response, often causing *failure*.

Remember, while people want to buy, they *do not* want to be taken advantage of. Buyers who cannot see how your offering will fulfill their needs ask questions and raise objections. If you cannot effectively answer the questions or meet the objections, you will not make the sale. It is *your* fault, not the buyer's fault, that the sale was not made, if you sincerely believe your offering fulfills a need but the prospect still will not buy. The salesperson who can overcome objections when they are raised and smoothly move back into a presentation will succeed.

WHAT ARE OBJECTIONS?

Interestingly enough, prospects who present objections are often more easily sold on your product. They are interested enough to object; they want to know what you have to offer.

Opposition or resistance to information or to the salesperson's request is labeled a **sales objection.** Sales objections must be welcomed because they show prospect interest and aid in determining what stage the prospect has reached in the buying cycle—attention, interest, desire, conviction, or readiness to close.

WHEN DO PROSPECTS OBJECT?

The prospect may object at any time during your sales call—from introduction to close. Imagine walking into a retail store (as once happened to me), carrying a sales bag, and the buyer yells out, "Oh no, not another salesman. I don't even want to see you, let alone buy from you!" What do you say?

I said, "I understand. I'm not here to sell you anything, only check your stock, help you stock your shelves, and return any old or damaged merchandise for a refund." As I turned to walk away, the buyer said, "Come on back here, I want to talk to you."

If I had simply said "OK" and left, I would not have made that sale. I knew that I could benefit that customer, and my response and attitude showed it. The point is: always be ready to handle a prospect's objections, whether at the approach, during the presentation, after a trial close, after you have already met a previous objection, or during the close of the sale.

OBJECTIONS AND THE SALES PROCESS

Objections can occur at any time. Many times, however, the prospect will allow you to make a presentation, often asking questions along the way. Inexperienced salespeople traditionally finish their presentation and wait for the prospect's response.

Experienced, successful salespeople have learned to use the system shown in Figure 9.1. After the presentation, they use a trial close to determine the prospect's attitude toward the product and if it is time to close.

Remember, the **trial close** asks for the prospect's opinion, not a decision to buy. Here, the trial close is asking about what was said in the presentation. Since you may not know the prospect's opinion, it is too early to close. Typically, this trial close causes the prospect to ask questions and/or state objections. The salespeople should be prepared to respond in one of four ways:

1. If there is a positive response to the trial close immediately after the presentation, move to the close as shown on the right side of Figure 9.1, moving from Step 5 to Step 9.
2. If an objection is raised, respond to it and ask another trial close to see if you have met the objection. If you have, then move to the close.

FIGURE 9.1   When objections occur, quickly determine what to do!

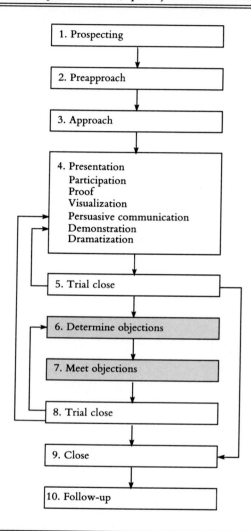

3. After meeting one objection, be prepared to determine if there are other objections. You may have to move from Step 8 back to Step 6.

4. If, after responding to the objection and asking a trial close you have not overcome the objection, move back to your presentation (Step 4) and further discuss the product relative to the objection.

Thus, there are several strategies a salesperson needs to master to handle objections. It is important to adapt to the situation. A big help to successfully handing objections is to thoroughly understand several basic points.

BASIC POINTS TO CONSIDER IN MEETING OBJECTIONS

No matter what type of objections are raised by the prospect, there are certain basic points to consider in meeting objections. The first involves planning.

Plan for Objections

Plan for objections that might be raised by your presentation. Consider not only the reasons prospects should buy but why they should *not* buy. Structure your presentation so as to minimize the disadvantages of your product. Be sure not to discuss disadvantages unless prospects bring them up in the conversation.

After each sales call, review the prospect's objections. Divide them into major and minor objections. Then develop ways of overcoming them. Your planning for and rehearsal of overcoming objections will allow you to respond to them in a natural and positive manner. Planning for and review of the sales call allows you to anticipate and forestall objections.

Anticipate and Forestall

Forestalling the objection involves the salesperson discussing an objection before it is brought up by the prospect. It is often better to forestall or discuss objections before they arise. The sales presentation can be developed to directly address anticipated objections.

Take a manufacturer's salesperson selling exterior house paint who learns that a not-too-ethical competitor has been telling retail dealers that his paint starts to chip and peel after six months. Realizing the predicament, this salesperson develops a presentation that quickly points out, "Three independent testing laboratories have shown that this paint will not chip or peel for eight years after application." The salesperson has forestalled or answered the objection before it is raised by using a proof statement. This technique can also prevent a negative mood from entering the buyer-seller dialogue.

Another way to anticipate objections is to bring disadvantages out before the prospect does. Many products have flaws, and they sometimes surface as you try to make a sale. If you know of an objection that comes up consistently, you ought to bring it up. If you discuss it first, you don't have to defend it.

On the other hand, a customer who has an objection feels compelled to defend that objection. For example, you might be showing real estate property. En route to the location you say, "You know, before we get out there, I just want to mention a couple of things. You're going to notice that it needs a little paint in a few places, and I noticed a couple of shingles on the roof the other day that you may have to replace." When you arrive, your customer may take a look and say, "Well, those shingles aren't so bad . . . and I can see . . . we're going to paint it anyway." Yet, if you reached the house without a little prior warning of small defects, those items are often the first things a customer notices.

A third way of using an anticipated objection is to brag about it and turn it into a sales benefit. You might say, "I want to mention something important before we go any further. Our price is a high one because as you are beginning to see, it is quality merchandise, and we're proud of the fact that we put this price on it. This allows us to build in the quality that we know has to go in it to give you the service and type of product that will fulfill your needs. Our customers are happy when they buy it from us because we're able to stand behind our product."

You have taken the sting out of the price objection because you have brought it up. It is difficult for a buyer to come back and say, "It's too high," because you have already mentioned that. So there are times when you can anticipate objections and use them advantageously.

Handle Objections as They Arise

At times, situations arise in which you feel it is best to postpone your answer to an objection. When the objection raised will be covered later in your presentation, or when you build up to that point, it is best to pass over it for awhile. As a general rule, however, it is best to meet objections as they arise; postponement may result in a negative mental picture or reaction such as the following:

• The prospect may stop listening until you address the objection.
• The prospect may feel you are trying to hide something.
• You also feel it's a problem.
• You cannot answer because you do not know how to deal with this objection or you do not know the answer to the objection.
• It may appear that you are not interested in the prospect's opinion.

The objection could be the only thing left before closing the sale. So, meet the objection, determine if you have satisfied the prospect, use another trial close to uncover other objections, and if there are no more objections, move toward closing the sale.

Be Positive

When responding to an objection, use positive body language such as a smile. Strive to respond in a manner that keeps your prospect friendly and in a positive mood. Do not take the objection personally. Never treat the objection with hostility. Take the objection in stride by responding respectfully and showing sincere interest in your prospect's opinion.

At times, the prospect may raise objections based on incorrect information. Politely deny objections that are false. Be realistic; all products have drawbacks, even yours. If a competitor's product has a feature yours does not have, point out the overriding benefits of your product.

Listen—Hear Them Out

Many salespeople leap on an objection before the other person has a chance to finish saying it. The prospect barely gets five words out—and already the salesperson is hammering away as though the evil thing will multiply unless it's stomped out. "I have to prove he is mistaken, or he won't take the product," is a panicky reaction to the first hint of any objection.

Not only does the prospect feel irritated to be interrupted, the prospect also feels pushed and uneasy. "Why's he jumping on that so fast and so hard?" your prospect will ask; "I smell a rat." Suppose you run south when the prospect hits north, and you answer the wrong objection or even raise one the prospect hadn't thought of? The listening guidelines discussed in Chapter 4 apply here. You might want to review them.

Understand Objections

When customers give you an objection, they do one of three things, as shown in Figure 9.2. They are either requesting more information, setting a condition, or giving you a genuine objection. The objection can be hopeless or true.

Request for Information. Many times, prospects appear to make objections when they are actually requesting more information. That is why it is important to listen. If prospects request more information, chances are they are in the conviction stage. You have created a desire; they want the product,.but they are not convinced you have the best product or that you are the best supplier of that product. If you feel this is or may be the case—supply the information that has been requested indirectly.

A Condition. At times, prospects may raise an objection that turns into a **condition of the sale.** They are saying, "If you can meet my request, I'll buy" or, "Under certain conditions I will buy from you."

FIGURE 9.2   What does a prospect mean by an objection?

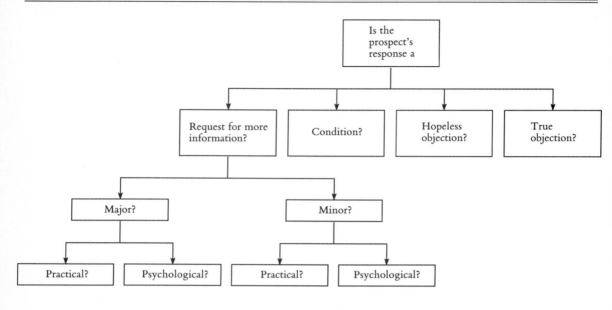

If you sense that the objection is a condition, you must quickly determine if you can help the prospect meet the condition. If you cannot, then politely close the interview. Take the following real estate example:

> PROSPECT: It's a nice house, but the price is too high. I can't afford a $1,000 a month house payment. [You do not know if this is an objection or a condition.]
>
> SALESPERSON: I know what you mean [acknowledging the prospect's viewpoint]. If you don't mind my asking, what is your monthly salary?
>
> PROSPECT: My take-home pay is $1,400 a month.

In this case, the prospect has set a condition on the purchase that cannot realistically be met by the salesperson; it is not an objection. Attempting to continue the exchange by bargaining would waste time and possibly anger the prospect. Now that the prospect's income is known, the salesperson can show a house in the prospect's price range.

Negotiation Can Overcome a Condition. Often, conditions stated by the prospect are overcome through **negotiation** between buyer and seller. Prospects may say things like, "I'll buy your equipment if you can deliver it in one month instead of three" or, "If you'll reduce your price by 10 percent, I'll buy."

If you determine that this type of statement is a condition rather than an objection, through negotiation you may make the sale with further discussion and an eventual compromise between you and the buyer. In the example above, you might ask the manufacturing plant if equipment can be shipped to the prospect in two months instead of three. This arrangement may be acceptable to the prospect. You may have a present customer who has that piece of equipment but is not using it. You might arrange for the prospect to lease it from your customer for three months.

If the prospect sets a price condition, saying, "I will buy your typewriter only if you reduce your price 10 percent," you might determine if your company will reduce the price if the buyer is willing to purchase a larger quantity of typewriters. Consider this example. As a state agency, Texas A&M University purchases much of its office equipment on a bid system. The IBM salesperson could not sell the Texas A&M Marketing Department a word processor because the cost of a single machine was too high for that department's budget. The department wanted the machine; however, they could not afford it. Instead of giving up, the salesperson went to other departments in the university and found a need for a total of 16 machines (at a price of $4,000 per word processor less than the price of one machine). IBM could substantially lower the price because of the large number of machines purchased. The salesperson determined that price was a condition, found a way to overcome the condition, and make the sale. Through initiation and inquiry, a potentially lost sale was turned into a multiple victory beneficial to all parties.

There are two broad categories of objections. One of them is called "hopeless." A hopeless objection is one that cannot be solved or answered. Examples of a hopeless objection are: "I already have one," "I'm bankrupt," and "I'd like to buy your life insurance, but the doctor only gives me 30 days to live." So there are objections you could call hopeless. You cannot overcome them.

If your prospect does not buy and no condition exists or the objection is not hopeless, it is your fault you did not make the sale because you could not provide information to show how your offering would suit the buyer's needs.

The second category is the objection that can be answered. It is a "true" objection. The true objection has two types: the major and the minor objection.

Major or Minor Objection.   Once you determine that the prospect has raised a true objection, you need to determine its importance. If it is of little or no importance, then quickly address it and return to selling. Be careful not to provide a long response or blow a minor objection up into a major

TABLE 9.1 Examples of objections

Practical	Psychological
• Price	• Resistance to spending money.
• Not what is needed	• Resistance to domination
• Has overstock of your or competitor's products	• Predetermined beliefs
	• Negative image of salespeople
• Delivery schedules	• Dislike of making buying decision

discussion item. The minor objection is often a defense mechanism of little actual importance to the prospect. Concentrate on objections directly related to the prospect's important buying motives.

Practical or Psychological Objection. Objections, minor or major, can be **practical** (overt) or **psychological** (hidden) in nature. Table 9.1 gives some examples. A real objection is tangible, such as a high price. If this is a real objection, and the prospect says so, you can show that your product is of high quality and worth the price, or you might suggest removing some optional features and reducing the price. As long as the prospect clearly states the real objection to purchasing the product, you should be able to answer the objection.

However, prospects will not always be so agreeable as to clearly state their objections. Rather, they will often give some excuse about why they are not ready to make a purchase, which conceals real objections. Usually, the prospect will not purchase the product until hidden objections are rectified. It is up to you to uncover a prospect's hidden objections and eliminate them.

Meet the Objection

Once you fully understand the objection, you are ready to respond to the prosect. How to respond depends on the objection. During the year, a salesperson will hear hundreds of various objections. Prospects will object to various items in different ways.

Generally, objections are placed in six categories. By grouping objections, you can better plan for how to respond. Let's examine these six categories and discuss specific techniques for meeting objections.

SIX MAJOR CATEGORIES OF OBJECTIONS

Most objections salespeople encounter are placed into the six categories shown in Figure 9.3. Know how you will handle each situation before it occurs. An advance decision on how you will handle these objections will

FIGURE 9.3   Six major categories of objections

Hidden objections	Stalling objections	No-need objections	Money objections	Product objections	Source objections

help you become a better salesperson by improving your image as a problem solver.

The Hidden Objection

Prospects who ask trivial, unimportant questions or conceal their feelings beneath a veil of silence have **hidden objections.** They are unwilling to discuss their true objections to a product because they may feel they are not your business; they are afraid objections will offend you; or they may not feel your sales call is worthy of full attention.

Such prospects may have a good conversation with you without revealing their true feelings. You have to ask questions and carefully listen to know what questions to ask to smoke out their real objections to your product. Learning how to determine what questions to ask a prospect and how to ask them are skills developed by conscious effort over a long period. Your ability to ask probing questions will improve with each sales call if you consciously try to develop this ability.

Smoke Out Hidden Objections. With prospects who are unwilling to discuss their objections or who may not know why they are reluctant to buy, be prepared to "smoke out" objections by asking questions. Do what you can to get the objections out in the open. Consider the following questions:

- "What would it take to convince you?"
- "What causes you to say that?"
- "Let's consider this, suppose my product would . . . [do what prospect wants] . . . then you would want to consider it, wouldn't you?"
- "Come on now, tell me, what's really on your mind?"

Uncovering hidden objections is not always easy. Observe the prospect's tone of voice, facial expressions, and physical movements. Pay close attention to what the prospect is saying. You may have to "read between the lines" occasionally to find the buyer's true objections. All of these factors will help you discover whether objections are real or simply an excuse to cover a hidden objection.

Prospects may not consciously know what their real objections are. Sometimes they will claim that the price of a product is too high. In reality, they may be reluctant to spend money on anything. If you attempt to show that your price is competitive, the real objection will remain unanswered and no sale will result. Remember, you cannot convince anyone to buy until you understand what a prospect needs to be convinced of.

If, after answering all apparent questions, the prospect is still not sold, you might attempt to subtly uncover the hidden objection. You might ask the prospect what the real objection is. Direct inquiry should be used as a last resort because it may indirectly amount to calling the prospect a liar, but if it is used carefully, it may enable the salesperson to bring out the prospect's true objection. Smoking out hidden objections is an art form developed over time by skillful salespeople. Its successful use can greatly increase your sales. This approach should be used carefully, but if it enables the salesperson to uncover a hidden objection, then it has served its purpose.

The Stalling Objection

When your prospect says, "I'll think it over. . . ." or, "I'll be ready to buy on your next visit," you must determine if the statement is the truth or if it is a smoke screen designed to get rid of you. The **stalling objection** is a common type of tactic.

What you discovered when developing your customer profile and customer benefit plan will aid you in determining how to handle this type of objection. Suppose that before seeing a certain retail customer you had checked the supply of your merchandise in both the store's stockroom and on the retail shelf and this occurs:

BUYER: I have enough merchandise for now. Thanks for coming by.

SALESPERSON: Ms. Marcher, you have 50 cases in the warehouse and on display. You sell 50 cases each month, right?

You have forced her hand. This buyer will either have to order more merchandise from you or tell you why she is allowing her supply of the product to dwindle. An easy stall to handle is illustrated in Figure 9.4. When the prospect says, "I'm too busy to see you now," you might ask, "When would be a good time to come back today?"

One of the toughest stalls to overcome arises when selling a new consumer product. Retail buyers are reluctant to stock consumer goods that customers have not yet asked for, even new goods produced by large, established consumer product manufacturers. The following excerpt is taken from a sales call made by an experienced consumer goods salesperson on a reluctant retail buyer. This excerpt begins with an interruption made by the buyer during a presentation of a new brand of toothpaste:

FIGURE 9.4   Imagine you walk up to your prospect, who says, "I'm too busy
to see you now." What would you say?

BUYER: Well, it sounds good, but I have 7 brands and 21 different
sizes of toothpaste now. There is just no place to put it. [A false objection—smoke screen.]

SALESPERSON: Suppose you had 100 customers walk right down the
aisle and ask for Colgate 100 Toothpaste. Could you find room
then?

BUYER: Well, maybe. But I'll wait until then. [The real objection.]

SALESPERSON: If this were a barbershop and you did not have your barber pole outside, people wouldn't come in because they wouldn't know it was a barbershop, would they?

BUYER: Probably not.

SALESPERSON: The same logic applies to Colgate 100. When people see it, they will buy it. You would agree that our other heavily advertised products sell for you, right? [Trial close.]

BUYER: Yeah, they do, all right. [Positive response; now reenter your selling sequence.]

The salesperson eliminated the stall in this case through a logical analogy.

A third common stall is the alibi that your prospect has to get approval from someone else, such as a boss, buying committee, purchasing agent, or home office. Since the buyer's attitude toward purchasing your product will influence the firm's buying decision, it is important you determine the buyer's attitude toward your product.

When the buyer stalls by saying, "I will have to get approval from my boss," you can counter by saying, "If you had the authority, you would go ahead with the purchase, wouldn't you?" If the answer is "yes," chances are the buyer will exert a positive influence on the firm's buying decision. If not, then you must uncover the real objections. Otherwise, chances are you will not make the sale.

Two additional responses to the "I've got to think it over" stall are: "What are some of the issues you have to think about?" Or, you may directly focus on the prospect's stall by saying, "Would you share with me some of the things that are holding you back?"

Another effective response to "I've got to talk to my boss," is "Of course you do. What are some of the things you would talk about?" This allows you to agree with the reluctant prospect. You are now on the buyer's side. It helps encourage the buyer to talk and to trust you. This empathic response ("Of course you do.") puts you in the other person's position.

Sometimes, the prospect will not answer the question. Instead, the response is, "Oh, I just need to get an opinion." You can follow up with a multiple choice question such as: "Would you be exploring whether this is a good purchase in comparison with a competitor's product or would you be wondering about the financing?" This helps display an attitude of genuine caring.

As with any response to an objection, communicate a positive attitude. Do not get demanding, defensive, or hostile. Otherwise, your nonverbal expressions may signal a defensive attitude—reinforcing the prospect's defenses.

Your goal in dealing with a stall is to help prospects realistically examine reasons for and against buying now. If you are absolutely sure it is not in their best interest to buy now, tell them so. They will respect you for it. You will fell better about yourself. The next time you see these customers, they will be much more trusting and open with you.

SELLING TIPS

Stalling Objections

A. "I have to think this over."

   1. "Let's think about it now while it is fresh in your mind. What are some of the items you need to know more about?"

   2. "I understand that you want more time to think. I would be interested in hearing your thoughts about the reasons for and the reasons against buying now."

   3. "You and I have been thinking this over since the time we first met. You know that this is a terrific opportunity, you like the product, and you know it will save you money. Right? [If prospect says "yes":] Let's go ahead now!"

B. "I'm too busy."

   1. "I appreciate how busy you are. When could we visit for just _____ minutes." [Stop, or add a benefit for seeing you.]

C. "I'm too busy. Talk to _____ first."

   1. "Does he/she have the authority to approve the purchase of _____ ? [If prospect says "yes":] Thank you. I'll tell him/her you sent me. [If prospect says "no":] Well, then, why should I talk with him/her?"

   2. "We almost never deal with purchasing managers. This is an executive-level decision. I need to talk with you."

D. "I plan to wait until next fall."

   1. "Why?"

   2. "Some of my best customers said that. Once they bought, they were sorry they waited."

   3. "You promise me you will buy this fall?" [If prospect says "yes," then:]

     a. "OK, let's finalize the order today and I'll have it ready to arrive October 1."

     b. "Great! Should I call you in September or October so we can set it up?"

   4. "What if I could arrange for it to be shipped to you now, but you didn't have to pay for it until the fall?"

However, the main thing to remember is not to be satisfied with a false objection or a stall. Tactfully pursue the issue until you have unearthed the buyer's true feelings about your product. If this does not work, (1) you should present the benefits of using your product now; (2) if there is a special price deal, mention it; and (3) if there is a penalty or delay, mention it. Bring out any or all of your main selling benefits and keep on selling!

The No-Need Objection

The prospect says, "Sounds good. I really like what you had to say, and I know you have a good product, but I'm not interested now. Our present product [or supply or merchandise] works well. We will stay with it." Standing up to conclude the interview, the prospect says, "Thanks very much for coming by." This type of objection can disarm an unwary salesperson.

SELLING TIPS

No-Need Objections

A. "I'm not interested."

1. "May I ask why?"

2. "You are not interested now or forever?"

3. "I wouldn't be interested if I were you, either. However, I know you'll be interested when you hear about. . . . It is very exciting!" [If prospect still says "no":] "What would be a better time to talk?"

4. "Some of my best customers first said that until they discovered . . . [state benefits]."

5. "You are not interested? Then who should I talk to who would be interested in . . . [state benefits]."

B. "The . . . we have is still good."

1. "Good compared to what?"

2. "I understand how you feel. Many of my customers said that before they switched over. However, they saw that this product would . . . [discuss benefits of present product or service versus what you are selling]."

3. "That's exactly why you should buy—to get a good trade now."

4. "What stops you from buying?"

C. "We are satisfied with what we have now."

1. "Satisfied in what way?"

2. "What do you like most about what you have right now? [then compare to your product]."

3. "I know how you feel. Often we're satisfied with something because we have no chance [or don't have the time] to compare it with something better. I've studied what you are using and would like _____ minutes to compare products and show you how to . . . [state benefits]."

4. "Many of our customers were happy with what they had before they saw our product. There are three reasons they switched . . . [state three product benefits]."

The **no-need objection** is widely used because it politely gets rid of the salesperson. Some salespeople actually bring it on themselves by making a poor sales presentation. They allow prospects to sit and listen to a sales pitch, without getting them to participate by showing true concern and asking questions. Therefore, as soon as the presentation is over, prospects can quickly say, "Sounds good, but . . ." In essence, they say no, making it difficult for the salesperson to continue the call. While not always a valid objection, the no-need response strongly implies the end of a sales call.

The no-need objection is especially tricky because it may also include a hidden objection and/or a stall. If your presentation was indeed a solo performance or a monologue, your prospect might be indifferent to you and your product, having tuned out halfway through the second act. Aside from departing with a "Thanks for your time," you might attempt to resurrect your presentation by asking questions.

The Money Objection

The **money objection** encompasses several forms of economic excuses: "I have no money"; "I don't have that much money"; "It costs too much"; or the ever-popular, "Your price is too high." These objections are simple for the buyer to say, especially in a recessionary economy.

Often, prospects want to know the product's price before you begin the presentation, and they will not want you to explain how the product's benefits outweigh its costs. Price is a real consideration and must be discussed, but it is risky to discuss product price until it can be compared to product benefits. If you successfully postpone the price discussion, you must eventually come back to it because your prospect will seldom forget it. Some prospects are so preoccupied with price that they will give minimal attention to your presentation until the topic reemerges. Others will falsely present price as their main objection to your product, which conceals the true objection.

By observing nonverbal signals, asking questions, listening, and positively responding to the price question when it arises, you can easily handle price-oriented objections.

Many salespeople think that offering the lowest price gives them a greater chance of sales success. Generally, this supposition is not valid. Once you realize this, you will become even more successful. You might even state that your product is *not* the least expensive one available because of its benefits and advantages, and the satisfaction it provides. Once you convey this concept to your buyer, price becomes a secondary factor that usually can be dealt with successfully.

Do not be afraid of price as an objection; be ready for it and welcome it. Quote the price and keep on selling. It is usually the inexperienced salesperson who blows this often minor objection into a major one. If the price objection becomes major (as shown in Figure 9.5), prospects can become excited and overreact to your price. The end result is loss of the sale. If prospects overreact, slow down the conversation; let them talk it out and slowly present product benefits as related to cost.

The Price/Value Formula. The price objection is a bargaining tool for a canny buyer who wants to be sure of getting the best, absolutely lowest price. But often there is more to it than shrewd bargaining.

If the buyer is merely testing to be sure the best possible price is on the table, it's a strong buying signal. But perhaps the prospect sincerely believes the price is too high. Two different situations, aren't they?

Let's see if we can define why one buyer might already be convinced the product is a good deal—fair price—but is just testing to make sure it's the best price, while another buyer may sincerely believe the asking price is more than the goods are worth.

Remember that cost is what concerns the buyer, not just the price. Cost

FIGURE 9.5   Price seems to have excited this buyer!

• 1. "Your price . . .

• 2. is . . .

• 3. how . . .

• 4. high!?"

is arrived at in the buyer's mind by considering what is received compared to the money paid. In other words price divided by value equals cost:

$$\frac{\text{Price}}{\text{Value}} = \text{Cost}$$

In this price/value formula, the value is what the prospect sees the product doing for them and/or their company. "Value" is the total package of benefits you have built up for the prospect. "Value" is the solution you provide to the buyer's problems.

SELLING TIPS

Money Objections

A. "Your price is too high."
1. "Compared to what?"
2. "How much did you think it would cost?"
3. "We can lower the price right now, but we need to make a decision on what options to cut from our proposal. Is that what you really want to do?"
4. "Our price is higher than the competition. However, we have the best value (now explain)."
5. "How high is too high?"
6. "If it were cheaper, would you want it?"

B. "I can't afford it."
1. "Why?"
2. "If I could show you a way to afford this purchase, would you be interested?"
3. I sincerely believe that you cannot afford *not* to buy this. The benefits of . . . far outweighs the price. Right?"
4. "You cannot afford to be without it! The cost of not having it is greater than the cost of having it. Think of all the business you can lose, the productivity you can lose, that lost income from not having the latest, best, and most reliable technology. You'll love it! You'll wonder how you've gone without it! Lets discuss how you can afford it—OK?"
5. "Do you mean you can't afford it now, or forever?"

C. "Give me a 10 percent discount, and I'll give you an order today."
1. "I always quote my best price."
2. "If you give me an order for 10, I can give you a 10 percent discount. Would you like to order 10?"
3. "[Prospect's name], we build our product up to a certain quality and service standard—not down to a certain price. We could produce a lower-priced item, but our experience shows it isn't worth it. This is a proven product that gives 100 percent satisfaction—not 90 percent."

D. "You've got to do better than that."
1. "Why?"
2. "What do you mean by better?"
3. "Do you mean a longer service warranty? A lower price? Extended delivery? Tell me exactly what you want."

The price will not change. The company sets that price at headquarters. The company has arrived at the price scientifically—computers were used—based on costs, competition, and other salient factors. It is a fair price, and it's not going to change. So, the only thing to change is the prospect's perception of the value. For example, assume the buyer viewed the cost as follows:

$$\frac{\text{Price 100.}}{\text{Value 90.}} = \text{Cost 1.11}$$

The price is too high. You have to solve the prospect's problem with the product by translating product benefits into what it will do for the buyer. You have to build up the value:

$$\frac{\text{Price 100.}}{\text{Value 110.}} = \text{Cost .90}$$

Now, that is more like it. The cost went down because the value went up.

The price/value formula is not the answer to "your price is too high." It is only a description of the buyer's thinking process and an explanation of why the so-called "price objection" is heard so often. It does tell us what we must do to answer the price objection.

The salesperson is usually the one who identifies a statement or question from the prospect as an objection. Rarely does the prospect say, "This is my objection." So the first step is to ask, "Why did the buyer say that?" If you ask that question you can probe, get the prospect to say more, and tell why he or she made that objection.

Remember, at one extreme the buyer may be sold on the product and simply testing to see if there is an extra discount. At the other extreme, the buyer may not see any benefit in the product or service but only see the price. When this is the case, "it costs too much" is a legitimate objection to be overcome by translating features into advantages into benefits to the buyer. Use the SELL sequence technique.

The Product Objection

All salespeople encounter **product objections** that relate directly to the product. Everyone does not like even the best-selling product on the market. At times, most buyers have fears over risks associated with buying a product—the product will not do what the salesperson says it will do; or the product is not worth the time or energy required to use it, plus actual cost.

You also sell against competition. The prospect either already uses a competitive product, has used one, would like to use one, has heard of one, or knows people who have used one.

Your reaction to a product objection must use a positive tone. The use of a guarantee, testimonial, independent research results, and demonstrations are helpful in meeting the product objection.

The Source Objection

The **source objection** is the last major category of objections typically faced by salespeople. Source objections relate loyalty to a present supplier or salesperson. It can also be that the prospect does not like you or your company.

Prospects will often discuss their like for a present supplier or salesperson. They may tell you that they do not like your company. Seldom, however, will someone directly say "I don't want to do business with you."

SELLING TIPS

Handling Product Objections

A. "Your competitor's product is better."
   1. "You're kidding!!" [Act surprised.]
   2. "Better in what way?" [Have customer list features liked in the other product; then show how your product has the same or better features.]
   3. "I'm interested in hearing your *unbiased* opinion on the two products."
   4. "You've had a chance to look at their product. What did you see that impressed you?"
   5. "Are you referring to quality, service, features, or the product's value after five years of use?"

B. "The machine we have is still good."
   1. "I understand how you feel. Many of my customers have said that before they switched over. However, they found that the reason a new model makes an old model obsolete is not that the old one is bad, but that the new one is so much more efficient and productive. Would you like to take a look at what these businesses found?"
   2. "That's exactly why you should trade now. Since your machine is still good, you still have a high trade-in value. When it breaks down, your trade-in value will go down, too. It's less expensive to trade in a workable machine than to wait for it to fail."

C. "I'll buy a used one."
   1. "When you buy a used product, you take a high risk. You buy something that some-one else has used and possibly abused. Do you want to pay for other people's mistakes?"
   2. "You may save a few dollars on your monthly payments, but you'll have to pay much more in extra service, more repairs, and downtime. Which price would you rather pay?"
   3. "Many of our customers thought about getting a used product before they decided to get a new one. Let me show you why they decided that new equipment is the best buy. The cost comparisons will make it clear."
   4. "I understand you want to save money. I like to save money. But, you have to draw the line somewhere. Buying a used product in this field is like shopping for a headache. Perhaps you should consider the smaller model for starters. At least you won't have any worries about its reliability!"

D. "I don't want to take risks."
   1. "You feel it's too risky? We rarely hear that. What do you mean by risky?"
   2. " 'Risky' compared to what?"
   3. "What could we do to make you feel more secure?"
   4. "[Prospect's name], it may be more risky for you *not* to buy. What is the price you may pay for low productivity in your plant?"

Usually, handling a source objection requires calling on the prospect routinely, over a long period. It takes time to break this resistance barrier. Get to know the prospect and the prospect's needs. Show your true interest. Do not try to get all of the business at once—go for a trial run, a small order. It is important to find out exactly what bothers the prospect. Some examples are shown in the "Selling Tips" box.

SELLING TIPS

The Source Objection

A. "I'm sorry; we won't buy from you."

1. "Why?"

2. "Obviously, you must have a reason for feeling that way. May I ask what it is?"

3. "Are you not going to buy from us now or forever?"

4. "What could we do to win your business in the future?"

5. "Is there anyone else in your company who might be interested in buying our cost-saving products? Who?"

6. "I respect the fact that you aren't buying from us this one time. However, I suspect that as you hear more about our fantastic products in the news and from customers, you will buy something from us in the future. Do you mind if I stop by periodically to keep you up-to-date on our new products?"

7. "Would you like to work with someone else in our company?"

8. "Is there anything about me that prevents you from doing business with our company?"

B. "I want to work with a more established company. We've done business with . . . for five years. Why should I change?"

1. "I understand how safe you feel about a relationship that goes back five years. And yet, I saw your eyes light up when you looked at our products. I can see that you're giving serious consideration to diversity. Just out of curiosity, could we compare the pros and cons of the two choices? Let's take a piece of paper and list the reasons for and against buying from us. The first reason against us is that we haven't worked with you for the past five years. What are some reasons *for* giving us a chance to prove ourselves?"

2. "I can only say good things about my competitor and if I were you, I would go with him or her—unless, of course, you want a better product at a better price."

TECHNIQUES FOR MEETING OBJECTIONS

Having uncovered all objections, a salesperson must answer them to the prospect's satisfaction. Naturally, different situations require different techniques; several techniques shown in Figure 9.6 apply in most situations. You can:

- Pass up the objection.
- Rephrase an objection as a question.
- Forestall (postpone) the objection.
- Boomerang the objection.
- Ask questions regarding the objection.
- Directly deny the objection.
- Anticipate the objection.
- Compensate for the objection.
- Obtain a third-party answer to the objection.

FIGURE 9.6   Techniques for meeting objections

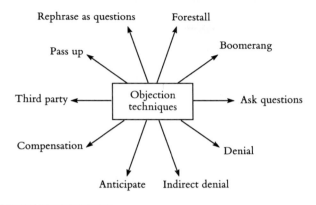

Don't Be Afraid to Pass Up an Objection

Occasionally, you may have a prospect raise an objection or make a statement that requires going around it without directly addressing it. After introducing yourself, for example, a prospect may say, "I'm really not interested in a service such as yours."

You have two options. First, you can take the "sissy" approach, **pass up the objection,** and say "Well, if you ever do, here is my card. Give me a call." Or, you could take the approach used by top salespeople and say something that allows you to move into your presentation, such as immediately going to the customer benefit approach or simply asking "why?"

As you gain selling experience, you will be confident in knowing when to pass up or stop and respond to the objection. If you pass up an objection and the prospect brings it up again, then treat this as an important objection. Use your questioning skills to uncover the prospect's concerns.

Rephrase an Objection as a Question

Since it is easier to answer a question than to overcome an objection, **rephrase** (an objection) **as a question** when you can do so naturally. Most objections are easily rephrased. Table 9.2 presents examples of several procedures for rephrasing an objection as a question. Each procedure, except the objection based on a bad previous experience with the product by the prospect, has the same first three steps: (1) acknowledging the prospect's viewpoint, (2) rephrasing the objection into a question, and (3) obtaining agreement on the question. Here is an example:

TABLE 9.2   Examples of rephrasing objections as a question

Facts Are Incorrect	Facts Are Incomplete	Facts Are Correct	Based on Bad Personal Experience
1. Acknowledge viewpoint.	1. Acknowledge viewpoint.	1. Acknowledge viewpoint.	1. Thank prospect for telling you.
2. Rephrase objection.	2. Rephrase objection.	2. Rephrase objection.	2. Acknowledge viewpoint.
3. Obtain agreement.	3. Obtain agreement.	3. Obtain agreement.	3. Rephrase objection.
4. Answer question providing information supported by proof— third party.	4. Answer question by providing the complete facts.	4. Answer question, outweigh with benefits.	4. Obtain agreement.
5. Ask for present viewpoint.	5. Ask for present viewpoint.	5. Ask for present viewpoint.	5. Answer question.
6. Move back into selling sequence.	6. Move back into selling sequence.	6. Move back into selling sequence.	6. Move back into selling sequence.

> BUYER: I don't know—your price is higher than competitors.
>
> SALESPERSON: I can appreciate that. You want to know what particular benefits my product has that make it worth its slightly higher price. [or, "What you're saying is that you want to get the best product for your money."] Is that correct?
>
> BUYER: Yes, that's right.

Now discuss product benefits versus price. Once you have done so, attempt a trial close by asking for the prospect's viewpoint to see if you have overcome the objection.

> SALESPERSON: Do you see how the benefits of this product make it worth the price? [trial close]

A variation of this sequence is M&M—Mars' Bruce Scagel's "Feel-Felt-Found" method, in which he first acknowledges the prospect's viewpoint, saying: "John, I understand how you *feel.* Bill at XYZ store *felt* the same way, but he *found,* after reviewing our total program of products and services, that he would profit by buying now."

Bruce refers to rephrasing the objection as a question as his "Isolate and Gain Commitment" method. He gives as an example: "Mary, as I understand it, your only objection to our program is the following. . . . If I can solve this problem, then I'll assume that you will be prepared to accept our program."

Bruce knows he can solve the problem or he would not have asked the question. When Mary says "yes," he has isolated the main problem. He is not handling an objection; he is answering a question. He now shows her how to overcome the problem and then continues his selling. If Mary says "no," Bruce knows he has not isolated her main objection. He must start over in attempting to uncover her objections. He might say, "Well, I guess I misunderstood. Exactly what is the question?" And now, when Mary responds, it will usually come back as a question. "Well, the question was about. . . ." You need to involve the customer and find out what is happening internally. You can do this with the proper use of questions.

Postponing Objections Is Sometimes Necessary

Often, the prospect may skip ahead of you in the sales presentation by asking questions that you address later in the presentation. (See Figure 9.7.) If you judge that the objection will be handled to your prospect's satisfaction by your customary method, and that the prospect is willing to wait until later in the presentation, you politely **postpone the objection.** Five examples of postponing objections are:

PROSPECT: Your price is too high.

SALESPERSON: In just a minute I'll show you why this product is reasonably priced, based on the savings you will receive compared to

FIGURE 9.7 Suppose you sit down to show your prospect computer software, and the prospect says, "How much does this piece of software cost?" What would you say?

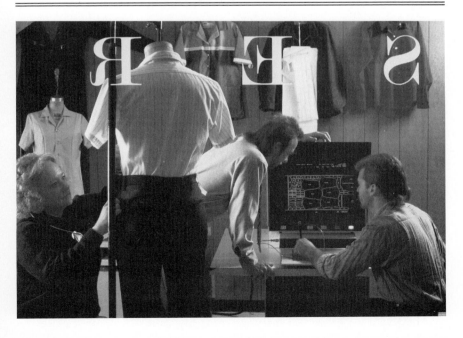

SELLING TIPS

Be Positive in Discussing Price

All prospects are sensitive to how price is presented. This is a typical list of negative and positive ways to deal with price issues during the business proposition phase:

Negative Words	Positive Words
• This costs two thousand three hundred dollars.	• This is only twenty-three hundred dollars.
• Your downpayment. . .	• Your initial investment. . .
• Your monthly payment. . .	• Your monthly investment. . .
• You can pay the purchase price over a series of months.	• We would be happy to divide this investment into small monthly shares.
• How much would you like to pay us every month?	• What monthly investment would you feel comfortable with?
• We'll charge you two points above the prime rate.	• Your rate will be only prime plus two.
• We'll take off sixty-seven hundred to trade-in your used car.	• We are offering you six thousand seven hundred dollars to trade your existing model.

what you presently do. That's what you're interested in, savings, right? [trial close]

or

SALESPERSON: Well, it may sound like a lot of money. But let's consider the final price when we know the model you need, OK? [trial close]

or

SALESPERSON: There are several ways we can handle your costs. If its all right, let's discuss them in just a minute. [Pause. This has the same effect as the trial close. If no response, continue.] First, I want to show you. . . .

or

SALESPERSON: I'm glad you brought that up [or, "I was hoping you would want to know that."] because we want to carefully examine the cost in just a minute, OK? [trial close]

or

SALESPERSON: High? Why, in a minute I'll show you why it's the best buy on the market. In fact, I'll bet you a Coke that you will believe it's a great deal for your company! Is it a deal? [trial close]

Tactfully used, postponing can leave you in control of the presentation. Normally, respond to the objection immediately. However, occasionally it is not appropriate to address the objection. This is usually true of the price objection. Price is the primary objection to postpone if you have not had the opportunity to discuss product benefits. If you have fully discussed the product, then immediately respond to the price objection.

Send It Back with the Boomerang Method

Be ready at any time to turn an objection into a reason to buy. By convincing the prospect that an objection is a benefit, you will have turned the buyer immediately in favor of your product. This is the very heart of the **boomerang method.** Take, for example, the wholesale drug salesperson, working for a firm like McKesson and Robbins, who wants to sell a pharmacist a new container for prescription medicines. Handling the container, the prospect says:

PROSPECT: They look nice, but I don't like them as well as my others. The tops seem hard to remove.

SALESPERSON: Yes, they are hard to remove. We designed them so that children couldn't get into the medicine. Isn't that a great safety measure? [trial close]

Or, consider the industrial equipment salesperson who is unaware that a customer is extremely dissatisfied with a present product:

PROSPECT: I have been using your portable generators, and do not want to use them anymore.

SALESPERSON: Why?

PROSPECT: Well, the fuses kept blowing out and causing delays in completing this project! So get out of here and take your worthless generators with you.

SALESPERSON: [with a smile] Thank you for telling me. Say, you and our company's design engineers have a lot in common.

PROSPECT: Oh yeah? I'll bet! [sarcastically]

SALESPERSON: Suppose you were chief engineer in charge of manufacturing our generators. What would you do if valued customers—like yourself—said your generators had problems?

PROSPECT: I'd throw them in the trash.

SALESPERSON: Come on, what would you really do? [with a smile]

PROSPECT: Well, I would fix it.

SALESPERSON: That's why I said you and our design engineers have a lot in common. They acted on your suggestion—don't your think? [trial close]

You have used reverse psychology. Now the prospect is listening, giving you time to explain your product's new features and to make an offer to repair the old units. You are ready to sell more products, if possible.

Another example is the industrial salesperson who responded to the prospect's high price objection by saying, "Well, that's the very reason you should buy it." The prospect was caught off guard and quickly asked, "What do you mean?" "Well," said the salesperson, "for just 10 percent more you can buy the type of equipment you really want and need. It is dependable, safe, and simple to operate. Your production will increase so that you have paid back the price differential quickly." The prospect said, "Well, I hadn't thought of it quite like that. I guess I'll buy it after all."

Boomeranging an objection requires good timing and quick thinking. Experience in a particular selling field, knowledge of your prospect's needs, a positive attitude, and a willingness to stand up to the objection are necessary attributes for successful use of this technique.

Ask Questions to Smoke Out Objections

Intelligent questioning impresses a prospect in several ways. Technical questions show a prospect that a salesperson "knows the business." Questions relating to a prospect's particular business show that a salesperson is concerned more with the prospect's needs than with just making a sale. Finally, people who **ask intelligent questions,** whether they know much about the product, the prospect's business, or life in general, often receive admiration. Buyers are impressed with the sales professional who knows what to ask and when to ask it! Examples of questions are:

PROSPECT: This house is not as nice as the one someone else showed us yesterday.

SALESPERSON: Would you tell me why?

or

PROSPECT: This product does not have the . . . [feature].

SALESPERSON: If it did have the . . . [feature], would you be interested?

[This example is an excellent questioning technique to determine if the objection is a smoke screen, a major or minor objection, or a practical or psychological objection. If the prospect says "no" to the response you know the feature was not important.]

or

PROSPECT: I don't like your price.

SALESPERSON: Will you base your decision on price or on the product offered you . . . at a fair price?

TABLE 9.3 Five-question sequence method of overcoming objection

Question 1:	There must be some good reason why you're hesitating to go ahead now. Do you mind if I ask what it is?
Question 2:	In addition to that, is there any other reason for not going ahead?
Question 3:	Just supposing you could convince yourself that. . . . Then you'd want to go ahead with it? [If positive response, go back to selling; if negative response, go to Question 4.]
Question 4:	Then there must be some other reason. May I ask what it is? [After response, move back to Question 2. Can go directly to Question 5 or complete the sequence one or two more times before going to Question 5.]
Question 5:	What would it take to convince you?

[If the prospect says "price," show how benefits outweigh costs. If the decision is based on the product, you have eliminated the price objection.]

Five-Question Sequence Method of Overcoming Objections. Buyers state objections for numerous reasons. From time to time, all salespeople sense that a buyer will not buy. As you gain sales experience, you will be able to feel it. It may be the buyer's facial expressions or a tone of voice that tips you off. When this occurs, quickly find out why a prospect doesn't want to buy. For doing this, consider using a preplanned series of questions as shown in Table 9.3.

Let's assume you have finished the presentation. You try to close the sale and see the buyer is not willing to go any further in the conversation. What do you do? Consider using the following **five-question sequence.**

First, use this question: "There must be some good reason why you're hesitating to go ahead now; do you mind if I ask what it is?" When the reason is stated, or even if it is an objection, immediately double-check the objection with one more question by using question number two: "In addition to that, is there any other reason for not going ahead?" The buyer may give the real reason for not buying, or may give the original objection. No matter what is said, you have set up a condition for buying.

Now use question number three, which is a "just supposing" question: "Just supposing you could . . . then you'd want to go ahead?" If the answer is yes, discuss how you can do what is needed. If you get a negative response, then use question number four: "Then there must be some other reason. May I ask what it is?" Respond with question number two again. Then ask, "Just supposing . . . you'd want to go ahead?" Should you get another negative response, use question number five by saying, "What would it take to convince you?"

What often happens will surprise you. The buyer will often say, "Oh, I don't know, I guess I'm convinced. Go ahead and ship it to me." Or, you might be asked to go back over some part of your presentation. The important thing is that this series of questions keeps the conversation going and gets the real objections out in the open, which helps increase your sales. Imagine you are the salesperson in this example:

SALESPERSON: Should we ship the product to you this week or next?

BUYER: Neither; see me on your next trip. I'll have to think about it.

SALESPERSON: You know, there must be some good reason why you're hesitating to go ahead now. Would you mind if I asked what it is? [Question 1]

BUYER: Too much money.

SALESPERSON: Too much money. Well, you know, I appreciate the fact that you want to get the most for your money. In addition to the money, is there any other reason for not going ahead? [Question 2]

BUYER: No.

SALESPERSON: Well, just suppose that you could convince yourself that the savings from this machine would pay for itself in just a few months, and that we could fit it into your budget. Then you'd want to go ahead with it? [Question 3]

BUYER: Yes, I would.

Now you go back to selling by discussing the return on investment and affordable payment terms. You went from the first objection to the "double-check" question ("In addition to the money, is there any other reason for not going ahead?"). Then you used the "just supposing" question. You met the condition, the machine's cost. Then you went to the "convince" question. The buyer said "yes," so you can keep selling. Now, let's role-play as if the buyer had said "no." (Again, you are the salesperson.)

BUYER: No, I wouldn't go ahead.

SALESPERSON: Well, then there must be some other reason why you're hesitating to go ahead now. Do you mind if I ask what it is? [Question 4]

BUYER: It takes too much time to train my employees in using the machine.

SALESPERSON: Well, you know, I appreciate that. Time is money. In addition to the time, is there any other reason for not going ahead?

[Question 2]

BUYER: Not really.

SALESPERSON: Just supposing that you could convince yourself that this machine would actually save employees time so they could do other things. You'd find the money then, wouldn't you?
[Question 3]

BUYER: I'm not sure. [another potential negative response]

SALESPERSON: Money and time are important to you, right?

BUYER: Yes they are.

SALESPERSON: What would it take for me to convince you this machine will save you time and money? [Question 5]

Now you have to get a response. The buyer has to set the condition. You, as the salesperson, are in control. The buyer is answering the questions. Remember, you want to help the person buy. When you get an objection, you are told what you must do to make the sale happen. So do not fear objections, welcome them!

Use Direct Denial Tactfully

You will often face objections that are incomplete or incorrect. Acknowledge the prospect's viewpoint, then answer the question by providing the complete or correct facts.

PROSPECT: No, I'm not going to buy any of your lawn mowers for my store. The Bigs-Weaver salesperson said they break down after a few months.

SALESPERSON: Well, I can understand. No one would buy mowers that don't hold up. Is that the only reason you won't buy?

PROSPECT: Yes it is, and that's enough!

SALESPERSON: The BW salesperson was not aware of the facts, I'm afraid. My company produces the finest lawn mowers in the industry. In fact, we are so sure of our quality that we have a new three-year guarantee on all parts and labor. [pause]

PROSPECT: I didn't know that. [positive buying signal]

SALESPERSON: Are you interested in selling your customers quality lawn mowers like these? [trial close]

PROSPECT: Yes, I am. [appears that you have overcome the objection]

SALESPERSON: Well, I'd like to sell you 100 lawn mowers. If even one breaks down, call me and I'll personally come over and repair it. [close]

As you see by this example, you do not say, "Well, you so-and-so, why do you say a thing like that?" Tact is critical in using a direct denial. A smart or huffy response can alienate a prospect. However, a **direct denial** based on facts, logic, and politeness can be effective in overcoming the objection.

If I say to you, "You're wrong. Let me tell you why," what happens to your mind? It closes! So if I tell you that you are wrong and this closes your mind, what would I have to tell you to open your mind? That you are right! But if what you said was indeed wrong, do I tell you it was right? No, instead, do what the example illustrated by saying, "You know, you're right to be concerned about this. Let me explain." You have made the buyer right and kept the buyer's mind open. Also, you could say, "You know, my best customer had those same feelings until I explained that. . . ." You have not made the customer wrong, but right.

The Indirect Denial Works

An **indirect denial** is different from a direct denial in that it initially appears as agreement with the customer's objection but then moves into a denial of the fundamental issue in the objection. The difference between the direct denial and the indirect denial is that the indirect denial is softer, more tactful, and more courteous. The direct denial should only be used—judiciously—to disconfirm especially damaging misinformation.

The typical example of indirect denial is the "yes, but" phrase. Here are several examples:

- "Yes, but would you agree that it takes information, not time, to make a decision? What kind of information are you really looking for to make a good decision?"
- "I agree. Our price is a little higher, but so is our quality. Are you interested in saving $1,200 a year on maintenance?"
- "Sure, it costs a little more. However, you will have the assurance that it will cost much less over its lifetime. Isn't that the way your own products are made?"
- "Your point is well taken. It does cost more than any other product on the market. But why do you think we sell millions of them at this price?"
- "I appreciate how you feel. Many of our customers have made similar comments prior to buying from me. However, they all asked themselves: 'Can I afford not to have the best? Won't it cost me more in the long run?'"

The indirect denial begins with an agreement or an acknowledgment of the prospect's position. "Yes, but . . . ," "I agree," "Sure . . . ," "Your point is well taken," or "I appreciate how you feel" are phases that allow the salesperson to tactfully respond to the objection. Done in a natural, conversational way, the salesperson will not offend the prospect.

Try this yourself. When someone you talk with says something you disagree with, instead of saying "I don't agree," say something like "I see what you mean. However, there's another way to look at it." See if this, as well as the other communication skills you have studied, helps you to better sell yourself—and your product.

Compensation or Counterbalance Method

Sometimes a prospect's objection is valid, and calls for the **compensation method** in overcoming objections. Several reasons for buying must exist to justify or compensate for a negative aspect of making a purchase. For example, a higher product price is justified by benefits such as better service or higher performance. In the following example, it is true that the prospect can make more profit on each unit of a competing product. You must develop a technique to show how your product has benefits that will bring the prospect more profit in the long run.

> PROSPECT: I can make 5 percent more profit with the Stainless line of cookware and it is quality merchandise.
>
> SALESPERSON: Yes, you are right. The Stainless cookware is quality merchandise. However, you can have an exclusive distributorship on the Supreme cookware line, and still have high quality merchandise. You don't have to worry about Supreme being discounted by nearby competitors as you do with Stainless. This will be the only store in town carrying Supreme. What do you think? [trial close]

If the advantages presented to counterbalance the objection are important to the buyer, you have an opportunity to make the sale.

Let a Third Party Answer

An effective technique for responding to an objection is to answer it by letting a **third party answer** and using someone else's experience as your proof or testimony. A wide range of proof statements are used by salespeople today. You might respond to a question in this way: "I'm glad you asked. Here is what our research has shown . . . ," or, "EPA tests have shown . . . ," or, "You know, my best customer brought that point up before making the purchase . . . but was completely satisfied." These are examples of proof statement formats. If you use a person or a company's name, be sure to obtain their approval first.

Secondary data or experience, especially from a reliable or reputable source, is especially successful with the expert or skeptical prospect. If after hearing secondary testimony, the prospect was still unsure about the product, one successful equipment salesperson would ask the buyer to directly contact a current user:

> SALESPERSON: I still haven't answered your entire question, have I?
>
> BUYER: Not really.
>
> SALESPERSON: Let's do this. Here is a list of several people presently using our product. I want you to call them up *right now* and ask them that same question. I'll pay for the calls.

A salesperson should use this version of the third-party technique only when certain that the prospect is still unsatisfied with how an objection has been handled, and that positive proof will probably clinch the sale. This dramatic technique allows the salesperson to really impress a prospect. It also shows a flattering willingness in going to great lengths to validate a claim.

AFTER MEETING THE OBJECTION— WHAT TO DO?

As shown in Figure 9.8, your prospect has raised an objection that you have answered and overcome; now what? First, as shown in Figure 9.9, use a trial close, then be prepared to either move back into your presentation or to close the sale.

First, Use a Trial Close—Ask for Opinion

After meeting an objection at any time during the interview, you need to know if you have overcome the objection. If you have not overcome it, your prospect may raise it again. Whether it resurfaces or not, if your prospect believes that an objection was important, your failure to handle it, or your mishandling of it, will probably cost you the sale. Ideally, all objections raised should be met before closing the sale. So the first thing to do after responding to the objection is to use a trial close to determine if you have overcome the objection. Ask things like:

- "That clarifies this point entirely, don't you agree?"
- "That's the answer you're looking for, isn't it?"
- "With that question out of the way, we can go ahead, don't you think?"
- "Do you agree with me that we've covered the question you raised, and given you a way to handle it?"
- "Now that's settled entirely, isn't it?"
- "That solves your problem with _____, doesn't it?"

Once you have confirmed overcoming an objection, immediately go to the next SELL sequence step. To signal that the last step is over, and that

FIGURE 9.8 Imagine you are this bank loan officer and you just answered this woman's objection. What should you do now?

you are moving on, use body language as you speak. That is, make an appropriate gesture, look in a new direction, turn the page of your proposal, or shift in your chair—make some small or large physical movement. Now, do one of two things (assuming you have handled the objection): either move back into your presentation or close the sale.

FIGURE 9.9 Procedure to follow when an objection is raised by a prospect

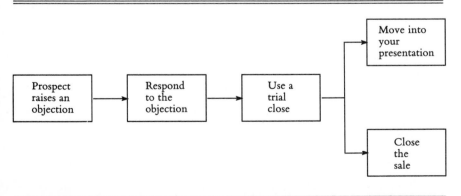

Move Back into Your Presentation

Once satisfied that you have answered and overcome an objection, make a smooth transition back into your presentation. As you nonverbally signal the last step is over, let the prospect know you are moving back into your presentation with a phrase such as, "As we were discussing earlier. . . ." Now, you can continue the presentation.

Move to Close Your Sale

If you have finished your presentation when the prospect raised an objection and the prospect's response to your trial close indicates you have overcome an objection, your next move is to close the sale. If the objection was raised during your close, then it is time to close again.

As you move on to the close with a gesture, you might summarize benefits previously discussed with a phrase such as, "Well, as we have discussed, you really like. . . ." Then, again ask the prospect for the order. The next chapter on closing will give you other ideas on how to ask for the order.

If You Cannot Overcome the Objection

If you cannot overcome an objection or close a sale because of an objection, be prepared to move back into your presentation and concentrate on new or previously discussed features, advantages, and benefits of your product. If you have determined that the objection raised by your prospect is a major one that cannot be overcome, admit it and show how your product's benefits outweigh this disadvantage.

If you are 100 percent sure that you cannot overcome the objection and that the prospect is not going to buy, go ahead and close. *Always ask for the order.* Never be afraid to ask your prospect to buy. The buyer says no, not you. Someone else may walk into the prospect's office after you with a product similar to yours. Your competitor also may be unable to overcome this person's objection, but he or she may get the sale nonetheless just by asking for it!

SUMMARY OF MAJOR SELLING ISSUES

People want to buy, but they do not want to be taken advantage of, so they often ask questions or raise objections during a sales presentation. Your responsibility is to be prepared to logically and clearly respond to your prospect's objections whenever they arise, whether during your approach or when you move to close the sale.

Sales objections indicate a prospect's opposition or resistance to the information or request of the salesperson. Basic points to consider in

SELLING TIPS

A Strategy for Handling Objections

One of the biggest hurdles to success for salespeople is how to handle objections. Here is a strategy top salespeople use to draw out, understand, and overcome objections:

1. Plan for objections.
2. Anticipate and forestall objections when needed.
3. Handle objections as they arise.
4. Be positive.
5. Listen to objections—hear them out.
6. Understand objection—ask questions to clarify.
7. Meet objection by selecting methods or techniques to use in responding to objection.
8. Confirm you have met objection—use a trial close.
9. Where am I? Decide if you need to keep on selling, handle another objection, or close the sale.

meeting objections are to: (1) plan for them, (2) anticipate and forestall them, (3) handle them as they arise, (4) listen to what is said, (5) respond warmly and positively, (6) make sure you understand, and (7) respond using an effective communication technique.

Before you can successfully meet objections, first determine if the prospect's response to your statement or close is a request for more information, a condition of the sale, or an objection. If it is a real objection, determine whether it is minor or major. Respond to it using a trial close, and if you have successfully answered it, continue your presentation based on where you are in the sales presentation. For example, if you are still in the presentation, then move back into your selling sequence. If you have completed the presentation, move to your close. If you are in the close and the prospect voices an objection, then you must decide whether to use another close or move back into the presentation and discuss additional benefits.

Be aware of and plan for objections. Objections may be classified as hidden, stalling, no-need, money, and product and source objections. Develop several techniques to help you overcome each of these types of objections, such as stalling the objection, turning the objection into a benefit, asking questions to smoke out hidden objections, denying the objection if appropriate, illustrating how product benefits outweigh the objection drawbacks, or developing proof statements that answer the objection.

Welcome your prospects' objections. They will help you determine if you are on the right track or guide you to uncovering what prospects' needs actually are, and if they believe your product will fulfill those needs. Valid objections should be viewed as beneficial for you and the customer. A true objection reveals the customer's need, allowing a salesperson to demonstrate how a product can meet that need. Objections also show inadequacies in a salesperson's presentation or product knowledge. Finally, objections make selling a skill that a person can constantly improve. Over time, a dedicated salesperson can learn how to handle every conceivable product objection—tactfully, honestly, and to the customer's benefit.

10

Close, Close, Close

Realizing my interest was in a career of selling, I interviewed with companies in many industries while a student at the University of Oklahoma. When I interviewed with the general agent of the Massachusetts Mutual Insurance Company in Oklahoma City prior to graduation, I became very fascinated with the opportunities the insurance business offered. The Mass Mutual was not then operating in Amarillo, my home town, and a friend suggested I talk to the manager of the Prudential Life Insurance Company for Fort Worth and the West Texas area. It appeared to me that I wanted to be associated with a major, reputable company, so while studying for final exams, I was simultaneously preparing to learn the Prudential Dollar Guide Presentation. I received my degree on June 11, 1950, and signed my contract the next day to start in the insurance business.

Mr. McCelvey, my first manager with Prudential, used to say the development of a sales presentation was simply fixing the prospect's problems and helping him accomplish his objectives. Thirty-one years later in the insurance business, I couldn't agree more! The sales presentation is the ability of the agent to build extremely close, personal relationships with people, learn about their objectives, desires, concerns, and commitments, and help accomplish them. If everything has been done to develop the sales presentation properly, the closing of the sale is simply the next logical sequence.

To be successful in an insurance career, a person needs a very deep commitment to the product of life insurance and what it will do. The insurance business will test a person's mettle and this abiding faith will be needed in times of discouragement and frustration. As you experience death claims and see what the product can and does do for families, corporations, partnerships, trusts, and other entities, the faith and commitment to the product are sure to come. This develops the philosophy of "you're not only in the insurance business, the insurance business is in you!"

A person who is interested in an insurance career should first overcome the negatives sometimes attached to the life insurance business. These negatives, however, are more than offset, in my opinion, by the limitless opportunity for a large income, ultimate respect and admiration from your clientele, complete independence to pursue your career as you feel best, and no dependence on the political whims of your superior; it's based totally on your capabilities and commitment. •

P R O F I L E

George W. Morris
Prudential Life Insurance

"My company," said one executive, "had done business for many years with a firm that helped us merchandise our industrial products. I persuaded our advertising manager to have another firm also submit a proposal on how to best handle our products. Both suppliers received enthusiastic consideration on their proposals from our executives, and submitted competitive bids on price.

"The salesperson for the new company had every reason," the executive went on to say, "to believe he would receive our business and so did I. However, our advertising manager felt the company should stay with the old firm because of the chance we would take by adopting something new. It was too risky for him. He knew what to expect from the old company." This executive had not discussed this concern with the newcomer's salesperson during his presentation. The salesperson failed to overcome objections and thus make the sale. He probably never found out why he lost the order. •

The point of this example is that successful salespeople do not give a presentation and then ask for the order. Successful salespeople develop selling techniques that aid them in developing a natural instinct, sensitivity, and timing for when and how to close each buyer. This chapter wraps up our discussion of the main elements of the sales presentation. We will begin by discussing when to close, showing examples of buying signals, and discussing what makes a good closer. Next is a discussion of the number of times you should attempt to close a sale, along with some problems associated with closing. Ten closing techniques are presented followed by an explanation of the importance of being prepared to close several times based on the situation.

WHEN SHOULD I POP THE QUESTION?

Closing is the process of helping people make a decision that will benefit them. You help people make that decision by asking them to buy. As successful salespeople know, there are no magic phrases and techniques to use in closing a sale. It is simply the end result of your presentation. As insurance agent George Morris says, "If everything has been done to properly develop a sales presentation, the closing of the sale is simply the next step in a logical sequence."

Although it seems obvious, some salespeople forget that prospects know that the salesperson is there to sell them something. So, as soon as the two meet, the prospect's mind may already have progressed beyond the major portion of the salesperson's presentation. At times, the prospect may be ready to make the buying decision early in the interview.

So when should you attempt to close a sale? Simply, *when the prospect is ready!* More specifically, when the prospect is in the "conviction stage" of

FIGURE 10.1   Close when the prospect is ready

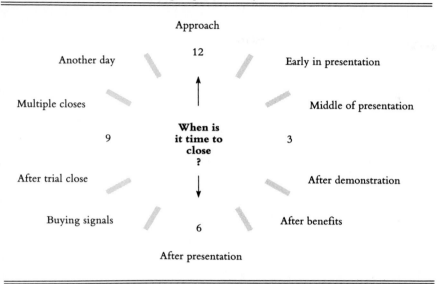

the mental buying process. A buyer can enter the conviction state at any time during the sales presentation. As shown in Figure 10.1, you might ask someone to buy as early as the "approach stage" or as late as another day. Ninety-nine percent of the time, however, the close comes after the presentation. An ability to read a prospect's buying signals correctly can aid a salesperson in deciding when and how to close a sale.

READING BUYING SIGNALS

After prospects have gone through each stage of the mental buying process and are ready to buy, they will often give you some type of signal. A **buying signal** refers to anything prospects say or do to indicate that they are ready to buy. Buying signals hint that prospects are in the conviction stage of the buying process, as seen in Figure 10.2. Several ways in which prospective buyers may signal that they are ready to buy are as follows:

- *Ask questions*—"How much is it?" "When is the earliest I can receive it?" "What are your service and return goods policies?" At times, you may respond to a buying signal question with another question, as shown in Table 10.1. This helps you better determine your prospect's thoughts and needs. If your question is answered positively, the prospect is showing a high interest level and you are close to closing the sale.

FIGURE 10.2 A positive response to the trial close indicates a move toward the close; a negative response means return to your presentation or determine the prospect's objections

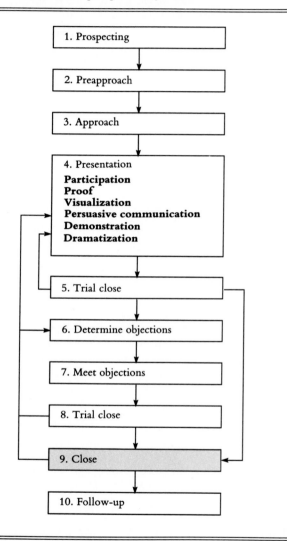

- *Asks another person's opinion*—The executive calls someone on the telephone and says, "Come in here a minute; I have something to ask you." Or the husband turns to his wife and says, "What do you think about it?"
- *Relaxes and becomes friendly*—Once the prospect decides to purchase a

TABLE 10.1   Answering a prospect's buying signal question with a question

Buyer Says:	Salesperson Replies:
• What's your price?	• In what quantity?
• What kind of terms do you offer?	• What kind of terms do you want?
• When can you make delivery?	• When do you want delivery?
• What size copier should I get?	• What size do you need?
• Can I get this special price on an order I place now and next month?	• Would you like to split your shipment?
• Do you carry, 8, 12, 36, and 54-foot pipe?	• Are those the sizes you commonly use?
• How large an order do I need to place to receive your best price?	• What size an order do you have in mind?
• Do you have the Model 6400 in stock?	• Is that the one you like best?

product, the pressure of the buying situation is eliminated. A state of visible anxiety changes to one of refreshed relaxation because your new customer believes you are a friend.

• *Pulls out a purchase order form*—If, as you are talking, your prospect pulls out an order form, it is time to move toward the close.

• *Carefully examines merchandise*—When a prospect begins to carefully scrutinize your product or seems to contemplate the purchase, this may be an indirect request for prompting. Given these indications, attempt a trial close: "What do you think about. . . ?" Should you obtain a positive response to this question, move on to close the sale.

A buyer may send verbal or nonverbal buying signals at any time before or during your sales presentation (remember Figure 10.1). The accurate interpretation of buying signals should prompt you to attempt a trial close. In beginning a trial close, summarize the major selling points desired by your prospect. If you receive a positive response to the trial close, you can move to Step 9 and wrap up the sale. A negative response should result in a return to your presentation, Step 4, or to determine objections, Step 6. This is illustrated in Figure 10.2. In any case, a successful trial close can save you and your prospect valuable time, while a thwarted trial close allows you to assess the selling situation.

WHAT MAKES A GOOD CLOSER?

In every sales force, there are individuals who seem better than others at closing sales. Some rationalize this difference of abilities by saying, "It comes naturally to some people," or, "They've just got what it takes." Well, what does it take to be a good closer?

Good closers have a strong desire to close each sale. They have a positive attitude about their product's ability to benefit the prospect. They know their customers and tailor presentations to meet each one's specific needs.

Good closers spend time in preparing for each sales call. They take the time to carefully ascertain the needs of their prospects and customers by observing, asking intelligent questions, and most of all, earnestly listening to them.

The successful salesperson does not stop on the prospect's first "no." If a customer says "no", determine the nature of the objection and then move back into the presentation. After discussing information relative to overcoming the objection, use a trial close to determine if you have overcome the objection, and then determine if there are other objections. If resistance continues, remain positive and remember that every time you attempt to close, you get closer to making the sale. Additionally, always ask for the order and then be silent.

Ask for the Order and Be Quiet!

No matter when or how you close, remember that when you ask for the order it is important to be silent. Do not say a single word. If you say something—anything—you increase your probability of losing the sale.

You must put the prospect in a position of having to: (1) make a decision; (2) speak first; and (3) respond to the close. If you say anything after your close, you take the pressure off the prospect to make that decision.

Imagine this situation. The salesperson has finished the presentation and says, "Would you want this delivery in two or four weeks?" The average salesperson cannot wait over 10 seconds for the prospect's reply without saying something like, "I can deliver it anytime," or starting to talk again about the product. This destroys the "closing moment." The prospect does not have to make the decision. There is time to think of reasons not to buy. By keeping quiet for a few seconds, the prospect can again escape making the decision.

All individuals experience the urge to say "no," even when they are not sure of what you are selling or may actually want what you are proposing. At times, everyone is hesitant in making a decision. To help the prospect make the decision, you must maintain silence after the close.

The professional salesperson "asks for the order and shuts up." The professional can stay quiet all day if necessary. Rarely will the silence last over 30 seconds. During that time, do not say anything or make a distracting gesture; merely project positive nonverbal signs. Otherwise, you will lessen your chances of making the sale. This is the time to mentally prepare your responses to the prospect's reaction.

It sounds simple, yet it is not. Your stomach may churn. Your nerves make you want to move. You catch yourself with a serious look on your face, instead of a positive one. You may look away from the buyer. Most

MAKING THE SALE

A Mark Twain Story

"Mark Twain attended a meeting where a missionary had been invited to speak. Twain was deeply impressed. Later he said, 'The preacher's voice was beautiful. He told us about the sufferings of the natives and pleaded for help with such moving simplicity that I mentally doubled the fifty cents I had intended to put in the plate. He described the pitiful misery of those savages so vividly that the dollar I had in mind gradually rose to five. Then that preacher continued. I felt that all the cash I carried on me would be insufficient. I decided to write a large check.' Then he went on, added Twain, and on and on about the dreadful state of those natives. 'I abandoned the idea of the check. Again, he went on, and I was back to five dollars. As he continued, I went to four, two, and then one dollar. Still, he persisted to preach. When the plate finally came around, I took ten cents out of it.'"[1]

of all, you want to talk to relieve the uncomfortable feeling that grows as the silence continues. Finally, the prospect will say something. Now you can respond based on the reaction to your close.

Constantly practice asking your closing question, staying silent for 30 seconds, and then responding. This will develop your skill and courage to close.

Get the Order and Get Out!

Talking can also lose the sale after the prospect has said yes. An exception would be if you ask the customer for names of other prospects. Once this is done, it is best to get the order and get out.

In continuing to talk, you may give information that changes the buyer's mind. Then ask for the order and remain silent until the buyer responds. If you succeed, finalize the sale and leave.

HOW MANY TIMES SHOULD YOU CLOSE?

Courtesy and common sense imply a reasonable limit to the number of closes attempted by a salesperson at any one sitting. However, salespeople call on customers and prospects to sell their products.

To sell, you must be able to use multiple closes. As the chapter title indicates, three closes is a minimum for successful salespeople. Three to five well-executed closes should not offend a prospect. Attempting several closes in one call challenges a salesperson to employ wit, charm, and personality in a creative manner. So always take at least three strikes before you count yourself out of the sale.

CLOSING UNDER FIRE

To effectively close more sales, never take the first no from the prospect to mean an absolute refusal to buy. Instead, you must be able to "close under fire." In other words, you must be able to ask a prospect who may be in a bad mood or even appear hostile toward you to buy.

Take the experience of a consumer goods salesperson who suggested that a large drug wholesaler should buy a six-month supply of the company's entire line of merchandise. Outraged, the purchasing agent threw the order book across the room. The salesperson explained to the furious buyer that the company had doubled its promotional spending in the buyer's area and that it would be wise to stock up because of an upcoming increase in sales. The salesperson calmly picked up the order book, smiled, and handed it to the buyer saying, "Did you want to buy more?"

The buyer laughed and said, "What do you honestly believe is a reasonable amount to buy?" This was a buying signal that the prospect would buy, but in a lesser quantity. They settled on an increased order of a two-month supply over the amount of merchandise normally purchased. This example illustrates why it is important for the salesperson to react calmly to an occasional hostile situation. That salesperson was your author. I will never forget that day!

DIFFICULTIES WITH CLOSING

Closing the sale is the easiest part of the presentation. It serves as a natural wrap-up to your sales presentation because you solidify details of the purchase agreement. Yet, salespeople sometimes have difficulty closing the sale for a number of reasons.

One reason salespeople may fail to close a sale and get an order is that they are not confident of their ability to close. Perhaps some earlier failure to make a sale has brought about this mental block. They may give the presentation and stop short of asking for the order. Obviously, the seller must overcome this fear of closing to become successful.

Second, salespeople often determine that the prospect does not need the quantity or type of merchandise, or that the prospect simply should not buy. So they do not ask the prospect to buy. The salesperson should remember that "it is the prospect's decision and responsibility whether or not to buy." Do not make that decision for the prospect.

Finally, the salesperson may not have worked hard enough in developing a customer profile and customer benefit plan—resulting in a poor presentation! Many times a poorly prepared presentation will fall apart. It is important to be prepared and develop a well-planned, well-rehearsed presentation.

MAKING THE SALE

Closing Is Not One Giant Step

Too many salespeople regard the close as a separate and distinct part of the sales call. "I've discussed benefits and features, answered some objections, handled price, and now it's time to close."

Chronologically, of course, the "close" does come at the end. You need to be closing all along. Closing is the natural outgrowth of the sales presentation. If the rest of the sales call has been a success, closing simply means working out terms and signing the order.

What about the salesperson who says, "I always have trouble closing. Everything's fine until it's time to close the sale." Chances are, there's no basis for the sale. "Everything's fine . . ." may merely be a way of saying, "I stated my case and the prospect listened. At least she never told me to pack up and go."

ESSENTIALS OF CLOSING SALES

While there are numerous factors to consider in closing the sale, the following are essential if you wish to improve your chances:

- Be sure your prospect understands what you say.
- Always present a complete story to ensure understanding.
- Tailor your close to each prospect. Eighty percent of your customers will respond to a "standard" close. It is the other 20 percent you need to prepare for. Be prepared to give the "expert" the facts requested, to give the egotist praise, to lead the indecisive prospect, and to slow down for a slow thinker.
- Everything you do and say should consider the customer's point of view.
- Never stop at the first "no."
- Learn to recognize buying signals.
- Before you close, attempt a trial close.
- After asking for the order—be silent.
- Set high goals for yourself and develop a personal commitment to reach your goals.
- Develop and maintain a positive, confident, and enthusiastic attitude toward yourself, your products, your prospects, and your close.

TWELVE STEPS TO A SUCCESSFUL CLOSING

Before we discuss specific techniques on how to ask for the order or close the sale, remember that you will greatly increase the number of sales you close by following 12 simple steps. These steps are:

1. Think *success!* Be enthusiastic!
2. *Plan* your sales call.
3. Confirm your prospect's *needs* in the approach.
4. Give a *great* presentation.
5. Use *trial closes* during and after your presentation.
6. Smoke out a prospect's *real* objections.
7. *Overcome* these real objections.
8. Use a *trial close* after overcoming each objection.
9. Summarize *benefits* as related to buyer's *needs*.
10. Use a *trial close* to confirm Step 9.
11. Ask for the *order* and then *be quiet*.
12. Leave the door *open!* Act as a professional.

As you see from these 12 steps, a successful close is the result of a series of steps you have followed before asking for the order. "Closing is not one giant step."

Should you not make the sale, always remember to act as a professional salesperson and be courteous and appreciative of the opportunity to present your product to the prospect. This allows the door to be open another time. Thus, Step 12 cannot be overlooked—always remember to leave the door open!

Often, salespeople believe there is some mystical art to closing a sale. Some believe that if they say the right words in the appropriate manner, the prospect will buy. They concentrate on developing tricky closing techniques and are often pushy with prospects in hopes of pressuring them into purchasing. Certainly, salespeople need to learn alternative closing techniques. However, what is most needed is a thorough understanding of the entire selling process and of the critical role that closing plays in that process.

A memorized presentation and a hurriedly presented product will not be nearly as successful as the skillful use of the 12 steps to a successful close. A close look at the 12 steps illustrates that a lot of hard work, planning, and skillful execution of your plan occurs before you reach Step 11 and ask for the order. The point is that if salespeople understand how each of the 12 steps applies to them and their customers, and if they are capable of performing each step, they will earn the right to close.

In fact, many times the close will occur automatically because it has become the easiest part of the sales presentation. Often the prospect will close for the salesperson, saying: "That sounds great! I'd like to buy that." All that the salesperson has to do is finalize the details and write up the order. Often, though, the prospect will be undecided on the product after the presentation, so the skillful salesperson develops multiple closing techniques.

PREPARE SEVERAL CLOSING TECHNIQUES

To successfully close more sales, be able to determine your prospect's situation, understand the prospect's attitude toward your presentation, and be prepared to instantly select a closing technique from several techniques you know based on your prospect. For example, suppose you profiled the prospect as having a big ego, so you planned to use the "compliment" closing technique. You find the prospect is eager to buy but undecided about which model or the number of products to buy, so you switch to using your "standing room only" closing technique. By changing to a closing technique that fits the situation, you can speed the sale and still keep your customer satisfied.

Successful salespeople adapt a planned presentation to any prospect or situation that may arise. Some salespeople have up to 10 closing techniques, each designed for a specific type of situation. The following are 10 common closing techniques:

- Alternative choice close.
- Assumptive close.
- Compliment close.
- Summary of benefits close.
- Continuous-yes close.
- Minor-points close.
- T-account or balance sheet close.
- Standing-room-only close.
- Probability close.
- Negotiation close.

Whatever product is sold, whether an industrial or consumer product, these closing techniques are used to ask a prospect for the order. (See Figure 10.3.)

The Alternative Choice Close Is an Old Favorite

The **alternative choice close** was popularized in the 1930s as the story spread of the Walgreen Drug Company's purchase of 800 dozen eggs at a special price. A sales trainer named Elmer Wheeler suggested to the Walgreen clerks that when a customer asked for a malted milk at a Walgreen fountain, the clerk should say, "Do you want one egg or two?" Customers had not even thought of eggs in their malteds. Now they were faced with the choice of *how many* eggs—not whether or not they wanted an egg. Within one week all 800 dozen of the eggs were sold at a profit. Two examples of the alternative close are:

Which do you prefer—one or two neckties to go with your suit?

Would you prefer the Xerox 6200 or 6400 copier?

FIGURE 10.3 Techniques for closing the sale. Which close should be used?

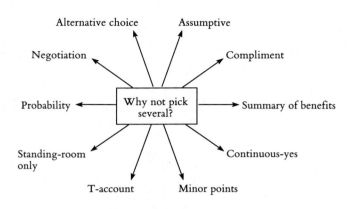

As you see, the alternative choice does not give the prospect a choice of buying or not buying, but asks which one or how many items they want to buy. It says, "You are going to buy, so let's settle the details on what you will purchase." Buying nothing at all is not an option.

Take, for example, the salesperson who says: "Would you prefer the Xerox 6200 or 6400?" This question: (1) assumes the customer has a desire to buy one of the copiers; (2) assumes the customer will buy; and (3) allows the customer to have a preference. If the customer prefers the Xerox 6400, you know the prospect is ready to buy, so you begin the close. A customer who says, "I'm not sure," is still in the desire stage, so you continue to discuss each product's benefits. However, you see that the customer likes both machines. Should the prospect appear indecisive, you can ask: "Is there something you are unsure of?" This question probes to find out why your prospect is not ready to choose.

If used correctly, the alternative choice close is an effective closing technique. It provides a choice between items, never between something and nothing. By presenting a choice, you either receive a "yes" decision or uncover objections, which if successfully met, allow you to come closer to making the sale.

The Assumptive Close

With the **assumptive close,** the salesperson assumes the prospect will buy (see Figure 10.4). Statements can be made such as, "I'll call your order in tonight," or, "I'll have this shipped to you tomorrow." If the prospect does not say anything, you can assume the suggested order has been accepted.

FIGURE 10.4   This banker hands the prospect a pen and slides a new account form in front of him. At the same time, he says, "Mr. Faber, just complete this form, sign it, and your account will be open by this afternoon." What closing technique did he use?

Many times the salesperson who has called on a customer for a long time can fill out the order form, hand it to the customer, and say, "This is what I'm going to send you," or, "This is what I believe you need this month." Many salespeople have earned customer trust to such an extent that the salesperson orders for them. Here, the assumptive close is especially effective.

The Compliment Close Inflates the Ego

Everyone likes to receive compliments. The **compliment close** is especially effective when you talk with a prospect who is a self-styled expert, who has a big ego, or who is in a bad mood. Would-be experts and egotistical prospects both value their own opinions. By complimenting them, you get them to listen and respond favorably to your presentation. The prospect with a low ego, low self-esteem, or one who finds it difficult to decide will also respond favorably to a compliment. Here is an example of a housewares salesperson closing a sale with a grocery retail buyer:

> SALESPERSON: It is obvious you know a great deal about the grocery business. You have every square foot of your store making a good profit. Ms. Stevenson, our products will also provide you with a good profit margin. In fact, our profit will exceed your store's average profit-per-square-foot. And they sell like hotcakes. This added benefit of high turnover will further increase your profits— which you have said is important to you. [He pauses, and when there is no response, he continues.] Given the number of customers coming into your store, and our expected sales of these products due to normal turnover, along with our marketing plan, *I suggest you buy*. . . . [He states the products and their quantities.] This will provide you with sufficient quantities to meet your customers' demands for the next two months, plus provide you the profit you expect out of your products. [Now he waits for the response or again asks for the order using the alternative choice or assumptive close.]

All buyers appreciate your recognition of their better points. Conscientious merchants take pride in their ways of doing business; customers coming into the retail clothing store take pride in their appearance; people considering life insurance take pride in looking after their families. So compliment prospects relative to something that will benefit them as you attempt to close the sale. Remember, always make honest compliments. No matter how trusting you may think people are, nearly anyone can detect insincerity in a compliment. When a compliment is not in order, choose to summarize the benefits of your product for a specific customer.

The Summary of Benefits Close Is Most Popular

During the sales presentation, it is important to remember the main features, advantages, and benefits of interest to the prospect to use them successfully during the close. Summarize these benefits in a positive manner so that the prospect agrees with what you say; then ask for the order.

Here is an example of using the **summary of benefits close** on a prospect. Assume that the prospect indicated to you during your sales presentation that she likes your profit margin, delivery schedule, and credit terms.

> SALESPERSON: Ms. Stevenson, you say you like our profit margin, fast delivery, and credit policy. Is that right? [Summary and trial close.]

PROSPECT: Yes, I do.

SALESPERSON: With the number of customers coming into your store and our expected sales of the products due to normal turnover, along with our marketing plan, *I suggest you buy.* . . . [State the products and their quantities.] This will provide you with sufficient quantities to meet customer demand for the next two months, plus provide you with the profit you expect from your products. I can have the order to you early next week. [Now wait for her response.]

You can easily adapt the FAB statements and SELL sequence for your "summary" close. The vacuum cleaner salesperson might say, "As we have discussed, this vacuum cleaner's high speed motor [feature] works twice as fast [advantage] with less effort [advantage], saving you 15 to 30 minutes in cleaning time [benefit] and the aches and pains of pushing a heavy machine [benefit of benefit]. Right! [trial close. If positive response, say] Would you want the Deluxe or the Ambassador model?"

The sporting goods salesperson might say, "As we have said, this ball will give you an extra 10 to 20 yards on your drive [advantage], helping to reduce your score [benefit] because of its new solid core [feature]. That's great—isn't it? [trial close. If positive response, say] Will a dozen be enough?"

The air-conditioning salesperson could say, "This air conditioner has a high efficiency rating [feature] that will save you 10 percent on your energy costs [benefit] because it uses less electricity [advantage]. What do think of that? [trial close. If positive response, say] Would you want it delivered this week or do you prefer next week?"

The summary close is favored by industrial product manufacturers like Xerox. Emmett Reagan, profiled in Chapter 7, says the major closing technique taught at the Xerox Training Center consists of the three basic steps of the summary close, which are: (1) determine the key product benefits that interest the prospect during the presentation, (2) summarize these benefits, and (3) make a proposal. The summary of benefits technique is useful when you need a simple, straightforward close rather than a close aimed at a specific prospect's personality.

The Continuous-Yes Close Generates Positive Responses

The **continuous-yes close** is like the summary close. However, instead of summarizing product benefits, the salesperson develops a series of benefit questions that the prospect must answer.

SALESPERSON: Ms. Stevenson, you have said you like our quality products, right?

PROSPECT: Yes, that's right.

SALESPERSON: And you like our fast delivery?

PROSPECT: Yes, I do.

SALESPERSON: You also like our profit margin and credit terms?

PROSPECT: That's correct.

SALESPERSON: Ms. Stevenson, our quality products, fast delivery, profit margin, and good credit terms will provide you with an excellent profit. With the large number of customers you have coming into your store. . . . [Salesperson completes the close as done in the summary of benefits close.]

In this example of the continuous-yes close, the salesperson recognized four product benefits that the prospect liked: (1) the product's quality, (2) fast delivery, (3) profit margin, and (4) favorable credit terms. After the presentation, three questions were used to give the prospect the opportunity to agree that she was impressed with each of the four product benefits. By stacking these positive questions, the salesperson kept the prospect continually saying, "Yes, I like that benefit."

The prospect has now placed herself in a positive frame of mind. Her positive stance toward the product makes it likely that she will continue to say "yes" when asked to buy.

Realize, of course, that some prospects may want to be "cute," and relish the thought of seeing the look of surprise on your face when, after they agree to all of your product benefit statements (yes . . . yes . . . yes), they respond to your order request with an unexpected no. Also, suspicious prospects may view your continuous-yes close as trickery or as an insult to their intelligence rather than as an aid in making a purchase decision. In either case, calmly handling the situation reflects a sales professionalism that will both surprise the trickster and impress the suspicious person.

The Minor-Points Close Is Not Threatening

It is sometimes much easier for a prospect to concede several minor points about a product than to make a sweeping decision on whether to buy or not to buy. Big decisions are often difficult for some buyers to make. By having the prospect make decisions on a product's minor points, you can subtly lead into the decision to buy.

The **minor-points close** is similar to the alternative-choice close. The alternative-choice close asks the prospect to make a choice between two products. To some people, this represents a high-risk decision that they may prefer not to make, whereas the minor-points close asks the prospect to make a low-risk decision on a minor, usually low-cost element of a single product such as delivery dates, optimal features, color, size, payment terms, or order quantity. Single or multiple product element choices may be presented to the prospect. The stereo salesperson says, "Would you prefer the single or multiple record changer for your stereo system?" The Lanier Business Products salesperson asks, "Are you interested in buying or leasing our equipment?" The automobile salesperson asks, "Would you like an air-conditioned car?"

This close is widely used when prospects have difficulty in making a decision or when they are not in the mood to buy. It is also effective as a second close. If, for example, the prospect says no to your first close because of difficulty in deciding whether or not to buy, you can close on minor points.

The T-Account or Balance Sheet Close Was Ben Franklin's Favorite

The **T-account close** is based on the process people go through when they make a decision. Some sales trainers refer to it as the Benjamin Franklin close. In his *Poor Richard's Almanac,* Franklin said, "You know, I believe most of my life is going to be made up of making decisions about things. I want to make as many good ones as I possibly can." So, in deciding on a course of action, his technique was to take pencil and paper and draw a line down the center of the paper. On one side, he put all the pros and on the other side he put all the cons. Now if there were more cons than pros, he would not do something. If the pros outweighed the cons, then he felt it was a good thing to do; this was the correct decision.

This is the process a customer uses in making a buying decision, weighing the cons against the pros. At times, it may be a good idea to use this technique. Pros and cons, debits and credits, or to act and not to act are common column headings. For example, on a sheet of paper the salesperson draws a large T, placing "to act" (asset) on the left side and "not to act" (liability) on the right side (debit and credit, in accounting terms). The salesperson reviews the presentation with the prospect, listing the positive features, advantages, and benefits the prospect likes on the left side, and all negative points on the right. This shows that the product's benefits outweigh its liabilities, and it leads the prospect to conclude that now is the time to buy. If prospects make their own lists, the balance sheet close can be quite convincing. Here is an example:

> SALESPERSON: Ms. Stevenson, here's a pad of paper and a pencil. Bear with me a minute and let's review what we have just talked about. Could you please draw a large T on the page and write "To Act" at the top on the left and "Not to Act" on the right? Now, you said you liked our fast delivery. Is that right?
>
> PROSPECT: Yes.
>
> SALESPERSON: OK, please write down "fast delivery" in the To Act column. Great! You were impressed with our profit margin and credit terms. Is that right?
>
> PROSPECT: Yes.
>
> SALESPERSON: OK, how about writing that down in the left-hand

column? Now is there anything that could be improved?

PROSPECT: Yes, don't you remember? I feel you have a narrow assortment with only one style of broom and one style of mop. [Objection.]

SALESPERSON: Well, write that down in the right-hand column. Is that everything?

To Act	Not to Act
Fast delivery Good profit Good credit	Narrow assortment

PROSPECT: Yes.

SALESPERSON: Ms. Stevenson, which in your opinion outweighs the other—the reason to act or not to act? [A trial close.]

PROSPECT: Well, the To Act column does. But it seems I need a better assortment of products. [Same objection again.]

SALESPERSON: We have found that assortment is not important to most people. A broom and mop are pretty much a broom and mop. They want a good quality product that looks good and will hold up under continuous use. Customers like our products' looks and quality. Aren't these good-looking products? [Trial close showing broom and mop.]

PROSPECT: Look OK to me. [Positive response—she didn't bring up assortment so assume you have overcome objection.]

SALESPERSON: Ms. Stevenson, I can offer you a quality product, fast delivery, excellent profit, and good credit terms. I'd like to suggest this. You buy one dozen mops and one dozen brooms for each of your 210 stores. However let's consider this first! The XYZ chain found that our mops had excellent drawing power when advertised. Their sales of buckets and floor wax doubled. Each store sold an average of 12 mops. [He pauses, listens, and notices her reaction.] You can do the same thing!

PROSPECT: I'd have to contact the Johnson Wax's salesperson and I really don't have the time. [A positive buying signal.]

SALESPERSON: Ms. Stevenson, let me help. I'll call Johnson's and get them to contact you. Also, I'll go by and see your advertising manager to schedule the ads. OK? [Assumptive close.]

PROSPECT: OK, go ahead, but this stuff had better sell.

SALESPERSON: [smiling] Customers will flock to your stores [he's building a picture in her mind] looking for mops, polish, and buckets. Say, that reminds me, you will need a dozen buckets for each store. [Continuous-yes, keep talking.] I'll write up the order. [Assumptive.]

Some salespeople recommend that the columns of the T-account be reversed so that the Not to Act column is on the left and the To Act column is on the right. This allows the salesperson first to discuss the reasons not to buy, followed by the reasons to buy, ending the presentation on the positive side. This decision depends on a salesperson's preference.

Modified T-Account or Balance Sheet Close.   Some salespeople modify the T-account close by only listing reasons to act in one column. They do not want want to remind the prospect of any negative reasons not to buy as they attempt to close the sale. This is similar to the continuous-yes close. The only difference is that the product benefits are written on a piece of paper.

This is a powerful sales tool because prospects are mentally considering reasons to buy and not to buy anyway. You may just as well get the reasons out in the open so you can participate and be a part of the decision-making process.

While this close can be used anytime, it is especially useful as one of your secondary or backup closes. For example, if the summary close did not make the sale, go on to your next close, the T-account close. A contrary idea in the prospect's mind is like steam under pressure—explosive. So when you remove the pressure by getting an objection out in the open, opposition vaporizes. An objection often becomes a minor one or goes away. Remember, however, if the customer says, "Well, I'm going to buy it," do not say, "Well, let's first take a look at the reasons not to buy." Go ahead and finalize the sale.

The Standing-Room-Only Close Gets Action

What happens if someone tells you that you cannot have something that you have an interest in or would like to have? You instantly want it! When you face an indecisive prospect or if you want to have the prospect purchase a larger quantity, indicate that if they do not act now they may *not* be able to buy in the future. To get the prospect to act at once, you can use the **standing-room-only close:**

- "I'm not sure if I have your size. Would you want them if I have them in stock?"
- "My customers have been buying all we can produce. I'm not sure if I have any left to sell you."
- "Well, I know you are thinking of ordering X amount but we really need to order . . . (a larger amount) . . . because we now have it in stock and I don't think we will be able to keep up with demand and fill your summer order."
- "The cost of this equipment will increase 10 percent next week. Can I ship it today or do you want to pay the higher price?"

For the right product, person, and situation, this is an excellent close. Both retail and industrial salespeople can use this technique to get the prospect so excited they cannot wait to buy. However, it should only be used honestly. Prospects realize that factors such as labor strikes, weather, transportation, inflation, and inventory shortages could make it difficult to buy in the future. You can do them a favor by encouraging them to buy now using the standing-room-only close.

The Probability Close

When the prospect gives the famous, "I want to think it over" or some variation of that objection, try saying, "Ms. Prospect, that would be perfectly fine. I understand your desire to think it over, but let me ask you this—when I call you back next week, what is the probability, in percentage terms out of a total of 100, that you and I will be doing business?" Then pause, and don't say another word until the prospect speaks.

The prospect's response can generally be divided into three possible categories:

1. More than 50 percent but less than 85 percent for buying. If your prospects respond in this range, try to ask what the remaining percent is against buying, then pause and don't say a word. When you become skilled in this technique, you will see prospects blink as they focus on their real objections.

Many times, we hear that prospects want to think things over. It is not because they want to delay the decision; it is because they don't fully understand what bothers them. The **probability close** permits your prospects to focus on their real objections. Once you have a real objection, convert that objection with a persuasive sales argument.

2. Above 85 percent but not 100 percent for buying. If they're in this range, recognize that there is a minor probability against you. You might want to say, "As it is almost certain that we're going to do business together, why wait until next week? Let's go ahead now; and if you decide in the next couple of days that you want to change your mind, I'll gladly tear up your order. But let's get a running start on this project together."

When prospects indicate a very high percentage of probability, you can use their own statements as a lever to push them over the top.

3. Less than 50 percent for buying. This is a signal that there is little, if any, chance that you will ever close this particular sale. The only appropriate tactic is to go back to square one and start the reselling process. It is amazing how many professional salespeople take a look at a closing situation and expect the prospect to say 80–20 as a probability in their favor, and instead hear "80–20 . . . against."

SELLING TIPS

Your Prospect's Name Is a Powerful Closing Tool

Dale Carnegie, author of *How to Win Friends and Influence People,* taught his students, "If you remember my name, you pay me a subtle compliment; you indicate that I have made an impression on you." Your prospect's name is one of the most powerful closing tools because most of us are more interested in ourselves than anyone else.

Repeat your prospect's name several times— but don't overdo it—during your sales call. *Connect your prospect's name with the major benefit statements* like:

- "This automatic dialing feature, Jim, will save you a lot of time."
- "Our warranty is designed to give you peace of mind, Susan."

Your prospect will not know that you are using a powerful psychological strategy referred to as "learned association or positive pairing." If you have connected your prospect's name with three or four prominent product benefits, your customer will expect to hear something positive when you merely mention his or her name. When you approach the close, remember to use your prospect's name. Chances are that the sound of her or his name will again evoke positive feelings. By using this little known secret of master sales closers, you will quickly close more sales than you ever thought possible.

The probability close permits prospects to focus on their objections. It allows the true or hidden objections to surface. The more prospects fight you and the less candid they are about the probability of closing, the less likely they are to buy anything.

The Negotiation Close

Every sale is a negotiation. Most sales negotiations focus on two major themes: value and price. Customers often demand more value and lower prices. In their quest for more value at lower cost, prospects often resort to unfair tactics and put heavy pressure on the salesperson. The purpose of a good sales **negotiation close** is not to haggle over who gets the larger slice of pie, but to find ways for everyone to have a fair piece of the pie. Both the buyer and seller should win. Here are two examples of a negotiation close:

- "If we could find a way in which we would eliminate the need for a backup machine and guarantee availability, would you be happy with this arrangement?"
- "Why don't we compromise? You know I can't give you a discount, but I could defer billing until the end of the month. That's the best I can do."

When you hit a tennis ball over the net, the kind of spin you put on the ball determines the type of return shot you will receive. In a negotiation, the attitude you project determines the attitude you receive. Be positive! Be helpful! Be concerned! Show your interest in helping the prospect.

PREPARE A MULTIPLE CLOSE SEQUENCE

By keeping several difficult closes ready in any situation, you are in a better position to close more sales. Also, the use of a multiple close sequence, combined with methods to overcome objections, greatly enhances your chance of making a sale.

For example, you could begin with a summary close. Assuming the buyer says no, you could rephrase the objection and then use an alternative close. If again the buyer says no, you could use the five-question sequence method for overcoming objections, cycling through it two or three times.[*]

Table 10.2 gives an example of multiple closes incorporating techniques to overcome objections. The successful closing of the sale often requires both methods to overcome objections and closing techniques.

CLOSE BASED ON THE SITUATION

Since different closing techniques work best for certain situations, salespeople often identify the common objections they encounter and develop specific closing approaches designed to overcome these objections. Table 10.3 lists some ways in which different closing techniques are used to meet objections.

Assume, for example, that a buyer has a predetermined belief that a competitor's product is needed. The salesperson could use the T-account approach to show how a product's benefits are greater than a competitor's product. In developing the sales presentation, review your customer profile and develop your main closing technique along with several alternatives. By being prepared for each sales call, you will experience increased confidence and enthusiasm, which results in a more positive selling attitude. You can both help the customer and reach your goals.

RESEARCH REINFORCES THESE SALES SUCCESS STRATEGIES

This chapter ends the discussion on the various parts of the sales presentation. While it is difficult to summarize all sales success strategies discussed throughout this book one research report reinforces several key procedures that improve sales performance. This research sought to exam-

---

[*]See Chapter 9 for correct procedures on overcoming objections.

TABLE 10.2   Multiple closes incorporating techniques for overcoming objections

SALESPERSON: John, we have found that the Octron bulb is going to reduce your storage space requirements for your replacement stock. It offers a higher color output for your designers reducing their eye fatigue and shadowing. [Summary benefits.] Should I arrange for delivery within the week?

BUYER: Well, those are all good points, but I'm still not prepared to buy. It's too costly.

SALESPERSON: What you're saying is, "You want to know what particular benefits my product has that make it worth its slightly higher price?" Is that correct?

BUYER: Yes, I guess so.

SALESPERSON: Earlier we saw that considering the extended life of the lamps and their energy savings you can actually save $375 each year by replacing your present lamps with GE Watt-Misers. This shows, John, that you actually save money using our product. Right? [Trial close.]

BUYER: Yes, I guess you're right.

SALESPERSON: Great! Do you prefer installation this weekend or after regular business hours next week? [Alternative close.]

BUYER: Neither. I need to think about it more.

SALESPERSON: There must be some good reason why you're hesitating to go ahead now. Do you mind if I ask what it is? [Question 1 in sequence.]

BUYER: I don't think I can afford relamping all at one time.

SALESPERSON: In addition to that, is there another reason for not going ahead? [Question 2 in sequence.]

BUYER: No.

SALESPERSON: Just supposing you could convince yourself that group relamping is less expensive than spot replacing . . . then you'd want to go ahead with it? [Question 3.]

BUYER: I guess so.

SALESPERSON: Group relamping is not an absolute necessity; however, it does allow you to realize immediate energy savings on all of your fixtures. It actually saves you much of the labor costs of spot replacement because the lamps are installed with "production line" efficiency. See what I mean? [Trial close.]

BUYER: Yes, I do.

SALESPERSON: Would you like installation at night or on the weekend? [Alternative close.]

BUYER: I'd still like to think about it.

SALESPERSON: There must be another reason why you're hesitating to go ahead now. Do you mind if I ask what it is? [Question 1.]

BUYER: We just don't have the money now to make that kind of investment.

SALESPERSON: In addition to that, is there any other reason for not going ahead? [Question 2.]

BUYER: No. My supervisor just will not let me buy anything.

SALESPERSON: You agree you could save money for your company on this purchase—right?

BUYER: Yes.

SALESPERSON: Well, John, how about calling your supervisor now and telling him about how much money we can save him in addition to reducing your storage space and the eye fatigue of your employees? Maybe both of us could visit your supervisor.

ine two key questions all salespeople frequently ask themselves: What makes one sales call a success and another a failure? Do salespeople make common mistakes that prevent success?

To answer questions such as these, Xerox Learning Systems enlisted a team of observers to monitor and analyze more than 500 personal sales calls of 24 different sales organizations. The product and services sold ranged from computers to industrial refuse disposal.

TABLE 10.3   Closing techniques based upon situation

Situation	Alternative	Compliment	Summary	Continuous-Yes	Minor-Points	Assumptive	T-Account	Standing-Room-Only	Probability	Negotiation	Reason Why
Customer is indecisive	X		X	X	X		X	X	X	X	Forces a decision
Customer is expert or egotist		X					X		X	X	Lets "expert" make the decision
Customer is hostile		X	X						X	X	Positive strokes
Customer is a friend						X			X	X	You can take care of the small things
Customer has predetermined beliefs							X		X	X	Benefits outweigh disbeliefs
Customer is greedy, wants a deal								X	X	X	Buy now

Mike Radick, the Xerox senior development specialist overseeing the study, stated that the average successful sales call observed was 33 minutes long. During that call, the salesperson asked 13.6 questions and described 6.4 product benefits and 7.7 product features. Meanwhile, the customer described 2.2 different needs, raised 1.0 objections, made 2.8 statements of acceptance, and asked 7.7 questions.

The observers noted that it does not seem to matter whether the salesperson is 28 or 48 years old, male or female, or has 2 or 20 years of experience. What matters is the ability to use certain skills and avoid common errors. These are six common mistakes that prevented successful sales calls:

Tells Instead of Sells; Doesn't Ask Enough Questions.   The salesperson does most of the talking. Instead of asking questions to determine a customer's interest, the salesperson charges ahead and rattles off product benefits. This forces the customer into the passive role of listening to details that may not be of interest. As a result, the customer becomes increasingly irritated.

For example, a person selling a computerized payroll system may tell a customer how much clerical time could be saved by using this service. However, if clerical time is not a concern, then the customer has no interest in learning about ways to reduce time spent on payroll processing. On the other hand, the same customer may have a high need for more accurate recordkeeping and be extremely interested in the computerized reports generated by the system.

Over-Controls the Call; Asks Too Many Closed-End Questions. This sales dialogue resembles an interrogation, and the customer has limited opportunities to express needs. The over-controlling salesperson steers the conversation to subjects the salesperson wants to talk about without regarding the customer. When the customer does talk, the salesperson often fails to listen or respond, or doesn't acknowledge the importance of what the customer says. As a result, the customer is alienated and the sales call fails.

Doesn't Respond to Customer Needs with Benefits. Instead, the salesperson lets the customer infer how the features will satisfy his or her needs. Consider the customer who needs a high-speed machine. The salesperson responds with information about heat tolerance, but doesn't link that to how fast the equipment can turn out the customer's product. As a result, the customer becomes confused, loses interest, and the call fails.

Research shows a direct relationship between the result of a call and the number of different benefits given in response to customer needs; the more need-related benefits cited, the greater the probability of success.

Doesn't Recognize Needs; Gives Benefits Prematurely. For example, a customer discussing telephone equipment mentions that some clients complain that the line is always busy. The salesperson points out the benefits of his answering service, but the customer responds that busy lines are not important since people will call back. In this case, the customer is not concerned enough to want to solve the problem.

Doesn't Recognize or Handle Negative Attitudes Effectively. The salesperson fails to recognize customer statements of objection (opposition), indifference (no need), or skepticism (doubts). What isn't dealt with effectively remains on the customer's mind, and left with a negative attitude, the customer will not make a commitment. The research also shows that customer skepticism, indifference, and objection are three different attitudes. Each attitude affects the call differently; each one requires a different strategy for selling success.

Makes Weak Closing Statements; Doesn't Recognize When or How to Close. In one extreme case, the customer tried to close the sale on a positive note, but the salesperson failed to recognize the cue and continued selling until the customer lost interest. The lesson is that successful salespeople are alert to closing opportunities throughout the call.

The most powerful way to close a sales call involves a summary of benefits that interest the customer. Success was achieved in three out of four calls that included this closing technique.

KEYS TO IMPROVED SELLING

How is the bridge from average to successful salesperson made? Xerox found it involves learning and using each of the following skills:

- Ask questions to gather information and uncover needs.
- Recognize when a customer has a real need and how the benefits of the product or service can satisfy it.
- Establish a balanced dialogue with customers.
- Recognize and handle negative customer attitudes promptly and directly.
- Use a benefit summary and an action plan requiring commitment when closing.[2]

Learning and using these five selling skills, using other skills emphasized throughout the book, and your natural ability and positive mental attitude combine to make you a successful, professional salesperson.

SUMMARY OF MAJOR SELLING ISSUES

Closing is the process of helping people make decisions that will benefit them. You help people make those decisions by asking them to buy. The close of the sale is the next logical sequence after your presentation. At this time, you finalize details of the sale (earlier, your prospect was convinced to buy). Constantly look and listen for buying signals from your prospect to know when to close. It is time to close the sale anytime the prospect is ready, whether at the beginning or end of your presentation.

As you prepare to close the sale, be sure you have presented a complete story on your proposition and that your prospect completely understands your presentation. Tailor your close to each prospect's personality and see the situation from the prospect's viewpoint. Remember that you may make your presentation and close too early, causing the prospect to say no instead of "I don't understand your proposition and I don't want to be taken advantage of." This is why you should never take the first no. It is another reason to use a trial close immediately before the close. But no matter when or how you close, do so in a positive, confident and enthusiastic manner to better serve your prospect and help reach your goals. Learn and abide by the 12 steps to a successful closing.

Plan and rehearse closing techniques for each prospect. Develop natural closing techniques or consider using closes such as the alternative, compliment, summary, continuous-yes, minor decision, assumption,

T-account, or the standing-room-only close. Consider the situation and switch from your planned close if your prospect's situation is different than anticipated.

A good closer has a strong desire to close each sale. Rarely should you accept the first no as the final answer. If you work in a professional manner, you should be able to close a minimum of three to five times.

Do not become upset or unnerved if a problem creeps up when you are ready to close. Keep a cool head, determine any objections, overcome them, and try to close again—you can't make a sale until you ask for the order!

11

Winning in the Long Run
Building a Relationship through Service

"After graduating from Ohio State University majoring in history, I worked in the retail clothing business for two years," says Irwin's Jeff Christopher. "Then, I went to work with an industrial sales firm selling fiberglass-reinforced plastics to food processing manufacturers such as Heinz in Pittsburgh."

Jeffrey S. Christopher
Richard D. Irwin, Inc.

In 1976, Jeff began selling textbooks to college professors for Business Publications, Inc. (BPI). In 1988, BPI merged with its parent company—Richard D. Irwin, Inc.

Over the years, Jeff's outstanding sales performance earned him numerous awards such as Salesperson of the Year. He is one of a select group of people in the company's President's Club—earning this recognition for high performance over an extended period. For this honor, he receives such things as a better car, bonus plans, and consults with the company's president on sales and business matters.

"The key to success in my business," says Jeff, "is getting to know the customer. Once you get to know the customer, it's a lot easier to sell a book. A friend will buy from you easier than a stranger. To do this, I like to get people away from their offices. It is hard to get to know someone with so many interruptions such as the telephone ringing or students and instructors coming by. So I try to take them to lunch or go out and have a cup of coffee.

"Giving the customer the best service I can provide is also important in my job; this is something my competitors do not always do. For example, I'll often hand deliver something a customer needs to help them and to show that I care about their needs.

"A third key to success is providing customers with competitive information. I try to make our product look positive without making competitor's products look negative. It is important to effectively compare products so the customer understands the differences between textbooks. This makes the decision to use my products easier for the instructor. It is important to know all of the decision makers or people who actually select textbooks and others who can provide information about the book selection process such as the department head, secretary, or the professor's teaching assistant. Once the person is using the product, it is doubly important to follow up and keep them using the textbook for the next term. If I do my job right, they'll often not even talk with my competition because their mind is already made up to use my product. It is important for me to stay in touch in person or by telephone and letters to ensure complete satisfaction." •

"A key to my success is being concerned with both the short-run and long-run relationship I have with the customer," says Jeff Christopher. "I need to get the business now. However, if I can't close someone now there is always tomorrow. So, I act in a professional manner if I lose out and continue to regularly make sales calls. For example, a few years ago someone switched from my book to a competitor's. I continued to call on them for the three years they used their book. When it came time to consider a new book, my competitor was late in sending the new edition. I showed them my new edition.

"My new edition, plus the relationship with the person over those three years, resulted in selling books for 1,700 students. That was a $54,000 sale. People will often use the product of the representative they liked best if choosing between several similar books. That is why getting to know the customer, service, and follow-up are so important in my business.

"In selling people, I say, 'I'll give you good service and take care of whatever you need. I've shown you that. We'd love to have your business! What do you say? Will you use my book?' I close a lot of people that way. It is not what I say, but my past actions that close the sale. They know I'll be there for them! I've proved it by calling on them routinely, providing outstanding service, and following through. They trust me!" •

The often used cliché, "last but not least," applies to this chapter, which ends our discussion of the elements of the selling process. As Irwin's Jeff Christopher indicates, follow-up and service are important to the success of a salesperson in today's competitive markets. This chapter discusses the importance of follow-up and service, ways of keeping your customers, methods of helping them increase sales, and handling customer complaints, and ends by emphasizing the need to act as a professional salesperson when servicing your accounts.

SUPER SALESPEOPLE DISCUSS SERVICE

Providing service after the sale to customers is important, no matter what type of company, product, or service you represent.[1] To illustrate the importance of service to the professional salesperson, three men, each of whom has been referred to as one of America's greatest salespeople, discuss the importance of service in selling real estate, steel, and information systems.

Rich Port built a successful real estate business in Chicago that now consists of 28 offices, 375 salespeople, and generates over $300 milion a year in sales. How? Rich explains:

In most fields, a salesperson can offer the customer a product that has some differences from competitive products. But when we sell a residential property, we're often selling the same product that the buyer can purchase from the real estate office down the street. So, in order for us to offer something better, we must give more service. The key to success in the n real estate business is service.[2]

In discussing service, Mike Curto, a retired group vice president of the United States Steel Corporation, says:

You've got to realize that what we're selling isn't a whole lot different from what our competitor can produce. In steel, we take some iron ore, refine it, and eventually end up with a product of a semifinished nature . . . we have to sell *service*. Our salesperson must convince the customer that we're the best in our industry, and that over the long run, better off doing business with us.

 A salesperson has to develop a customer's confidence; the customer must believe that U.S. Steel products are not only equal to what the competition sells, but are the best that can be produced in that particular line. And the salesperson better be sure that the products are as good as he says they are, because he's going to be calling back on that customer many times throughout the year. [3]

These two men both stated that their service or product is similar to those offered by the competition. What about a product like computers sold by such companies as IBM, Honeywell, Burroughs, and Amdahl? Francis G. ("Buck") Rogers, a recent vice president of marketing for IBM, believes one of the keys to success at IBM is service. He says:

IBM means service. With IBM, nothing is successfully sold until it's successfully installed. Now, the salesperson goes through the installation phase, including educating the customer, teaching people how the products will actually perform, and showing them how to properly apply the product. Finally, the equipment is delivered; this can be almost a year later. At any rate, that's the installation phase of the sale.

 Beyond that, we take it much further. We're dealing with customers on a continual basis, for example, trying to find new applications to further justify the equipment. At IBM, we're often leasing a fairly expensive piece of equipment, and unless we continue to give customers the best possible service, always looking out for their best interests, we're taking the risk of losing them.[4]

Based on statements from these three successful sales-oriented individuals alone, it is easy to see the importance of customer service before, after, and between sales. Know as much as possible about each of your accounts to provide the amount of service necessary to keep buyers happy.

ACCOUNT PENETRATION IS A SECRET TO SUCCESS

Follow-up and service create goodwill between a salesperson and the customer, which in the long run increases sales faster than a salesperson who does not provide such service. By contacting the customer after the sale to see that the maximum benefit is derived from the purchase, a salesperson lays the foundation for a positive business relationship. Emmett Reagan of Xerox says:

> It should be borne in mind that there is still much work to be done after making the sale. Deliveries must be scheduled, installations planned, and once the system is operational, we must monitor to assure that our product is doing what is represented. This activity gives us virtually unlimited access to the account, which moves us automatically back to the first phase of the cycle. We now have the opportunity to seek out new needs, develop them, and find new problems that require solutions. Only this time it's a lot easier because, by now, we have the most competitive edge of all, a satisfied customer.

The ability to work and contact people throughout the account, discussing your products, is referred to as *account penetration*. Successful penetration of an account allows you to properly service that account by uncovering its needs and problems. Achieving successful account penetration is dependent on knowledge of that account's key personnel and their situation. If you do not have a feel for an account's situation, you reduce chances of maximizing sales in that account.

Tailor the presentation to meet buyers' objectives in a manner that benefits them. By knowing your buyers, their firms, and other key personnel, you will better uncover their needs or problems and develop a presentation that fulfills the needs or solves the problems. Account penetration is determined by:

- Your total and major brand sales growth in an account.
- Distribution of the number of products in a product line, including sizes, used or merchandised by an account.
- Level of cooperation you obtain, such as reduced resale prices, shelf space, advertising and display activity, discussion with their salespeople, and freedom to visit with various people in the account.
- Your reputation as the authority on your type of merchandise for the buyer.

As a general rule, the greater your account penetration, the greater your chances of maximizing sales within the account. Earning the privilege to freely move around in the account allows you to better uncover prospect needs and to discuss your products with people throughout the firm. As people begin to know you and believe that you are there to help them, they allow you to do things that ultimately increase sales, such as increasing shelf space or talking with the users of your industrial equipment in the account's manufacturing facilities. A good sign that you have successfully penetrated an account is when a competitor dismally says to another, "Forget that account; it's already sewn up."

SERVICE CAN KEEP YOUR CUSTOMERS

You work days, weeks, and sometimes months to convert prospects into customers. What can you do to ensure they will continue to buy from you in the future? After landing a major account, there are six factors to consider:[5]

1. Concentrate on improving your account penetration. As discussed earlier, account penetration is critical in uncovering prospect needs or problems and consistently recommending effective solutions through purchasing your products. This allows you to demonstrate that you have a customer's best interests at heart and are there to help.

2. Contact new accounts on a frequent and regular schedule. In determining the frequency of calls, consider:

- Present sales and/or potential future sales to this account.
- Number of orders you expect to be placed in a year.
- Number of product lines sold to the account.
- Complexity, servicing, and redesign requirements of the products purchased by the account.

Since the amount of time spent servicing an account may vary from minutes to days, be flexible in developing a call frequency for each customer. Typically, invest sales time in direct proportion to the actual or potential sales represented by each account. The most productive number of calls is reached at the point where additional calls do not increase sales to the customer. This relationship of sales volume to sales calls is referred to as the "response function" of the customer to the salesperson's calls.

3. Handle customers' complaints promptly. This is an excellent opportunity to prove to customers that they and their businesses are important, and you sincerely care about them. The speed with which you handle even the most trivial complaint will show the value you place on that customer.

4. Always do what you say you will do. Nothing can destroy your relationship with a customer faster than not following through on what you have promised. Promises made and subsequently broken are not tolerated by professional buyers. They have placed their faith (and sometimes reputation) in you by purchasing your products, so you must be faithful to them to ensure their future support.

FIGURE 11.1

5. Provide service as you would to royalty. By providing your client with money-saving products and problem-solving ideas, you can become almost indispensable. You are an advisor to listen to rather than an adversary to haggle with. Provide all possible assistance. As State Farm Insurance agent Charlotte Cornett says in Figure 11.1, "We're there to help."[6]

6. Show you appreciation. A buyer once said to a salesperson, "I'm responsible for putting the meat and potatoes on your table." Customers contribute to your success, and in return you must show appreciation. Thank them for their business, do them favors. Here are several suggestions:

SELLING TIPS

Can Someone Please Help Me!?

CUSTOMER: May I speak to Frank, please? I want to reorder.

SUPPLIER: Frank isn't with us anymore. May someone else help you?

CUSTOMER: What happened to Frank? He has all my specs; I didn't keep a record.

SUPPLIER: Let me give you to Roger: he's taken over Frank's accounts.

CUSTOMER: Roger, you don't know me, but maybe Frank filled you in. I want to reorder.

SALESPERSON: You want to reorder what?

CUSTOMER: I want to repeat the last order, but increase your number 067 to 48.

SALESPERSON: What else was in the order?

CUSTOMER: Frank had a record of it. It's got to be in his file.

SALESPERSON: Frank isn't here anymore, and I don't have his records.

CUSTOMER: Who does?

SALESPERSON: I don't know. I'm new here, so you'll have to fill me in on your requirements. Are you a new customer?

CUSTOMER: Does four years make me new?

SALESPERSON: Well, sir, you are new to me. How long ago did you place your order?

CUSTOMER: Last month.

SALESPERSON: What day last month?

CUSTOMER: I don't remember; Frank always kept track of it. Maybe I could speak to the sales manager?

SALESPERSON: You mean Mort?

CUSTOMER: No, I think his name is Sam.

SALESPERSON: Sam left us about the same time as Frank. I can ask Mort to call you, but I'm sure he doesn't have your file either.

CUSTOMER: Roger, have you ever heard that your best prospect is your present customer?

SALESPERSON: Is that true?

CUSTOMER: I don't think so.

Multiply this conversation by a thousand, and you have the biggest deterrent to sales.

- Although you may be hundreds of miles away, phone immediately whenever you've thought of something or seen something that may solve one of your customer's problems.
- Mail clippings that may interest your customers even if the material has no bearing on what you're selling. They could be items from trade journals, magazines, newspapers, or newsletters.
- Write congratulatory notes to customers who have been elected to office, promoted to higher positions, given awards, etc.
- Send clippings about your customers' families such as marriages, births, and activities.
- Send holiday or special occasion cards. If you limit yourself to just one card for the entire year, send an Easter card, Fourth of July card, Thanksgiving card, etc. This makes a big impression on customers.

- Send annual birthday cards. To start this process, subtly discover in what months your prospects were born; this can be done easily.
- Prepare and mail a brief newsletter, perhaps quarterly, that keeps customers informed on important matters.
- When a professor gets promoted or tenured, Jeff Christopher of Irwin has a brass wall plaque made in his or her honor. He also brings croissants to customers' offices. Jeff feels these are noticed more than donuts. Occasionally, for holidays, he'll ask a meat market to gift wrap and deliver steaks to the professor's home.

These are just a few of the many practical, down-to-earth ways you can remember customers. Undoubtedly, you'll think of others. The important thing is to personalize whatever you send.

More specifically, it doesn't take much thought, energy, or time to send a card, newspaper clipping, or copy of an article. The secret of impressing customers is to personalize the material with a couple of sentences in your handwriting. Be sure it's legible! Print a short message, if necessary.

YOU LOSE A CUSTOMER—KEEP ON TRUCKING!

All salespeople suffer losses, either through the loss of a sale or an entire account to a competitor. Four things can win back a customer:

1. Visit and investigate. First, contact the buyer and your friends within the account to determine why the customer did not buy from you. Be sure to get the real reason.
2. Be professional. If you have completely lost the customer to a competitor, let the customer know you have appreciated past business, that you still value the customer's friendship, and that you are still friendly. Remember to assure this lost account that you are ready to earn future business.
3. Don't be unfriendly. Never criticize the competing product your customer has purchased. If it was a bad decision, let the customer discover it. Sales is never having to say, "I told you so!"
4. Keep calling. Treat a former customer like a prospect. Continue to make calls normally, presenting your product's benefits without directly comparing them to the competition.

Like a professional athlete, a professional salesperson takes defeat gracefully, moving on to the next contest, and performing so well that victories overshadow losses. One method of compensating for the loss of an account is to increase sales to existing accounts.

INCREASING YOUR CUSTOMER'S SALES

To maximize your sales to a customer, develop a customer benefit program. This means the account uses in business, or sells to customers, a level of merchandise equal to its maximum sales potential. The salesperson has only two methods to do this:

1. Have present customers buy *more* of a product that they currently use.

2. Have present customers buy the same products to use for different purposes. A Johnson & Johnson retail sales representative may encourage accounts to stock the firm's baby shampoo in both the infant care *and* adult toiletries sections of their establishments.

It is often not difficult to sell repeat orders; however, to maximize sales in an account, for example, with a retailer, you must persuade the customer to consistently promote your product through advertisements, displays, and reduced prices. To increase sales with a customer, the following steps can be taken. Each step cannot be used in all situations, but some can help increase sales:

Step 1:

Develop an account penetration program. Develop a "master plan" for each account consisting of specific actions to take toward developing friends within the account and increasing sales.

Step 2:

Examine your distribution. Review the merchandise currently used or carried in inventory. If the account is not using or carrying some of your merchandise, concentrate on improving your distribution. For example, if you have four sizes of a product and the account only carries one or two of them, develop a plan to persuade the customer to carry all four sizes. A general goal may be having each account carry all sizes of your products.

Step 3:

Keep merchandise in the warehouse and on the shelf. Never allow the account to run out of stock. "Stockouts" result in lost sales for your firm and account. Routine calls on customers help to avoid stockouts. If the account is critically low on merchandise, telephone in an emergency order. Quick service can maintain, or even increase, your credibility as a sales professional.

Step 4:

Fight for shelf space and shelf positioning. If you are selling consumer goods, constantly seek the best shelf space and aisle position. On each sales call, stock the shelf, keep your merchandise clean, and develop merchandising ideas. For example, during a routine visit to a client's store, a consumer goods salesperson found that a product the salesperson represented with a list price of $2 was sold for $1.79. This enterprising salesperson taped a small sign to the shelf showing both prices and discovered later that sales of the product had increased. This device is now routine for all of this salesperson's products.

Step 5:

Assist the product's users. If you sell industrial products, help users learn to operate products properly. Make users aware of product accessories that might aid them in performing a function in a safer, better, or more profitable manner. This type of account servicing can increase both account penetration and sales.

Step 6:

Assist retailer's salespeople. To ensure enthusiastic promotion of your firm's products, work closely with your account's sales force. Experience indicates that manufacturer's salespeople who cultivate the friendship of the reseller's salespeople and provide them with product knowledge and selling tips are more successful than the salesperson who calls only on the account's buyer.

A successful pharmaceutical salesperson suggested to all retail salespeople involved in a certain account that as they hand a customer a prescription for an antibiotic they say, "In taking these antibiotics you should also double up on taking your vitamins." Well, most customers were not taking vitamins, so when they said, "I don't have any vitamins," the salesperson would hand them a bottle of vitamins, saying, "I take these myself and highly recommend them to you." Of course, this manufacturer's salesperson had previously given the retail salesperson a sample bottle of vitamins. This sales tip accounted for an increase of over 300 percent in vitamin sales for this reseller.

Step 7:

Demonstrate your willingness to help. On each sales call, demonstrate your willingness to help the account through your actions. Your actions—not just words—are what build respect or distaste for you. Pull off your coat and dust, mark, stack, and build displays of your merchandise, and return damaged merchandise for credit. Let the buyer know that you are there to help increase retail sales.

Step 8:

Obtain customer support. By working hard to help your customers reach their goals through doing the items just discussed, you will find they help and support you. You help them; they help you. This type of relationship results in benefits to both you and the customer.

TABLE 11.1 Super sales success secret

Think positively	. . . and follow up
Plan carefully	. . . and follow up
Present thoroughly	. . . and follow up
And follow up	. . . and follow up
. . . and follow up	. . . and follow up
. . . and follow up	. . . and follow up
. . . and follow up	. . . and follow up

Again, there is no guarantee that doing everything suggested in this text will always result in a sale. Conscientious use of sound selling principles *will* increase your likelihood of overall success, though.

Vincent Norris of Scientific Equipment Corporation sent us a copy of what he feels is the secret to sales success. While "follow-up" is at the bottom of Vincent's list of secrets shown in Table 11.1, it is extremely important, as you can see.

As mentioned earlier in this chapter, a key characteristic of a sales professional is the ability to accept failure or rejection gracefully, and to then quickly move to the next objective.

WHEN YOU DO NOT MAKE THE SALE

A group of purchasing agents were asked their biggest gripes about poor sales procedure. One item on their list was this: "They [salespeople] seem to take it personally if they don't get the business, as though you owe them something because they are constantly calling on you."[7]

Although you should try, you cannot always sell everyone as much as you would like to or expect them to place special emphasis on *all* of your products *all* of the time. When you have done the best you can to persuade prospects or customers to make a purchase, and they still will not buy or do what you wish, remember there is always tomorrow. Act as a professional, adult salesperson, and do not take the buyer's denial personally, but recognize it as a business decision that the buyer must make given the circumstances. Be courteous and cheerful, be grateful for the opportunity to discuss your business proposition. The proper handling of a no-sale situation actually helps build a sound business relationship with your customers by developing a spirit of cooperation.

RETURN GOODS MAKE YOU A HERO

One of the best ways to help customers is through careful examination of merchandise you have sold in the past to see if it is old, out-of-date, or unsalable due to damage. If any of these conditions exist, the salesperson should cheerfully return the merchandise following the company's returned goods policies.

Some companies allow you to return any amount of merchandise, whereas other firms have limits on unauthorized returns. A firm may allow no more than $100 of merchandise to be returned at a time without the company's approval. Some companies require a reciprocal replacement order. Thus, if $100 worth of merchandise is returned, the customer must place an order for $100 of new merchandise. You do not want the customer to display or sell damaged goods, so it is in your best interest to return faulty merchandise, an action that aids you in building friendship with each customer.

HANDLE COMPLAINTS FAIRLY

Customers may be dissatisfied with products for reasons such as:

- The product delivered is a different size, color, or model than the one ordered.
- The quantity delivered is less than the quantity ordered—the balance is "backordered" (to be delivered when available).
- The product does *not* arrive by the specified date.
- Discounts (trade, promotional payment, etc.; see Chapter 5) agreed on are not rendered by the manufacturer.
- The product does not have a feature or perform a function that the customer believed it would.
- The product is not of the specified grade or quality (does not meet agreed-on specifications).

Whenever you determine that the customer's complaint is honest, make a settlement that is fair to the customer. "The customer is always right" is a wise adage to follow. Customers actually may be wrong, but if they honestly believe they are right, no amount of haggling or arguing will convince them otherwise. A valued account can be lost through temperamental outbursts.[8]

Occasionally, a customer is dishonest, which may require you and your company not to honor a request. A retailer (A) once purchased some of my firm's merchandise from another retailer (B), who had a "fire sale" and eventually went out of business. Retailer A insisted he purchased it from me and that I return close to $1,000 of damaged goods to my company for full credit. He had actually paid ten cents on the dollar for it at the fire sale. I told Retailer A that I would have to obtain permission from the company to return such a large amount of damaged goods.

That afternoon, a competitive salesperson told me that Retailer A had asked him to do the same thing. I informed my sales manager of the situation. He investigated the matter and found out about Retailer B, who sold most of his merchandise to Retailer A—who happened to be my customer. I went back and confronted Retailer A with this and said it was

FIGURE 11.2   Servicing your accounts is critical to your success

• *Working out of his home in Columbus, Ohio, Irwin's Jeff Christopher calls Professor Tim Hartman at Ohio University to set up an appointment. Before making the call, Jeff examines his records to see what course Dr. Hartman is teaching. In selling college textbooks, just as selling other products, Jeff shows the textbook and discusses its features, advantages, and benefits to Professor Hartman and others in his territory.*

company policy only to return merchandise that was purchased directly from me. This was a rare situation; yet, you must occasionally make similar judgments considering company policy and customer satisfaction.

Customers should get the benefit of the doubt. Always have a plan for getting to the bottom of the problem. Some procedures to follow are:

• Obtain as much relevant information from your customer as possible.
• Express sincere regret for the problem.
• Display a service attitude (a true desire to help).
• Review your sales records to make sure the customer purchased the merchandise.
• If the customer is right, quickly and cheerfully handle the complaint.
• Follow up to make sure the customer is satisfied.

Take care of your customers—especially large accounts. They are difficult to replace and are critical to success. When you take care of accounts, they take care of you. Servicing your accounts, as shown in Figure 11.2, demonstrates a professional attitude.

BUILD A PROFESSIONAL REPUTATION

Implied and directly stated throughout this chapter and text is the concept of sales professionalism. Sales professionalism directly implies that you are a professional person—due the respect and ready for the responsibilities that accompany the title. In speaking before a large class of marketing students, one sales manager for a large college textbook publishing company continually brought up the concept of sales professionalism. This man stated that a professional sales position is not just an 8 to 5 job. It is a professional, responsible, and adult position promising both unlimited opportunity and numerous duties. This veteran publishing sales manager emphasized that in the 1990s, a sales job is an especially good vocational opportunity because people are looking for "someone we can believe in; someone who will do what she says—a sales professional."

To be viewed as a professional and respected by your customers and competitors, consider these eight important points:

- First, be truthful and follow through on what you tell the customer. Do not dispose of your conscience when you start work each day.
- Second, maintain an intimate knowledge of your firm, its products, and your industry. Participate in your company's sales training and take continuing education courses.
- Third, speak well of others, including your company and competitors.
- Fourth, keep customer information confidential; maintain a professional relationship with each account.
- Fifth, never take advantage of a customer by using unfair, high-pressure techniques.
- Sixth, be active in community affairs and help better your community. For example, live in your territory, be active in public schools, and join such worthwhile organizations as the Lions Club or Chamber of Commerce.
- Seventh, think of yourself as a professional and always act like one. Have a professional attitude about yourself and your customers.
- Eighth, provide service "above and beyond the call of duty." Remember that it is easier to maintain a relationship than to begin one. What was worth attaining in the first place is worth preserving. Remember, if you do not pay attention to customers, they will find someone who will. The professional salesperson never forgets a customer after the sale.

DOS AND DON'TS FOR INDUSTRIAL SALESPEOPLE

What does a purchasing agent expect of industrial salespeople? A survey of purchasing agents showed that they expect results. The following list shows some specific traits purchasing agents found in their top industrial salespeople. The most important traits are:

TABLE 11.2 The seven deadly sins of industrial selling

1. *Lack of product knowledge.* Salespeople must know their product line as well as the buyer's line or nothing productive can occur.
2. *Time wasting.* Unannounced sales visits are a nuisance. When salespeople start droning about golf or grandchildren, more time is wasted.
3. *Poor planning.* A routine sales call must be preceded by some homework—maybe to see if it's really necessary.
4. *Pushiness.* This includes prying to find out a competitor's prices, an overwhelming attitude, and backdoor selling.
5. *Lack of dependability.* Failure to stand behind the product, keep communication clear, and honor promises.
6. *Unprofessional conduct.* "Knocking" competitors, boozing at a business lunch, sloppy dress, and poor taste aren't professional.
7. *Unlimited optimism.* Honesty is preferred to the hallmark of the "Good News Bearers" who promise anything to get an order. Never promise more than you can deliver.

Here are a few actual comments purchasing agents made on these deadly sins:
- "They seem to take it personally if they don't get the business; it's as though you owe them something because they are constantly calling on you."
- "I don't like it when they blast through the front door like know-it-alls and put on an unsolicited dog-and-pony show that will guarantee cost saving off in limbo somewhere."
- "Many salespeople will give you any delivery you want, book an order, and then let you face the results of their 'short quote.'"
- "They try to sell *you,* rather than the product."
- "After the order is won, the honeymoon is over."
- "Beware the humble pest who is too nice to insult, won't take a hint, won't listen to blunt advice, and is selling a product you neither use nor want to use, yet won't go away."

- Willingness to "go to bat" for the buyer within the supplier's firm.
- Thoroughness and follow-through after the sale.
- Knowledge of the firm's product line.
- Market knowledge and willingness to "keep the buyer posted."
- Imagination in applying one's products to the buyer's needs.
- Knowledge of the buyer's product line.
- Preparation for sales calls.
- Regularity of sales calls.
- Diplomacy in dealing with operating departments.
- Technical education (knowledge of specifications and applications).

The survey also asked purchasing agents what they did not like salespeople to do in sales calls. The results, shown in Table 11.2, are "The Seven Deadly Sins of Industrial Selling."[9] Purchasing agents want sales-

TABLE 11.3   We are a customer-oriented company

Salesperson's Checklist of Dos	Salesperson's Checklist of Don'ts
1. Know the current products/services and their applications in your area. Look for the new techniques/services your customers want.	1. Never bluff; if you don't know, find out.
2. Maintain an up-to-date personal call list.	2. Never compromise your, or anyone else's, morals or principles.
3. Listen attentively to the customers.	3. Don't be presumptuous—never with friends.
4. Seek our specific problems and the improvements your customers want.	4. Never criticize a competitor—especially to a customer.
5. Keep calls under five minutes unless invited to stay.	5. Do not take criticisms or turndowns personally—they're seldom meant that way.
6. Leave a calling card if the customer is not in.	6. Do not worry or agonize over what you cannot control or influence. Be concerned about what you *can* affect.
7. Identify the individual who makes or influences decisions, and concentrate on that person.	7. Do not offend others with profanity.
8. Entertain selectively; your time and your expense account are investments.	8. Do not allow idle conversation to dominate your sales call. Concentrate on your purpose.
9. Make written notes as reminders.	9. Don't try to match the customer drink-for-drink when entertaining. Drink only if you want to and in moderation.
10. Plan work by the week, not by the clock. Plan use of available time. Plan sales presentations. Have a purpose.	10. Don't be so gung ho that you use high-pressure tactics.
11. Ask for business on every sales call.	11. Never talk your company down—especially to customers. Be proud of it and yourself.
12. Follow through with appropriate action.	12. If you smoke, never do so in the customer's office unless invited to smoke.

people to act professionally, to be well trained, to be prepared for each sales call, and to keep the sales call related to *how the salesperson can help the buyer.*

Professional selling starts in the manufacturer's firm. A professional attitude from the manufacturer reinforces professionalism among the sales force. One such company is B. J. Hughes, a division of the Hughes Tool Company.[10] The B. J. Hughes company manufactures and sells oil field equipment and services to companies in the oil and gas industry. Table 11.3 presents Hughes' checklists of *dos* and *don'ts* for their salespeople. By providing these checklists, the company encourages them to act in a professional manner.

SUMMARY OF MAJOR SELLING ISSUES

Providing service to customers is important in all types of selling. Follow-up and service create goodwill between salesperson and customer that allows the salesperson to penetrate or work throughout the customer's organization. Account penetration helps the salesperson to better service the account and uncover its needs and problems. A service relationship with an account leads to increases in total and major brand sales, better distribution on all product sizes, and customer cooperation in promoting your products.

To serve customers best, improve account penetration. Contact each customer frequently and regularly; promptly handle all complaints. Always do what you say you will do, and remember to serve customers as if they were royalty. Finally, always remember to thank sincerely all customers for their business, no matter how large or small, to show you appreciate them.

Should customers begin to buy from a competitor or reduce their level of cooperation, continue to call on them in your normal professional manner. In a friendly way, determine why they did not buy from you, and develop new customer benefit plans to recapture their business.

Always strive to help your customers increase their sales of your product or to get the best use from products you have sold them. In order to persuade a customer to purchase more of your products or use your products in a different manner, develop a sales program to help maximize sales to that customer. This involves developing an account penetration program; increasing the number and sizes of products purchased by the customer; maintaining proper inventory levels in the customer's warehouse and on the shelf; achieving good shelf space and shelf positioning; clear communication with persons who directly sell or use a product; a willingness to assist wholesale and retail customers' salespeople in any way possible; a willingness to help customers; and an overall effort to develop a positive, friendly business relationship with each customer. By doing these eight things, your ability to help and properly service each customer increases.

Today's professional salesperson is oriented to service. Follow-up and service after the sale greatly maximize your territory's sales and help attain personal goals.

IV

Special Selling Topics

12

Retail Selling Is Challenging and Rewarding

Jack Pruett is a sales specialist with Bailey Banks & Biddle, a division of the Zale Corporation, the world's largest retailer of jewelry. He works in Atlanta, Georgia. Jack has sales responsibility and assists others in the store. I asked him about his sales and he said, "My customers typically spend a minimum of $2,500 to $5,000. The largest sale to a single customer I have had so far was $120,000 in diamonds, rings, and a gold and diamond bracelet. My highest sales for one month have been $278,000 and for a year, $820,000. I expect to sell over $1 million this year.

Jack's previous job was as a Pepsi-Cola truck driver, driving from Augusta, Georgia into South Carolina. Jack says, "This is where I learned a lot about people, and this contributed to my sales success. I learned to deal with people equally and fairly no matter who they are, where they come from, or what their background.

"Sales is a joy to me. I would really rather sell jewelry than anything in the world. It is both personally and financially rewarding. It takes hard work to earn serious money. Today, retailers recognize the importance of salespeople to their success and many are compensating on a commission basis, which allows good salespeople to make high salaries.

"I realize there are sales techniques, and many of us use parts of some techniques. But selling is a people business, and there are no two people with the same fingerprints or needs. So you can't treat people exactly the same. The most important factor to my success is my belief that I can do the best job taking care of a person's needs. I've studied hard, worked hard, and developed a selling process that works for me. It didn't happen overnight—it was my second year in the business before I became comfortable in jewelry sales." •

Jack Pruett
Bailey Banks & Biddle

"Many professions offer personal and financial rewards," says Jack Pruett. "A salesperson doesn't save lives, like a physician, or build the largest bridge in the world, like an engineer. But we do receive a tremendous amount of joy out of what we do.

"Sales is really personally and financially rewarding. I know people selling shoes who earn $60,000 a year; who sell men's clothes and earn $70,000; who sell jewelry and earn more than $100,000. These people are professionals making a substantial salary. The secret is to believe in what you're doing and what you're selling—then develop a method to serve your customers.

"Another secret of my success is that I've learned how to create business. One afternoon, a young couple came in. They looked awhile, and they weren't really interested in buying anything. So I asked them if they knew anyone who might need one of our products. The man said, 'Yes, I have a friend who has expressed an interest in an 18-carat Rolex watch.' 'That sells for over $9,000,' I replied. This shopper felt comfortable enough to say, 'Why don't you call him' before I could ask if I could contact his friend.

"So I called him and got him to come into the store. He bought the watch, plus a women's diamond watch for $12,000, a $30,000 three-carat diamond, and two gold watches for his children. Without farming (prospecting) I'd never have found this customer. This happens to me more than you think. Actually, it doesn't just happen—I make it happen." •

Jack puts major emphasis on understanding buyers' needs, qualifying customers, becoming their friend, having customers introduce him to prospects, giving person service, playing down features and advantages while concentrating on benefits. Having made a sale, he shows customers he is thankful for their business and provides all of the service they need to be satisfied with their purchase. These are some of the things that have made him successful.

Retail selling, as in Jack Pruett's case, can be both challenging and rewarding. This chapter covers retailing opportunities, the retail sales process, and the "dos and don'ts for retail selling."

WHAT IS RETAILING?

Retailing refers to any individual or organization that sells its goods or services directly to final consumers for their personal, nonbusiness use.

The distinguishing characteristic of a retail sale is that a retail transaction involves the final consumer—the retail customer. A retail sale may occur over the telephone, through the mail, on a street corner, in a private residence, or in a traditional retail store.

Goods and services sold to final consumers for their personal, nonbusiness use vary from items such as T-shirts and jogging shoes to

TABLE 12.1 Rules for retail clerks in 1882

1. This store must be opened at Sunrise. No mistake. Open 6 o'clock A.M. Summer and winter. Close about 8:30 or 9:00 P.M. the year round.

2. Store must be swept—dusted—doors and windows opened—lamps filled, trimmed and chimneys cleaned—counters, base shelves, and show cases dusted. Also the coal must be brought in before breakfast, if there is time to do it and attend to all the customers who call.

3. The store is not to be opened on the Sabbath day unless absolutely necessary and then only for a few minutes.

4. Should the store be opened on Sunday the clerks must go in alone and get tobacco for customers in need.

5. The clerk who is in the habit of smoking Spanish Cigars—being shaved at the barbers—going to dancing parties and other places of amusement and being out late at night—will assuredly give his employer reason to be ever suspicious of his integrity and honesty.

6. Clerks are allowed to smoke in the store provided they do not wait on women with a "stogie" in the mouth.

7. Each clerk must pay not less the $5.00 per year to the Church and must attend Sunday School regularly.

8. Men clerks are given one evening a week off for courting and two if they go to prayer meeting.

9. After the 14 hours in the store the leisure hours should be spent mostly in reading.

Reprinted by permission from Delbert J. Duncan, Charles F. Phillips, and Stanley C. Hollander, *Modern Retailing Management* (Homewood, Ill.: Richard D. Irwin, 1972), p. 184.

stocks and bonds, legal services, singing telegrams, and wedding cakes. A person selling panty hose to a department store shopper is engaged in retailing, as is a real estate agent selling a $90,000 house. This chapter focuses on retail transactions that occur in a retail store.

Retail stores account for some $900 billion in sales each year or about 18 percent of all business generated by America's economy.[1] The roughly 3 million salespeople associated with retailing are employed by firms as large and diverse as Macy's in New York City, which boasts of being the world's largest store, to small "mom and pop" stores.

Although people unfamiliar with modern retailing might think otherwise, retailing as a career is very attractive. It is not like 100 years ago when the rules in Table 12.1 were posted.[2]

Financial Rewards Are Excellent

The financial rewards and promotional opportunities for the retail salesperson are excellent. There are retail firms that pay only the minimum wage, but many pay excellent salaries to qualified people.

As in other forms of professional selling, the financial rewards and promotional opportunities for the retail salesperson are excellent. Earnings, as a retail salesperson, vary depending on the type of product sold, the

FIGURE 12.1   A possible retail career path

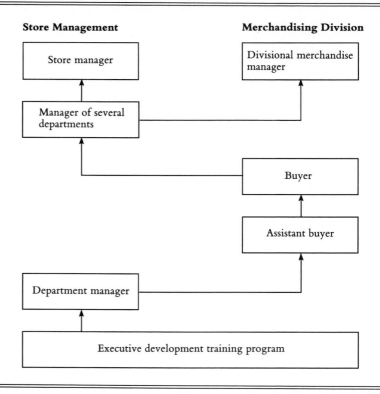

compensation plan (straight salary, salary plus commission, or straight commission), and the organization.

Figure 12.1 illustrates a career path for a large chain of department stores. After completing the initial executive development training program, the individual is given a department to manage, such as women's clothing, and is responsible for training salespeople and efficiently handling operations. The person next moves to assistant buyer and then to buyer, followed by a promotion to manager of several departments. At this time, the individual can elect to stay in store management or move into merchandising.

Along with increased responsibility and authority, promotions within larger retailing companies yield increases in salary. Retail store managers may earn salaries ranging from $50,000 to $150,000 per year, depending on the type of store and compensation program.[3]

Enterprising retail managers may earn bonuses or share in the profits of a store that performs beyond expectations. Successful store managers may eventually move into corporate managerial positions—planning, market-

TABLE 12.2 Compensation of selected retail chief executives

Company	Compensation
Dayton-Hudson	$1,233,000
Federated Department Stores	1,171,000
Great A&P Tea Co., Inc.	2,014,000
J.C. Penney Co.	1,214,000
K mart Corp.	1,672,000
Kroger	2,379,000
Limited	1,154,000
May Department Stores	2,717,000
Sears, Roebuck & Co.	1,994,000
Wal-Mart Stores	6,085,000

ing, training, and expansion schemes for the entire chain! Table 12.2 illustrates the annual compensation for some corporate managers.[4]

Nonfinancial Rewards Are Many

Financial compensation is only one part of the reward received as a retail salesperson. Nonfinancial rewards offered by a retail career are numerous. They include excellent training programs, rapid assumption of responsibility, recognition, opportunity for personal growth and development, travel, and satisfaction from work.

RETAILERS SELL LIKE INDUSTRIAL SALESPEOPLE

Fundamental sales principles apply to all types of persuasive situations including retailing. Of course, basic differences exist between retail and industrial sales; the main difference is that most retailers have customers enter their store to purchase a product or service. However, retailers who sell products such as appliances, carpeting, and building supplies frequently send salespeople out to call on customers at home. Whether the retail salesperson is selling in the store, over the telephone, or outside the store, basic selling techniques can be used effectively when adapted to a particular retailing situation.

THE RETAIL SALESPERSON'S ROLE

The role of the retail salesperson varies greatly in what is required. Some jobs require the salesperson to act only as an order taker. Other jobs require highly skilled people who can successfully identify and arouse the customers' needs and persuade them to purchase and satisfy those needs. Generally, a retail salesperson is involved, to some extent, in completing transactions, handling customer complaints and merchandise returns,

MAKING THE SALE

Stanley Marcus: The Lost Art of Salesmanship

Americans used to be known as the world's best salespersons.[5] Recently, it has become difficult in most stores to encounter that quality of salesmanship, if you can even find a salesperson.

A few years back, I made up my mind I wouldn't buy anything I didn't urgently need unless a salesperson was convincingly persuasive. As a result of this self-imposed discipline, I saved $46,734.

Want to know a few things I didn't buy? An automobile, for one. I called a dealer I knew and inquired whether his new models had arrived. "Yes," he said. "How are they?" I asked. "Fine," he replied. I said, "Thank you." He made no suggestion of having a salesperson drive me around the block or of lending me one to drive on the weekend. He never called back, nor did I receive a phone call from one of his salespersons. So, I didn't buy a car.

I visited a luggage shop in search of some lightweight luggage. A salesperson started to show me some pieces when he was summoned to the telephone. He came back and embarked on the merits of his product when the phone rang again. I waved good-bye to him. He knew me, but he never called to apologize for his poor service. That night when the manager asked what sort of day he had, he probably replied, "There weren't many buyers, today; only lookers." I don't blame him, but I do fault his management, which had not em-phasized that the customer at hand takes precedence over the one on the telephone.

The advertisements of the new thin watches impressed me, but since I had a perfectly good 25-year-old watch, I was looking for some compelling reason to junk it and buy a new one. When I asked a jewelry salesperson why I should buy it, he looked around and finally said, "It's newer." That, I knew, but that was not sufficient reason to make a purchase.

The volume of lost business to retailers and industry as a whole is appalling. Some merchandise can be sold without a salesperson, but many products require an introduction and presentation. If stores are dedicated to self-service, then it is incumbent on them to organize displays and stocking for easy shopping, but if they profess to supply service, then they must provide adequate, well-versed sales assistants. Otherwise, they should resort to vending machines, which are more efficient and less costly than humans who don't know their stock or why it's worth buying.

Stores and sales staffs have been spoiled by years of easy selling. During the depression, I learned that the best way to sell anything was to encourage the prospective customer to feel the article while I discussed the benefits received from it. We treated every prospect as though we wouldn't see another all day. And, some days, we didn't.

working stock, and personal selling. The following sections will elaborate on each of these four retail sales functions.

Accurately Completing Transactions Is a Must

When a customer is ready to make a purchase, the salesperson must complete the transaction before the sale can be completed. A retail transaction should be handled smoothly and quickly with a great degree of accuracy to avoid frustrating the customer and possibly losing the sale. A good checklist to follow when transacting a sale is listed below:

- Write the sales slip clearly and accurately.
- Accept payment or arrange for credit.
- If change is required, count it accurately, and do not place the money received from the customer in the cash drawer until you have made change.
- When accepting a check or credit card, make sure all forms are signed by the customer.

Many retailing institutions encourage the use of charge accounts by qualified customers. In such an instance, you may encourage new customers to participate in your store's charge program by asking them to fill out a credit application. Later that day, you could drop these customers a short thank-you card requesting their regular patronage. This type of retail service builds long-lasting relationships between salespeople and customers.

Handling Complaints Satisfies Customers

The retailer sometimes encounters customers who are unhappy with their purchases, and no matter how good a salesperson might be in meeting the needs of the consumer, something can go wrong. The product may be faulty, does not fit, or the customer has decided against the purchase. In general, customers find fault with the product, not themselves.

As in other types of selling, the retail salesperson represents a manufacturer to customers. In the role of representative, the retail salesperson must be courteous and gracious, treating customers as "guests of the house." Such an attitude might be displayed in a willingness to completely answer questions and anticipate customers' needs.

An effective retail salesperson displays an interest in the welfare of each customer. An objective, service attitude is the best approach to take.

Working Stock Is Necessary

Maintaining a variety of neatly displayed items for sale to consumers, and reordering or replacing stock items when depleted is a tedious, time-consuming, and important function of many retail salespeople. The appearance of a store, or a department within a large store, reflects on the retail salesperson and helps the consumer to develop a good first impression, thereby boosting the retailer's chance for making sales. Working stock also aids a retail salesperson in gaining knowledge of the company's products and their location within the store.

Personal Selling Is Where It's At

Of the four functions of the retail salesperson, personal selling is most important. In most cases, the retail salesperson should consider using the

FIGURE 12.2   "Take good care of your customers, and they'll come back," says
Mr. Marcus, "Take good care of your merchandise, and it
doesn't come back."

same major parts of the sales presentation used by the industrial salesperson,
beginning with the approach. A more detailed explanation of the retail
selling process is discussed next.

We have all been customers wanting the salesperson to *sell* us on the
product. In the box about "The Lost Art of Salesmanship" (also see Figure
12.2), the situation is corrected with the proper selection of personnel,
training, a reward program, and an evaluation system. To be a professional
retail salesperson requires a knowledge of, and the proper application of, the
basic retail selling process.

BASIC RETAIL SELLING PROCESS

Why do you shop at a particular retail store? Why do you buy from a
particular salesperson? Your reasons will differ depending on the type of
product you shop for, such as gasoline, a bank account, a wedding ring, or
an automobile. There are many basic reasons why people shop a particular
store. Here are some of the most important reasons:

- *The salesperson*—Is this the right salesperson for me to trust and from
  whom to buy? Does this salesperson have integrity, judgment, and
  knowledge concerning my situation?

- *Company*—Is this the store for me?
- *Product*—Will this product fulfill my needs?
- *Price*—Should I shop around for price? Will this store lower the price shortly? What about terms and returns?
- *Time to buy*—Should I buy now?
- *Service*—Will the company and salesperson help me if I need further help?
- *Trust*—Can I trust this salesperson, store, and product?

You probably have other reasons to add to the list on why you shop at various retailers. However, these seven patronage motives should be considered when developing your basic retail selling process. Successful retail salespeople, such as Jack Pruett, consider these patronage motives when using a selling process similar to these 10 steps:

1. Prospecting.
2. The approach.
   a. Attitude.
   b. Appearance.
   c. Manner.
3. Presentation.
   a. Agreement of need.
      (1) Bring sales presentation into focus on product needed.
   b. Selling the store.
      (1) Your reputation.
      (2) Company reputation.
   c. Fill the need.
      (1) Stress benefits of features and advantages of product and store using SELL sequence.
4. Use a trial close.
5. Respond to objection.
6. Use your trial close to determine if you've handled objection.
7. Close the primary sale.
8. Suggestion selling.
   a. Suggest other items to buy.
9. Wrap it up.
   a. Remove fears, uncertainties, doubts.
   b. Complete the transaction.
10. Follow-up and service after the sale.

Carefully orchestrated and executed, these ten steps can bring you success and satisfied customers.

Prospecting Is Important in Retail Sales

Yes, you can prospect for customers in retail selling. Most retailers don't prospect because they do not have the sales staff for it; they do not know of the benefits from prospecting; and they do not know how to prospect. However, successful salespeople, such as Jack Pruett, are excellent prospectors. Prospecting can occur by mail, telephone, and personal visits outside of the store. More retailers are realizing they can increase sales and profits through the prospecting methods discussed in Chapter 6.

The Approach Is Critical

"A lot of times," says Jack Pruett, "customers come in and say 'I'm just looking.' It's OK to look, but why are they just looking? What is it that they might need? Is it something they would like to have that they feel like they can't afford? We might have the perfect terms. Without talking to the customer and getting close to them, making them feel comfortable, feel at home, and not pressured, you will never find out. You have to work at learning how to do that—and that comes with trying it and experience."

The approach consists of activities engaged in to gain your prospects' attention, interest, and willingness to listen to your discussion of a product. Often, you already have their attention from the time customers walk in the door looking for assistance. As you walk up to the counter, they say, "Do you have this or that?"

In other cases, customers do not want immediate assistance. Never force what you have to say on a customer because this leads to resentment. Only when you have the customer's willing attention should you proceed with a presentation.

In capturing a customer's interest, react to nonverbal signs. Nonverbal signs help quickly determine whether prospects are willing to listen to what you have to say, and if they want your help. Learn from these signs what prospects' real objectives are, and if they are seriously considering a purchase.

No matter what type of approach is used, it is important to greet customers in a warm, friendly manner and make them feel welcome. Treat them as guests in your home. Be sure to project positive nonverbal signals, such as a smile.

The guiding rule in determining the approach used is to avoid having the customer immediately say no to you. This frequently happens when the salesperson says, "May I help you?" Every shopper has heard "May I help you?" so many times. Though it sounds polite, it is impersonal and allows the customer to reject you. Communication barriers between you and the customer are quickly erected.

The Service Approach. The **service approach** is used to indicate a desire to serve the customer. Do not get in the habit of saying, "Have you been waited on?" "Do you need help?" or, "May I help you?" These can be answered "No." Greet your customers by saying "Hello! How are you today?" Very likely, you will receive a positive response such as "Hello," "Hi," or "Just fine."

Some salespeople use their names as an introduction to customers. Customers sometimes tell you their names in return. Now you are on a first-name basis. Pause for the customer's next comment. Chances are, you will learn what the customer wants.

The Question Approach. Asking questions is often an effective approach. At certain times of the year, such as December, it is easy to use the **question approach** after the saluation or pause. This question should be a direct, situation-type question, such as "Are you looking for a Christmas or Hannukah gift?"★ Someone may be examining a product as you walk up. You might say, "Is this radio for you?" or, "Are you looking for a complete stereo system or speakers?" Customers will usually tell you their needs.

The situation question is also used to further clarify customers' needs when they tell you the product they are shopping for. The customer says, "Hi. I'm looking for a personal computer." You can respond, "Is it for home or office?" Continue using questions until you determine the customer's needs.

If the customer says, "I'm not sure what I'm looking for," quickly show a product to establish a reference point. Maybe you have a stereo system on sale. Show it and ask, "Is this what you had in mind?" Now, most customers will direct you to their real needs.

Watch for buying signals. For example, if they say "Yes" to the question, "Is this what you had in mind?" you may be ready to move towards the close instead of discussing the product's features, advantages, and benefits.

The Merchandise Approach. This third approach, the **merchandise approach,** is used with two types of customers:

1. The customer who is "just looking."
2. The customer who has stopped browsing, and is intently scrutinizing a particular group of goods.

An alert salesperson quickly recognizes the mannerisms of the individual who is "just looking." A looker usually wanders aimlessly, avoids eye contact with the salesperson, and keeps a safe distance from retail salespeople. Once the looker stops to examine a product, the salesperson should move in and start talking about the product, giving the customer some information without making it obvious.

★Refer to the Chapter 7 discussion of the SPIN approach and the use of questions.

In cases where a customer is clearly interested in a product, the salesperson, if possible, can prompt the customer with a question. A person who peers intently into the window of an auto on a showroom floor might be asked by a salesperson: "Why don't you get behind the wheel?" [a sports car, in this case]. To the individual who is carefully examining an article of clothing, a salesperson might say, in a slightly encouraging tone, "Why don't you try it on? The dressing room is right back here."

The Retail Sales Presentation Requires Creativity

Following a successful approach in a retail situation is the sales talk or presentation. Customers buy products to meet their needs or solve their problems, and because of the limited amount of time you have to spend with customers, you must use clear, concise, and persuasive language to sell benefits that are meaningful to customers. These benefits must relate to customers' needs and be stated in terms that they understand.

Agreement of Needs.   The major ways to identify customers' wants, needs, or problems are to ask questions, present alternatives, make suggestions, and use demonstrations.

Ask Those Questions. The first way to uncover a customers' needs or problems is to ask a revealing question. Suppose that an observant shoe salesperson notices that a customer's shoes are too narrow, causing the leather to stretch out of shape. The customer asks for a pair of shoes in the style selected, stating the size and width. In turn, the salesperson asks, "Do you find your shoes stretching out of shape after a few months of wear?" "Yes . . . most of my shoes tend to do that, and eventually the leather begins to crack." The customer has always selected shoes that were too narrow, without realizing it.

In this example, the salesperson discovers a problem that the customer is not even aware of. In many cases, a salesperson learns about customers' problems and needs through questioning. This may eventually lead to a sale. A salesperson might ask questions such as:

"How will you use this . . . ?"
"Would you be satisfied with . . . ?"
"Do you have trouble with . . . ?"
"Do you always do that . . . ?"

The use of perceptive questioning in retail sales aids in uncovering customer needs and solving customer problems that are not readily apparent.

Present Alternatives. The second way to make a customer aware of a need or problem is to present alternatives. Take, for example, the customer whose jeans appear too short. The salesperson asks: "Do you prefer wearing your jeans so that they just touch the top of your shoes, or would you prefer them to cover the top of your shoe?" The customer replies, "They do seem a little too short, don't they?" The salesperson then recommends that the customer wear preshrunk jeans to avoid shrinkage due to machine washing and drying. By presenting the customer with a useful alternative, this salesperson tactfully makes the customer aware of a problem, and provides a solution.

Make Suggestions. Another way to point out a need or problem is to make a suggestion. The following example shows this approach. The customer's slacks are too long, causing the bottom of the trousers to wear out. The salesperson asks, "Have you ever tried a 32-inch length slack? The bottom won't drag on the ground and wear out." This salesperson points out the problem to the customer by suggesting a shorter length slack.

Use Demonstrations. The fourth way to point out a need or problem to a retail customer is through a demonstration. A shoe store customer insists that she knows what size shoes she wears. The salesperson suggests that the customer should have her feet measured, as shoe size varies with the style of shoe. (Few customers refuse the request when given this reason.) Once the person's foot is measured, the salesperson shows the size to the customer, who agrees to try on that size shoe.

Demonstrations of products such as televisions, automobiles, stereo systems, appliances, and clothes are common in retail sales because such a demonstration is an excellent way to make the customer aware of needs or problems.

Sell the Store. Retail salespeople should be aware that many customers have concerns about the store they buy from. It is common to wonder if a store will go out of business, change ownership, or stop carrying a line of merchandise. To buy an item, we want to know that it is quality merchandise and that we will receive our money's worth.

Because of customer concerns such as these, salespeople should "sell their store." "I always talk about my company and reputation" says Jack Pruett. "We started out as silversmiths. We made the first class rings for West Point and the Naval Academy. We designed the Purple Heart, the Medal of Honor, and the United States Seal as it is today. We are cutting a stone today that's helped me in a lot of sales because it will be the largest single cut diamond in the world—it's called the Zale diamond and I tell customers about it.

SELLING TIPS

Use of Questions in Retail Selling

A retail salesperson in a men's clothing store notices a prospect looking at the sport coats. As the salesperson approaches the customer, he says:

SALESPERSON: Hello, looking for a suit or sport coat?

PROSPECT: I'm not really sure what I'm looking for.

SALESPERSON: Something basic for everyday use or something special?

PROSPECT: Well, I have to be able to wear it to work.

SALESPERSON: Where do you work?

PROSPECT: Oh, I'm a funeral director, but I'm looking for something different—sporty. I sort of like this coat.

SALESPERSON: Would you like to try that on? [*Puts on a red, white, and blue sport coat.*]

PROSPECT: Well, it's sporty. What do you think?

SALESPERSON: Well, you certainly would be sporty. Are you sure this is what you want?

PROSPECT: Well, I'm not sure. I'm used to dressing so conservatively. Maybe I'd better shop around.

SALESPERSON: Do you want to be sporty—yet conservative?

PROSPECT: Yeah, that's it!

SALESPERSON: I think I have something you'd really like. [*Brings out and tries on a navy blue sport coat.*]

PROSPECT: This looks sharp!

SALESPERSON: Step over here and let's select your slacks and shirt. I have a tie that would really set off that blazer!

"I take a lot of time to discuss the credibility of the company, and the history of the company. This makes the customer more interested in who they are doing business with and helps them want to do business with us and me. They are far less likely to go down the mall and buy from another store. If they do shop around they will remember me, my interest in them, and our organization because other retail salespeople don't do this. I greatly increase my chances of a prospect coming back to me by selling them on my store." See Figure 12.3.

Fill the Need—Use the SELL Sequence. Whether you ask questions, present alternatives, make suggestions, or use demonstrations, it is important to concentrate on emphasizing the benefits of your product. *Show the feature, explain the advantage, lead into the benefit, and let the customer talk by asking a question about the benefit (trial close).*

S	E	L	L
Show feature	Explain advantage	Lead into benefit	Let customer talk

FIGURE 12.3 Jack Pruett sells the customer on himself, his product, the store, and his company

Listen to what your customer says and you will discover the customer's "hot button." Once you determine the customer's needs, match your product's benefits to those needs. Concentrate on discussing benefits that the customer has indicated are important.★

HANDLING OBJECTIONS

Because a retail store handles such a large number of products, the retail salesperson must respond to a multitude of objections. Objections must be answered in a way that does not lead to an argument. In some cases, this is accomplished by rephrasing an objection as a question. This example, and other techniques for overcoming objections (discussed in Chapter 9), are easily adopted to the retail selling situation.

Some objections are valid. If an objection is a valid one, don't deny it. You gain status in the eyes of your customer by responding *truthfully* to an objection.

If the objection is invalid, you may deny it or ignore the objection if it is not important to make the sale. Since customers usually feel obligated to defend their objections, you may make them mad and lose them if you tell them they are wrong.†

★Refer to Chapter 9 for a detailed discussion of handling objections.
†See Chapter 3 for a complete discussion of FAB and Chapter 8 on the SELL sequence.

FIGURE 12.4   Imagine that this prospect says, "I really like this outfit but I'm going to shop around." Using the echo technique—what would you say?

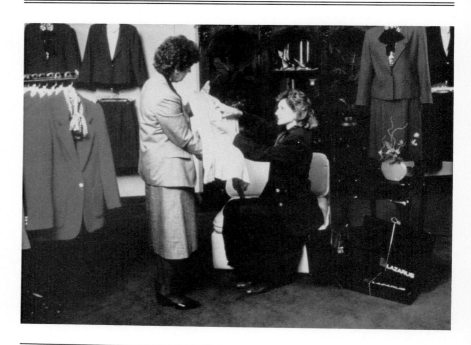

The LAIR Approach

One approach retail salespeople might consider in handling objections is the LAIR, which stands for:

- Listen—Hear the objection.
- Acknowledge—Repeat the objection. This is the "echo" technique. The customer says "This is not what I'm looking for," and you say, "It's not what you're looking for?" Sounds unreasonable at first, but try it. Your customer will react to your question by explaining the objection. Then you know how to help. See Figure 12.4.
- Identify the objection—"Is that the only thing keeping you from buying today?" or "In other words, if it were not for [whatever the objection is] you would take it home with you today—right?"
- Reverse the objection—"Yes, but!"

Objections are the stepping stones to closing the sale. Work hard and learn how to handle them; it will pay off for you.

CLOSING THE SALE

Of all the steps in the selling process, closing the sale is often the most difficult for a new retail salesperson, especially when multiple closes are involved.

An experienced retail salesperson senses when a customer is favorably disposed toward a product. Questions a customer asks, such as, "How soon could I have this product?" or, "What type of warranty does this item have?" are indicators of willingness to buy. Of course, the customer who approaches a retail sales counter, product in one hand and wallet or credit card in the other, is already sold! In less obvious cases, a trial close can ascertain a customer's readiness to buy.

Types of Closes

While each close discussed in Chapter 10 can be used in a retail situation, there are four closes used most frequently in retail selling: the assumptive close, the physical action close, the minor point close, and the inducement close.

The Assumptive Close. If you have completed your sales talk, have responded to all of your customer's objections, have used a trial close, and have received a positive response, the customer is ready to buy. Going on this **assumptive close,** it is often best to ask the questions needed to write up the sales ticket, such as:

"Shall I go ahead and have this wrapped up for you?"

"May I have your name and address?"

"Will you need help taking this to your car?"

Customers who are not ready to buy will stop you from finishing the sales slip. If they let you continue, you have made the sale and can go on to your next customer. See Figure 12.5.

The Physical Action Close. This requires that the salesperson make some **physical action close** indicating to the customer an understanding that the sale has occurred. An automobile salesperson may hand the customer the keys to a new car. A department store clerk may start wrapping the goods.

Such actions can make the decision for a wavering customer. However, this close requires finesse and intuition from the salesperson. A premature physical close may make the salesperson appear "too pushy."

The Minor Point Closing. On product lines in which the customer must make a choice on features such as color, size, delivery, and terms of the sale, the salesperson may use the **minor point close** by asking which of the two characteristics the customer wants, such as:

FIGURE 12.5   Using the assumptive close, what would you say if the prospect said, "I really like this new Avon product!"

"Would you prefer this in red or blue?"
"Will this be cash or charge?"

Always present a limited number of alternatives to allow the customer a choice between "something" and "something." If only one choice is presented, the customer may respond with, "No." (No to the color, or no to the purchase.) But a choice between alternatives cannot be answered "No." Don't present *too many* alternatives, because your customer may become confused.

The Inducement Close.   Assuming you have the authority to offer inducements, a good way to close the sale is to encourage the customer to buy by offering something extra or something free. The **inducement close** may be extended warranties at no charge, a price reduction, a free bonus, free delivery, or free installation.

One stereo salesperson often offers a discount if the customer purchases a stereo combination by saying, "If you purchase this system today, I'll give you a 10 percent discount over what it would cost you to buy each component separately." Often, this inducement convinces the customer to cross the line and make the purchase. After all, who can resist getting something for nothing?

MAKING THE SALE

A Retail Salesperson Earns Millions in Commission

Martin Shafiroff's gross commissions are in the millions of dollars and rank him as one of the top retail salespeople in the United States. Martin sells investments in securities, real estate, and tax shelters to various people such as professional entertainers, board chairpersons, and presidents of corporations.

Martin says, "Product and conviction are only half of my success formula; the other half stresses cold calls and contacts." He strives to convert cold calls into legitimate prospects and turn prospects into accounts—building an investment portfolio for each account. That's the "lifeblood of my business," Shafiroff says. But carefully planning his day to concentrate *solely* on selling activities, Martin telephones up to 60 clients and prospects each day. By the way, he enters his office before eight in the morning and leaves at about seven in the evening.

Martin is a great believer in using questions to uncover prospect objections, and he carefully listens to the prospect's responses to determine his needs. He spends little time on his introduction, only a few minutes on why he called or on an explanation of what he wants the prospect to buy, leaving 70 to 80 percent of his time to asking for the order. Unlike most telephone salespeople who hang up after one no, Martin believes in closing at least three times. He believes the first couple of no answers force the prospect into sincerely listening to his investment philosophies and concepts and lower his defense mechanism.

Martin believes he can help customers and often must take a strong position. After all, he is selling corporate presidents, who are strong-willed men and women with large egos. He says, "I am very persistent . . . I recall one individual that I called perhaps 15 times . . . before he became my customer."

Martin's success revolves around properly planning his time, using multiple closes, determining the prospect's real objection, knowledge of his product, understanding his clients' needs, and many hours of hard work each day.[6]

FOLLOW UP WITH SERVICE AFTER THE SALE

The sale of high-priced durable goods (cars, appliances, etc.) and intangible (insurance, stocks, and bonds) implies customer contact after the sale.

Proper service and handling of complaints cannot be over-emphasized. It is essential for repeat sales. Joe Girard, the world's greatest automobile salesperson, believes one secret of his success is that when the customer returns with a complaint or needs service, he drops everything and makes sure the customer gets the best service available. He says, "The sales begin 'after' the sale . . . . If the customer was good enough to buy from you, then the customer deserves service."[7]

Customers returning merchandise with a complaint are seldom happy. The salesperson must handle this situation in a calm, diplomatic way. It is the salesperson's responsibility to provide service after the sale. If the customer is not carefully handled, the salesperson will probably lose any chance of making a sale to this buyer in the future. Also, word could spread, and future sales could be hurt. It is always important to listen to the customer's complaint and ask questions to discover the real problem.

TURN FOLLOW-UP AND SERVICE INTO A SALE

High-performing salespeople have the ability to convert follow-up and service situations into sales. Jack Pruett gives several examples:

> I send customers a thank-you card immediately after the sale; and after two weeks, I call again to thank them and see if they are pleased with their purchase. If the purchase is a gift, I wait on contacting the customer or contact the spouse at the office. This has been a key to my success in building a relationship and in farming or prospecting. Very often I get a lead.
>
> Here is how it works: In two weeks they have shown it around to someone who has made a comment. I start with, "Is everything OK?" Then I say, "Well, I know Judy [or Jack] is real proud of it and I'm sure she's [he's] shown it to someone—parents, family, friends. I was curious if there is anyone I could help who is interested in something. I'd like to talk to them or have you call and see if they'd like me to call them." If I've done a good job, the customer feels good about letting me call this individual and will help me. If I wait too long to call they say, "Well, someone was asking about it, but I've forgotten who it was." (See Figure 12.6.)
>
> My biggest sale to a single customer was $120,000. It took about two weeks. A man initially called asking for 12 diamonds to give two stones to each of his children. In handling this, I found some other pieces I felt were good for him—a ruby ring, a 4.62 sapphire ring, a gold and diamond bracelet, and two other rings. He bought everything. Thus, much of my success comes from follow-ups, suggestion selling [when someone comes in for something and they end up buying other things], or service situations. Once you realize that you can turn routine situations into sales, retail selling becomes exciting and challenging.

CHALLENGING SITUATIONS IN RETAIL SELLING

The examples of retail selling presented so far are common: one customer interacting with one salesperson for a short time period. A retail sales situation is complicated by a number of factors and occurrences. The following sections relate several challenging situations commonly encountered in retail selling.

Selling to Several Customers at the Same Time

A confusing situation may arise when a retail salesperson is required to wait on more than one customer at a time. It is the salesperson's responsibility to

FIGURE 12.6   How could this salesperson follow Jack Pruett's example and follow up after this jewelry was purchased?

attend to as many customers as possible without causing any resentment. Often, while the salesperson waits on a customer who is slow and deliberate in making a decision, another customer, who is pressed for time, enters the store. The salesperson should offer a greeting or somehow acknowledge the second customer's presence. The salesperson can usually speak to the second customer out of listening range of the first customer. A common greeting is: "Good morning. Someone will be with you soon."

If the first customer is looking at products that the salesperson has displayed, the salesperson may politely leave the first customer and attend to the second customer. If the new customer's needs cannot be attended to quickly, the salesperson faces the dilemma of handling both customers at once. The only way to resolve this problem is to move back and forth between each customer. A successful salesperson can effectively wait on several customers at once. It is better to make two sales than to wait on only one customer at a time.

The Group Shopper

Many retail salespeople dread the prospect of waiting on customers who shop in pairs or in larger groups **(group shoppers)** as they believe their efforts to make a sale may be drastically reduced. In such situations, the important thing for the salesperson is to identify both the primary decision maker and the person for whom the product is being purchased.

If they are the same person, the salesperson has a smaller problem.

More often than not, the friend or relative is viewed as a "purchase pal," offering the customer a more unbiased view of the situation than a salesperson. A study conducted analyzing the purchase pal's effects on buyer behavior showed that the presence of a purchase pal increased the likelihood of a sale when the customer was attended by a salesperson with high expertise.[8]

Substitutions Are Sometimes Necessary

There are two types of situations in which a salesperson may desire to make a **substitution** of one product for another: (1) when the article requested by the customer is in stock, but the salesperson feels it possible to sell another instead, and (2) when the article the customer asks for is out of stock or not carried in inventory. A substitute product should only be presented when its performance or functional capabilities equal or exceed the item requested. The salesperson must make valid claims about the substitute item. The auto tire salesperson may recommend the Uniroyal Fastrak Belted tire because: "For only two dollars more you get 5,000 added miles."

Never should a salesperson present a substitute only saying, "It's just as good." Such a weak statement makes no valid case for a product, and it may put a customer on the defensive. In summary, when substituting a product for either of these two cases, the salesperson must quickly present the substitute to the customer, relating it to the product originally requested.

Turning the Customer over to Another Salesperson

Occasionally, a salesperson finds it impossible to answer a customer's questions regarding a particular product. In such a case, rather than fabricating an answer, a salesperson must obtain help from another employee better versed in the technical aspects of the product in question. The person summoned can be referred to as the manager or as the resident expert on that product.

In a recent search for a set of new stereo speakers for my car, I had shopped around, comparing various brands sold at specialty stores and general retailers. Most of the salespeople with whom I spoke either knew little about car stereo speakers or pushed the top-of-the-line model—to the exclusion of all others.

Shortly after entering one store, I noticed that they divided the speakers into two groups. When I asked about the difference between the two types, the salesperson confessed ignorance, but courteously suggested that I might speak to the store owner. As it turned out, the store manager discussed the matter with me, explaining under what circumstances each type of speaker should be used, and I left the store content, having purchased a new set of car stereo speakers.

In retail selling, some salespeople are trained to "turn over" the customer to another salesperson if they feel they cannot make the sale. Salesperson A excuses herself or himself and returns with salesperson B. The introduction may be: "This is Ms. Jones our store manager, who is most familiar with our merchandise," or "This is Mr. Berry our buyer. He has recently returned from market. He's our expert on. . . ."

Often, nonverbal signs are planned to aid in turnover. Salesperson B slowly takes over the entire presentation. If salesperson A does not get an opportunity or the hint to leave, salesperson B slowly moves between the customer and salesperson A. Salesperson A leaves the area. This is a successful selling strategy.

The Customer Who Does Not Buy

A retail salesperson often finds customers who are shopping at various stores prior to purchasing a particular product. In such cases, the salesperson's objective becomes one of getting the customer to return to the store when a decision has been reached. By pointing out the exclusive benefit of one or two brands of a product, the salesperson avoids confusing the prospect, and may even attempt a few "soft closes." Rather than following the easy way out, and ignoring customers who are shopping around, the professional salesperson attempts to uncover customer needs, to smoke out objections, and to use multiple closes to make a sale that solves a customer's problem or satisfies a need.

Trading Up Increases Sales

Often, buyers enter the store looking for a product that, if purchased, would probably not satisfy their needs. After looking, they may not find the ideal product at the low, low price they have in mind, and they leave the store.

The salesperson's challenge is to determine such buyers' actual needs, and suggest a product that will satisfy them. This activity may result in customers' **trading up,** by suggesting that they purchase:

- A higher quality product—a new car instead of a used one; a standard typewriter rather than a portable one; a Texas Instruments TI-2500 III with several mathematical functions instead of a calculator with only a few functions.
- Several products instead of one—slacks and a tie to go with a new sport coat; automobile front-end alignment to go with new tires.
- More of the same product—buy two—one to give away, one to keep; buy two pair of jeans instead of one while they are on sale.

Trading up is an effective method of helping both the customer and the salesperson.

MAKING THE SALE

Creative Suggestion Selling

"I witnessed an outstanding example of creative suggestion selling one day in a Neiman-Marcus men's store," says Stanley Marcus.[9] "A salesperson approached a young buyer and asked if she could help her by writing up the sale of a $15 necktie, so she could wait on another customer. She handed the buyer the $15 tie and quickly introduced the customer to another salesperson at the counter.

"As he began writing up the sale, he looked up and said, 'This is a beautiful tie you have selected. What is he going to wear it with?' The woman reached into her purse and pulled out a swatch of fabric. He looked at it a moment and said, 'There's an ancient madder pattern which comes in two color combinations that would go very well with this suit.' He pulled out the two ties as he was talking with her. She readily agreed and took both of them—at $22.50 each.

"He asked, 'Doesn't he need some new shirts to go with his new suit?' The customer replied, 'I'm glad you asked; he does need some, but I haven't been able to find any white ones with French cuffs. Do you have any size fifteen thirty-three?' He showed her two qualities, pointing out the difference in the cloths. She selected three shirts at $40 each. 'Doesn't he ever wear colored shirts?' he inquired. 'Yes; if you have this same shirt in blue I'll take two.'

"The sale progressed from there to include gold-filled cuff links, a travel robe to match the ancient madder ties, pajamas, and slippers. The total sale was $615—a 4,000 percent increase over the $15 the original salesperson was willing to settle for. Of even more importance, he made a firm new customer for the department. That is creative suggestion selling at its very best.

"Not once in the course of the sale did he oversell. He related to the customer's desires and wants and knew the content of the stock well enough to fulfill her requirements. Above all, he had the heart of a salesperson who not only thoroughly enjoys the excitement of meeting the expressed request of the customer but had the imagination to conceive of other things the buyer might find of interest. This type of selling technique can be taught; unfortunately, it doesn't happen very often. Americans have prided themselves on their selling ability, but lack of management attention to selling has dulled those skills."

Return Goods Selling Is a Must

All retail salespeople have customers return purchases from time to time, and when this happens, one of four things occur:

1. Refund the customer's money.
2. Credit the customer's charge account (if appropriate).
3. Exchange the product for the same type.
4. Sell the customer another product.

The salesperson should first attempt to sell the customer another product or to exchange the product **(return goods selling),** and if this is not possible, attempt to credit the customer's account. Cash refunds are a last resort.

On my last birthday, my wife gave me a pair of jeans and an umbrella, each valued at $35. She purchased these items from two different stores at which I had never shopped. When I sought to return the gifts, the clerks at both stores cheerfully refunded my money, neither one suggesting that I exchange the item or buy something else.

Why didn't one of the clerks say, "I know your wife would like you to have a nice birthday present. What is it you need in clothing?" With $70 in my pocket, I could have purchased shoes, socks, ties, or could have made a down payment on a sport coat or suit. When I left the two stores, their money was gone forever. If this happens three to five times a week, a store has lost a great deal of sales revenue. Remember that you can sell at any time—even when the customer is dissatisfied and wants a refund on another item.

Selecting a Price Line to Show

When several price ranges of merchandise are available to show a customer, the salesperson often becomes perplexed, unable to decide which product line to show first. Although it may seem insulting, an honestly phrased question such as, "What price range do you have in mind?" eases the uncertainty of the situation. However, the more sensitive, price-conscious customer may be offended by this question. Also, do not limit the customer to a certain price range unnecessarily.

Some salespeople prefer to show the top-of-the-line product first, hoping that the customer will appreciate the better-quality product, placing value before price. This approach may, however, scare away the price-conscious shopper. Other salespeople prefer to bring out the popular-priced product (moderately priced, best-selling) first, and then move up or down in price according to the customer's reaction.

In stores that carry few **price lines** (a common merchandising policy is to carry three lines), the salesperson may present the customer with a sample of each price range and monitor the response. This procedure allows the customer to choose the price range that is most attractive. It is important to clear out unwanted products once the customer has narrowed the selection. It is confusing to choose between too many products.

Suggestion Selling Is Persuasive

The astute salesperson generally suggests complementary or related products before the original transaction is complete. ("Would you like some stockings or polish to go with your new shoes?") The reason merchants stress **suggestion selling** is obvious: it increases the size of sale, adding sales that would otherwise be missed. Once a product is chosen, the salesperson must suggest additional merchandise that complements the purchase. Often, stores will provide salespeople with a list of products related to each other, known as "tie-in" goods. In addition to the examples used by Jack Pruett, consider the success story of Stanley Marcus in determining if you, as a retail salesperson, should routinely use suggestion selling.

Two other forms of suggestion selling are: suggesting purchase of a larger quantity of the item, or suggesting some unrelated item. To suggest that the customer buy more at one time, the salesperson might say "There is a saving in buying three," or "Shall I send you the larger one? It's really more economical."

Suggesting an unrelated item generally focuses on products that are either on sale or for some reason are uniquely featured. Items on sale that offer a desirable savings to customers must always be mentioned. In addition, customers should be alert to newly stocked items. Even if they don't buy at the time, they will know that the store carries the product. Now that you know what to do in a retail selling situation, note a few items to avoid as a successful salesperson.

DOS AND DON'TS OF RETAIL SELLING

There are a multitude of ways to lose sales in retailing. The following list points out a few reasons that sales are lost, and it offers suggestions on how to avoid them:

- A lack of enthusiasm. Enthusiasm in a salesperson often generates positive feelings in the customer regarding the salesperson's product. An uncertain customer can be encouraged by an enthusiastic salesperson. Show enthusiasm when talking with the customer.
- Arguing. This is a deadly sin. Arguing with the customer will only result in a lost sale. Avoid arguing with a customer whenever possible!
- Vocabulary. Don't talk over your customer's head. Remember to **k**eep **i**t **s**imple, **s**alesperson. For example, if you are selling a stereo system, don't talk about the technical aspects unless the prospect wants to. Use words that people understand. Technical words will usually lead to confusion on the part of customers who are not experts. They may get too much information and leave, only to buy from someone who explains the product at their level of understanding.
- Disregard questions. When customers ask questions, they are looking for answers—don't sidestep issues. If a question is difficult to answer, get help from another salesperson or your manager.
- Overtalk. Don't confuse this with communication. Communication requires two factors: talking and listening. Overtalking causes you to miss when customers are saying, "I'm ready to buy." Usually, it's best to ask questions first, listen, and then talk.
- Run down a customer's judgment. *Never* tell customers they are wrong! Such a blatant statement may lead to an argument, and it shows a lack of respect for customers. So be a diplomat, politely and delicately showing prospects your point of view.

SELLING TIPS

Example of a Retail Sales Presentation

Customer is looking at a display of Cross gold pens and pencils:[10]

SALESPERSON: [*giving a big smile*] Hello. My name is _____. Are you looking for a pen and pencil set for yourself or for a gift?

CUSTOMER: I'm looking for a graduation gift for my brother, but I'm not necessarily looking for a pen and pencil set.

SALESPERSON: Is your brother graduating from college or high school?

CUSTOMER: He is graduating from college this spring.

SALESPERSON: I can show you quite a few things that would be appropriate gifts. Let's start by taking a look at this elegant Cross pen and pencil set. Don't they look impressive? [Trial close.]

CUSTOMER: They look too expensive. Besides, a pen and pencil set doesn't seem like an appropriate gift for a college graduate. [Objection.]

SALESPERSON: You're right, a Cross pen and pencil set *does* look expensive. [Acknowledge objection.] Just imagine how impressed your brother will be when he opens your gift package and finds these beautiful writing instruments. Even though Cross pen and pencil sets look expensive, they are actually quite reasonably priced, considering the total value you are getting.

CUSTOMER: How much does this set cost?

SALESPERSON: You can buy a Cross pen and pencil set for anywhere from $15 to $300. The one I am showing you is gold-plated and costs only $28. For this modest amount you can purchase a gift for your brother that will be attractive, useful, last a lifetime, and show him that you truly think he is deserving of the very best. Don't you think that is what a graduation gift should be like? [Trial close.]

CUSTOMER: You make it sound pretty good,

but frankly I hadn't intended to spend that much money. [Objection.]

SALESPERSON: I can show you something else. However, before I do that, pick up this Cross pen and write your name on this pad of paper. [Demonstration.] Notice that in addition to good looks, Cross pens offer good writing. Cross is widely acclaimed as one of the best ball point pens on the market. It is nicely balanced, has a point that allows the ink to flow on the paper smoothly, and rides over the paper with ease.

CUSTOMER: You're right, the pen writes really well. [Positive buying signal.]

SALESPERSON: Each time your brother writes with this pen he will remember that you gave him this fine writing instrument for graduation. In addition, Cross offers prestige. Many customers tell us that Cross is one of the few pens they have used that is so outstanding that people often comment on it by brand name. Your brother will enjoy having others notice the pen he uses is high in quality.

CUSTOMER: You're right. I do tend to notice when someone is using a Cross pen. [Positive buying signal.]

SALESPERSON: You just can't go wrong with a Cross pen and pencil set for a gift. Shall I wrap it for you? [Close.]

CUSTOMER: It's a hard decision.

SALESPERSON: Your brother will be very happy with this gift.

CUSTOMER: OK. Go ahead and wrap it for me.

SALESPERSON: Fine. Would you like me to wrap up another set for you to give yourself? [Suggestion selling.]

CUSTOMER: No, one is enough. Maybe someone will buy one for me someday.

- Don't be repetitive. Customers usually hear your point the first time. After the second or third time, they may leave.
- Don't keep a customer bottled up. Let your customers speak their minds, so that if they have a comment or complaint, it comes out. Keeping them bottled up through an elaborate sales pitch can lead to frustration. You may never know their problems, and they may never tell you what they want or what their real objections are if you don't give them the opportunity to speak.

SUMMARY OF MAJOR SELLING ISSUES

The retailer is extremely important to the U.S. economy, contributing approximately 18 percent of the nation's total revenue. As a career, retailing offers excellent financial and personal rewards to people who are willing to work hard, have the ability to manage people, and understand the principles of selling.

The retail salesperson's job activities vary from store to store, yet they usually include making transactions, contacting customers, handling complaints, working stock, and personal selling. The fundamentals of selling discussed in earlier chapters and mentioned in this chapter are used by the retail salesperson just as they are used by the industrial salesperson.

In the retail sales presentation, the salesperson should stress product benefits; ask questions; and present alternatives, suggestions, and demonstrations. Objections raised by the customer must be handled quickly. Many times, questions are used to smoke out hidden objections. Assumptive, physical action, minor point, or inducement techniques are used to close the sale.

Retail selling is a challenging and demanding vocation that requires finely honed skills to help handle difficult situations such as selling to several customers at the same time, the group shopper, trading up, or return goods selling. The individual who wants to succeed in retailing must begin by learning and practicing good personal selling techniques.

13

Selling in the Industrial Setting

My name is Mike Impink, and I am a sales representative with the Aluminum Company of America. I have worked for Alcoa as a sales representative in four different sales assignments since graduating from Lehigh University in 1977 with an MBA degree. My career began with an intensive training program approximately 12 weeks long, and it included a tour of Alcoa's manufacturing facilities. I have moved through progressively responsible sales assignments over the past nine years, and I look forward to moving into sales management.

Alcoa recently implemented a major corporate restructuring that included the decentralization of the sales and marketing function to ensure that our individual business units are even more responsive and attuned to our customer needs and requirements. My role as a sales representative for Alcoa's Extrusion and Tube Division is complex and involves responsibility for total annual sales of $15 million. My job is working with customers and prospects to help them improve products, lower costs, and increase efficiency of the manufacturing processes. I work with and sell to developmental engineers, production managers, and corporate officers, as well as with buyers and purchasing agents. I evaluate each aspect of my customer's business and develop persuasive recommendations for using aluminum. I negotiate contracts, assist in making credit arrangements, and suggest proper packaging and delivery methods.

Alcoa is known for its effective and innovative industrial marketing. In large measure, this reputation results from people who represent the company—people who are first and foremost professionals in their ability to identify and solve customer problems.

I have found three sales techniques critical in a successful sales effort. First, you must bring creativity and innovation to solving the customer's problems. In addition, you must take risks in developing your approach to selling. If you are not willing to try new approaches, you will not achieve personal and professional growth. Finally, and most importantly, you must be persistent. Rarely is success easily achieved. Thus, you must persevere, because even if you are creative and take risks, you will have to overcome seemingly unlimited hurdles. Persistence is critical. •

P R O F I L E

Mike Impink
Alcoa

"My greatest triumph" says Jim Gibbons, president, Manufacturers' Agents National Association, "occurred when I was representing a small bearings manufacturer in Wisconsin whose salespersons had been tossed out of an industrial heating and air-conditioning manufacturer's plant. Their bearing requirements were substantial—on the order of $300,000 a year—and with considerable effort, I was able to discover exactly where the problem was and sit down and renegotiate the contract. This was not a major account at the time, but it did have a lot of potential.

"The reason I was able to renegotiate the contract had to do with some really in-depth research I did at the company. In this case, it wasn't the vice president of purchasing who had the beef, but an engineer who happened to be one of the last people on the totem pole. He had very little clout title-wise, but management listened to him.

"I had to start with the purchasing people and work my way through the company from there. Over a period of four or five months, I did a lot of detective work to find the right person. Along the way, I met a lot of engineers who were skeptical, but never the right guy. Finally, I located the engineer who was causing the problem. We sat down and totally re-engineered the bearings, which actually ended up increasing the price a little.

"As a result, the manufacturer sent me a big medal and a certificate, and I brought them about $1 million worth of business by satisfying both my principal and their customers. This happened very early in my career, and I'm glad it did because it taught me the importance of being persistent."[1] •

Jim Gibbons' example, and the profile of Alcoa's Mike Impink, illustrate the key function of the industrial salesperson. Mike is a problem solver for customers. He is involved in examining the customer's business operation, locating any unnoticed or potential problems, and aiding the buyer in determining methods for solving problems or improving business operations. The industrial salesperson has many duties, but by helping to perceive a real need, the salesperson can explain best how her or his products benefit the buyer.

This chapter examines the industrial goods market. The demand for industrial products, types of industrial purchases, and the characteristics of industrial products are first discussed. Next, the eight steps in the industrial buying decision are detailed. This is followed by an examination of why purchasing agents buy, including the use of value analysis, which is common in industrial sales presentation.

WHAT'S DIFFERENT ABOUT THE INDUSTRIAL MARKET?

The **industrial market,** sometimes called the business or producer market, consists of all industrial users. Industrial users are profit and nonprofit organizations that buy goods and services for one of three purposes:

- *To make other goods and services:* Campbell's buys fresh vegetables to make soup, and American Airlines buys airplanes to transport people.
- *To sell to consumers or other industrial users:* Kroger's buys canned tuna to sell to customers, and Boeing sells their airplanes to organizations such as American Airlines or the Air Force.
- *To conduct the organization's operation:* Texas A&M University buys office supplies and electronic office equipment for the registrar's office, and a dentist buys supplies to use in the office.

In the industrial market, salespeople can deal with both consumer products and industrial products. **Industrial marketing** is the marketing of products and services to industrial users—as contrasted to ultimate consumers.

Because the industrial market is largely unknown to average consumers, they are apt to underrate its significance. Actually, this market is huge in terms of total sales volume and the number of firms involved in it. About 50 percent of all manufactured products are sold to the industrial market. In addition, about 80 percent of all farm products and virtually all minerals, forest, and sea products are industrial goods. These are sold to firms for further processing. The U.S. government is the largest purchaser of products and services in the world.

The basic types of goods and services purchased by buyers in the producer market are shown in Table 13.1.[2] In addition to raw materials and components, producers purchase facilities (such as buildings), capital equipment, and a wide array of periodic services such as repair, legal services, and advertising.

Demand for Industrial Products

Three important factors distinguish the demand for industrial products from the demand for consumer goods. When selling in the industrial market, consider the influences on the demand for your products and services to properly plan a sales presentation. Customer demand for industrial products is: (1) derived, (2) inelastic, and (3) joint.

Derived Demand. The demand for many industrial goods and services is linked to consumer demand for other products—it is a **derived demand.** For example, the Whirlpool Corporation buys small electric motors for its

TABLE 13.1   Classification of goods and services in the industrial market

I. Entering goods.
   A. Raw materials.
      1. Farm products (wheat, cotton, livestock, fruits, and vegetables).
      2. Natural products (fish, lumber, crude petroleum, iron ore).
   B. Manufactured materials and parts.
      1. Component materials (steel, cement, wire, textiles).
      2. Component parts (small motors, tires, castings).
II. Foundation goods.
   A. Installations.
      1. Buildings and land rights (factories, offices).
      2. Fixed equipment (generators, drill presses, computers, elevators).
   B. Accessory equipment.
      1. Portable or light factory equipment and tools (hand tools, lift trucks).
      2. Office equipment (typewriters, desks).
III. Facilitating goods.
   A. Supplies.
      1. Operating supplies (lubricants, coal, typing paper, pencils).
      2. Maintenance and repair items (paint, nails, brooms).
   B. Business services.
      1. Maintenance and repair services (window cleaning, typewriter repair).
      2. Business advisory services (legal, management consulting, advertising).

refrigerators because consumers purchase the refrigerator; the motor's demand is based on the demand for the refrigerator. People do not buy motors in this case; they buy refrigerators. There would be little demand for refrigerator motors, and other associated components, if no one bought refrigerators.

Other industrial sellers are affected by a change in demand for a particular product. If, for example, the demand for Whirlpool's refrigerators declined, the demand for production equipment would decline. Lower demands for steel would lead to a lower demand for iron ore. A change in a product's demand can set in motion a wave of changes affecting the demand for all firms involved in production.

Inelastic Demand.   The demand for many industrial products is **inelastic demand.** An increase or decrease in the price of a product will not usually generate a proportionate increase or decrease in sales for the product. The Whirlpool refrigerator has many parts. The cost of each part represents a fraction of the total cost for producing the refrigerator. If there is an increase or decrease in the price of a single part, such as the motor, the demand for the appliance is not significantly influenced. Even if the cost of its motor doubled (assuming it did not represent a large proportion of production costs), and was passed along to the consumer, the refrigerator's sales price would increase by a small amount, having little effect on consumer demand.

Joint Demand. The demand for many industrial products is also affected by **joint demand.** Joint demand occurs when two or more products are used together to produce a single product. For example, a firm that manufactures automobiles needs numerous component parts—tires, batteries, steel, glass, etc. These products are demanded jointly.

The salesperson selling products that are demanded jointly must understand the effect of joint demand on the market. When a customer purchases a product, there is an opportunity to sell companion products. An example is the grocery retailer who purchases computerized cash registers. The IBM 3660 Supermarket System shown in Figure 13.1 also requires the purchase of associated items such as a small computer, cash registers, product scanners, and other supplies for operating the equipment in the grocery store.[3]

Industrial goods have three types of demand—derived, inelastic, and joint. By understanding the demand for the product, a salesperson is better able to sell successfully.

Major Types of Industrial Purchases

Industrial purchases are usually one of three general types—new task purchases, straight rebuy purchases, or modified rebuy purchases.

The **new task purchase** is made when a product is bought in conjunction with a job or task newly performed by the purchaser. A long period is frequently needed for the salesperson to make this type of sale since the buyer is often cautious, especially when confronted with an expensive product or large quantities. This is the most challenging selling situation, since buyers want to consider all alternative suppliers and may need substantial information from each supplier. The salesperson may have to submit a prototype of the product, a price bid, and make several presentations over an extended time period before the final purchase decision. New task purchases include buying capital equipment, construction materials for a new job site, and even an entire plant facility.

The **straight rebuy purchase** is a routine purchase of products bought regularly. This sale is normally casual order taking. Often, buyers negotiate a blanket purchase order (BPO) agreement, which establishes the price and terms of the sale for a set period. Buyers require little time and information to make a purchase decision. This type of purchase might include continually used raw materials, office supplies, or MRO (maintenance, repair, and operations items such as spare parts for machinery).

The **modified rebuy purchase** is somewhat like the straight rebuy purchase procedure. The buyer seeks a similar product, but wants or needs to negotiate different terms. The buyer may want a lower price, faster

FIGURE 13.1   The IBM 3660 Supermarket System

delivery, or better quality. For example, a firm that buys oil field drilling bits from a supplier each month (straight rebuy situation) decides it needs a better-quality drilling bit. The firm goes to the same supplier and others to see whether a better-quality bit is available and at what price (modified rebuy situation). The drilling company still wants drill bits, but looks for a slightly different product to suit its present needs.

Product Characteristics

Industrial products, like industrial markets, have certain characteristics that a salesperson must consider when selling to buyers of these goods. These product characteristics differ from consumer product characteristics. Industrial products often are: (1) technical, (2) in need of specifications and bids, (3) complex in pricing, and (4) standardized.

Technical Products.   Compared to consumer goods, industrial sales are more technical. The industrial salesperson must have more product knowledge training than a salesperson of consumer goods. Discussing complex product information with knowledgeable customers, which demands considerable expertise, is essential to success.

Specifications and Bids.   Many industrial goods are bought based on specifications. These specifications may be determined by the industrial customer, or they may be commonly accepted industry standards. They may be tremendously complex, such as the design of a specialized hydraulic pump, or as simple as stating a particular color to use.

Bids, based on stated specifications, are usually submitted by several selling firms to the purchasing firm. Each seller bids on a homogeneous, similar product. Depending on the buyer's wishes, bids may range from a simple oral quote given over the phone to a formalized written quotation or a sealed bid held in the buyer's office and opened on a specific closing date along with all other bids. If the purchasing agent does not want to accept any of the bids, suppliers may be asked to submit second bids. Purchasing firms typically use this system to identify the product's true market price.

If all other factors are equal, the company submitting the lowest bid wins the contract. However, other factors often affect the buying decision. The product's performance and quality level, for example, may be important considerations in the buying decision. Del Monte Corporation may pay a supplier several cents more per bushel for a higher grade of tomatoes so that they can charge a premium price for canned tomatoes at the retail level.

Complex Pricing. Because of the product's technical nature, its inelastic demand characteristic, the buyer's expertise, and the fact that competitive bidding is often involved in the purchase process, pricing in the industrial market is complex. Final price to the customer can be based on estimates of long-term agreements, present and future labor and material costs, availability of materials, expected salvage value of present equipment, product service agreements, cost-effectiveness of production facilities, and return–on–investment.

A bid under complex pricing may include progressive payments whereby the buyer makes periodic payments to the supplier as a down payment, with the remainder paid when the product is delivered; escalator clauses, such as if the cost of manufacturing the product increases, the product's price also increases; specific foreign currency exchange rates; and letters of credit. In addition, the quote will probably include cash terms and delivery terms (discussed in Chapter 5).

In considering the many factors affecting the price of an industrial product, a sales manager may give the company's sales force a range of prices to use in negotiations. Avoid trying to use low price alone to make a sale. After all, your selling skills will determine success in the long run.

Standardization. Many industrial products tend to be homogeneous. When compared to competing products, they often show high similarity. When a new product or product feature is introduced to the market, its initial advantage may quickly be lost. It is easy for competitors to improve a product slightly and market it as their own. Most of the time, the industrial salesperson sells products that are similar to a competitor's products.

WHO MAKES THE DECISIONS AROUND HERE?

Industrial goods have market and product characteristics that differ from consumer goods. Therefore, the buying decision is somewhat different for industrial goods than for consumer goods. The industrial buying process, like the consumer buying process, is a series of steps. The eight steps

TABLE 13.2 Industrial buying process and situations

	Type of Buying Situation		
Steps in Industrial Buying Process	New Task	Modified Rebuy	Straight Rebuy
1. Recognition of a problem or need	yes	yes	yes
2. Determination of characteristics of the needed product	yes	yes	no
3. Determination of product specifications	yes	yes	no
4. Search and qualification of potential sources	yes	yes	no
5. Acquisition and analysis of proposal	yes	yes	no
6. Selection of supplier(s)	yes	yes	no
7. Selection of an order routine	yes	yes	no
8. Evaluation of product performance	yes	yes	yes

involved in purchasing industrial products are: (1) recognition of the problem or need; (2) determination of the characteristics of the needed product; (3) determination of product specifications; (4) search and qualification of potential sources; (5) acquisition and analysis of proposal; (6) selection of supplier(s); (7) establishment of an order routine; and (8) evaluation of product performance.

Table 13.2 shows the steps in the industrial buying process, along with the three industrial buying situations. For the straight rebuy, steps 2 through 7 can be eliminated. In this situation, a need is recognized, such as a low inventory of a product, and the order is automatically processed. The salesperson supplying a product on a straight rebuy basis contacts the customer periodically to check inventory, and to make sure that the order processed quickly. This procedure strengthens a customer's loyalty to and reliance on a seller, indirectly warding off competition. Salespeople must continually watch for the possibility that present customers may reassess their needs and find some problem with a product, and thus seek another supplier. By routinely contacting the customer, the salesperson becomes aware of changes in the buyer's attitude.

In the new task and modified buying situations, several competing suppliers' salespeople may present the prospect with information. The salesperson helps determine the buyer's needs and shows the buyer how they are fulfilled by a product. The salesperson needs to work closely with everyone who has an influence on the buying decision. When no firm has an initial edge on an industrial order, the salesperson who spends the *right* amount of time with the *right* people often walks away with the order. This person probably spent some time learning *whom* to talk to. Knowing the right people in an organization is vital to a salesperson's existence. With experience, most good salespeople learn whom they need to contact. But how does the beginning salesperson find these influential people? The next section provides some answers.

WHOM SHOULD I TALK TO?

Salespeople must locate people in the buying firm who will influence and make the buying decision. Industrial salespeople may talk with several people about the product before making a sale.

Emmett Reagan of Xerox is an excellent example of a person who finds the decision maker. As shown in Figure 13.2, the salesperson (Emmett Reagan) approaches the receptionist, signs in, and asks to see the purchasing agent. As he greets her, he presents his business card. In this situation, the purchasing agent does not permit the salesperson to come to his office. Instead, he comes to the lobby where the business will be discussed. This is a defense mechanism often employed by purchasers.[4]

The salesperson is seated in the lobby reviewing details of his presentation while waiting for the prospect. The prospect arrives in the lobby and is greeted by the salesperson. Then, the prospect and salesperson discuss the proposed transaction, after which the purchaser agrees to witness a product demonstration. The buyer also says that the ultimate decision will be made by the vice president of finance.

After the product is demonstrated to the purchasing agent, he agrees that the product has merit and that the vice president of finance may be interested. Now, the purchasing agent and the salesperson make a joint presentation to the vice president of finance.

In determining whom to see and how much time to spend with each person, the salesperson should learn who influences the purchase decision and the *strength of each person's influence*. People who may influence the purchase of a product include:

- **Initiator**—the person proposing to buy or replace the product.
- **Deciders**—the people who are involved in making the actual decision—such as the plant engineer, purchasing agent, and someone from top management.
- **Influencers**—plant engineer, plant workers, and research and development personnel who develop specifications needed for the product.
- **Buyers**—the purchasing agent.
- **Gatekeepers**—people who influence where information from salespeople goes and with whom salespeople will be allowed to talk. Receptionists, secretaries, and purchasing agents are gatekeepers.
- **Users**—those people that must work with or use the product, for example, plant workers or secretaries.

It is crucial that the salesperson get by the **gatekeepers** and talk to the initiators, users, influencers, buyers, and deciders. For example, users of a company's copy machine (initiators) may become dissatisfied with its quality of copies. A secretary (influencer) mentions that Xerox makes an

FIGURE 13.2   Xerox salesperson Emmett Reagan illustrates initial industrial sales call

• *Emmett signs in at the reception desk.*

• *He asks to see the purchasing agent.*

• *He reviews his presentation while waiting.*

• *He meets the purchasing agent.*

• *He discusses the proposed transaction.*

• *He demonstrates the product.*

excellent copier that the firm can afford. After a conference with several major users of the present duplicating machine, the office manager (decider) confers with the representatives of several competing copy machine firms and decides to lease the Xerox machine. A purchase order is forwarded to the corporate home office, where a purchasing agent (buyer) approves the purchases. Which person should the Xerox salesperson have visited in selling the machine? In this example, each person who participates in the purchase decision should have been contacted—the secretary, major users, and office manager—and the salesperson should have explained the product's benefits to each person.

Often, a new salesperson is not allowed in the plant nor allowed to talk to people within the company other than the purchasing agent. Hundreds of

FIGURE 13.2 *(concluded)*

· *Emmett meets the company's vice president of finance (the decision maker).*

· *He again discusses the proposed transaction.*

· *The purchasing agent and the vice president talk it over.*

· *Emmett asks the vice president to see a demonstration.*

· *Emmett answers all questions . . .*

· *. . . and carefully shows and discusses features, advantages, and benefits.*

other salespeople may have already called on the company wanting the same thing. Large manufacturers, like General Motors, have salespeople stop at the receptionist's desk. Whomever the salesperson has asked to see is telephoned. Purchasing agents and other influential individuals will often see only those salespeople who have appointments, or with whom they are well acquainted. A new salesperson calling on GM must plan ahead. It is essential to call ahead for an appointment, not just drop by.

If a buyer's secretary is reluctant to make an appointment, or if the buyer refuses to establish a meeting time, the salesperson must either give up or use creativity and charm. Sending a reluctant buyer a personalized novelty, such as a small figure of a salesperson holding a sample case along with a note saying, "This salesperson has something that will benefit you" is a creative way of gaining an appointment.

After being turned away by a head nurse (gatekeeper), a pharmaceutical salesperson put a stethoscope around his neck, obtained a small doctor's bag, and proceeded to the tenth floor of a large hospital to see the hospital's chief of surgery about a new drug. He told the doctor what he had done and why, and was asked not to do it again. All was not for naught, however, because he arranged to have future conferences with the surgeon in the doctor's lounge on request. This salesperson would not take no for an answer. While you do not want to offend any clients with persistence, you may open the door on a sale that a gatekeeper tried to keep closed.

Ask yourself, when you do something creative, how many others have been stopped by the gatekeeper? Buyers, like all of us, appreciate people who give them special attention or go out of their way for them, especially if they believe someone understands their needs, sincerely wants to help them, and acts professionally.

PURCHASING AGENTS ARE RATIONAL BUYERS

When selling to the producer market, the salesperson deals with well-trained, knowledgeable, and rational buyers. Industrial purchasing agents in large corporations are often specialists. They are expert professionals in dealing with professional salespeople.

Purchasing agents carefully examine information presented to them. Quality sales presentations are expected from salespeople they see. Buying decisions are made based on practical, business reasons. Emotional reasons for buying play a less important role in purchasing decisions than in decisions made by a consumer. As a result, the time required to make a purchase decision is usually longer than in the consumer setting. This is because industrial buyers carefully compare their firm's needs with the features, advantages, and benefits of competing products—a process that takes time.

WHY DO PRODUCERS BUY?

Buyers in the producer market seek to buy for many reasons. Some common reasons usually evolve from an aspect of the product's cost and quality. Specific primary buying needs or motives include:

- Increasing profits.
- Increasing sales.
- Producing a quality product.
- Improving the operation's efficiency (resulting in cost reductions).
- Helpfulness of the salesperson.

- Service.
- Payment.
- Trade-in allowances.
- Delivery.
- Buying a product at the lowest price.

To be a successful salesperson, determine each buyer's important buying needs. Then, develop a sales presentation emphasizing your product's features, advantages, and benefits, and how they can fulfill those needs. One of the best and most often used methods of presenting your product's benefits to the buyer is value analysis.

Value Analysis: A Powerful Selling Tool

Industrial salespeople often include a value analysis in the sales presentation. A **value analysis** determines the best product for the money. It recognizes that a high-priced product may sometimes be a better value than a lower-priced product. Many firms routinely review a value analysis before deciding to purchase a product.

The value analysis evaluates the product in terms of the buying company's specific needs. It addresses such questions as:

- How do your product's features, advantages, and benefits compare to the product currently used?
- Can your product do the same job as your buyer's present product at a lower price?
- Does the buyer's current equipment perform better than required? (Is equipment "too good" for present needs?)
- On the other hand, will a higher-priced, better-performing product be more economical in the long run?

As you can see from the examples in this chapter, you are often required to analyze the buyer's present operation carefully before suggesting how your product might improve efficiency, enhance the quality or quantity of the product produced, or save money.

In discussing how to present a value analysis to a buyer, Patrick Kamlowsky, who sells drilling bits for oil and gas wells, said:

> It's not as simple as it may appear to make a recommendation and have the oil company adhere to it. You must be thorough in the presentation and present the facts in an objective manner. After all, their money is at stake. The presentation must be logical and based on facts that are known; it must be made with as little speculation as possible.
>
> What is difficult is presenting a recommendation to one who has spent 30 or more years in the oil field and has drilled all over the world. I am confronted with the challenge of explaining to this man that the methods he

has employed for years may not be the best application where he is currently drilling. The presentation of the recommendation must therefore be thorough and to the point. When talking to him, I do not imply that his method is outdated or wrong, but that I believe I can help him improve his method. To be successful, I must establish two things very quickly—his respect and my credibility. Showing him my proposal and supporting evidence, and permitting him the time to evaluate it are vital. I don't wish to come on to him too strong, just show him that I genuinely want to help.

There are numerous types of value analyses that a salesperson can develop for a prospective buyer. Three types frequently used are: (1) product cost versus true value, (2) unit cost, and (3) return on investment.

Compare Product Costs to True Value. All buyers want to know about costs. The value analysis developed for a customer should present cost in a simple, straightforward manner. A product's costs are always relative to something else; thus, cost must be judged in terms of "value" and results. The base cost of your product should never be the determining factor of the sale. Buying a product solely on cost could cause a customer to lose money.

Never discuss costs until you have compared them to the *value* of a product. In this manner, the customer intelligently compares the true worth of the proposed investment in your product to its true monetary cost. In effect, a good purchase involves more than initial cost; it represents an investment and you must demonstrate that what you sell is a good investment.

Table 13.3 provides an example of how a salesperson might compare the cost of a copier (product X) with a competitive copier. The difference between the purchase prices of the two copiers is $305. Product X saves $200 on monthly copy costs, assuming the buyer's firm makes 10,000 copies a month. The buyer receives a savings of two cents per copy. This savings makes up the difference in the initial purchase price in only six weeks. In 15 months, savings on the monthly copy costs will equal the purchase price of product X. Therefore, product X is less expensive in the long run.

The copier example illustrates how you can demonstrate to a buyer that your product is a better value than one would think from looking only at purchase price. Another value analysis technique is to further break down a product's price to its unit cost.

Unit Costs Break Price Down. One method of presenting a product's true value to a buyer is to break the product's total costs into several smaller units or the **unit cost.** Assume you sell a computer system that costs $1,000 per month and processes 50,000 transactions each month. The cost per

TABLE 13.3   Example of cost versus value of a small copier

	Product C	Product X
Initial cost	$2,695	$3,000
Type of paper	Treated paper	Plain paper
Copy speed	12 copies per minute	15 copies per minute
Warm up time	Instant	Instant
Cost of each copy	3¢ a copy	1¢ a copy
Monthly cost (assuming 10,000 copies)	$300	$100

Conclusion: The difference in the purchase price of the two copiers is $305 ($3,000 − $2,695). Product X saves $200 on monthly copy costs. The savings on monthly copy costs pays for the higher priced product X in one and one-half months. In 15 months, savings on the monthly copy costs will equal the purchase price of product X.

transaction is only 2 cents. Figures 13.3 and 13.4 present six additional examples of how value analysis reduces costs.[5]

Return on Investment Is Listened to. **Return on investment** refers to an additional sum of money expected from an investment over and above the original investment. Buyers are interested in knowing the percentage return on their initial investment. Since the purchase of many industrial products is an investment in that it produces measurable results, the salesperson can talk about the percentage return that can be earned by purchasing your product.

Again, assume you sell computer equipment requiring a $10,000 per month investment. Benefits to the buyer are measured in hours of work saved by employees, plus the resulting salary saving. First, have the buyer agree on an hourly rate, which includes fringe benefit cost; let's say salaries average $5 an hour for employees. The hours saved are then multiplied by this hourly rate to obtain the return on investment. If hours saved amounted to 2,800 per month, it is a savings of $14,000 per month (2,800 hours × $5 hourly rate). You could develop a table to show the potential return on investment:

Value of hours saved	$14,000 per month
Cost of equipment	− 10,000 per month
Profit	$ 4,000 per month
Return on investment ($14,000 ÷ $10,000)	140 percent

Subtracting the $10,000 cost per month from the return of $14,000 per month provides a $4,000 a month profit or a 140 percent return on

FIGURE 13.3   How value analysis reduces costs

Weights mounted on a rotor ring were curved to match the ring curve. Did it need this feature? No. Using a straight piece, the cost dropped from 40 cents to 4 cents.

Field coil supports were machined from stock, but the original design blended nicely into a casting operation. The change resulted in lowering the cost from $1.75 to 36 cents each.

This insulating washer was made from laminated phenolic resin and fiber. Machined from individual pieces of material, it cost $1.23. A supplier with specialty equipment now fly-cuts the parts, nesting them on full sheets, at 24 cents each.

Standard nipple and elbow required special machining to fit a totally enclosed motor. Casting a special street "L" with a lug eliminated machining and a special assembly jig. The cost dropped from 63 cents to 38 cents.

An insulator costing $4.56 was originally porcelain, leaded extra heavy. Now molded from polyester and glass, it is lighter and virtually indestructible. New cost: $3.25.

investment. This is taken one step further by considering return on investment after taxes — calculated like this:

$$\frac{\$14,000 \ (1 \ - \ \text{Tax rate})}{\$10,000}$$

This return on investment presents the buyer with a logical reason to buy. Remember to let the customer make the cost estimates. The buyer must agree with the figures used for this to be effective in demonstrating the real value of buying your product.

FIGURE 13.4 A value-analyzed assembly for directing steel cable through an angle top

1. Left- and right-hand coupling was eliminated.
2. Cover was changed from brass to plastic.
3. Special tapping operation was eliminated by using only one screw captive to cover. Tapped hole was made concentric with body recess.
4. Pulley was made as screw machine piece rather than a machined casting and made captive to body to simplify field installation.
5. Specialty suppliers with high-speed equipment were used.
6. Cost of unit was reduced 60 percent.

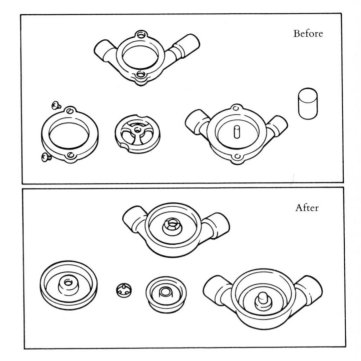

SUMMARY OF MAJOR SELLING ISSUES

Industrial goods include the raw materials, supplies, equipment, and services used in production, as well as finished goods and services intended for the producer, reseller, and government markets. The producer market contains individuals and organizations that purchase products and services for the production of other goods or services. Characteristics of the producer market include: derived demand, inelastic demand, and joint demand. Product characteristics are technical in nature and have frequent requirements for specifications and bid, complex pricing, and standardization.

The industrial buying decision may be a complex and lengthy process. It usually involves eight basic steps, depending on whether it is a new task, a modified rebuy, or a straight rebuy situation. It is important for the salesperson to locate individuals who influence the buying decision and determine the strength of each one's influence to allocate the right amount of time and effort needed to solve a customer's problems. Buyers are concerned about costs and product quality, which can result in increased profits and more efficient operations. A value analysis can be used to show the buyer that the salesperson's product is cost efficient.

14

Time and Territory Management Is a Key to Success

Twelve years have passed since Terry Fingerhut attended a Tupperware party as a favor to a friend. Terry, with her B.A. in secondary education, was teaching junior high students and her husband, Paul, with his M.S. in mathematics, was teaching in high school. Today Terry and Paul operate a $4 million Tupperware distributorship.

Terry began as a salesperson holding an average of two parties per week. She then became a manager with a unit of four dealers that ultimately grew to a unit of 45 dealers. "During this time," says Terry, "I promoted 12 dealers from my unit to managership. Each took into their new units an average of 3 dealers from my unit. In my third year as a manger, our unit had sales of $500,000.

"In my fourth year with the Tupperware company, the ultimate goal of having a Tupperware distributorship became a reality for Paul and me. Steamboat Party Sales, Inc., became the fourth distributorship servicing the St. Louis metropolitan area. We began with a sales force of eight managers and 86 dealers, selling $1 million in our first year. Today, we have a sales force of 50 managers and 480 dealers selling $4 million. We are ranked number four in Tupperware on sales volume.

"One of the keys to success is time management," says Terry. "When the desire is there and the discipline of doing the job *now* to create the series of positive results is ever-present, priorities are set and followed. In fact, these priorities need to be worked with, evaluated, and perhaps readjusted as the day/week/month progresses. What is the best use of this time *now?* Planning the day—on paper—allows you to see what is effective use of time. Ask yourself, 'Is this the best use of me—*now?*' 'Will I get the best and most results from what I am doing right *now?*' "

"Self-discipline is a vital part of time management," say Terry and Paul Fingerhut. "Establish what is your best use of time. Determine the amount of hours to be spent in the week that allows time to reach your chosen goals. Look at the days of the week that will give the best results for your efforts and schedule the various phases of your job on the days that give the best results for time spent. Within each day, analyze the best use of time. For example, if I need to make phone calls to solidify upcoming appointments—isn't it better time management to determine ahead of time with the customer what is the best time for that call—specifically 11:00 A.M.—rather than calling at random until the party is reached? and *you* determine when calls or contacts are made. Give the action choice—'I'll be in your area Monday. Would ten be good for you or perhaps one?'—not 'When can we make contact?' " •

Terry and Paul Fingerhut
Steamboat Party Sales, Inc. (Tupperware)

All successful salespeople recognize the importance of time and territory management. Terry says, "Understand the value of your time. Time is the essence of life and because of time management, you have productive time for whatever you choose to do."

In recalling his early days as a salesperson, Shelby H. Carter, Jr., Xerox's senior vice president of sales of U.S. field operations, said, "I placed a sign on my car's visor that read, 'Calls are the guts of this business.' We lived in Baltimore," he recalls, "and I drove 40 miles every day to get to Annapolis." His wife fixed him a jug of lemonade so he would not have to stop for lunch.

"You've got to make extra calls," he now tells his salespeople, "because 1 more call a day is 5 a week, 20 a month, and 240 calls a year. If you close 10 percent of the people you contact, you have an extra 24 sales a year. You have to be tough on yourself to make that extra call."[1] •

Terry and Paul Fingerhut and Shelby Carter voice the sentiments of sales managers about the importance of working hard and making extra calls on prospects and customers. The importance of planning the work day and managing your time and territory is important to success.

According to a national survey of thousands of salespeople across the nation, managing time and territory is the most important factor in selling.[2] Because of such things as the rapidly increasing cost of direct selling, decreasing time for face-to-face customer contact, continued emphasis on profitable sales, and the fact that time is always limited, it is no wonder that many companies are concentrating on improving how salespeople manage time and territory.[3]

WHAT IS A SALES TERRITORY?

A **sales territory** comprises a group of customers or a geographical area assigned to a salesperson. The territory may or may not have geographical boundaries. Typically, however, a salesperson is assigned to a geographical area containing present and potential customers.

Why Establish Sales Territories?

Companies develop and use sales territories for numerous reasons. Seven important reasons are:

To Obtain Thorough Coverage of the Market. With proper coverage of territories, the company will reach the sales potential of its markets. The sales person analyzes the territory and identifies customers. At the individual territory level, the salesperson better meets customers' needs. Division into territories also allows management to easily realign territories as customers and sales increase or decrease.

To Establish Salesperson's Responsibilities. Salespeople act as business managers for their territories. They are responsible for maintaining and generating sales volume. Salespeople's job tasks are clearly defined. They know where customers are located and how often to call on them. They also know what performance goals are expected. This can raise the salesperson's performance and morale.

To Evaluate Performance. Performance is monitored for each territory. Actual performance data are collected, analyzed, and compared to expected performance goals. Individual territory performance is compared to district performance, district performance compared to regional performance, and regional performance compared to the performance of the entire sales force. With computerized reporting systems, the salesperson and a manager can monitor individual territory and customer sales to determine the success of selling efforts.

To Improve Customer Relations. Customer goodwill and increased sales are expected when customers receive regular calls. From the customer's viewpoint, the salesperson is, for example, Procter & Gamble. The customer looks to the salesperson, not to Procter & Gamble's corporate office, when making purchases. Over the years, some salespeople build up such goodwill with customers that customers will delay placing orders because they know the salesperson will be at their business on a certain day or at a specific time of the month. Some salespeople even earn the right to order merchandise for certain customers.

To Reduce Sales Expense. Sales territories are designed to avoid duplicating efforts so that two salespeople do not travel in the same area. This lowers selling cost and increases company profits. Such benefits as fewer travel miles and fewer overnight trips, plus regular contact of productive customers by the same salesperson can improve the firm's sales–cost ratio.

To Allow Better Matching of Salesperson to Customer's Needs. Salespeople are hired and trained to meet the requirements of the customers in a territory. Often, the more similar the customer and the salesperson, the more likely the sales effort will succeed.

Benefit to Salespeople and the Company. Proper territory design aids in reaching the firm's sales objectives. Thus, the company can maximize its sales effort, while the sales force can work in territories that allows them to satisfy personal needs (e.g., good salary).

Why Sales Territories May Not Be Developed

In spite of advantages, there are disadvantages to developing sales territories for some companies, such as in the real estate or insurance industry. First, salespeople may be more motivated if they are not restricted by a particular territory and can develop customers anywhere. In the chemical industry, for example, salespeople may sell to any potential customer. However, after the sale is made, other company salespeople are not allowed to contact that client.

Second, the company may be too small to be concerned with segmenting the market into sales areas. Third, management may not want to take the time, or may not have the know-how for territory development. Fourth, personal friendship may be the basis for attracting customers. For example, life insurance salespeople may first sell policies to their families and friends. However, most companies establish sales territories.

ELEMENTS OF TIME AND TERRITORY MANAGEMENT

For the salesperson, time and territory management (TTM) is a continuous process of planning, executing, and evaluating. The seven key elements involved in time and territory management are shown in Figure 14.1.

Salesperson's Sales Quota

A salesperson is responsible for generating sales in a territory based on its sales potential. The salesperson's manager typically establishes a total sales quota that each salesperson is expected to reach.

Once this quota is set, it is the salesperson's responsibility to develop territorial sales plans for reaching the quota. While there is no best planning sequence to follow, Figure 14.1 presents seven factors to consider in properly managing the territory for reaching its sales quota.

Account Analysis

Once the salesperson has set a sales goal, it is important to analyze each prospect and customer to maximize the chances of reaching that goal. First, a salesperson should identify all prospects and present customers, and second, estimate present customers' and prospects' sales potential. This makes it possible to allocate time between customers, to decide what products to emphasize for a specific customer, and how to better plan the sales presentation.

Two general approaches to **account analysis**—identifying accounts and their varying levels of sales potential—are the undifferentiated selling approach and the account segmentation approach.

FIGURE 14.1 Elements of time and territory management for the salesperson

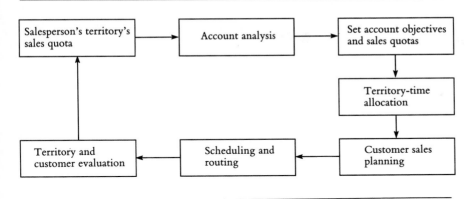

The Undifferentiated Selling Approach. An organization may see the accounts in its market as similar. When this happens and selling strategies are designed and applied equally to all accounts, the salesperson uses an **undifferentiated selling** approach. Notice in Figure 14.2 that the salesperson aims a single selling strategy at all accounts. The basic assumption underlying this approach is that the accounts needs for a specific product or group of products are similar. Salespeople call on all potential accounts, devoting equal selling time to each of them. The same sales presentation may be used in selling an entire product line. The salesperson feels it can satisfy most customers with a single selling strategy. For example, many door-to-door salespeople use the same selling strategies with each person they contact (stimulus-response sales presentation).

Salespeople whose accounts have homogeneous needs and characteristics may find this approach useful. The undifferentiated selling approach was popular in the past, and some firms still use it. However, many salespeople feel that their accounts have different needs and represent different sales and profit potentials. This makes an account segmentation approach desirable.

The Account Segmentation Approach. Salespeople using the **account segmentation** approach recognize that their territories contain accounts with heterogenous needs and differing characteristics that require different selling strategies. Consequently, sales objectives, in terms of overall sales and sales of each product, are developed for each customer and prospect. Past sales to the account, new accounts, competition, economic conditions, price and promotion offerings, new products, and personal selling are among key elements in the analysis of accounts and territories.

FIGURE 14.2   Undifferentiated selling approach

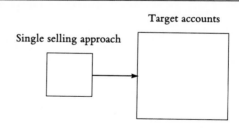

Salespeople classify customers to identify profitable ones. This in turn determines where the salesperson's time is invested. One method of defining accounts is:

1. Key account.
   a. Buys over $200,000 from us annually.
   b. Loss of this customer would substantially affect the territory's sales and profits.
2. Unprofitable account.
   a. Buys less than $1,000 from us annually.
   b. Little potential to increase purchases above $1,000.
3. Regular account.
   a. All other customers.

The unprofitable accounts would not be called upon. The **key accounts** and regular accounts become target customers.

Once the accounts are classified broadly, categories or types of accounts are defined in terms such as: extra large (key), large, medium, and small, which we will refer to as the **ELMS system.** For example, management may divide the 3,000 total accounts in the firm's marketing into these four basic sales categories, as shown in Table 14.1. As seen in the table, there are few extra large or large accounts, but they often account for 80 percent of a company's profitable sales even though they represent only 20 percent of total accounts. This is known as the **80/20 principle.** The number of key accounts in an individual territory varies, as does responsibility for them. Even though the key account is in another salesperson's territory, a key account salesperson may call on the "extra-large" customer. Typically, this is done because of the account's importance or because of an inexperienced local salesperson.

Accounts can be segmented whether or not the firms are actual customers or prospects. As shown in Table 14.2, actual customers are further segmented based on sales to date and sales potential. Prospects are

TABLE 14.1 Example of account segmentation based on yearly sales

Customer Size	Yearly Sales (actual or potential)	Number of Accounts	Percent
Extra large	over $200,000	100	3.3
Large	$75,000–200,000	500	16.6
Medium	$25,000–75,000	1,000	33.3
Small	$1,000–25,000	1,400	46.6

TABLE 14.2 Basic segmentation of accounts

Account Classification	Customers		Prospect Potential Sales
	Sales to Date	Potential Sales	
Extra large			
Large			
Medium			
Small			

also segmented into the ELMS classification, and each account's potential sales are estimated.[4]

Multiple Selling Strategies. Figure 14.3 illustrates how multiple selling strategies are used on various accounts. Salespeople know the importance of large accounts; in fact, meeting sales objectives often depends on how well products are sold to these customers. As a result, companies often develop their sales force organizational structure to service these accounts— incorporating elements such as a key account salesperson.

As illustrated in Figure 14.3, selling strategies vary depending on the account. The bulk of sales force resources (such as personnel, time, samples, and entertainment expenses) should be invested in the key accounts, and the needs of these large accounts should receive top priority.

Company positioning relative to competition must receive careful consideration. Competitors will also direct a major selling effort toward these accounts. Thus, salespeople should strive to create the image that their company, products, and themselves are uniquely better than the competition. One way to accomplish this is to spend more time on each sales call and to make more total sales calls during the year, thus providing a problem-solving approach to servicing accounts.[5]

Selling larger accounts is different than selling medium and small accounts. However, these smaller accounts may generate 20 percent, and sometimes more, of a company's sales and must not be ignored.

FIGURE 14.3   Account segmental approach

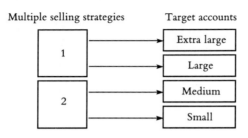

Multivariable Account Segmentation.   Multivariable account segmentation means using more than one criterion to characterize the organization's accounts. This is done because many sales organizations sell to several markets and use many channel members in these markets. Furthermore, different products, product sizes, or product lines may be emphasized to different channel members in various markets.

Figure 14.4 illustrates how firms might use several variables to segment their accounts. This allows sales personnel to develop plans for selling various products to specific segments of their accounts. For example, different selling strategies might be developed for the extra large and large accounts. There might be different sales plans developed for retailers, wholesalers, and government accounts. These three types of accounts might be further segmented. Retailers, for instance, could be segmented into mass merchandisers and specialty stores. Furthermore, different products might be emphasized in each account segment. The type of market, environment, account sales potential, and sales volume are major variables for segmenting accounts.[6]

Develop Account Objectives and Sales Quotas

The third element of time and territory management is developing objectives and sales quotas for individual products and for present and potential accounts. Objectives might include increasing product distribution to prospects in the territory or increasing the product assortment purchased by current customers.

Increasing the number of sales calls each day and the number of new accounts obtained for the year are other examples of objectives that are developed by the salesperson to help meet sales quotas.

FIGURE 14.4   Multivariable account segmentation

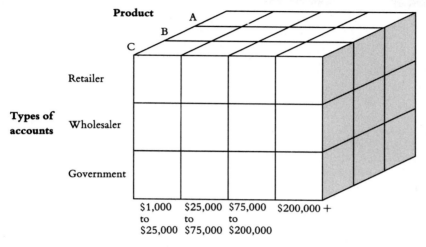

Territory-Time Allocation

The fourth element of time and territory management is how salespeople's time is allocated within territories. Time is the time spent by the salesperson traveling around the territory and in calling on accounts. There are seven basic factors to consider in time allocation:

1. Number of accounts in the territory.
2. Number of sales calls made on customers.
3. Time required for each sales call.
4. Frequency of customer sales calls.
5. Travel time around territory.
6. Nonselling time.
7. Return on time invested.

Analysis of accounts in the territory has resulted in determining the total number of territory accounts and their classification in terms of actual or potential sales. Now, the number of yearly sales calls required, the time required for each call, and the intervals between calls can be determined. Usually, the frequency of calls increases as there are increases in: (1) sales and/or potential future sales, (2) number of orders placed in a year, (3) number of product lines sold, and (4) complexity, servicing, and redesign requirements of products.

Since the time spent servicing an account varies from minutes to days, salespeople must be flexible in developing call frequencies. However, they can establish a minimum number of times each year they want to call on the various classes of accounts. For example, the salesperson determines the frequency of calls for each class of account in the territory, as shown in Table 14.3, where all but the small account are contracted once a month.

Typically, the sales person invests sales time in direct proportion to the actual or potential sales that the account represents. The most productive number of calls is reached at the point where additional calls do not increase sales. This relationship of sales volume to sales calls is the **sales response function** of the customer to the salesperson's calls.

Return on Time Invested.   Time is a scarce resource. To be successful, the salesperson uses time effectively to improve territory productivity. In terms of time, costs must also be accounted for. That is, what is the cost both in time and money of an average sales call?

Break–even analysis determines how much sales volume a salesperson must generate to meet costs in a territory. The difference between cost of goods sold and sales is the gross profit on sales revenue. Gross profit should be large enough to cover selling expenses. A territory's break–even point is computed in terms of dollars with this formula:

$$\frac{\text{Break-even point}}{\text{(in dollars)}} = \frac{\text{Salesperson's fixed costs}}{\text{Gross profit percentage}}$$

To illustrate the formula, let us use the values shown here for sales and costs, with gross profit being the difference between sales revenue of a salesperson and costs of goods sold in the territory, expressed as a ratio of gross profit to gross sales in percentage form:

Sales	$200,000
Cost of goods sold	− 140,000
Gross profit	$ 60,000
Gross profit (percentage)	(60,000 ÷ 200,000), or 30 percent

Assume the salesperson's direct costs are as follows:

Salary	$20,000
Transportation	4,000
Expenses	5,000
Direct costs	$29,000

and substitute in the formula:

$$\text{BEP} = \frac{\$29,000}{.30} = \$96,667$$

If the salesperson sells $96,667 worth of merchandise, it exactly covers the territory's direct costs. A sales volume of $96,667 means that the sales person produces a gross margin of 30 percent, or $29,000. Sales over $96,667 contribute to profit.

TABLE 14.3 Account time allocation by salesperson

Customer Size	Calls per Month	Calls per Year	Number of Accounts	=	Number of Calls per Year
Extra large	1	12	2		24
Large	1	12	28		336
Medium	1	12	56		672
Small	1 every 3 months	4	78		312
Total			164		1,344

Assume that the salesperson works 46 out of 52 weeks (considering time off for vacations, holidays, and illness) or 230 days each year; also assume a five-day week, and an eight-hour day in which six calls are made. There are 1,840 working hours per year and 1,380 sales calls (230 × 6 calls) made each year in the territory. To determine a salesperson's cost per hour, divide direct costs ($29,000) by yearly hours worked (1,840 hours). The cost per hour equals $15.76. The break-even volume per hour is as follows:

$$\begin{array}{l} \text{Break-even} \\ \text{volume} \\ \text{per hour} \end{array} = \frac{\text{Cost per hour}}{\text{Gross profit percentage}} = \frac{\$15.76}{.30} = \$52.53$$

Thus, the salesperson must sell an average of $52.53 an hour in goods or services to break even in the territory. Carrying this logic further, the salesperson must sell an average of $420.24 each day or $70.04 each sales call to break even.

This simple arithmetic shows that a sales territory is a cost- and revenue-generating profit center, and because it is, priorities must be established on account calls to maximize territory profits.

The Management of Time. "Time is money" is a popular saying that applies to our discussion because of the costs and revenue generated by the individual salesperson. This is particularly evident with a commission salesperson. This salesperson is a territory manager who has the responsibility of managing time wisely to maximize territorial profits. Thus, the effective salesperson consistently uses time well. How does the effective salesperson manage time?

Plan by the Day, Week, and Month. Many salespeople develop daily, weekly, and monthly call plans, or general guidelines of customers and geographical areas to be covered. The salesperson may use them to make appointments with customers in advance, to arrange hotel accommodations, and so forth. Weekly plans are more specific, and include the specific days that customers will be called on. Daily planning starts the night before as the salesperson selects the next day's prospects, determines the time to

TABLE 14.4 Daily customer plans

| Hours | Sales Calls | | | Service |
	Customers	Prospects	Customers
7:00– 8:00 A.M	Go by office; pick up order for Jones Hardware		
8:00– 9:00	Travel		
9:00–10:00	Zip Grocery		
10:00–11:00	Ling Television Corp.		
11:00–12:00	Ling Television Corp.		
12:00– 1:00 P.M.	Lunch and delivery to Jones Hardware		
1:00– 2:00	Texas Instruments		
2:00– 3:00		Ace Equipment	
3:00– 4:00	Travel		
4:00– 5:00			Trailor Mfg.
5:00– 6:00	Plan next day—do paper work		

contact the customer, organizes facts and data, and prepares sales presentation materials. Table 14.4 is an illustration of a daily plan, and Figure 14.5 shows that location of each account and the sequence of calls.

"It's been said," says Terry Fingerhut, "21 days make a habit—good or bad. In three weeks, the results of the work I did or didn't do today will show up. If I spent my time well, three weeks from today I'll have positive results. If I wasted my time, three weeks from today I'll have negative results. The conclusion—each day, every day, produce *now* at your best. In three weeks and every week thereafter you'll have a string of truly positive results." (See Figure 14.6.)

Qualify the Prospect. The salesperson must be sure that the prospect is qualified to make the purchase decision, and determine whether sales to this account are large enough to allow for an adequate return on time invested. If not, do not call on the prospect.

Use Waiting Time. Have you seen salespeople waiting to see buyers? Have you ever noticed their actions? Top salespeople do not read magazines. They work while waiting, studying material about their products, completing call reports, or organizing material for the sales presentation. Also, they quickly determine whether buyers they wait for will be free in a reasonable time. If not, they contact other customers.

Have a Productive Lunchtime. Salespeople often take prospects to lunch. However, the results of one study show that the business lunch does not lead directly to a sale, but to the buyer and seller knowing each other better, building confidence and trust. In turn, this may lead to sales in the long run.[7]

FIGURE 14.5 Example of a salesperson's daily customer plans

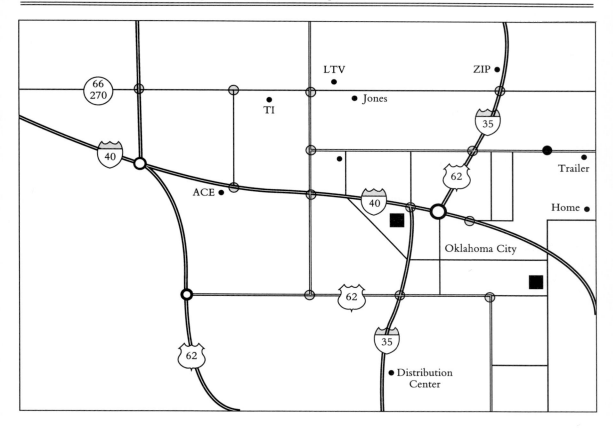

During a business lunch, salespeople must keep an eye on the clock and not monopolize too much of the buyers' time. They should not have a lunchtime cocktail. While it may seem customary to have a drink at lunch, the salesperson may be less alert in the afternoon as a result. In fact, in some companies, a luncheon cocktail is against company policy. A salesperson's lunch is time to review activities and further plan the afternoon. It is a time to relax and start "psyching up" for a productive selling afternoon.

Records and Reports. Records and reports are a written history of sales and of the salesperson's activities. Effective salespeople do paperwork during nonselling times; evenings are best. Many companies note these records and reports in performance evaluations of salespeople. However, paperwork should be held to a minimum by the company and kept current by the salesperson.

FIGURE 14.6 Time management is a key to the Fingerhut's success

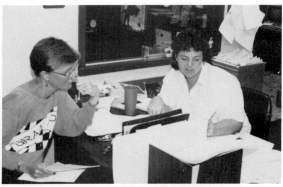

• *Careful planning is needed for running the business . . .*

• *. . . training salespeople . . .*

• *. . . recruiting successful salespeople and . . .*

• *. . . conducting sales meetings.*

Customer Sales Planning

The fifth major element of time and territorial management is developing a sales call objective, a customer profile, and a customer benefit program, including selling strategies for individual customers.* You have a quota to meet, have made your account analysis, have set account objectives and have established the time you will devote to each customer; now, develop a sales plan for each customer.

---

*Refer to Chapter 6 for further discussion of customer sales planning.

Scheduling and Routing

The sixth element of time and territory management is scheduling sales calls and planning movement around the sales territory.

Scheduling refers to establishing a fixed time (day and hour) for visiting a customer's business. **Routing** is the travel pattern used in working a territory. Some sales organizations prefer to determine the formal path or route that their salespeople travel when covering their territory. In such cases, management must develop plans that are feasible, flexible, and profitable to the company and the individual salesperson, and satisfactory to the customer. In theory, strict formal route designs enable the company to: (1) improve territory coverage; (2) minimize wasted time; and (3) establish communications between management and the sales force in terms of the location and activities of individual salespeople.

In developing route patterns, management needs to know the salesperson's exact day and time of sales calls for each account; approximate waiting time; sales time; miscellaneous time for contacting people such as the promotional manager, checking inventory, or handling returned merchandise; and travel time between accounts. This task is difficult unless territories are small and precisely defined. Most firms allow considerable latitude in routing.

Typically, after finishing a work week, the salesperson fills out a routing report and sends it to the manager. The report states where the salespeople will work (see Table 14.5). In the example, on Friday, December 16, you are based in Dallas and plan to call on accounts in Dallas for two days during the week of December 25. Then, you plan to work in Waco for a day, spend the night, drive to Fort Worth early the next morning and make calls, and be home Thursday night. The last day of the week, you again plan to work in Dallas. The weekly route report is sent to your immediate supervisor. In this manner, management knows where you are and, if necessary, can contact you.

Some firms may ask the salesperson to specify the accounts to be called on and at what times. For example, on Monday, December 26, the salesperson may write, "Dallas, 9 A.M., Texas Instruments; Grand Prairie, 2 P.M., L.T.V." Thus, management knows where a salesperson will be and what accounts will be visited during a report period. If no overnight travel is necessary to cover a territory, the company may not require any route reports, because the salesperson can be contacted at home in the evening.[8]

Carefully Plan Your Route. At times, routing is difficult for a salesperson. Customers do not locate themselves geographically for the seller's convenience. Also, there is the increasing difficulty of traveling throughout large cities. To help, companies are selling computerized mapping systems, as

TABLE 14.5   Weekly route report

Today's Date: December 16		For Week Beginning: December 26
Date	City	Location
December 26 (Monday)	Dallas	Home
December 27 (Tuesday)	Dallas	Home
December 28 (Wednesday)	Waco	Holiday Inn/South
December 29 (Thursday)	Fort Worth	Home
December 30 (Friday)	Dallas	Home

shown in Figure 14.7. There is also the problem caused by some accounts who will see you only on certain days and hours.

In today's complex selling situation, the absence of a well-thought-out daily and weekly route plan is a recipe for disaster. It's impossible to operate successfully without it. How do you begin?

Start by locating your accounts on a large map. Mount the map on some corkboard or foamboard, which can be obtained from an office supply store or picture framing shop. Use a road map for large territories or a city map for densely populated areas. Also purchase a supply of map pins with different colored heads. Place the pins on the map so that you can see where each account is located. For example, use:

· Red pins for "extra large" **(EL)** accounts.
· Yellow pins for "large" **(L)** accounts.
· Blue pins for "medium" **(M)** accounts.
· Black pins for "small" **(S)** accounts.
· Green pins for "best prospects."

Once all pins are in place, stand back and take a look at the map. Notice first where the **"EL"** accounts are located. This will help determine your main routes, or areas where you must go most frequently.

Now divide the map into sections, keeping the same number of **"EL"** accounts in each. Of course, each section should be a "natural" geographic division, that is, the roads should be located in such a way that allows you to drive from your home base to each section, as well as travel easily once you are there. Generally, your **"L," "M,"** and **"S"** accounts will fall into place near your **"ELs,"** with a few exceptions.

For example, if you work on a monthly or four-week call schedule for **ELs,** then divide your territory into four sections, working one section each week. In this way, you will get to all **ELs** while having the flexibility needed to get to your other accounts regularly.

FIGURE 14.7   The Etak Navigator

• *The Etak Navigator is a computerized mapping system, installed in cars, that in a glance shows a salesperson the current location and the future location.*

Section 1	Section 2	Section 3	Section 4
7 **EL**	9 **EL**	5 **EL**	10 **EL**
15 **L**	12 **L**	15 **L**	15 **L**
35 **M**	25 **M**	35 **M**	25 **M**
40 **S**	35 **S**	40 **S**	36 **S**

By setting up geographical routes this way, you could call on all **EL** accounts every four weeks, half of your **L** and **M** accounts (an 8-week call cycle) and 25 percent of your **S** accounts (a 16-week call cycle). Also, allow time for calls on prospective customers, too. Use the same procedure as for regular customers. The only difference might be that prospects would be contacted less frequently than customers, in most cases.

There is no right number of sections or routes for all salespersons. It depends on the size of your territory, the geographical layout of your part of the country, and the call frequencies you want to establish. Lay out your travel route so that you can start out from home in the morning and return in the evening—or, if you have a larger territory, make it a Monday to Friday route, or a two-day (overnight) route. Remember that the critical factor is travel time, not miles. In some cases, by using major nonstop highways, your miles may increase but your total travel time may decrease.

The actual route followed each day and within each section is important to maximize your prime selling hours each day. For this reason, make long drives early in the morning and in the late afternoon, if possible. For example, if most accounts are in a straight line from your home, get up early and drive to the far end of your territory before making your first call, then work your way back, so that you end up near home at the end of the day. Figure 14.8 illustrates three ways to route yourself, including the straight-line method just mentioned.[9]

Using the Telephone for Territorial Coverage

The telephone is both a great time-waster and time-saver. It all depends on how it is used. The increasing cost of a personal sales call, and the increasing amount of time spent traveling to make personal calls, are reasons for the efficient territory manager to look to the telephone as a territory coverage tool.

With field selling costs still rising and no end in sight, more companies are developing telephone sales and marketing campaigns to supplement personal selling efforts. These campaigns utilize trained telephone communicators and well-developed telephone marketing techniques. Usually, they require a company-wide effort. Here, though, we will concentrate on how an individual territory manager can use the telephone as a tool in territory coverage to save time.

Telephone use in the individual territory may be grouped into three categories: (1) sales generating, (2) order processing, and (3) customer servicing. These are some telephone applications in each category:

1. Sales generating
   a. Selling regular orders to smaller accounts.
   b. Selling specials, such as offering a recent price decrease on an individual product.
   c. Developing leads and qualifying prospects.
2. Order processing.
   a. Telephoning the order into the warehouse.
   b. Gathering credit information.
   c. Checking whether shipments have been made.
3. Customer servicing.
   a. Handling complaints.
   b. Answering questions.

FIGURE 14.8 Examples of three basic routing patterns

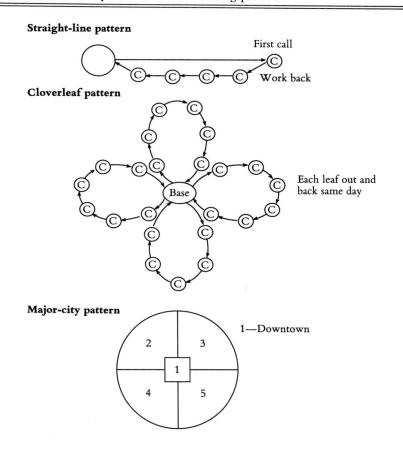

Straight-line pattern

First call

Work back

Cloverleaf pattern

Base

Each leaf out and back same day

Major-city pattern

1—Downtown

Although each salesperson has to decide which types of calls and which accounts lend themselves to telephone applications, most people benefit from adopting the following practices, as a minimum, in territory coverage:

- Satisfy part of the service needs of accounts by telephone.
- Assign smaller accounts, those that contribute less than 5 percent of business, to mostly telephone selling.
- Do prospecting, marketing data gathering, and call scheduling by telephone.
- Carefully schedule personal calls to distant accounts. If possible, replace some personal visits with telephone calls.

FIGURE 14.9   The telephone and the computer are effective selling tools

• *The telephone and computer are effective aids that keep salespeople connected to sales operations no matter where they travel.*

The telephone, coupled with the computer, are important selling tools for salespeople.[10] Many sales jobs require extensive travel. Even in airports, as shown in Figure 14.9, traveling salespeople can keep in contact with their offices, access computer files containing customer information, and record customer information.

Territory and Customer Evaluation

Territorial control is the establishment of performance standards for the individual territory in the form of qualitative and quantitative quotas or goals. Actual performance is compared to these goals for evaluation purposes. This allows the salesperson to see how well territory plans were executed in meeting performance quotas. If quotas were not met, new plans must be developed.

Many companies routinely furnish managers and individual salespeople with reports on the number of times during the year their salespeople have called on each account and the date of the last sales call. Management can monitor the frequency and time intervals between calls for each salesperson.

TABLE 14.6 Net sales by customer and call frequency: May 1, 1990

	Brown (GP, Houston)	Peterson (Pediatrics, Galveston)	Gilley (GP, Galveston)	Bruce (GP, Galveston)	Heaton (GP, Texas City)
Calls					
Month	2	1	1	0	2
Year to date	8	4	4	4	9
Last call	4/20	4/18	4/18	3/10	4/19
Net sales in dollars					
Current month	60	0	21	0	500
Year to date:					
This year	350	200	75	1,000	2,000
Last year	300	275	125	750	1,750
Entire last year	2,000	1,000	300	1,000	5,000

As an example, a national pharmaceutical company supplies its sales force with the "net sales by customer and call report" shown in Table 14.6. The report lists each customer's name, address, and medical specialty. The desired number of monthly calls on a given customer and the actual number of calls to date are noted. Net sales are broken down into last year's sales, the current month's sales, and year-to-date sales. Finally, the date the salesperson last called on each customer is reported.

Using the report, one can see that H. L. Brown is a Houston physician in a general practice. He should be called on twice a month, and for the four months that have gone by, he has been seen eight times to date. He purchased $60 worth of merchandise this month, and his purchases so far this year are $50 more than last year. He was last called on April 20 of the current year. Using this type of information, which might include 200 to 300 customers for each salesperson, management and salespeople can continually review sales call patterns and customer sales to update call frequency and scheduling.

SUMMARY OF MAJOR SELLING ISSUES

How salespeople invest their sales time is a critical factor influencing territory sales. Due to the increasing cost of direct selling, high transportation costs, and the limited resources of time, salespeople have to focus on these factors. Proper management of time and territory is an effective method for the salesperson to maximize territorial sales and profits.

A sales territory comprises a group of customers or a geographical area assigned to a salesperson. It is a segment out of the company's total market. A salesperson within a territory has to analyze the various segments, estimate sales potential, and develop a marketing mix based on the needs and desires of the marketplace.

Companies develop and use sales territories for a number of reasons. One important reason is to obtain thorough coverage of the market to fully reach sales potential. Another reason is to establish salespeople's responsibilities as territory managers.

Performance can be monitored when territories are established. A territory may also be used to improve customer relations so that customers receive regular calls from the salesperson. This also helps to reduce sales expense as duplicated effort in traveling and customer contacts is avoided. Finally, they allow better matching of salesperson to customer needs and benefit salespeople and the company.

There are also disadvantages to developing sales territories. Some salespeople may not be motivated if they feel restricted by a particular territory. Also, a company may be too small to segment its market or management may not want to take time to develop territories.

Time and territory management is continuous for a salesperson; it involves seven key elements. The first major element is establishment of the territory sales quota. The second element is account analysis, which involves identifying present and potential customers and estimating their sales potential. In analyzing these accounts, salespeople may use the undifferentiated selling approach if they view accounts as similar; or, if accounts have different characteristics, they use the account segmentation approach.

Developing objectives and sales quotas for individual accounts is the third element. How salespeople allocate time in their territories is another key element. Salespeople have to manage time, plan schedules, and use all spare time effectively.

The fifth element of time and territorial management is developing a sales call objective, profile, benefit program, and selling strategies for individual customers. Salespeople have to learn everything they can about customers and maintain records on each one. Once this is done, they can create the proper selling strategies to meet customers' needs.

Another major element is scheduling the sales calls at specific times and places and routing the salesperson's movement and travel pattern around the territory. Finally, objectives and quotas that were established are used to determine how effectively the salesperson performs. Actual performance is compared to these standards for evaluation purposes.

15

Social, Ethical, and Legal Issues in Selling

After completing my nursing education at Jameson Memorial Hospital in New Castle, Pennsylvania, and the University of Pittsburgh, I was a clinical instructor in pediatric nursing at Pittsburgh Children's Hospital and later a head nurse of the pediatrics department in a Florida hospital. Although happy with nursing, I decided to pursue a career in sales because of more opportunities, advancement, and challenge.

Sandra Snow
The Upjohn Company

Initially my job was calling on the physicians, hospitals, and drugstores in a general sales territory. After 3½ years, I was promoted to hospital sales specialist, responsible for three large hospitals and the University of Miami School of Medicine in Miami, Florida. In January 1983, I was promoted to a general sales district manager's position responsible for 14 people and $10 million in sales. In January 1985, I became sales manager for one of Upjohn's medical specialty representative groups; then in August 1986, I was moved into the home office as part of our professional training and development group.

It is imperative that I am knowledgeable not only about our products but also about the disease entities that our drugs treat. I have an obligation to provide this information in an honest and ethical way. Since we may alter the prescribing habits of physicians, it is important that they know not only the benefits of our products, but also the risks. Human health care is not an area where deceptive selling techniques can be used in any way.

I also have an obligation to the company to conduct myself in a professional manner while increasing sales. There is significant government regulation of the pharmaceutical industry and unethical practices by a salesperson reflect not only on that salesperson, but on the company for which he or she works, and the industry as a whole. Fortunately, I work for a company that is research-oriented and prides itself on having a knowledgeable sales force. We are constantly learning new things about old drugs, as well as preparing for the introduction of new products. •

"Even though it is a salesperson's job to inform, I feel that we are more effective salespeople if we establish a dialogue with physicians and find out their feelings and experiences with our products, rather than being didactic," said Sandra Snow of the Upjohn Company. "It is also important to disseminate this information to pharmacists and nursing personnel via a one-on-one discussion or a continuing education program for a small group. The pharmacist and nurse may not prescribe therapy, but they may pick up both drug toxicity and/or failure." •

As you see from Sandra Snow's comments, she is convinced of the need to be honest, ethical, and to act as a professional salesperson. This chapter addresses many of the important social, ethical, and legal issues in selling. We begin by defining the term *social responsibility* and discuss six reasons why firms want sales personnel to act responsibly. Then, we examine ethical issues involved in dealing with salespeople, employers, and customers. We end the chapter by presenting ways a company can help its sales personnel follow ethical selling practices.

THE SOCIAL RESPONSIBILITY OF BUSINESS

Social responsibility in business refers to profitably serving employees and customers in an ethical and lawful manner. This definition involves the individual salesperson, implying that the salesperson is an important resource in the firm and must be treated responsibly, just as it states that a salesperson must treat customers in an ethical manner.

Quite often, corporations operate solely to maximize profits. Certainly profits are important to a firm, just as a grade point average is important to a student. Profit provides the capital to stay in business, to expand, and to compensate for the risks of conducting business. There is a responsibility to make a profit to serve society.[1] Imagine what would happen to our society if large corporations (e.g., AT&T, General Motors) did not make a profit and went out of business. Thousands of people and the U.S. economy would be affected.

Sales managers and salespeople are occasionally accused of obtaining sales in any manner possible. The temptations to make sales at any cost are curbed both by laws designed to penalize wrongdoers and by the new professionalism of individuals selecting sales as a career. Let's briefly examine why business today must continue to act in a responsible manner and then review how managers view ethics.

Why Assume Social Responsibilities?

There are numerous reasons why a business must assume social responsibilities; six of the major reasons are:

1. It is expected by society.
2. It allows the business to operate better in the long run.
3. It shows community responsibility.
4. Salespeople are company representatives.
5. It minimizes competitors' retaliation.
6. It decreases government intervention.

Social Expectation. Sales managers must understand that they are in business to serve customers profitably and responsibly. Sales practices must not conflict with the interests of society. As the company grows, it increases its power in the industry and is expected to assume greater social responsibilities. This is the power–responsibility equation.

Better Operations in the Long Run. If the sales force works totally for short-run goals, irresponsible selling practices often result.[2] At the corporate level, executives view the firm as existing to make a profit in the long run, but sales personnel have trouble with this because they typically work in the short run. They have monthly, quarterly, and yearly sales goals that may create pressures to make the sale at any cost.

Sales executives must continually monitor their sales units to minimize the temptations to use unethical and illegal sales practices. Pressure on sales personnel must be kept at a reasonable level that allows them to use responsible selling techniques. High pressure to increase sales helps to force salespersons to make the sale no matter what. This is especially true if managers openly suggest or overlook unethical sales practices. Sales may increase in the short run, but in time, customers catch on and sales decrease.

Community Responsibility. Sales managers and their salespeople often participate in community activities and organizations. This includes working with groups such as the Lions Club, United Way, environmental work, and scouting. Many salespeople are also active in their industry's trade associations.

Salespeople as Company Representatives. Would you want salespeople giving kickbacks or cheating customers? Certainly not, because salespeople reflect the the company's image and, after a time, customers might expect all of the company's salespeople to act that way. Buyers could expect kickbacks before doing business with the company. Both actions are costly to the company, and sales managers cannot take the position of "Hear no

MAKING THE SALE

Assuming Community Responsibility

"One of the legacies we took from the Bell System philosophy," says AT&T's Bill Frost, "is being a visible community supporter in arts, education, health services, and civic and community clubs and organizations. We must be a strong corporate supporter of the communities in which we live and work. Beyond the obvious good of being a strong business partner in the community, it offers excellent opportunities for networking.

"It leaves a good feeling in a customer's mind to recall what AT&T has done for the community. When that customer is approached by competitors, one of the things in memory might be what AT&T has done in the public arena versus what the competition has done, and that memory again proves our value to the community—and by extension, to the customer.

"This entire positioning process is our biggest challenge. At divestiture, we explained it by calling AT&T the 'oldest new company in history.' For so many years, the Bell operating companies were the number one community leaders while AT&T itself took a back seat.

"We've been talking about information movement and management for years, and we're finally there. It is very important for AT&T to become the number one vendor in that arena and associating our name with quality organizations and events is one way to get there."

evil, see no evil, speak no evil." They must oversee the sales practices of their personnel so that the pressure of reaching sale quotas does not lead to unethical sales practices.

Minimizing Competitors' Retaliation. Often, in competitive industries, if one company decreases prices, others follow. The same thing happens when a company uses unethical practices. Maintaining ethical standards can cause competitors to do the same.

Decreasing Government Intervention. Sales managers prefer not to have the government intervene in their activities; but over the years, the business community has not acted totally responsibly. Consequently, government regulation has increased. To make government intervention less necessary, sales managers must develop a code of ethics and help govern their companies' sales practices. There are numerous ways a corporation can demonstrate social responsibility. Table 15.1 show actions that can be taken by all firms.[3]

How Managers View Ethics

Ethics are principles of right or good conduct, or a body of such principles, that affect good and bad business practices. Ethical principles govern the conduct of an individual or group. Over the years, surveys have determined managers' views of business ethics. In general, they have found the following:

TABLE 15.1   Ten actions a corporation can take to demonstrate social
responsibility

1. Take corrective action before it is required.
2. Work with affected constituents to resolve mutual problems.
3. Work to establish industrywide standards and self-regulation.
4. Publicly admit your mistakes.
5. Get involved in appropriate social programs.
6. Help correct environmental problems.
7. Monitor the changing social environment.
8. Establish and enforce a corporate code of conduct.
9. Take needed public stands on social issues.
10. Strive to make profits on an ongoing basis.

- All managers face ethical problems.
- Most managers feel they and their employers should be more ethical.
- Managers are more ethical with friends than with people they do not know.
- Even though they want to be more ethical, some managers lower their ethical standards to meet job goals.
- Managers are aware of unethical practices in their industry and company ranging from price discrimination to hiring discrimination.
- Business ethics can be influenced by an employee's superior and company environment.

The remainder of this chapter discusses some situations that may arise requiring managers and salespeople to search their consciences. It cannot be all-inclusive, but it is an attempt to give a feel for some difficult decisions faced by salespeople.[4]

ETHICS IN DEALING WITH SALESPEOPLE

Sales managers have both social and ethical responsibilities to sales personnel.[6] Salespeople are a valuable resource; they are recruited, carefully trained, and given important responsibility. They represent a large financial investment and must be treated in a professional manner. Yet, occasionally, a company may place managers and/or salespeople in positions that force them to choose between compromising their ethics, not doing what is required, or leaving the organization. The choice depends on the magnitude of the situation. At times, situations arise in which it is difficult to say whether a sales practice is ethical or unethical. Many sales practices are in the gray area, somewhere between completely ethical and completely unethical. Five ethical considerations faced by the sales manager are the level

MAKING THE SALE

Keep Your Sense of Humor

"It was my first call as a district manager in Washington, D.C.," says Alan Lesk, senior vice president, sales and merchandising, Maidenform. "One of the major department stores was not doing a lot of business with Maidenform, and we were looking to get some more penetration in the market. Surprisingly, the sale took only two sales calls.

"The first person I approached was a buyer. He was completely uncooperative. On the way out of the store, I popped my head into his boss's office and we set up a meeting with some higher level executives later in the week.

"So there I was, a young kid facing a committee of nine tough executives, and I had to make my presentation. I was in the middle of my pitch when the executive vice president stopped me. He told me that this was going to be a big program, about $500,000, and asked me point blank, how much of a rebate I was willing to give him to do business with their store, over and above the normal things like co-op ad money. He was actually asking me for money under the table!

"I had to make a decision fast. I stood up and said, 'If this is what it takes to do business here, I don't want anything to do with it.' I then turned to walk out the door, and the guy started cracking up. I guess he was just testing me to see what lengths I'd go to in order to get my sales program into the store.

"This one incident taught me some very important things: You can't compromise your integrity, and you can't let people intimidate you. Most importantly, don't lose your sense of humor. Needless to say, we got the program into the store, and today, we do more than $2 million of business a year with them."[5]

of sales pressure to place on a salesperson; decisions concerning a salesperson's territory; whether or not to be honest with the salesperson; what to do with the ill salesperson; and employee rights.

Level of Sales Pressure

What is an acceptable level of pressure to place on salespeople? Should managers establish performance goals that they know a salesperson has only a 50–50 chance of attaining? Should the manager acknowledge that goals were set too high? If circumstances change in the salesperson's territory—for example, a large customer goes out of business—should the manager lower sales goals?

These are questions all managers must consider. There are no right or wrong answers. Managers are responsible for group goals. There is a natural tendency to place pressure on salespeople so that the managers' goals are reached. Some managers motivate their people to produce at high levels without applying pressure, while others place tremendous pressure on salespeople to attain sales beyond quotas. However, managers should set realistic and obtainable goals. They must consider individual territory situations. If this is done fairly, and sales are still down, then pressure may be applied.

Decisions Affecting Territory

Management makes decisions that affect sales territories and salespeople. For example, the company might increase the number of sales territories, which often necessitates splitting up a single territory. A salesperson has spent years building the territory to its current sales volume. Customers are taken away. If the salesperson has worked on a commission basis, this would mean a decrease in earnings.

Consider a situation of reducing the number of sales territories. What procedures do you use? Several years ago a large manufacturer of health and beauty aids (shaving cream, toothpaste, shampoo) reduced the number of territories to lower selling costs. So, for example, three territories became two. Here is how one of their salespeople described it:

> I made my plane reservation to fly from Dallas to Florida for our annual national meeting. Beforehand, I was told to bring my records up to date and bring them to the regional office in Dallas; don't fly, drive to Dallas. I drove from Louisiana to Dallas with my bags packed to go to the national meeting. I walked into the office with my records under my arm. My district and regional managers were there. They told me of the reorganization and said I was fired. They asked for my car keys. I called my wife, told her what happened and then caught a bus back home. There were five of us in the region that were called in that day. Oh, they gave us a good job recommendation—it's just the way we were treated. Some people had been with the company for five years or more. They didn't go by tenure, but by where territories were located.

Companies must deal with the individual in a fair and straightforward manner. It would have been better for the managers of these salespeople to go to their hometowns and personally explain the changes. Instead, they treated the salespeople unprofessionally.

One decision affecting a territory is what to do with extra large customers, sometimes called key accounts. Are they taken away from the salesperson and made into **house accounts?** Here, responsibility for contacting the account rests with someone from the home office (house) or a key account salesperson. The local salesperson may not get credit for sales to this customer even though the customer is in the salesperson's territory. A salesperson states the problem:

> I've been with the company 35 years. When I first began, I called on some people who had one grocery store. Today, they have 208. The buyer knows me. He buys all of my regular and special greeting cards. They do whatever I ask. I made $22,000 in commissions from their sales last year. Now, management wants to make it a house account.

Here, the salesperson loses money. It is difficult to treat the salesperson fairly in this situation. The company does not want to pay large commissions and 90 percent of the 208 stores are located out of the salesperson's territory. They should carefully explain this to the salesperson. Instead of taking the full $22,000 away from the salesperson, they could pay a 20 percent commission as a reward for building up the account.

To Tell the Truth?

Should salespeople be told they are not promotable, that they are marginal performers, or that they are transferred to the poorest territory in the company so that they will quit? Good judgment must prevail. Sales managers prefer to tell the truth.

Do you tell the truth when you fire a salesperson? If a fired employee has tried and has been honest, many sales managers will tell prospective employers that the person quit voluntarily rather than being fired. One manager put it this way: "I feel she can do a good job for another company. I don't want to hurt her future."

The Ill Salesperson

How much help do you give to an alcoholic, drug addicted, or physically or mentally ill salesperson? Many companies require salespeople to seek professional help for alcohol or drug abuse. If they improve, companies offer support and keep them in the field. Yet, there is only so far the company can go. The firm cannot have an intoxicated or "high" salesperson calling on customers. Once the illness has a negative effect on business, the salesperson is taken out of the territory. Sick leave and workers' compensation will cover expenses until the salesperson recovers. The manager who shows a sincere, personal interest in helping the ill salesperson greatly contributes to the person's chances of recovery.

Employee Rights

The sales manager must be current on ethical and legal considerations regarding employee rights, and develop strategies for their organizations in addressing employee rights. Below are several important questions that all managers should know how to answer:

- Under what conditions can an organization fire sales personnel without committing a legal violation?
- What rights do and should sales personnel have regarding the privacy of their employment records and access to them?
- What can organizations do to prevent sexual and racial harassment in the workplace?

Employee rights are rights desired by employees regarding the security of jobs and the treatment administered by their employer while on the job, irrespective of whether or not those rights are currently protected by law or collective bargaining agreements of labor unions. Let's briefly examine these three questions.

Termination-at-Will.   Early in this century, many courts were adamant in strictly applying the common law rule to terminate-at-will. For example, the termination-at-will rule was used in a 1903 case, *Boyer* v. *Western Union Tel. Co.* [124 F 246, CCED Mo. (1903)], in which the court upheld the company's right to discharge its employees for union activities and indicated that the results would be the same if the company's employees were discharged for being Presbyterians.

Later on, in *Lewis* v. *Minnesota Mutual Life Ins. Co.* [37 NW 2d 316 (1949)], the termination-at-will rule was used to uphold the dismissal of the life insurance company's best salesperson—even though no apparent cause for dismissal was given and the company had promised the employee lifetime employment in return for his agreement to remain with the company.

In the early 1980s, court decisions and legislative enactments moved the pendulum of protection away from the employer and toward the rights of the individual employee through limitations on the termination-at-will rule.[7]

Although many employers claim that their rights have been taken away, they still retain the right to terminate sales personnel for poor performance, excessive absenteeism, unsafe conduct, and poor organizational citizenship. It is critical, however, for employers to maintain accurate records of these events for employees, and to inform employees on where they stand. To be safe, it is also advisable for employers to have a grievance process for employees to ensure that due process is respected. These practices are particularly useful in discharge situations that involve members of groups protected by Title VII, the Rehabilitation Act, or the Vietnam Era Veterans Act.

Privacy.   Today it is more important than ever to keep objective and orderly personnel files. They are critical evidence that employers have treated their employees fairly, with respect, and have not violated any laws. Without these files, organizations may get caught on the short end of a lawsuit.

Although there are several federal laws that influence recordkeeping, they are primarily directed at public employers. However, many private employers are moving on their own to give employees the right to access their personnel files and to prohibit the file information from being given to others without their consent. In addition, employers are casting out of their personnel files any nonjob-related information and ending hiring practices that solicit such information.

Cooperative Acceptance. The category of cooperative acceptance refers to the right of employees to be treated fairly and with respect regardless of race, sex, national origin, physical disability, age, or religion while on the job (as well as in obtaining a job and maintaining job security). Not only does this mean that employees have the right to not be discriminated against in· employment practices and decisions, but it also means that employees have the right to be free of sexual and racial harassment.

Today, the right to not be discriminated against is generally protected under Title VII, the Age Discrimination in Employment Act, the Rehabilitation Act, the Vietnam Era Veterans Readjustment Assistance Act, and numerous court decisions and state and local government laws. Through the right to be free of sexual harassment is found explicitly in fewer laws, it has been made a part of the 1980 EEOC guidelines, which state that sexual harassment is a form of sex discrimination. The equating of sexual harassment as a form of sex discrimination under Title VII is also found in numerous court decisions.

It is necessary for employers to prevent sexual harassment. This can be done with top management support, grievance procedures, verification procedures, training for all employees, and performance appraisal and compensation policies that reward persons who practice anti-harassment behavior and punish persons who do not.

Companies realize that sexual harassment can be expensive. For example, in a landmark decision, a federal judge in Madison, Wisconsin, approved a damages award of $196,500 to a man who said he was demoted because he resisted the sexual advances of his female supervisor. This was the first time a man ever won a sexual harassment case against a woman. The man also received $7,913 in back pay and $21,726 in attorney's fees, in addition to the damages award approved by U.S. Judge John Shabaz.[8]

Companies must recognize that there are important strategic purposes served by respecting employee rights. The main ones are:

- Providing a high quality of work life.
- Attracting and retaining good sales personnel. This makes recruitment and selection more effective and less frequent.
- Avoiding costly back pay awards and fines.
- Establishing a match between employee rights and obligations and employer rights and obligations.

Here, both organizations and employees benefit. Organizations benefit from reduced legal costs, since not observing employee rights is illegal, and their image as a good employer increases, resulting in enhanced organizational attractiveness. This makes it easier for the organization to recruit a pool of potentially qualified applicants. And although it is suggested that expanded employee rights, especially job security, may reduce needed management flexibility, and thus profitability, it may be an impetus for better planning, which results in increased profitability.

Increased profitability may also result from the benefits employees receive when their rights are observed; employees may experience feelings of being treated fairly and with respect, increased self-esteem, and a heightened sense of job security. Employees who have job security may be more productive and committed to the organization than those without job security. As employees begin to see the guarantees of job security as a benefit, organizations also gain through reduced wage increase demands and greater flexibility in job assignments.

ARE THESE SOCIALLY RESPONSIBLE ACTIONS?

Often, it is difficult to determine whether actions taken by sales executives are for profit or social motives. For example, take the following:

- Training and educational programs for salespeople.
- A company heavily dependent on government contracts hiring minority group members.
- Setting fair sales goals.
- Fairly rewarding salespeople's performance.
- Paying salaries above industry averages.
- Providing extensive medical and life insurance coverage.
- Holding sales meetings in resort areas.

Some people argue that these are responsible acts done unselfishly, while others say that these are good business practices that help maximize a firm's sales and profits. These are examples of good business practices implemented in a responsible manner. No longer can the sales function occur in anything other than a manner that is fair to salespeople, customers, and society.

SALESPEOPLE'S ETHICS IN DEALING WITH THEIR EMPLOYERS

Salespeople, as well as sales managers, may occasionally be involved in misusing company assets, moonlighting, or cheating; such unethical practices can affect co-workers.

Misusing Company Assets

Company assets that are most often misused are automobiles, expense accounts, samples, and damaged merchandise credits. All can be used for personal gain or as bribes and kickbacks to customers. For example, a credit for damaged merchandise can be given to a customer when there has been no damage, or valuable product samples can be given to a customer.

Moonlighting

Salespeople are not closely supervised and, consequently, they may be tempted to take a second job, perhaps on company time. Some salespeople attend college on company time. For example, a salesperson may enroll in an evening MBA program but take off in the early afternoon to prepare for class.

Cheating

A salesperson may not play fair in contests. If a contest starts in July, the salesperson may not turn in sales orders for the end of June and lump them with July sales. Some might arrange, with or without the customer's permission, to ship merchandise that is not needed or really wanted. The merchandise is held until payment is due and then returned to the company after the contest is over. The salesperson may also overload the customer to win the contest.

Affecting Other Salespeople

Often, the unethical practices of one salesperson can affect other salespeople within the company. Someone who cheats in winning a contest is taking money and prizes from other salespeople. A salesperson also may not split commissions with, or take customers away from, co-workers.

ETHICS IN DEALING WITH CUSTOMERS

Numerous ethical situations may arise in dealing with customers. Some common problems are discussed below.

Bribes

A salesperson may attempt to bribe a buyer. Money, gifts, entertainment, and travel opportunities may be offered. At times, there is a thin line between good business and misusing a bribe or gift. A $10 gift to a $10,000 customer may be merely a gift, but how do we define a $1,000 gift for a $1 million customer? Many companies forbid their buyers to take gifts of any size from salespeople. However, bribery does exist. The U.S. Chamber of Commerce estimates that, of the annual $40 billion in "white collar crime," bribes and kickbacks account for $7 billion.[9]

Buyers may ask for cash, merchandise, or travel payment in return for placing an order with the salesperson. Imagine that you are a salesperson working on 5 percent straight commission. The buyer says, "I'm ready to place a $20,000 order for office supplies with you. However, another salesperson has offered to pay my expenses for a weekend in Las Vegas in exchange for my business. You know, $500 tax-free is a lot of money." You quickly calculate that your commission is $1,000. You still make $500. It could be hard to pass up that $500.[10]

Misrepresentation

Today, even casual misstatements by salespeople can put a company on the wrong side of the law. Most salespeople are unaware that they assume legal obligations—with accompanying risks and responsibilities—every time they approach a customer. However, we all know that salespeople sometimes "oversell." They exaggerate the capabilities of their products or services and sometimes make false statements just to close a sale.

Often, buyers depend heavily on the technical knowledge of salespeople, along with their professional integrity. Yet, sales managers and staff find it difficult to know just how far they can go with well-intentioned sales talk, personal opinion, and promises. They do not realize that by using certain statements, they can embroil their companies in a lawsuit and ruin the very business relationship they are trying to establish.

When a customer relies on a salesperson's statements, purchases the product or service, and then finds that it fails to perform as promised, the supplier can be sued for misrepresentation and breach of warranty. Companies around the United States have been liable for million-dollar judgments for making such mistakes, particularly when their salespeople sold high-ticket, hi-tech products or services.

You can avoid such mistakes, however, if you're aware of the law of misrepresentation and breaches of warranty relative to the selling function, and follow strategies that keep you and your company out of trouble. Salespeople must understand the difference between "sales puff" (opinions) and statements of fact, and the legal ramifications of both. There are preventive steps for salespeople to follow; they must work closely with management to avoid time-consuming delays and costly legal fees.

What the Law Says. Misrepresentation and breach of warranty are two legal causes of action; that is, theories on which an injured party seeks damages. These two theories differ in terms of the proof required and the type of damages awarded by a judge or jury. However, both arise in the selling context and are treated similarly for our purposes. Both typically arise when a salesperson makes erroneous statements or offers false promises regarding a product's characteristics and capabilities.

Not all statements have legal consequences, however. When sales personnel loosely describe their product or service in glowing terms ("Our service can't be beat; it's the best around"), such statements are viewed as "opinions" and generally cannot be relied on by a customer, supplier, or wholesaler. Thus, a standard defense used by lawyers in misrepresentation and breach of warranty lawsuits is that a purchaser cannot rely on a salesperson's puffery because it's unreasonable to take these remarks at face value.

But, when a salesperson makes claims or promises of a "factual nature" regarding a product's or service's inherent capabilities (that is, the results, profits, or savings that will be achieved, what it will do for a customer, how it will perform, etc.), the law treats these comments as statements of fact and warranties.

There is a subtle difference between sales puffery and statements of fact; they can be difficult to distinguish. No particular form of words is necessary; each case is analyzed according to its circumstances. Generally, the less knowledgeable the customer, the greater the chances that the court will interpret a statement as actionable. The following is an actual recent case and illustrates this point:

> An independent sales rep sold heavy industrial equipment. He went to a purchaser's construction site, observed his operations, then told the president of the company that his proposed equipment would 'keep up with any other machine then being used,' and that it would 'work well in cooperation with the customer's other machines and equipment.'
>
> The customer informed the rep that he was not personally knowledgeable about the kind of equipment the rep was selling, and that he needed time to study the rep's report. Several weeks later, he bought the equipment based on the rep's recommendations.
>
> After a few months, he sued the rep's company, claiming that the equipment didn't perform according to the representations in sales literature sent prior to the execution of the contract and to statements made by the rep at the time of the sale. The equipment manufacturer defended itself by arguing that the statements made by the rep were nonactionable opinions made innocently by the rep, in good faith, with no intent to deceive the purchaser.
>
> The court ruled in favor of the customer, finding that the rep's statements were "predictions" of how the equipment would perform; this made them more than mere sales talk. The rep was held responsible for knowing the capabilities of the equipment he was selling, so his assertions were deemed statements of fact, not opinions. Furthermore, the court stated that it was unfair that a knowledgeable salesperson would take advantage of a naive purchaser.

Suggestions for Staying Legal. The following suggestions cover ways that management and sales staff can work together to minimize exposure to costly misrepresentation and breach of warranty lawsuits. Salespeople must always do the following:

1. Understand the distinction between general statements of praise and statements of fact made during the sales pitch (and the legal consequences). For example, the following statements, taken from actual cases, were made by salespeople and were determined legally actionable as statement of fact:

- "This refrigerator will preserve foods in the warmest weather."
- "This tractor has live power-take-off features."
- "Feel free to prescribe this drug to your patients, doctor. It's nonaddicting."
- "This mace pen is capable of instantaneous incapacitation for a period of 15 to 20 minutes."
- "This is a safe, dependable helicopter."

2. Thoroughly educate all customers before making a sale. Salespeople should tell as much about the specific qualities of the product as possible. The reason is that when a salesperson makes statements about a product in a field in which his or her company has extensive experience, the law makes it difficult for the salesperson to claim it was just sales talk.

This is especially true for products or services sold in highly specialized areas to unsophisticated purchasers who rely entirely on the technical expertise of the salesperson. However, if the salesperson deals with a customer experienced in the trade, courts are less likely to find that the salesperson offered an expressed warranty, since a knowledgeable buyer has a duty to look beyond the assertions of a salesperson and investigate the product individually.

3. Be accurate when describing a product's capabilities. Avoid making speculative claims, particularly with respect to predictions concerning what a product will do.

4. Know the technical specifications of the product. Review all promotional literature to ensure that there are no exaggerated claims. Keep abreast of all design changes as well.

5. Avoid making exaggerated claims about product safety. The law usually takes a dim view of such affirmative claims, and these remarks can be interpreted as warranties that lead to liability.

For example, the Minnesota Court of Appeals recently ruled that a salesperson's assurances that a used car had a rebuilt carburetor and was a "good runner" constituted an expressed warranty of the vehicle's condition. Someone had bought the car based on the salesperson's assurance of its good quality. The carburetor jammed, causing the car to smash into a tree, injuring the purchaser, who recovered sizable damages.

6. Know federal and state laws regarding warranties and guarantees.

7. Know the capabilities and characteristics of your products and services.

8. Keep current on all design changes and revisions in your product's operating manual.

9. Avoid offering opinions when the customer asks what results a product or service will accomplish unless the company has tested the product and has statistical evidence.

Statements such as, "This will reduce your inventory backlog by 40 percent" can get the company in trouble if the system fails to achieve the promised results. Stay away from that kind of statement.

If you don't know the answer to a customer's question, don't lead her on. Tell her you don't know the answer but will get back to her promptly with the information.

10. Never overstep authority, especially when discussing prices or company policy. Remember, a salesperson's statements can bind the company.

One final point: it's generally easy for customers to recover damages on the grounds of misrepresentation and breach of warranty. In many states, this holds even when a salesperson's statement is made innocently.[11]

Price Discrimination

Some customers may be given price reductions and promotional allowances and support, while others are not, even though under certain circumstances, this is in violation of the **Robinson–Patman Act of 1936.** The act allows sellers to grant what are called quantity discounts to larger buyers based on savings in the cost of manufacturing.

Individual salespeople or managers may practice **price discrimination** to improve sales. However, this can be illegal if it injures or reduces competition.

Tie-In Sales

In order to buy a particular line of merchandise, a buyer may be required to buy other products that are not wanted. This is called a **tie-in sale** and is prohibited under the **Clayton Act** when it substantially lessens competition. Yet, the individual salesperson or manager can do this. For example, the salesperson of a popular line of cosmetics tells the buyer, "I have a limited supply of the merchandise you want. If all of your 27 stores will display, advertise, and push my total line, I may be able to supply you. That means you'll need 10 items you have never purchased before." Is this good business? It's illegal!

MAKING THE SALE

Conflict of Interest ???

The real estate salesperson assured the young couple that she would work hard to find them the right house. "Consider me your scout," she said. "I'll find you the best house for the least money." The couple was reassured, and on the way home they talked about their good fortune. They had a salesperson working just for them. With prices so high, it was nice to think they had professional help on their side.

The family selling the house felt the same way. They carefully chose the broker because, they observed, with home prices all over the lot these days they hoped a good salesperson might win them several thousand dollars more. They had another reason to choose carefully: At today's prices, the 6 percent sales commission is a lot of money. "If we have to pay it," they reasoned, "we're better off paying it to the best salesperson."

It happens all the time, and it can have serious consequences. How can both parties expect the best deal? How can a salesperson promise the seller the most for the money and then make the same promise to the buyer?

In the same vein, how can a salesperson whose commission rises or falls with the price of the house being sold be expected to cut into her own income? Isn't her allegiance totally to the person paying her?

Confusion of this sort has existed in the marketplace for so long that critics are sometimes confounded that regulators haven't made greater efforts to clarify matters.

Two explanations are sometimes offered: First, it is more a human than a legal problem; even if warned, buyers will continue to assume that salespeople are working solely for them, rather than for the seller, who pays the salesperson a commission.

Second, a good salesperson sometimes can come close to serving the desires of both parties. The point is arguable, but the justification offered is that the salesperson's compromises may be necessary to save a sale from falling through.

A somewhat similar situation exists in the stock market, where many small investors view their stockbroker as a confidant and adviser.

Exclusive Dealership

When a contract requires a wholesaler or retailer to purchase products from one manufacturer, it is an **exclusive dealership.** If it lessens competition, it is prohibited under the Clayton Act.

Sales Restrictions

To protect consumers against sometimes unethical sales activities of door-to-door salespeople, there is legislation at the federal, state, and local levels. The Federal Trade Commission and most states have adopted **cooling-off laws.** They provide a cooling-off period (usually three days) in which the buyer may cancel the contract, return any merchandise, and obtain a full refund. The law covers sales of $25 or more made door-to-door. It also states that the buyer must receive from the seller a written, dated contract and/or receipt of the transaction and be told there is a three-day cancellation period.[12]

Many cities require persons selling directly to consumers to be licensed by the city in which they are doing business if they are not residents, and to pay a license fee. A bond may also be required. These city ordinances are often called **Green River ordinances** because the first legislation of this kind was passed in Green River, Wyoming, in 1933. This type of ordinance helps protect the consumer and aids local companies by making it more difficult for outside competition to enter the market.

Both the cooling-off laws and the Green River ordinances were passed to protect consumers from salespeople using unethical, high-pressure sales tactics. These statutes, and others, were necessary because some salespeople used unethical practices in sales transactions.[13]

WHAT TO DO?

Honest and conscientious sales force members need much courage to expose wrongdoing. They may risk their jobs, be responsible for another person's termination, or destroy friendships and working relationships.

The single most important factor in improving the climate for ethical behavior in a sales force is the actions taken by top-level managers. In addition to setting examples by their behavior, there are a number of steps to take:

1. Top management must establish clear policies that encourage ethical behavior. For example, goal-setting programs must yield realistic goals, so that no salesperson is pressured to do something unethical to meet impossible objectives.

2. Management must assume responsibility for disciplining wrongdoers. Inaction sets a poor example for the rest of the organization and can induce others to behave unethically. A company policy of dismissing violators of its ethical code, and of totally cooperating with law enforcement authorities in criminal situations, will deter most potential violators.

3. Companies can provide a mechanism for whistle-blowing as a matter of policy. All employees who observe or become aware of criminal practices or unethical behavior must be encouraged to report incidents to superiors, to a higher level of management, or to an appropriate unit of the organization, such as an audit committee. Formalized procedures for complaining can encourage honest employees to report questionable incidents. However, careful verification is necessary to guard against using such means to get even with other employees.

Management training seminars and orientation meetings that include discussions of actual situations can alert sales personnel to potential ethical conflicts and serve to communicate the organization's code of ethics. By offering courses in business ethics, colleges and universities create conscientious managers with a morally responsible approach to business. The need for responsible managers is acute, since questions of business ethics cannot be wholly determined by law or government regulation, but must primarily remain the concern of individual managers. [14]

Sales managers must help develop and support ethical sales standards. They should publicize these standards and their opposition to unethical sales practices to subordinate managers and salespeople. This can be done in sales meetings. Finally, control systems must be established, but an effective control system is difficult to implement. Methods must be established to determine whether salespeople give bribes, falsify reports, or pad expenses. For example, sales made through low bids could be checked to determine whether procedures were followed correctly. Dismissal, demotion, suspension, or reprimand are possible penalties; for example, commissions would not be paid on a sale associated with unethical sales practices.

SUMMARY OF MAJOR SELLING ISSUES

Social responsibility in business means profitably serving employees and customers in an ethical and lawful manner. Extra costs can accrue because a firm takes socially responsible action, but this is a part of doing business in today's society, and it pays in the long run.

Sales executives must assume socially responsible roles (1) because this is expected of them by society; (2) to operate better in the long run; (3) because of community responsibility; (4) because salespeople are company representatives; (5) to minimize retaliation by competitors; and (6) to decrease government intervention.

Salespeople and managers realize that their business practices must be implemented ethically. They must be ethical in dealing with their salespeople, employers, and customers. Ethical standards and guidelines for sales personnel must be developed, supported, and enforced. In the future, ethical selling practices will be even more important to conducting business profitably.

V

Functions of the Sales Manager

16

Planning, Organizing, Staffing of Successful Salespeople

My name is Martha Hill, and I am the director of national accounts for Hanes Knitwear, a division of Hanes Corporation. After college graduation, I held several sales positions before joining Hanes. I chose Hanes because of the apparent growth and career potential for me. I began as an entry-level salesperson in 1976, and progressed through three promotions to become a regional manager, and then zone manager en route to the director position.

Martha Hill
Hanes Knitwear

Hanes' underwear business has grown dramatically in recent years, primarily due to changes in sales and marketing strategy. These changes involved a direct sales force with heavy emphasis on retail activities combined with national and local advertising and promotion; the results were dynamic volume and market share gains.

My job as a field sales manager included responsibility for the hiring, training, and development of salespeople in addition to analyzing our business and developing sales strategies in order to capitalize on our opportunities. Through my many experiences in interviewing and hiring salespeople, I value this as one of the most difficult, yet important, aspects of my job. My general philosophy toward selection of candidates is to find the best person for the particular territory, and I systematically screen applicants before, during, and after interviews. I use a basic process to find people who are suitable, and I look for characteristics and/or experiences in an applicant's background that will either help to qualify or disqualify the person. I rely heavily on the use of personal interviews because face-to-face selling is exactly what our jobs involve, and the applicant must be able to sell me on hiring him/her in order to be successful at the job.

Orientation of new salespeople is another important phase of a manager's job; it is critical to get a new rep started on the right track in order to set the stage for future development. I encourage new reps to ask me their questions, but also to try to learn independently by probing their accounts, consulting their reference materials, and then reporting to me what they have learned. The initiative taken by new reps often indicates their degree of interest and commitment. The application of what they learn is the key to progress, therefore, my training strongly encourages trial of newfound techniques. •

"In order for a sales manager to be successful," says manager Martha Hill, "I believe the person must be flexible, interested in teaching and learning, and must be a versatile communicator. Certainly a manager needs good selling skills, as it is a constant selling situation to persuade salespeople to try techniques that will improve their job performance. But the most important skill a manager needs is to be a good listener; a manager must be keenly aware of the attitudes of the salespeople and of the accounts. It is common for a salesperson or manager to want to dominate a conversation by talking; however, much more is learned by listening, because a buyer gives the road map to the sale by what he or she says.

"Selection of good candidates and thorough orientation of new reps is an essential element of a successful manager's career. The sales team a manager builds is his or her strength or weakness; consequently, the components of that team are crucially important, individually and collectively.

"A manager can learn a great deal about interviewing via study and observation, but it is the actual participation and experience of interviewing and hiring that leads to this skill development." •

Sales managers, such as Martha Hill, are responsible for planning, organizing, staffing, directing, and controlling their sales forces' activities, strategies, and tactics to generate sales that meet corporate objectives. Part V examines these five job functions of the sales manager. This chapter discusses the planning, organizing, and staffing functions so important for the success of a sales manager. We begin by considering the transition of a salesperson to sales manager.[1]

TRANSITION FROM SALESPERSON TO SALES MANAGER

What happens when a salesperson is promoted into a management position? Often, the qualities that make a good sales manager are different from what is needed by a salesperson, particularly in terms of attitude toward the job and responsibility.

Salespeople are guided by management, but are on their own, not worrying about peers. They are responsible for their performance and often feel that they have control over their sales territory. However, the first-level sales manager is responsible not for one, but for eight to twelve sales territories. If a problem develops, for example, a decrease in sales, the manager may be tempted to take over the salesperson's job. Instead, the manager should be concerned with developing people who can hurdle problems themselves, and with accomplishing goals through other people, not alone. Instead of having responsibility for $1 million in sales, as a salesperson does, the manager is responsible for $10 to $20 million, and a regional manager might be responsible for 10 times that amount. Managers are responsible for the success of salespeople, and they must work through others to reach their objectives.

Salespeople generally work independently without much interaction with or control by their organization. The job of the sales manager necessitates working closely with many different people—for example, salespeople, superiors, and home office personnel. Managers must realize that they are no longer salespeople, but members of the management team. The sales manager has responsibilities to the company, such as recruiting new salespeople, running an office, visiting important clients, and relaying information to higher management. Although there are many technical skills a sales manager must learn to be successful, the first step in the transition from salesperson to sales manager is to understand and accept the differences and the increased responsibilities of the new position.

"At IBM," says Matt Suffoletto, "the typical sales line management career path is generally a series of alternating line and staff positions, each with progressively increasing responsibility. It is our philosophy that before taking the next level of line management responsibility, additional development will be gained through the experience of a staff assignment.

"It is in those staff positions that your horizons are broadened. You begin to work and see elements of the business other than direct sales. Your concept of available career paths will broaden and your personal preferences will develop as your horizons are expanded in the business."

WHAT IS THE SALARY FOR MANAGEMENT?

Why do people strive to achieve management positions? One reason is the personal reward of operating and managing an organization. The second reason is financial reward. A sales job is often a stepping-stone to higher positions. The assumption is that the larger a company's revenues, the heavier the responsibility of the chief executive, and thus the larger the compensation. Salary is usually related to:

- Annual sales volume of units managed.
- Number of salespeople supervised.
- Length of experience in sales.
- Annual sales volume of the firm.

Leaving aside compensation at the top echelons, both corporate and field sales managers typically receive higher salaries than others such as production, advertising, product, or personnel managers at the same organizational level. Moreover, salary is just one part of compensation. For example, many firms offer elaborate packages that include extended vacation and holiday periods; pension programs; health, accident, and legal insurance programs; automobiles and compensation for auto expenses;

payment of professional association dues; education assistance for themselves and sometimes for their families; financial planning assistance; company airplanes; home and entertainment expenses; and free country club membership. The higher the sales position, the greater the benefits offered.

OVERVIEW OF THE JOB

Sales managers are responsible for planning, organizing, staffing, directing, and controlling sales force activities, strategies, and tactics to generate sales that meet corporate objectives. They do this through a process called management. Sales managers work with and through individuals and groups in the company, in the sales force, and outside the firm to accomplish their goals. The sales manager's main goal is to achieve the levels of sales volume, profits, and sales growth desired by higher levels of management.

The factor underlying a manager's success in achieving this goal is the ability to influence the behavior of all parties involved. This includes the ability to influence salespeople to do things that they would not do on their own. The manager must recruit good people and provide proper motivation and effective leadership. The sales manager is held responsible for the success of her or his salespeople. Consequently, sales managers are performance-oriented. They look for ways to make salespeople efficient and effective.

Managerial Skills

Successful managers must have three types of skills—technical, human, and conceptual. These skills are defined as:

> **Technical skill**—Ability to perform specific tasks; have great depth of product knowledge, skilled in all phases of selling.
> **Human skill**—Ability to lead, build morale and effort, motivate, and manage conflict among subordinates.
> **Conceptual skill**—Ability to understand how one's area of responsibility relates to the total operation of the organization; also ability to diagnose and assess management problems.

As shown in Figure 16.1, these skills are needed at all management levels. First-line managers, such as the district sales manager, need highly technical skills because they recruit and train salespeople, and they make sales calls with their salespeople. The higher the level (such as national sales manager), the better a manager must understand and relate sales management func-

FIGURE 16.1   Managerial skills and their importance at varying management
              levels

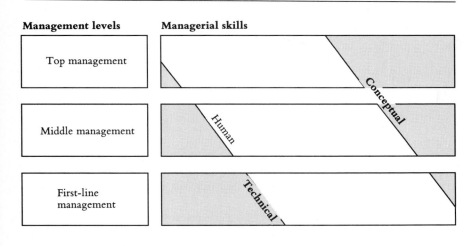

tions to accomplishing corporate goals. Human skills are equally important
at each managerial level.

A successful sales manager must have excellent "human skills." John D.
Rockefeller once stated, "I will pay more for the ability to deal with people
than any other ability under the sun." Many feel that the most important
skill of a manager—even more important than decisiveness, intelligence,
job skills, or knowledge—is the ability to get along with people. In fact,
when salespeople were asked what were the important qualifications for the
district sales manager's job, leadership was singled out as most important.[2]

SALES MANAGEMENT FUNCTIONS

This discussion of the sales manager's functions applies to each of the three
basic levels of management. Whether the sales manager is in a top, middle,
or first-line managerial position, there are five basic functions to be fulfilled,
as indicated in Figure 16.2. These are:

Planning—Establishing a broad outline for goals, policies, and
procedures that will accomplish the objectives of the organization.

Organizing—Setting up an administrative structure through which
work activities are defined, subdivided, and coordinated to
accomplish organizational goals.

Staffing—Recruiting, hiring, and training.

FIGURE 16.2   Sales management functions

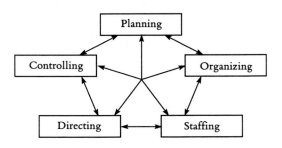

Directing—Dealing with people, positively and persuasively, from a leadership position.

Controlling—Comparing actual performance to planned performance goals to determine whether to take corrective action if goals are not achieved, or to continue using the same methods if goals are met.

First-line managers, such as district sales managers who hire salespeople, spend more time directing salespeople than higher-level managers. In comparison, top-level sales managers spend more time planning and organizing. This is seen clearly if we compare the job functions of the corporate sales executive to those of the district sales manager:

Corporate Sales Executive Job Functions:
- Planning—developing and implementing total organization sales goals, strategies, tactics, and policies.
- Organizing—developing the sales structure.
- Staffing—promoting and training divisional sales managers.
- Directing—developing leadership and motivational strategies for the entire sales organization.
- Controlling—evaluating performance of the total sales force.

District Sales Manager Job Functions:
- Planning—developing and implementing specific, individual objectives, strategies, and tactics.
- Organizing—developing sales district for effective account coverage.
- Staffing—recruiting, hiring, and training salespeople.
- Directing—leadership and motivation of sales district personnel.
- Controlling—evaluating individual and sales district performance.

SALES FORCE PLANNING

A firm's corporate management, including the national sales manager, develops sales goals for the company. As discussed in Chapter 2, the marketing department develops plans, strategies, and tactics that allow the company to reach its sales objectives. In turn, the sales force also develops plans, strategies, and tactics for meeting their sales objectives and quotas. Two important elements of planning are the development of sales forecasts and budgets.

Sales Forecasting

Sales forecasting is one method used to predict a firm's future revenues when planning the company's marketing and sales force activities. Since customer satisfaction is the purpose of every business, the forecast of customer needs is of primary importance. Forecasting is an integral part of planning that contributes to overall organizational effectiveness.

Uses of Sales Forecasts. Sales forecasting involves the prediction of future events that may influence the demand for a firm's goods or services. Total industry sales, total company sales, industry product categories, company product lines, and individual products are major elements that must be noted in estimating future demand. These forecasts are made for customer, sales territory, region, division, the entire country, and sometimes world sales. Forecasts are made for short-range (three to six months), medium-range (six months to one to two years), and long-range (over two years) demand.

The firm's sales forecast depends on many factors. The planned marketing activities of the firm have a major impact on the level of sales obtained in the marketplace. As shown in Figure 16.3, the firm's marketing plans have an influence on sales forecasts and budgets. Marketing plans can increase sales, which can increase budgets and quotas. From sales forecasts, sales goals are generated for products and product lines, individual salespeople, or company divisions. Typically, sales goals are slightly higher than sales forecasts. Once plans have evolved into sales forecasts, the company develops its sales budgets.

The Sales Manager's Budget

The **sales force budget** is the amount of money available or assigned for a definite period, usually one year. It is based on estimates of expenditures during that time and proposals for financing the budget. Thus, the budget depends on the sales forecast and the amount of revenue expected to be generated for the organization during that period. The budget for the sales

FIGURE 16.3   Planning—Forecasting—Budgeting Sequence

force is a valuable resource that the sales manager reassigns among lower-level managers. Budget funds must be appropriated wisely to properly support selling activities that allow sales personnel and the total marketing group to reach performance goals.

Purposes of the Budget.   The budget is an extremely important factor in successful operation of the sales force. Top sales managers spend much time attempting to convince corporate management to increase the size of their budgets. Budgets are formulated for many reasons, especially including planning, coordination, and control.

Planning.   Corporations and their functional units develop objectives for future periods, and budgets determine how these objectives will be met. For example, alternative marketing plans, the probable profit from each plan, and the individual budget for each will be considered before management decides on future marketing programs.

Coordination.   The budget is a major management tool for coordinating the activities of all functional areas and subgroups within the total organization. For example, sales must be coordinated with production to ensure that there are enough products to meet demand. The production manager can use sales forecasts and the sales department's marketing plans to determine the necessary production level. Budgeting allows the financial executive to determine the firm's revenues and expenses (e.g., accounts receivable, inventory, raw materials, labor) and provide enough capital to finance all business operations.

It is important that there is some flexibility in the budget so that plans may be changed in response to market conditions. Many companies allocate a lump sum dollar amount to their sales managers, allowing the managers to invest in the selling activities dictated by the sales and marketing plans. Thus, each sales group (e.g., division, region, district) has a budget.

Control. Allocation of budgeted funds gives management control over the use of funds. Sales managers estimate their budget needs, are given funds to operate their units, and then are held responsible for reaching their stated goals by effectively using their budgets. As the sales program is implemented and income and expenses are generated, results are assessed in terms of the amount budgeted and whether objectives are met.

Methods of Developing Sales Force Budgets. How much money does the sales manager receive to operate the sales force? While there are no fixed financial formulas to use in appropriating funds, there are three general methods of determining how money should be allocated. First, some firms use an arbitrary percentage of sales. Second, other firms may use executive judgment. Third, a few companies estimate the cost of operating each sales force unit, along with costs of each sales program over a specified time to arrive at a total budget.

In Table 16.1, some typical costs in operating a sales force are listed. Whatever method is chosen, the actual amount budgeted will be based on the organization's sales forecast, marketing plans, projected profits, top management's perceived importance of the sales force in reaching corporate objectives, and the sales manager's skills in negotiating with superiors. Budgets are often modified several times before the final dollar figures are determined.

Budgets Should Be Flexible. It is difficult to allocate exact dollar amounts to the sales group because market conditions may fluctuate. Sales, costs, prices, or the competition's marketing efforts may be higher or lower than expected. The sales force must react to market conditions; thus, the budget must not be fixed in concrete.

> Never ask of money spent
> Where the spender thinks it went.
> Nobody was ever meant
> To remember or invent
> What he did with every cent.
> — *Robert Frost*

ORGANIZING THE SALES FORCE

Organizing the sales force involves developing an administrative structure through which work activities of all sales personnel are defined, subdivided, and coordinated to accomplish organizational goals. This is further divided into two important parts, design and structure. **Organizational design** is the determination of job tasks carried out by the employees and groups within the firm, whereas **organizational structure** is the relatively fixed,

TABLE 16.1   Sales force operating costs

1. Base salaries	4. Special incentives
a. Management	5. Office expenses
b. Salespeople	6. Product samples
2. Commissions	7. Selling aids
3. Other compensation	8. Transportation expenses
a. Social security	9. Entertainment
b. Retirement plan	10. Travel
c. Stock options	
d. Hospitalization	

formally defined relationships of jobs within the firm, as reflected in a company's **organizational chart.**

The Organizational Chart

A company's chart is a graphic representation of its formal structure at a given time. The chart shows: (1) jobs at the various hierarchical levels; (2) specialization of functional areas within the firm; (3) how departments relate to one another; (4) lines of authority or chain of command; and (5) line and staff relationships.

METHODS OF ORGANIZATION

Companies organize using various designs. There is the simple line organization; there is organization by the various functions of the company; by the geography of their markets; by the type of customers served; and by the products sold. Many firms use some combination of these designs. Let's first discuss each design and then show how a combination of elements is used to allow the firm to better serve its customers.

The Line Organization

In the pure **line organization,** the chief executive, usually the president, has complete authority over decision making for the firm. Within the firm, there may be no specialists or advisors. There are many small sales firms with this structure. For example, the Compute Corporation is a Texas-based organization that sells used computers. Figure 16.4 shows the firm's line organization.[3] The company was begun by its president, Lewis Stoner, in 1975. He and two salespeople did the selling and bookkeeping. Mr.

FIGURE 16.4 Compute Corporation's line organization

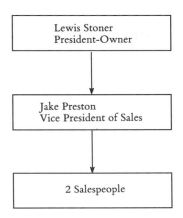

Stoner buys late-model computers and sells them to companies without a computer or in need of a larger computer. As the business grew, Jake Preston was promoted to vice president of sales as a line assistant and another salesperson was hired. An outside accounting firm maintains the financial records.

The advantages of this type of organization are that it is simple, has low overhead, decisions are made rapidly and communicated quickly, and salespeople tend to feel that they make a major individual contribution to the firm.

In this type of "solo" leadership organization, it is difficult to replace key people. In addition, executives may be so busy with the day-to-day operations that little time is devoted to planning. Also, because everyone is a jack-of-all-trades, lack of specialization can hinder the firm's growth. Finally, growth is difficult unless the number of employees is greatly increased, which would lead to a change in structure—usually to a specialized organizational structure.

Specialized Design

The structure of an organization is based on a variety of factors such as function, geography, product, customers, or a combination. It is common for large companies to begin with a functional structure, develop geographical departments, split along product division lines, and end with a customer-focused structure. While a firm may be organized along any of these lines, typically, a combination of these structural methods is used.

FIGURE 16.5 Alarm System Corporation's functional organizational design

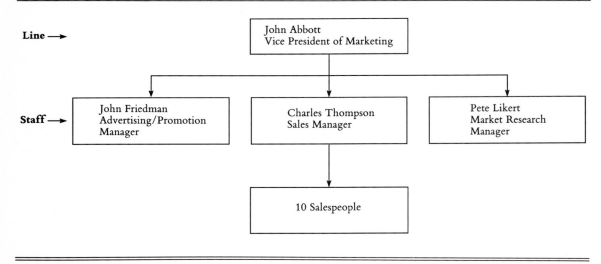

Functional Specialization. The **functional organization,** sometimes called line and staff organization, is the grouping of work according to its characteristics. It is the most common organizational design. Firms need special expertise to develop advertising, sales, and marketing research units or departments, then group all related activities (such as sales and advertising) together, thus introducing specialization into the organizational design. This type of organization is often used by firms that have a small number of similar products.

No single chief executive, no matter how brilliant and dynamic, can effectively handle all responsibilities of a relatively large and complex organization. Figure 16.5 shows the functional organizational design of the sales and related units of Alarm System, an industrial and home security firm based in Kansas City, Missouri.[4] Note the difference between this figure and Figure 16.4. The line component of the organization still runs from the chief executive directly down to the salespeople. However, the staff reports directly to the vice president of marketing. The sales manager has staff authority equal to the advertising and marketing research managers. However, neither the advertising and marketing research manager has authority over the salespeople. Persons in staff positions aid the vice president of marketing in marketing planning and operations.

The functional organization structure is suitable when a firm outgrows one type of organization and begins to add specialized positions. For example, as a firm grows, it adds more salespeople to call on an increasing number of customers, to sell a larger number of products or services, and to expand into multiple sales regions or a national market. This design is useful for medium-to-large organizations because it allows them to take advantage of specialization.

However, the functional organization structure also involves high overhead because a large number of management positions must be created that are not directly involved in generating income. Such an organization operates more slowly than the line organization, taking longer in responding to changes in the business environment. However, these disadvantages are overshadowed by the advantages.

Geographical Specialization. Many large corporations are organized by geographical territory. This type of organization is generally used by companies that have anything other than strictly local distribution of their products. It is also commonly combined with other methods of organization, such as by product or customer. With **geographical specialization,** each territorial unit can be treated as a separate company or profit center. The sales manager of a given territory often has complete responsibility for meeting a unit's sales objectives. The unit can be called a division, region, branch, or district. Let us consider the organizational chart shown in Figure 16.6.[5] Texton Chemical primarily sells industrial chemicals used in manufacturing plastics. Texton has three geographical sales divisions. Each division sells the same products. Each division is given the same support by the home office and each has its own performance goals, which are passed down from higher management.

Each of the regional sales managers works at a regional distribution or warehouse center. Although having 18 regional distribution centers is a costly duplication of facilities, the cost is offset by efficiency. For example, sales managers feel that with this organization there is improvement in: (1) control of activities; (2) market coverage; (3) customer service; (4) response to local conditions; and (5) direction of salespeople's efforts in achieving unit goals. Companies selling multiple product lines, with depth of assortment, often organize based on geographical specialization combined with product specialization.

Product Specialization. Another common type of organization in large companies is based on the firm's product. The entire company may be organized by product, with separate sales, advertising, marketing staffs, etc., for each, or some functional units may remain centralized (e.g., advertising) while a separate support staff is created for each product. With the former organization, there would be a separate sales force and sales management for each product group. These sales divisions are treated as a separate company or profit center, as are geographical divisions. It is common for large companies to use a combination of product and geographical departmentalization. In fact, it is difficult to find medium-

FIGURE 16.6   Texton Chemical Corporation's geographical specialization

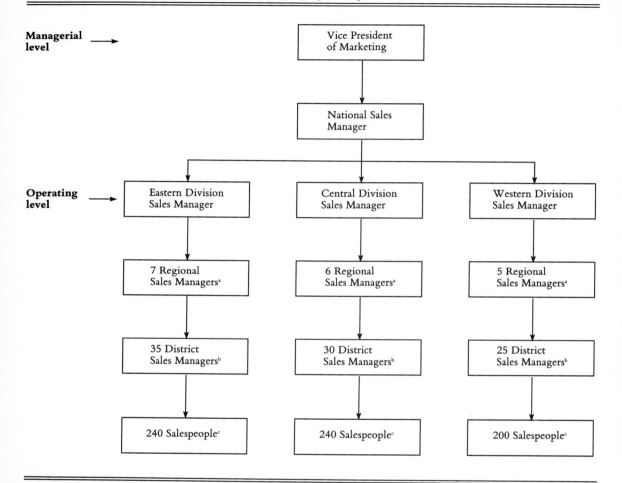

aDifferent number of sales regions due to population differences.
bFive district sales managers per region.
cApproximately eight salespeople per sales district.

to-large companies organized solely by product. The Procter & Gamble Packaged Soaps and Detergents organizational chart shown in Chapter 2 is an example of organizing according to **product specialization.**

Product specialization is necessary, or a least useful, when: (1) the products are very technical or complex; (2) there are many similar but separate products; (3) products are relatively simple but completely different; (4) product lines are distributed through entirely different trade channels; or (5) different products are sold to similar markets. When any combination of these factors is present, a company should investigate product specialization of the sales force.

The advantage of product specialization is that each product receives close attention from the salesperson. In the case of complex products, the salesperson can master the necessary information to sell the product effectively. The advantages of the organization based on geographical specialization also apply.

The drawbacks of product specialization, similar to geographical specialization, are the increased costs of executive personnel, sales personnel, and sales personnel time. A company that is organized by product specialization will often have different sales personnel calling on the same customers trying to sell them different products. Repeated calls by salespeople are costly in time both for the company and for the customer. Thus, if product specialization of the sales force can be avoided, either by hiring better sales personnel or by upgrading the training program, then these steps should be taken; but if not, product specialization should be introduced.

Customer Specialization. Companies that have several separate and distinct markets that account for major portions of their sales often base their organization on these markets or customers. Firms frequently shift from the product organization structure to **customer specialization.** Markets become the major sales emphasis. Figure 16.7 shows an industrial firm, Electro Corporation, organized in terms of its electronic and aerospace markets.[6] Here, the staff positions function for both divisions. Larger firms may create separate divisions with individual staff managers for each.

Many companies, such as Hewlett-Packard, IBM, Xerox, NCR, Burroughs, Gulf Oil, General Foods, and Bell Telephone, have evolved into more market-centered organizations. For example, Bell Telephone has systems salespeople specializing in 26 different markets, such as the oil companies. One senior salesperson may be assigned only one account— Exxon, located in Houston. Consequently, that salesperson becomes very knowledgeable about the oil industry and about Exxon's communication systems needs. This is the best method of specialization in use today.

Combination of Design Elements

Many companies organize based on some combination of function, geography, product, or customer design elements. Figure 16.8 illustrates a company with production, marketing, and engineering functional specialists; the firm sells consumer and industrial goods in both U.S. and international markets. The consumer goods division sells three categories of products through three geographically organized sales force divisions.

FIGURE 16.7　Electro Corporation customer specialization

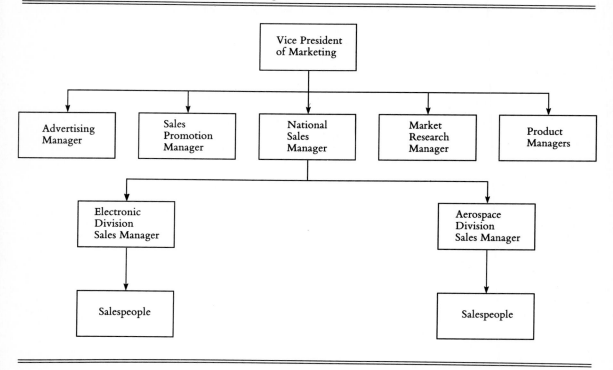

Organizing for Selling to Major Customers.　Companies realize the need to pay special attention to major customers. Different companies refer to major customers using different terms—house accounts, corporate accounts, key accounts, or national accounts. The loss of this customer would substantially affect a firm's sales and profits. Four basic organizational methods firms use with their major customers are:

1. A separate division to deal with major accounts.
2. The use of select members of the present sales force.
3. The use of sales managers.
4. A combination of 1 and 2.

　　Let's look at an example of how a firm can organize for selling to their major accounts. As director of the national accounts group for Hanes Knitwear, Martha Hill's responsibilities include sales to four distinct groups of customers: national chain department stores (Sears, J.C. Penney, etc.), national chain mass merchandise stores (Wal-Mart, Target, etc.), national food/drug chain stores (Walgreen's, Eckerds, etc.), and the entire military system (Army, Navy, Marines, etc.).

FIGURE 16.8 Multiple design factors

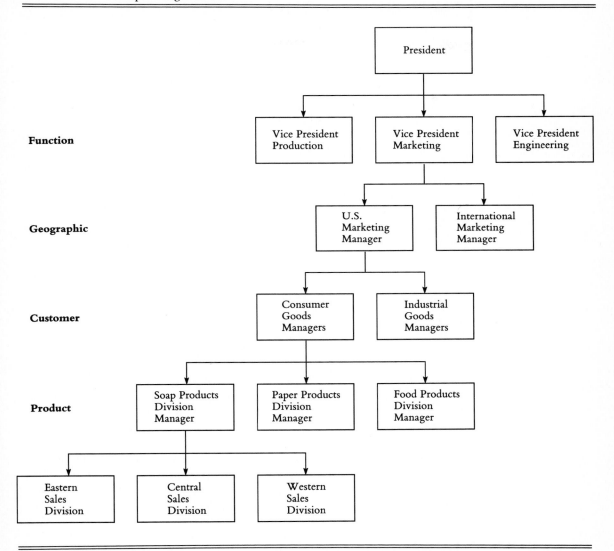

"I utilize four sales managers who have accountability and focus on each of the business segments," says Martha. "We approach each segment separately. For example, we have a tailored program to sell to food/drug and a separate program for J.C. Penney. The military business is completely different from the civilian business. There is some crossover between the groups, but we are positioned for the premise that each group of customers has specific needs."

STAFFING THE SALES FORCE

Sales force staffing is the entire personnel process of matching the right people to the right sales jobs and sales territory, thereby providing human resources capable of achieving sales force objectives. Staffing involves both personnel planning and employment planning.

Personnel Planning

Sales force **personnel planning** is the process of determining the kind and number of salespeople needed. Personnel planning for the sales force is an outgrowth of corporate, marketing, and sales force objectives. As shown in Figure 16.9, sales force staffing needs are based on the objectives and strategies assigned to the sales force. Determination is based on answers to questions such as: Will we have intensive or sparse coverage of existing and potential customers? Will the sales force be the major element in our promotion mix or the least important part? How many salespeople do we need to accomplish our objectives?

The current sales force is reviewed to forecast the total number of salespeople needed to reach sales management's objectives. Individual units, (i.e., divisions, regions, or district sales areas), are reviewed to determine their personnel requirements. It is then necessary to determine financial requirements. Sales force plans, as related to personnel needs, and the sales budget are submitted to the sales manager's superiors for corporate approval. The plans may be accepted or changed. For example, the budget may be reduced, which might result in a reduction of the planned sales force size. Once personnel requirements and the budget are finalized, employment planning begins. This entire process is monitored and evaluated to determine whether these requirements are aiding the sales force in reaching objectives.

Job Analysis and Descriptions.   After the number of salespeople to be hired is decided, it is necessary to determine the type of salesperson to recruit for each sales job. Accordingly, sales managers analyze their salespeople's jobs, develop job descriptions, and create job specifications.

A **job analysis** is the definition of a sales position in terms of specific roles or activities to be performed, and the determination of personal qualifications suitable for the job. **Job descriptions** are formal, written statements describing the nature, requirements, and responsibilities (e.g., sales volume, territory, product line, customers, supervisory duties) of a specific sales position. They officially establish what the salesperson will do, how it will be done, and why these duties are important, as well as indicate the salary range for the position. Table 16.2 gives a partial job description for a position selling automotive replacement parts.[7]

FIGURE 16.9 Sales force personnel planning model

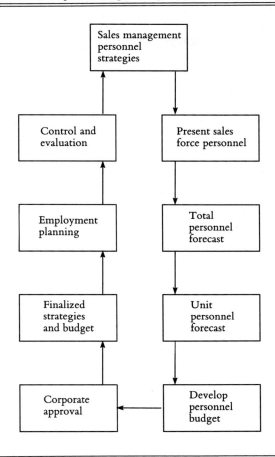

This description has five basic parts. The "nature of job" section is a statement of responsibilities involved. The next section, "principal responsibilities," states the specific end results or performance expected from someone holding the position. They explain how to implement the nature of job section. In the "dimensions" section, job duties are discussed. Finally, there is an explanation of the supervisory responsibilities involved.

Job Specifications. **Job specifications** convert job descriptions into the people qualifications (e.g., abilities, behavior, education, skills) the organization feels are necessary for successful job performance. Often, job specifications are determined by management in compliance with governmental regulations. This includes qualifications for initial employment and

TABLE 16.2   Formal job description, Transtex Automotive Supply Corporation

Position: Sales representative	Organizational Unit: Replacement parts
Reports to: District manager	Date: (When job was described)

Nature of job:
  Responsible for developing new accounts and reaching profitable sales goals in assigned territory.

Principal responsibilities:
  Meeting total sales goals for product lines and individual products.
  Maintaining an average of six daily sales calls.
  Maintaining an average of one monthly product presentation to wholesalers.

Dimensions:
  Develop strong promotional support from retail and wholesale customers.
  Plan effective territory coverage resulting in high sales-call ratio.
  Inform management of activities by submitting daily and weekly call and sales reports to district manager.

Supervision received:
  General and specific tasks are assigned for each sales period. Every two months, works with supervisor for a minimum of one day.

Supervision exercised:
  None

for training as a successful salesperson. Increasingly, however, statistical analyses also assist in generating job specifications. By this means, the relation of successful sales performance to certain personal characteristics such as education, specific aptitudes, communication skills, personality type, and experience is statistically determined.

Job Specifications for Successful Salespeople.   Sales managers often express frustration over the difficulty of selecting potential salespeople. Typical comments include the following: "What are the characteristics necessary for successful salespeople in my industry and my company? If I knew," states one sales manager, "I'd have fewer staffing problems." "We think we know," says another sales manager. "We hire them. Some do well, others don't." Another manager said: "The company gives us job specifications but they are difficult to use. I have to hire in a short time. I find the best people I can in the job market at that time who have good personality characteristics, background, and potential, and hire them. I don't really use job specifications."

Let us review the desirable characteristics to include in job specifications. We know the selling job is people-oriented. Thus, salespeople must deal with people positively and effectively.

The successful salesperson should have the proper empathy and ego drive for a specific sales job. Empathy is needed for identifying and understanding the other person's situation. Ego drive is the desire to make the sale, to overcome "no" sales, and to continue calling on customers.

TABLE 16.3 Selected characteristics of successful salespeople

1. High energy levels.	8. Good physical appearance.
2. High self-confidence.	9. Likable.
3. Need for material things.	10. Self-disciplined.
4. Hard working.	11. Intelligent.
5. Requires little supervision.	12. Achievement-oriented.
6. High perseverance.	13. Good communication skills.
7. Competitive.	

Other desirable characteristics reported are shown in Table 16.3.[8] A point can be made that the individual company should determine the job specifications and sales personnel characteristics necessary for successful performance. They must be updated continually. Most sales managers say the minimum components of a successful salesperson are:

1. Education. The individual should be an above-average student.
2. Personality. A good salesperson is achievement-oriented, tactful, mature, self-confident, a self-starter with a positive outlook on life, and has a realistic career plan.
3. Experience. A good salesperson works hard and goes beyond the call of duty; if a recent graduate, this person will have participated in school organizations and developed above-average class projects.
4. Physical Attributes. A good salesperson has a neat appearance, good personal habits, is physically fit, and makes a good first impression.

Guidelines for Job Descriptions and Job Specifications. Critics of job descriptions and job specifications point out that many are so unclear and ambiguous that they are useless in the staffing process. However, companies must develop useful job descriptions and job specifications. The following list provides suggestions for clarifying job descriptions and specifications:

• Decide on job objectives and state them in the form of activities (what sales personnel actually do).
• List the tasks required for desired performance.
• Differentiate between routine and critical tasks.
• List alternative methods of performing tasks.
• Specify criteria used to determine whether the job has been performed successfully.
• Specify favorable and unfavorable conditions for attainment of objectives.
• Specify other general information regarding the job (for example, title, salary, supervisor).

- List work qualifications, education, and/or experience levels required.
- Develop techniques for validating sales job analysis.

Employment Planning

Employment planning refers to the locating, recruiting, evaluation, and hiring of applicants for sales jobs. Recruitment begins with the initiation of a search, i.e., prospecting for applicants. Once all of the activities leading up to and including the actual decision by the applicant to accept or reject the final job are over, the recruitment process ends for the individual applicant. In essence, recruiters attempt to close sales by getting applicants to accept employment offers. On the other side, applicants attempt to sell themselves to the prospective employer, while searching for a job that will fulfill their needs and expectations.

Figure 16.10 illustrates the seven basic steps a recruiter may take in hiring a salesperson. Typically, candidates complete a job application blank, and undergo an initial interview. If applicants appear to be good candidates, they go through several in-depth interviews. Some companies have applicants work with salespeople to show them what the job is like. If applicants are married, the manager may also meet with spouses to further explain job requirements.

Tests are frequently given to applicants to determine their intelligence and aptitude for sales jobs.[9] Applicants submit names of people who can provide character references, which are checked. The final step is the physical examination.

Both the applicant and the sales manager have the option to say no at any of the seven steps in the selection process. During the process, the applicant and the sales manager collect enough information about each other to make a decision.

Legal Framework for Employment. The sales manager faces an increasing number of laws governing employment practices. Although a number of federal agencies are involved, the **Equal Employment Opportunity Commission (EEOC)** is the principal government agency responsible for monitoring discriminatory practices. As such, the EEOC has a major influence on sales force staffing. Changing social values, attitudes toward minorities and women entering the work force, a recognition of the traditional advantages enjoyed by white males, and an increasing number of government regulations necessitated creation of the commission.

The legislation affecting employment practices ranges from the Constitution to more recent laws such as the 1963 Equal Pay Act, which specifically prohibits sex discrimination in pay. The provisions of this act were broadened under the 1972 Education Amendments Act, which states that "Any employee employed in a bona fide executive, administrative, or professional capacity . . . or in the capacity of outside salesman" is entitled to equal pay. The most far-reaching recent legislation in this context is the

FIGURE 16.10   Major steps in the sales personnel selection process

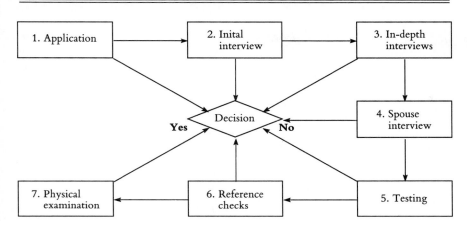

Civil Rights Act of 1964, especially Title VII of the act as amended by the Equal Employment Opportunity Act of 1972, which prohibits discrimination based on race, sex, religion, or national origin.

Remember that what might be labeled discrimination is allowed if an employer can show that a given action is "reasonably necessary to the operation of that particular business or enterprise" and that the employment decision is based on a "bona fide occupational qualification." Included in this context are such things as age, testing, and inquiries into pre-employment background. However, there are few cases in which this argument can stand up against charges of discrimination.

The government has many ways of influencing employment practices. Consequently, the sales manager must have continually updated information on government regulations and must have specific guidelines to follow. Broadly speaking, the equal employment opportunity criteria are based on two questions:

1. Are the employment practices equally applied and do they have the same effect on all potential employees, regardless of race, sex, religion, or national origin?
2. Are the employment practices job related?

A Sales Manager's View of the Recruit

Given a sales manager's way of training recruiters, interview sessions, and the post-interview comments of hundreds of students, the following sales manager's views of the recruit and the recruiting process is representative. This particular sales manager had 20 years' experience recruiting for a manufacturer of computer equipment. The following discussion is based on a tape recording of a talk given to a graduate class in sales management.

Is Sales the Right Job for the Applicant? The search for the sales job begins with the applicant. To obtain any job, applicants must "sell" themselves. If applicants are excited and enthusiastic about the future, recruiters will be, too.

Applicants should ask themselves what they look for in a job. They should be honest and realistic. They need to ask themselves:

- What are my past accomplishments and future goals?
- Do I want the responsibility of a sales job?
- Do I mind travel? How much travel is acceptable?
- How much freedom do I want in the job?
- Do I have the personality characteristics for the job?

These are questions recruiters attempt to answer about the applicant during the interview.

Job Analysis. Applicants need to determine which industries, types of products or services, and specific companies they are interested in. Find out what recruiters from different companies may look for in an applicant to better prepare yourself.

Recruiters look for outstanding applicants who are mature and intelligent. They must handle themselves well in the interview, demonstrating good interpersonal skills. They should have well-thought-out career plans and discuss them rationally. They must have friendly, pleasing personalities. A clean, neat appearance is a must. They should have positive attitudes, be willing to work hard, be ambitious, and demonstrate interest in the employer's business field. They should have good grades and other personal, school, and business accomplishments. Finally, they must have clear goals and objectives in life. The more common characteristics on which applicants for our company are judged are: (1) appearance, (2) self-expression, (3) maturity, (4) personality, (5) experience, (6) enthusiasm, (7) and interest in the job.

The Application Letter. The application letter introduces the applicant to the prospective employer. It should not totally rehash the information in the resume. It should be neat and personalized. The letter should begin by mentioning the job for which the person is applying. In the next paragraph, the applicant states reasons for interest in the position and the company. It indicates knowledge of the company. If currently in school, applicants must explain how their education qualifies them for the position. The same should be done with school activities and work experience. In the third paragraph, the resume can be mentioned, possibly pointing out the relevant factors not previously discussed, e.g., grade point average, honors, graduation date. The last paragraph should ask positively for an interview at a time and place convenient to the company.

The Resume.   The application letter serves to arouse the recruiter's interest and develops the desire to review the resume. Again, neatness is a must. Printed copies may be made with a picture attached. There are many resume formats, but, in general, they should contain information such as:

- Personal data—including address and phone number.
- Job objective.
- Education—listing most recent degree first.
- Work experience—listing most recent job first.
- Activities.
- Reference section—stating that references will be furnished upon request.

This information summarizes the applicant's life in one to two pages. In a few minutes, the recruiter should have a good idea of the applicant's background. Recruiters are busy people. If the resume is mailed and there has not been a response in one to two weeks, the applicant should call and/or write the company.

The Interview.   Applicants should be prepared. They should anticipate interview questions, prepare for them, and practice. Be prepared for questions such as:

- What can you tell me about yourself?
- Why do you want to be in sales?
- What do you know about my company?
- Why do you want to work for my company?
- What problems have you had and how you solved them?
- Where do you want to be in five years?

Some recruiters may ask the applicant to sell them something, for example, an ashtray or a pencil. The applicant cannot always prepare for everything. However, the recruiter knows when the applicant is prepared. When being interviewed, it is important to be early to review plans for the interview. The recruiter should be addressed by name.

Interview Follow-Up.   A letter immediately following the interview is not always necessary. However, if the recruiter has set a time for notifying the applicant of a decision and if it has passed, a follow-up letter or call is appropriate.

The Second Interview.   An applicant invited for a second interview has passed the first major step in the job search. The recruiter feels that this individual may be what the company seeks in a salesperson. Now, the applicant should prepare for this visit by doing everything from reviewing information to planning what to wear.

Job Offers. If a company offers the applicant a job, it is important to respond positively in one of three ways. First, accept the offer and stop interviewing. Second, reject the offer tactfully but give the reasons for your decisions; this should be done as soon as possible. Third, request more time to either complete the job search or consider the offer.

No Job Offer. If the recruiter feels that there is no match and does not make a job offer, the applicant may write a letter of appreciation for the opportunity to be interviewed. If still interested in the job, the applicant can express hope for future consideration.[10]

TRAINING THE SALES FORCE

Sales training is the effort put forth by an employer to provide the opportunity for the salesperson to acquire job-related attitudes, concepts, rules, and skills that result in improved performance in the selling environment.

John H. Patterson, founder of the National Cash Register Company and known as the "father of sales training," used to say, "At NCR, our salespeople never stop learning." This philosophy is the reason that even today successful companies thoroughly train new salespeople and have ongoing training programs for experienced sales personnel, in which even the most successful salespeople participate.

Basically, sales training changes or reinforces behavior to make salespeople more efficient in achieving job goals. Salespeople are trained to perform activities they would not normally undertake. In addition, training reinforces successful sales practices.

Purposes of Training

Companies are interested in training primarily to increase sales, productivity, and profits. As the chair and chief executive officer at United States Steel expressed it:

> We support training and development activities to get results. . . . We're interested in specific things that provide greater rewards to the employee, increased return to the stockholder, and enable reinvestment to meet the needs of the business. In other words, [we're interested in] those things that affect the "bottom line." Although you cannot always evaluate training as readily as some other functions, as people improve their performance, it is reflected in on-the-job results as well as all aspects of their lives.

Edward G. Harness, chair of the board of Procter & Gamble, says: "We grow our own managers, and it starts with finding the right people through an extremely intensive selection process, followed by continuing on-the-job training." There are specific purposes of training other than improving general sales volume. They relate to the type of training offered and include:

- Helping salespeople become better managers.
- Orienting the new salesperson to the job.
- Improving knowledge in areas such as product, company, competitors, or selling skills.
- Lowering absenteeism and turnover.
- Positively influencing attitudes in such areas as job satisfaction.
- Lowering selling costs.
- Informing salespeople.
- Obtaining feedback from the salespeople.
- Increasing sales in a particular product or customer category.

Yet, the primary purpose of training is to "invest" in the sales organization's most valuable resource—its salespeople. Training is an ongoing process and the responsibility of the trainee, the trainer, and the organization.

Training Methods

The three basic training methods are discussion, role playing, and on-the-job training.

Discussion. The discussion approach to sales training can be used in several ways including case studies and/or discussion groups. Case studies are usually included in presession assignments. At a session, small discussion groups may be formed to further analyze the case and to report findings to the group. Lectures incorporating discussion and demonstration are the most common and effective method of training. Filmed cases are more effective then written cases.

Role Playing. In **role playing,** the trainee acts through the sale of a product or service to a hypothetical buyer. Often the trainee's presentation is videotaped and replayed for critique by a group, the trainee, and the trainer. The role-playing procedure is generally a variation of the following:

1. "Define the sales problem." The trainee is told the company is coming out with a new shaving cream.
2. "Establish the situation." The trainee is asked to think about, and then describe, the largest potential account and its buyer.

3. "Cast the characters." The trainer or a trainee is selected to play the buyer.
4. "Brief the participants." Each person learns a role. In addition, the "buyer" may be briefed separately from the salesperson, and given certain specific objections to raise.
5. "Act out the buyer–seller situation." The salesperson goes through a sales presentation with interaction from the buyer.
6. "Discuss, analyze, and critique the role playing." This is important to the learning process. If videotaped, the presentation is shown to the group. Trainers often ask the group for their comments first. Then, the participants discuss the situation. A critique from the trainer is next. Trainees may be asked to repeat the exercise.[11]

On-the-Job Training. On-the-job training may take several forms. New salespeople may accompany their manager and observe sales calls. At first, the manager makes all sales presentations for some period. Then, typically, a customer is selected who will be easy to call on, and the trainee makes a first sales presentation with little or no assistance. This is an exciting and important time for the trainee, and the experience must be critiqued in a positive manner to establish a good relationship between salesperson and manager.

If a sale was not made, the manager should reassure the salesperson that selling is based on percentages. If the manager maintains a positive attitude, so will the trainee. As Fran Tarkenton, the former Minnesota Vikings quarterback, states, "We're all reinforcing agents and feedback agents for each other, each and every one of us. I'm a great believer in feedback, positive or negative. When something isn't right, tell the performer what and why and how to correct it. And when it's right, deliver the positive reinforcement and positive feedback."

For the experienced salesperson, on-the-job training includes observation by the trainer and curbside counseling by the sales manager. This way, the salesperson gets immediate feedback. When the manager and salesperson leave the customer's office, the manager can critique the sales presentation. If needed, corrections are made. Imagine yourself making six sales presentations in the presence of your manager and having each critiqued. The next day, you are prepared to use what you have learned to make more effective sales presentations.

There are many variations in critiquing the salesperson. Some managers prefer to have salespeople critique themselves. For example, "Judy, that was a very good sales presentation. Can you think of anything that should have been changed or improved on?" Then, the manager asks whether the trainee would like any help toward becoming more successful, such as more selling aids and samples, or having the manager make the next presentation so that the salesperson can watch and learn.

Where Does Training Take Place?

A salesperson may receive some form of training any place, any time of day or night. Sales training is continuous. In a broad sense, training occurs any time the superior does things such as commenting on a salesperson's reports, talking on the phone to the salesperson, working in the field with the salesperson, or conducting a meeting. The two broad categories of sales training are centralized and decentralized training. Companies often are divided on whether training should be totally centralized, using corporate staff trainers, or both centralized *and* decentralized.

Centralized Training. Training at a central location is primarily intended for instruction of salespeople from all geographical areas served by the company. Programs typically are held at or close to the home office/manufacturing plant, in a large city, or at a resort. **Centralized training programs** supplement the basic training done by sales personnel in the field. A survey of selling costs shows that 100 percent of the industrial products managers questioned use their home office as a training site, while 93 percent of the consumer products and 71 percent of service companies use home office sites.

A salesperson may attend a centralized training program when first starting work, after six months to a year of employment, or at stipulated intervals. The new salesperson may initially be trained in the field, then after one year, be sent to the home office for training and to tour the firm's manufacturing facilities. There may be further training at the home office every five years.

Centralized training programs usually involve excellent facilities and equipment such as classrooms, videotapes, closed circuit television, and sales laboratories designed for role playing. Trainees get to know each other and corporate executives. Because they are away from home, they can concentrate on learning. Training content can be standardized so that the entire sales force has a common body of knowledge.

Decentralized Training. The main form of sales force instruction, **decentralized training,** may be conducted anywhere. It can be done in a branch office, in the salesperson's car, at the customer's place of business, in a motel room, or at the salesperson's home.

There are numerous advantages to decentralized training. For one thing, costs are usually lower. For example, if a branch office is used as the training site, travel costs are less. The sessions are typically shorter, saving on motel and meal expenditures. Salespeople's geographical territories are such that often they see one another only during meetings and training programs. Many sales managers feel their salespeople receive as much knowledge and motivation from their peers in informal sessions as in regular training. Salespeople can informally discuss their problems in making sales and how they overcome sales resistance. The success stories particularly benefit the inexperienced salesperson. Of course, these informal talks also occur when salespeople attend centralized training sessions. Finally, supplies, samples, and tools can be provided to take home after the session.

There are several disadvantages to either type of training. A potential major weakness in decentralized training is that a branch manager may not be an able trainer, which can hurt salespeople. On the other hand, centralized training is expensive due to the cost of travel, meals, and facilities. Also, it is expensive for salespeople to be out of their territories, and trainees may not want to be away from their families for a prolonged time. Common disadvantages include the fact that salespeople may come to the meeting unprepared, really only wanting to get away from regular work. Trainers understand this, and overcome it by having training sessions that are well prepared, interesting, informative, and that encourage participation. Finally, customer sales may be lost. The cost of lost sales must be offset by increasing productivity and efficiency through training.

When Does Training Occur?

For new sales personnel, training begins the first day they report to work. Basic company, product, and selling skill information is usually given to the trainee to study. In a recruiting brochure, Procter & Gamble states: "Your training begins the day you join us and will continue throughout your career, regardless of your responsibility or job level." The firm gives new salespeople a two-day orientation conducted by an immediate supervisor. Company, product, and customer information are presented. Salespeople also receive a company car, equipment, and supplies. After the orientation session, salespeople call on customers with their manager. This procedure is common for persons selling consumer goods.

Training does not end with this initial session, but continues throughout the professional salesperson's career. Some firms want their salespeople to be thoroughly trained before they are assigned a sales territory. Conversely, some firms feel that new employees can relate to and retain more from training if they have been in the sales territory for a short time.

Companies also provide training for experienced salespeople through periodic sales meetings. Many companies have regular sales meetings once every month or two. In addition, materials are mailed to the homes of sales personnel. Training involves working with a manager in the sales territory.

FIGURE 16.11   Basic sources of sales training

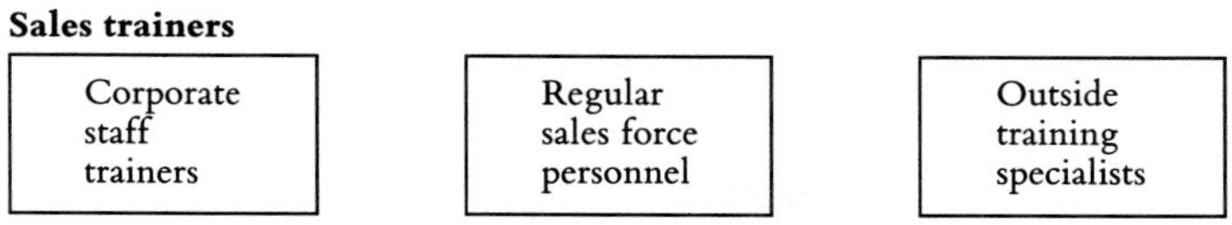

Sales trainers

Corporate staff trainers	Regular sales force personnel	Outside training specialists

Salespeople also periodically attend training programs at company head-quarters.

Who Is Involved in Training?

Typically, there are three basic kinds of sales trainers: corporate staff personnel, regular sales force personnel, and specialists from outside the company. These are shown in Figure 16.11.

Corporate Staff Trainers.   Staff trainers are responsible for the creation, administration, and coordination of a firm's sales management and sales force training and development programs. Typically, the training manager and staff are separate from the personnel department. They have an ongoing relationship with all staff departments and the field organization. The training manager usually reports to someone at the upper corporate level, such as the vice president of sales.

The duties and responsibilities of the training manager can be narrow or broad, depending on the size of the organization and the importance placed on centralized training. The following are some major duties:

- The foremost duty of the manager and the manager's staff is to assist sales management in identifying training "needs" and developing programs to meet those needs.
- They organize, coordinate, and schedule the training.
- They determine who will conduct the training and, if needed, provide them with support material.
- The training manager may help evaluate the training and report results to corporate and field management.
- The trainer often coordinates and administers follow-up training.
- The manager prepares an annual budget to meet the goals and needs of each training program.

Sales Force Personnel.   Senior sales representatives and district and regional sales managers often are the main trainers of the sales force. These people bring to the training program years of sales experience that leads the trainee to relate quickly to the instructor and the material. The sales manager possesses power and authority, which aids in getting the sales personnel to cooperate and to exert greater effort in training sessions. The manager is in a position to train salespeople in the best methods of working and selling. A good rapport between the manager and the sales force can be established if the salesperson sees the trainer as imparting knowledge and teaching skills that aid the trainee in obtaining personal sales goals.

Management must provide sales force personnel with adequate time, support, and rewards to do training. Otherwise, training personnel may not perform adequately, which can create low morale among salespeople and decrease effectiveness of the training program. Often, the trainer receives support from the home office personnel (for example, product managers or technical support personnel who discuss product strategies or product information).

The trainer must be an effective salesperson and a competent teacher. A company should use a senior salesperson as a trainer not on the basis of sales ability, but because of effective communication skills. People with both sales and teaching abilities can usually be found, but management must seek them out. An assignment at the corporate level as a trainer can be a step up the career ladder for the salesperson in the field.

Outside Training Specialists. Trainers drawn from outside the company may be consultants specializing in sales training or representatives of programs such as Toastmasters, Dale Carnegie Sales Courses, and the Xerox Sales Learning Programs. Some universities also offer courses for salespeople and sales managers.

Often, the company pays all or part of the cost to the salesperson for completing, for example, a college-level sales methods course. One endorsement of such sales training courses came from a vice president of engineering in the Cross Company: "As a result of taking the course, our people have new, positive attitudes toward their jobs, along with a better understanding of the company's goals. They also have a better appreciation of one another's problems, and they show better teamwork in resolving day-to-day situations."

Smaller firms may rely heavily on outside trainers. This practice affords them the training without the cost of maintaining a training staff. The courses may be standardized or customized for the company. A company must carefully select outside trainers based on individual needs.

Combination of Training Sources. Firms large and small use a combination of training sources. A firm may use its sales force personnel to do a large percentage of the training with a sales training director and staff. The latter organize and coordinate training efforts among the staff and trainers. The training director might arrange for a product manager to attend a sales meeting to give technical information and discuss future promotional plans for the product. Firms often hire consultants, such as university professors, to put on in-house seminars dealing with such subjects as the psychological aspects of why industrial buyers purchase goods or effective selling techniques. The firm may also purchase ongoing motivational programs such as the Earl Nightingale motivational phonograph record program. With this program, the salesperson receives a training record every month in the mail or at a sales meeting.

SUMMARY OF MAJOR SALES MANAGEMENT ISSUES

A salesperson who is promoted to sales manager becomes involved in sales planning, organizing, staffing, directing, and controlling sales force activities. This chapter discussed the need to understand how to make sales forecasts and budgets, how to determine the number of salespeople to hire, how to recruit and train salespeople, and the legal aspects of staffing. The sales manager uses this knowledge to achieve the sales volume, profits, and growth desired by higher levels of management. Technical, human, and conceptual skills aid in reaching these goals.

Today, firms design their organizational structure to best serve their customers. Small companies use a simple line organizational design, whereas large firms design specialized structures based on geography, the products they market, customers, or a combination of these elements.

Sales managers are frequently involved in forecasting their firm's sales. They also are involved in developing budgets and allocating money to various sales units, all of which ultimately serve as input into planning and aid in coordinating and controlling sales unit activities.

The contemporary sales manager is knowledgeable in personnel practices involving the recruiting and hiring of salespeople. Government laws need to be considered so that the firm can abide by EEOC guidelines. The staff function involves both personnel planning—the determination of the kind and number of needed salespeople; and employment planning—the locating, recruiting, evaluation, and hiring of applicants for the sales job.

Once the hiring is done, the sales manager becomes involved in training salespeople on things such as product knowledge and selling skills. Training begins immediately, usually in the salesperson's territory and at company training facilities.

The sales manager is a salesperson first, but also something of a jack-of-all-trades due to the various functions required for the job. The next chapter will discuss directing and controlling functions.

17

Motivation, Compensation, and Evaluation of Salespeople

My name is Bob James. I'm vice president and southwestern area general manager for American Scientific Products Biomedical division, an operating unit of American Hospital Supply Corporation. From my base in Dallas, I am responsible for some 500 people. They include two area managers, six regional sales managers, about 75 sales representatives, and 420 office, warehouse, and distribution personnel.

I grew up in Evanston, Illinois, my corporation's home base. At Marquette University, where I majored in business and philosophy, I was in the Naval ROTC. I planned to be a pilot, but had to give up that dream when I broke my neck on my way to Marine air training.

I was 21, a college graduate and an ex-serviceman. I needed a career. My father said an Evanston company—American Hospital Supply Corporation—looked promising. After talking with American's personnel director, I was hired as a sales trainee. That was in 1958. I've been with American Scientific Products Biomedical division ever since.

The sales rep traditionally has been the backbone of America. Sales is an ideal place to demonstrate your abilities quickly, to differentiate yourself from the crowd.

After working three territories, I was one of the division's top salespeople. But I knew management offered long-term career growth and potentially greater compensation. I could stay with sales and continue developing my territory or I could choose the more varied route of management. I chose management, worked my way up, and have been in my present position since 1970. •

P R O F I L E

Bob James
*American Scientific
Products*

"A manager's most important job is hiring good people," says Bob James. "I look for someone who cares for others, who listens well and is empathetic—someone I would be proud to bring into my home.

"Salespeople should be incisive and able to respond quickly when someone tries to steer them away from their objective. Honesty is essential. We entrust the corporation's reputation and assets to our salespeople.

"I want salespeople who are self-starters, who constantly strive to improve themselves, who lay plans with short- and long-term goals. To motivate such people, a manager must respond quickly to factors that might deter high-level performance. You need to make sure people are doing all that is necessary to become further entrenched in their accounts. If someone gets sloppy, or needs too much direction, bring such matters to their attention constructively. At the same time, compliment people when they do well.

"In evaluating salespeople, you look at sales performance and how well customers' needs are being met. You also look at a person's flexibility, at how well they implement new ideas within their territories.

"A manager needs these same qualities, and more. They must be able to plan, organize, motivate, and control. They should have good people skills. And they should have the drive and self-confidence necessary to be comfortable taking me through their game plans for meeting our objectives.

"In the final analysis, the better people you surround yourself with, the better manager you'll be." •

Bob James' comments on what it takes to be a successful sales manager lead us into the important areas of motivating, compensating, and evaluating salespeople. Much of a sales manager's job involves these three managerial functions. This chapter discusses the motivation, compensation, and performance evaluation of salespeople. We begin by presenting five factors that can be used to motivate salespeople.

MOTIVATION OF THE SALES FORCE

Sales managers are concerned with motivating salespeople at two levels. The first is the motivation of the individual salesperson and the second is the motivation of the entire sales force. At both levels, managers should determine how much motivation is needed if the sales personnel are to successfully accomplish their assigned job goals, and they should determine the methods of motivation that are best for the situation at hand. Finally, they should develop a well-designed motivation program that is coordinated with other sales management activities.

Motivation is a term originally derived from the Latin word *movere,* which means "to move," but it has been expanded to include the various factors by which human behavior is activated. Let us define *motivation* as the arousal, intensity, direction, and persistence of effort directed toward job tasks over a period. The sales manager strives to increase the motivation of salespeople toward performing their job activities at a high level through the development of a motivation mix.

THE MOTIVATION MIX: CHOOSE YOUR INGREDIENTS CAREFULLY

What can the sales manager do to motivate salespeople? A review of sales management literature reveals five broad classes of factors, all five referred to as the **motivation mix,** used to motivate salespeople, as shown in Figure 17.1. Examples of each factor follow:

1. The basic compensation plan.
   a. Salary.
   b. Commissions.
   c. Fringe benefits.
2. Special financial incentives.
   a. Contests.
   b. Bonuses.
   c. Promotion.
3. Nonfinancial rewards.
   a. Achievement awards.
   b. Challenging work assignments.
   c. Psychological rewards.
      (1) Praise.
      (2) Recognition.
4. Leadership techniques.
   a. Style.
   b. Personal contact methods (feedback).
      (1) National, regional, district meetings.
      (2) Individual meetings.
      (3) Letters, telephone calls.
5. Management control procedures.
   a. Performance evaluation.
   b. Quotas.
   c. Reports.

Each of these five factors is discussed in this chapter, beginning with compensation.

FIGURE 17.1   Sales manager's motivation mix

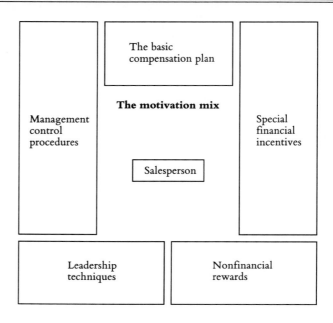

METHODS OF COMPENSATING SALESPEOPLE

Salespeople are compensated by one of three methods: (1) straight salary, (2) straight commission, or (3) a combination of straight salary and incentives, such as commissions, bonuses, or contests.

Straight Salary

Of all compensation plans, the **straight salary plan** is the simplest. The salesperson is paid a specific dollar amount at regular intervals, usually weekly, semimonthly, or monthly. For example, as shown in Figure 17.2(A), the salesperson earns $22,000 annually regardless of whether that person sells $100,000 or $500,000 in merchandise.

Advantages to the Salesperson.   This salary plan provides the sense of security that a person may require for effective selling because it ensures a regular income. In theory, pay is independent of sales performance in the short run (a month, three months). However, if performance is low for a prolonged period, the company can take corrective action to improve sales or replace the salesperson. High sales performance can be rewarded by a periodic salary increase (every six or twelve months). New recruits and

FIGURE 17.2 Examples of salary plans

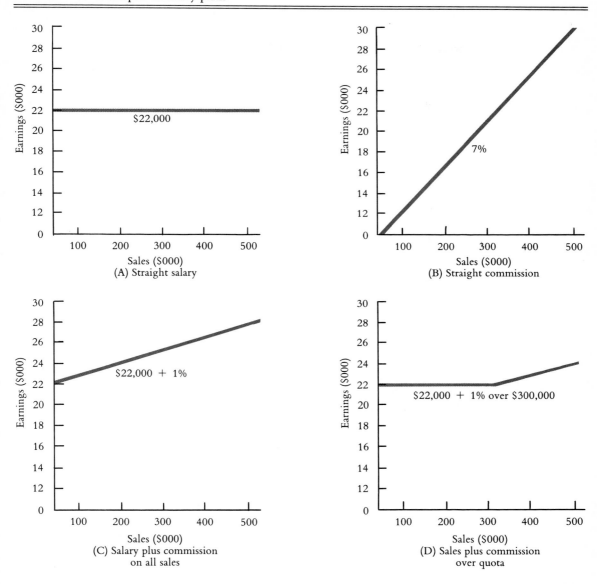

(A) Straight salary

(B) Straight commission

(C) Salary plus commission
on all sales

(D) Sales plus commission
over quota

younger salespeople with little sales experience often prefer a compensation
plan that gives them a known income.

Advantages to Management. From management's point of view, the plan
is simple and economical to administer. Salespeople can be directed toward
tasks the company believes are important much more easily than if they

were on a straight commission plan. Management can direct selling duties that may not immediately result in sales, such as contacting nonproductive accounts or routinely calling on customers who purchase the company's products from a distribution center or wholesaler outside the territory.

Management also usually finds less resistance to reassignments of accounts and personnel transfers with this arrangement. Salespeople are less likely to use high-pressure selling tactics or to overload customers with merchandise that may bring rewards to the salesperson, but not be best for the buyer or the company. Finally, management can project compensation expenses for several years in the future because sales costs are relatively fixed. This can make salary budgeting much more accurate. However, because there is no direct relationship between salary and sales performance, it is difficult to estimate salary expenses as a percentage of sales.

Disadvantages of the Straight Salary Plan. The straight salary plan has several potentially undesirable features. The major disadvantage is the lack of direct monetary incentive. The salesperson who meets certain job goals is rewarded by an increase in salary. However, salary adjustments are usually made at specified intervals, so that the increase may be given long after the goal was met. In addition, salary adjustments are not always based on specific performance. Often, everyone is given the same salary increase or there is little difference in the pay adjustment received by the higher performers and by the lower performers. Because salaries are usually kept secret, even if the top performers were given substantially higher raises, they may not perceive them as rewards for good performance. This lack of incentive may cause better salespeople to change jobs.

It can also create lowered work norms within the sales group. Salespeople often perceive that they are in competition with other salespeople and not with their firm's competitors. This is because their performance is compared with other salespeople in their sales district. They may only want to do an average job and meet or not greatly exceed sales quotas. This arrangement can thus favor the less productive sales people. If not closely supervised, salespeople may accomplish their monthly goals quickly—for example, in three weeks—and not work the rest of the month.

Another problem with the plan is that salary is not distributed in proportion to sales made. One salesperson may sell $500,000 of merchandise and be paid $22,000, while another sells $1 million and also earns $22,000. Also, since salaries are a fixed expense for the firm, they cannot be adjusted for downturns in the economy. This can increase direct selling costs as compared to other plans. When sales decline, the firm may have to dismiss people. Salespeople who are kept on often have the most job tenure and receive the larger salaries. However, they may not necessarily be the best salespeople. Another problem of using a straight salary compensation plan is that salespeople may emphasize products that are easiest to sell, especially if this allows them to meet their sales quota.

Many companies increase the number of sales managers to offset these problems. Each manager has fewer salespeople to supervise, helping to ensure that each salesperson works at maximum capacity. However, this approach usually results in an increase in sales expenses rather than selling effort. The amount of supervision has less effect on performance than on supervision quality.

When to Use Straight Salary Plans. A straight salary plan is best for jobs in which a high percentage of the work day is devoted to nonselling activities, and for which management finds it cannot effectively evaluate performance. Straight salary can be used effectively for routine selling jobs (selling milk, bread, or beverages), extensive missionary and educational sales (pharmaceutical selling), or sales jobs requiring lengthy presale and postsale service and negotiations (selling technical and complex products). Firms sometimes use this method when the person is in training. For example, some insurance firms pay a salary the first year. After one year, the salesperson is placed on a straight commission.

Straight Commission Plans

The **straight commission plan** is a complete incentive compensation plan. If you do not sell anything, you do not earn anything. There are two basic types of commission plans: straight commission and draw against commission.

There are three basic elements of the straight commission plan. First, pay is related directly to a performance unit such as a dollar of sales, a type or amount of product sold, a dollar of profit, type of purchaser, credit terms, or season of the sales. Second, a percentage rate of commission is attached to the unit. Third, a level at which commissions begin or change is established.

Figure 17.2(B) shows a 7 percent commission on all sales. The salesperson must generate approximately $314,000 in sales to earn the same $22,000 earned by the person under the straight salary plan.

In addition to the single commission plan, multiple commission rates sometimes are used. For example, a 10 percent commission may be paid on the first $100,000 of sales and 12 percent on sales over that amount in the same year. A person who sold $300,000 would receive $34,000 in commissions (($100,000 × .10) + ($200,000 × .12) = $34,000). When the commission rate increases, it is a "progressive" commission plan.

On the other hand, some companies use a "regressive" plan where commission rates decrease as sales increase, such as paying 12 percent on the first $100,000 and 10 percent on sales over that amount. For sales of

$300,000, the salesperson would receive $32,000. The regressive system is used to help place an upper limit on a salesperson's earnings to encourage top producers to accept management positions if they want to increase their earnings beyond the level attainable in a sales job. In some companies, a top salesperson can earn more than a boss.

Drawing Accounts.   One version of the straight line commission plan is known as the drawing account. It combines the incentive of a commission plan with the security of a fixed income. The firm establishes a monetary account for each salesperson. The amount may be based on the individual needs of the salesperson, a base level set by the company, or a base level that considers the individual salesperson's needs, background, and selling potential.

The salesperson may believe that $2,000 a month is needed to meet base expenditures for that period. Thus, at the beginning of the month, a draw of $2,000 against commission for that month is given. If sales for a particular month resulted in commissions of $2,100, at the end of the month, the company would pay $100 in commissions. Conversely, if commissions earned for that month amounted to only $1,300, the salesperson would owe the company $700.

Management must monitor each salesperson closely to prevent a negative balance on salary from becoming so large that it is difficult, if not impossible, to repay it. Should the balance become large, the possibility of repayment may be so discouraging that the salesperson might feel compelled to quit the job. Though many firms have contractual agreements calling for repayment of negative balances against a drawing account, collecting an overdraft can be difficult. Some firms use a guaranteed drawing account plan in which the salesperson does not have to pay back overdrafts. Such a plan is actually a salary plus commission.

Advantages of Straight Commission Plans.   Many sales managers believe that the commission plan provides maximum incentive for salespeople. They know that earnings are contingent on selling the firm's products. This expectancy of reward based on performance should direct salespeople to use their sales time wisely and to perform at maximum capacity. It is the reason many people are attracted to commission sales jobs. Only their abilities limit earning potential and no arbitrary earnings decisions can be made by management. See Figure 17.3.

Salespeople often feel that they are in business for themselves. This is a benefit. If they are fired or leave their employer voluntarily, they can often continue the same business relationship with their customers after taking a job with another company. In addition, more people are attracted to part-time commission sales jobs, such as selling real estate or consumer products (e.g., Mary Kay Cosmetics) because of the earning potential.

FIGURE 17.3   Straight commission provides a maximum incentive

· *Salespeople earning the highest income are on commission programs. Helen McVoy earned $1,000,000 from Mary Kay Cosmetics due to her excellent sales performance on a straight commission system.*

They can call on accounts that they feel are productive, determine their work schedules, and set their hours.

Many organizations prefer to use the commission plan because it is simple to administer and selling costs are kept in proportion to sales. This is important to a new firm that cannot afford to pay a portion of its salespeople a salary if they are not profitably productive, or in case of an economic recession that could cause sales costs to severely affect profits. The firm with limited capital can hire as many salespeople as needed and have no salary costs until sales are made.

Payment is made to the salesperson at time of the sale, when the order is shipped, or when the order is paid for. For some sales, the salesperson may continue to receive payment in the future as long as the product or service is purchased by the consumer. Commissions for life insurance policy premiums are an example.

Disadvantages of the Commission Plan.   Straight commission plans have several potential disadvantages. One, particularly for the person who has never sold before, is the uncertainty and insecurity of the plan. The salesperson must sell to be paid. This is fine for the company, but may discourage people from seeking sales careers.

With some big sales volume items, a long time may elapse before a person makes a sale. For example, in commercial real estate, it is common for a person to make only one, two, or three sales a year. These sales often result in large commissions, but the individual must have enough funds to live on between commissions. The uncertainty and insecurity of straight commission sales jobs can lead to high turnover and high expenses and sales costs for recruiting, selection, and training of new salespeople.

Often, salespeople on commission develop little loyalty for the company. While feeling that they are in business for themselves can have benefits for salespeople, the company may have difficulty in controlling or channeling salespeople's efforts. Salespeople on commission select their customer and their products, and in a few cases they may use high-pressure techniques to close sales because they will not see their customers again.

Under the straight commission plan, salespeople are much more reluctant to split territories or move their present territory to another territory. They may have spent time building a rapport with their customers and do not want to relinquish it. This can pose difficulties for the employer. In addition, with straight commission, service after the sale may be neglected.

The cost of sales may be somewhat greater with a straight commission plan even though a greater sales volume is produced. Salespeople can earn more pay per dollar of sale on straight commission than they can on salary plans. Commissions can fluctuate greatly. In good times, salespeople may earn large commissions, but in an economic recession, their earnings may drop drastically.

Because of the disadvantages of the straight commission plan for employees, sales managers often take for granted a high turnover of sales personnel. Such turnover makes it difficult to build an experienced sales force. Sales managers may hire salespeople quickly, without thorough selection and recruitment, because they realize that if the people do not produce, they will not be with the company for long. This lack of recruitment, training, and supervision results in an increase in sales costs and loss of potential sales.

The firm using the straight commission plan must work with the salespeople to set realistic sales goals that will allow the salesperson and the firm to meet their objectives. Because performance or sales activities to some extent are dictated by the marketplace and the salesperson's customers, management must reward the behavior or selling activities it seeks from the sales force. For example, different commission rates on different products deter the salesperson from concentrating on the easy-to-sell, low profit margin items. A lower commission rate could be placed on easy-to-sell products and higher commission rates paid on harder-to-sell products. Bonuses could also be established for the products that the company wants the sales force to concentrate on or a higher commission rate could be placed on these products.

Administrative Problems with the Commission Plan. With today's complex distribution channels and exchange processes, the proper allocation of commissions to salespeople can be a problem. The company must carefully examine the process through which the sales exchange is made to determine their commission compensation policies. Administrative policies must be developed for each of these circumstances to provide proper compensation of sales personnel and to prevent morale problems. For example, if two or more salespeople are involved in a sale, the fair distribution of commissions can be a problem. Should two salespeople put an equal amount of time and effort into the sale, the commission can easily be split on a 50-50 basis. However, if the two salespeople differ in their perception of each person's input, a dispute may arise over the percentage each should earn. One solution is for management to base all commissions that are made by two or more salespeople on the number of sales in which they were involved during that period.

Another potential problem is what to do when there are bad debts. A salesperson may have sold a product or products to a customer who is unable to pay or goes bankrupt. If the salesperson is not directly responsible for the extension of credit to accounts, most firms will not withdraw a commission. The same is true for sales returns. If a small number of items sold are returned, the company may not deduct money from commissions. However, many firms look at net sales. If, for example, a salesperson sold $11,000 worth of merchandise this month and had returns of $1,000, the company would pay a commission based on sales of $10,000.

Combination Plans

Under a **combination salary plan,** a proportion of the salesperson's total pay is guaranteed while some of it can come from commissions. The most commonly used percentage split is 80 percent base salary and 20 percent incentive. A 70/30 and 60/40 split are the next most common combinations.

Various combinations of salary plus incentives can be used by a company. The more popular plans are the following:

- Salary and commission.
- Salary and bonus: individual bonus or group bonus.
- Salary, commission, and bonus: individual bonus or group bonus.

Figure 17.2(C) and (D) illustrate the two popular versions of a combination plan. Figure 17.2(C) shows earnings of $22,000, plus 1 percent commission on all sales. Sales of $300,000 earn the salesperson an extra $3,000. Figure 17.2(D) illustrates a salary plus commission over a sales quota. In this example, the salesperson who sells $300,000 earns 1 percent on all additional sales. The quota of $300,000 may be based on meeting last year's actual sales or it may represent a sales quota above last year's actual sales.

Bonus: Individual or Group

In addition to combination plans based on salary and commissions, many firms use a bonus system. Bonuses can be used with any basic compensation plan. A **bonus** is something given in addition to what is usually earned by the salesperson. Typically, it is money earned over an extended period, such as one year.

Across-the-Board Bonus. One type of bonus includes the Christmas or year-end bonus, which is given to all salespeople regardless of their productivity. An equal sum of money may be paid to each salesperson or the bonus may be based on present salary and tenure with the organization. The Upjohn Company pays a Christmas bonus of 1.5 percent of the annual salary to salespeople who have been with the firm for one to two years and 2 percent to those who have been with the firm for two or three years. The percentage may go as high as 8 percent. The bonus is paid on an individual basis and is not related to employee performance.

Performance Bonus. The second type of bonus is related to performance. Numerous bonus plans of this type can be devised, but they fall into two general categories according to whether they are awarded on an individual or group basis. Bonuses can be awarded not only on the basis of sales or units sold, but also on the basis of gross profit margins, on sales performance appraisals, on new accounts acquired, on company or geographical sales unit earnings or sales, and on sales of specific products.

A sales region may be given a bonus amount based on its performance as compared to that of other sales regions in the organization. The regional sales manager would then allocate a certain amount to each sales district according to performance. The district manager could distribute the district bonus equally among all salespeople, or use a merit system based on individual performance.

Sales Contests. Another compensation variable for influencing salespeople's performance is the sales contest. **Sales contests** are special sales programs offering salespeople incentives to achieve short-term sales goals. The incentives may include items that indicate recognition of achievement (e.g., certificates, cash, merchandise, or travel). Occasionally, contests may run for as long as a year; examples include the insurance or real estate industry's "Million Dollar Club." The incentives are given in addition to regular compensation.

Billions are spent on sales contests each year. Industry typically spends 35 percent on sales incentives, with 78 percent spent on merchandise awards and 22 percent on incentive travel programs. Until the late 1960s, there was little use of incentive travel programs. However, as corporations attempted to find means of motivating salespeople to top the previous year's performance, travel was used increasingly to glamorize sales programs. Offering merchandise and cash keeps such programs flexible.[1]

The sales contest is an effective incentive method that is used to intensify, direct, and make salespeople more persistent in their work over time. Salespeople work harder to meet contest goals and thereby earn rewards. Management can direct salespeople to sell specific products or to perform activities they would not normally do through contest incentives. Contests can also cause salespeople to work harder for longer periods (persistence) to achieve the contest goals and earn extra rewards. As one executive in the cosmetics industry stated, "Our incentive program allows us to apply no direct sales pressure while motivating the salespeople, and to reward those who reach company-approved goals. Contests have helped this company increase sales from $7.8 million to over $31 million in five years."[2]

Sales contests can have several indirect influences on salespeople. Many sales managers feel that these contests, as well as bonuses, can increase the "team spirit" of their sales group, interest in the job, and job satisfaction, and can discourage absenteeism and turnover.

THE TOTAL COMPENSATION PACKAGE

People choose a sales career for both nonfinancial and financial reasons. The salesperson receives numerous forms of financial compensation. Table 17.1 illustrates the dollar value one company places on its total compensation for the beginning salesperson.

Monthly salary, including fringe benefits, equals $2,428.67, $628.67 a month above the base salary of $1,800. Also, the salesperson participates in an incentive bonus plan, plus 10 additional benefits. Thus, it is not surprising that a sales career is attractive to thousands of people.

NONFINANCIAL REWARDS ARE MANY

Nonfinancial rewards are effective in motivating salespeople. The sales manager can reward a salesperson for achieving sales goals with bonuses and other awards. Achievement or recognition awards are commonly presented at sales meetings. While there are usually no financial benefits associated with achievement awards, winning salespeople receive recognition from their managers and other salespeople that tends to motivate them to work harder.

TABLE 17.1 Example of a company's salary and fringe benefits for a new representative (based on starting salary of $1,800 per month, with automatic increases to $1,900 at training completion

Starting Salary before Completion of Training (annual):

$21,600.00	($1,800.00/month)—base salary
1,944.00	Company contribution to pension plan for future service only (9 percent)
1,000.00	Company contribution to group health insurance, major medical and life insurance plans
100.00	Telephone allowance
4,500.00	Estimated value of having a car at your disposal
$29,144.00	Total salary
$ 2,428.67	Monthly salary including fringe benefits

Plus, an incentive bonus plan determined on relative attainment of sales forecast. Additional benefits that are not measured in dollars, but contribute materially to your standard of living, security, and development:

1. Under 5 years, two weeks' vacation; after 5 years, three weeks' vacation; after 15 years, four weeks' vacation; after 25 years, five weeks' vacation.

2. Seven paid holidays

3. Christmas furlough.

4. Pension plan rated as one of the best in the industry.

5. Group health insurance and major medical plan cover not only the representative but also spouse and unmarried children under 19, and student children to age 26. Continuance of 20 percent of life insurance after retirement at age 60 or later without cost to employee.

6. Liberal sick pay plan.

Total Period Covered		
Years of Service	*Full Base Pay (weeks)*	*Half Base Pay (weeks)*
Under 5 years	4	12
Over 5 years	8	12
Over 10 years	10	12
Over 15 years	12	12
Over 21 years	16	12

7. New long-term disability (LTD) plan. LTD provides financial security for you and your family for period of continuous total disability extending beyond the benefits provided under the sick and accident plan or the company workmen's compensation supplement.

8. Employees' education fund pays half tuition for approved courses successfully completed, if the representative is employed less than one year; 75 percent of tuition after one year.

9. Twenty weeks' intensive training followed by constant supervision and guidance by district sales manager.

10. Regular reviews of job performance for salary consideration.

Salespeople who do well may be transferred to larger, more challenging sales territories or promoted to key account manager. This recognizes their contribution to the company and serves as further motivation. Furthermore, little personal things such as a sales manager's praise, can motivate a salesperson to improve performance.

It is up to the manager to develop ways of creating a work environment in which performing well is a rewarding experience to the salesperson, even though no pay raise, bonus, or contest is involved. Good job performance

FIGURE 17.4   Top Mary Kay Cosmetic salespeople attend annual national sales meeting to receive recognition and $1,500,000 in prizes earned through sales performance

should give the salesperson a feeling of accomplishment and satisfaction. Special nonfinancial awards, certificates, medals, and praise are an important part of the manager's motivational mix.

Mary Kay Cosmetics is an excellent example of a company rewarding performance financially and nonfinancially. At Mary Kay's annual sales meeting, over 30,000 salespeople receive training, inspiration, and rewards. As shown in Figure 17.4, salespeople are brought on stage to receive recognition and receive sales contest prizes.[3]

I [your author] attended a recent meeting as a guest to see over $1.5 million in money and prizes given to thousands of salespeople. Salespeople receive such things as furs, diamonds, and pink Cadillacs. Mary Kay presents top sales producers with numerous diamond sales prizes.

LEADERSHIP IS IMPORTANT TO SUCCESS

In a recent survey, nearly 500 sales and marketing managers working for some 450 companies of all sizes were asked to rank the most important factors in managing their firms' sales force. Leadership was ranked first. The second most important factor was the sales manager's ability to motivate salespeople.[4]

Leadership is the process by which the sales manager attempts to influence the activities of salespeople. Figure 17.5 is an illustration of the basic influence process involved in leadership. As shown, the leadership process begins with an intent on the part of person A, followed by an attempt to influence person B, who then reacts in some way that fulfills the intent of person A. An example is the sales manager attempting to influence each salesperson toward attaining certain performance goals. The manager who possesses leadership capabilities that influence all salespeople to reach their sales goals will attain the goals assigned to the whole group.

What makes a person a successful leader? How can a potentially successful sales manager be identified? Three major approaches have been explored to answer these questions: (1) the trait approach, (2) the behavioral approach, and (3) the situational approach.

Trait Approach

Up until 40 years ago, most people assumed that leaders were born, not made, and that a person became a leader because of certain characteristics. Consequently, researchers attempted to identify the traits that differentiated leaders from followers. According to the **trait leadership approach,** there is a set of characteristics that distinguishes successful from unsuccessful leaders. This was the simplest, oldest, and, until the late 1940s, the main method of determining the elements of effective leadership.

This approach asked the question: "What are the traits of successful leaders?" Once these traits were determined, it was felt that a firm could hire people who have these characteristics and therefore have effective leaders. A long and growing list of traits has been investigated—for example, a person's physical characteristics, social background, intelligence, and personality. Yet, no traits have been established as universally characteristic of successful leaders.

Behavioral Approach

Because the attempt to identify the traits that distinguish leaders was unsuccessful, from the late 1940s to the early 1960s, attention was turned to studying styles of leadership. This meant behavior that could be learned, behavior that was not innate. It was felt that successful leaders may be recognized by behavior patterns. The **behavioral leadership approach**

FIGURE 17.5 Leadership influence process

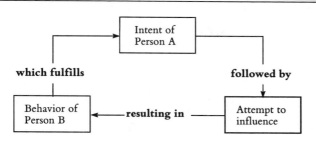

assumes that effective leaders are distinguished by their particular style of leadership in various situations.

The Ohio State University Studies. In the late 1940s, two major studies of leadership were begun at Ohio State University and the University of Michigan. As a result of the work done at Ohio State, two major dimensions of leadership behavior were identified: **initiating structure** and **consideration.**

Initiating Structure. This is referred to as a "task–oriented" leadership style because the leader's behavior is aimed at getting the job or task done. A sales manager of this type:

- Emphasizes reaching sales goals.
- Offers new approaches to selling a prospect.
- Criticizes poor work.
- Assigns salespeople to particular tasks.

Consideration. This is a "salesperson–oriented" leadership style. The leader's behavior indicates trust, warmth, respect, and concern for the salesperson's welfare. This kind of leader:

- Is friendly and easily approached.
- Backs up salespeople in their actions.
- Helps salespeople with personal problems.
- Sees that salespeople are rewarded for jobs well done.

As shown in Figure 17.6, a leader can be rated in terms of these two leadership styles. Research in this area found no single best leadership style. A combination of the initiating structure and consideration behavior based on the individual situation resulted in the highest performance. Thus, one sales manager might find the high-high style (high initiating structure-

FIGURE 17.6   Leadership styles: initiating structure and consideration

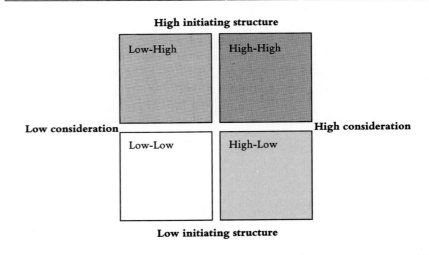

high consideration) successful, whereas another manager might use the same style and be unsuccessful. Furthermore, the manager successfully using the high-high style in one situation may find it ineffective in another situation.

The University of Michigan Studies.   At the University of Michigan, what were called "job-centered" and "employee-centered" leadership styles were studied. These are similar to the initiating structure and consideration styles, respectively, of the Ohio State studies. The results showed that the employee-centered leadership style was best. Both styles actually improved performance; however, a leader using a job-centered style created tensions and pressures that resulted in lower job satisfaction and increased turnover and absenteeism. As with the Ohio State results, the style of behavior of leaders changes from situation to situation. The leader may be friendly and helpful to subordinates if all is going well, but criticize poor work if performance decreases.

Situational Approach

The trait and behavioral approaches provide background for the study of leadership in individual situations. The key to a sales manager's effectiveness, according to the **situational approach,** is based on the ability to diagnose a salesperson's situation, and then to select the leadership style that will influence that salesperson to reach the desired performance.

Researchers have identified a number of leadership styles used by sales

FIGURE 17.7 Different participative styles of sales managerial behavior

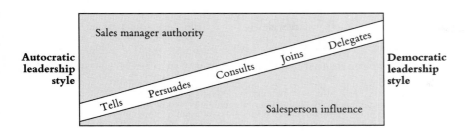

managers. Four of the basic styles are: (1) an **achievement style,** which involves establishing performance goals that are challenging, while letting salespeople know the manager has confidence that they will achieve goals; (2) a **supportive style,** characterized by concern for salespeople's welfare, needs, and well-being; (3) an **instrumental style,** involving telling salespeople what is expected of them—the sales manager is primarily concerned with salespeople performing their tasks effectively to reach their job goals; and (4) a **participative style,** in which salespeople take part in setting job goals, and use their ideas and creativity in accomplishing them.

There are five different styles of participative behavior, shown in Figure 17.7. The behavior at the left is an **autocratic style,** and the behavior at the right is a **democratic style.** Depending on the situation and subordinates, the manager can choose a participative behavior style ranging from highly autocratic to highly democratic. The salesperson has more influence over the job as the sales manager's leadership style moves to the right. These five participative styles of leadership behavior are described as follows:

• *Telling.* The sales manager identifies problems and opportunities, makes all decisions, and tells salespeople what to do. A "do it or else" approach is usually used.

• *Persuading.* As above, the sales manager makes decisions; however, the salesperson's cooperation is sought.

• *Consulting.* The sales manager presents the problem or situation and asks the salesperson for suggestions on how to act. The sales manager decides what is the most appropriate action.

• *Joining.* Within the restrictions imposed by superiors, the sales manager is part of the "sales team," and acts as a participant in the decision-making process. The sales manager agrees in advance to support the group decision.

• *Delegating.* The sales manager presents the problem or situation and allows the salesperson to act, giving total support to the salesperson's decision. The success or failure of the action is the responsibility of the salesperson.[5]

Choosing a Leadership Style

While there is no one best way to lead salespeople in all situations, there are leadership techniques that can improve a manager's effectiveness. These are:

- Be familiar with each salesperson's territory, customers, and personal circumstances to properly diagnose the person's situation.
- Have the flexibility to be autocratic or democratic when dealing with a salesperson based on the situation—for example, be democratic with the high-performing salesperson and autocratic with the low performer.
- Clearly show salespeople the way to reach their goals.
- Play the role of a coach whose aim is to aid salespeople to reach their personal and territorial goals.
- Develop technical, human, and conceptual skills.

A more specific example of how one chooses a leadership style based on the situation is seen in this example. A district sales manager (we will call him Bruce) for a large national consumer goods manufacturer discussed the four styles of leadership he uses in leading his sales group. These four styles are illustrative of some situational influences that dictate a particular leadership style.

First, Bruce uses "management by objectives." He develops no more than two yearly objectives for each of his salespeople (such as placing major emphasis on a single product or concentrating on accomplishing certain objectives for a single large account) based on the situation in an individual territory. In this context, Bruce uses instrumental, participative, and achievement-oriented leadership techniques.

Second, Bruce uses "management by the objective." In all companies, there are times when the home office tells the sales force that they must meet certain sales goals. The directive is given to Bruce by upper management and he informs his people that they are expected to reach certain sales goals (such as a 10 percent increase in sales of all sizes of a particular product). He uses instrumental and achievement-oriented leadership techniques in this instance.

Third, Bruce uses "management by motivation." The salespeople who do what is expected receive recognition. Having reached a certain level of performance, salespeople become members of an "All-Star Team." Letters are also sent to Bruce's boss, Joe, informing him of a salesperson's success. Joe writes personal letters to the salespeople congratulating them on their performance. These are short-term motivators; raises, commissions, and promotions are used as long-term motivators. Supportive and achievement-oriented techniques are applied here.

Fourth, Bruce uses "management by terror." Behavioral researchers have long known that people are motivated not only by a need to achieve, but also by a fear of failure. Twice each year, he evaluates performance and continually gives salespeople feedback on their strengths and on where they can improve. Of course, there are times when managers have to inform people that, unless their performance improves, they should look for another job. This involves instrumental and achievement-oriented techniques.

Only one leadership style is consistently used by Bruce: the achievement-oriented technique. This is typical in sales positions because of the great emphasis placed on performance.

PERFORMANCE EVALUATIONS LET PEOPLE KNOW WHERE THEY STAND

Achieving acceptable levels of performance is essential for the organization to stay in business and for the salesperson to reach personal goals. A major part of the manager's job is to lead and motivate salespeople to perform at an acceptable level. At the end of each performance period, such as the end of the year, the manager evaluates each salesperson's performance. This creates a **management control system** that establishes performance goals, evaluates the goals compared to the salesperson's accomplishments, and then rewards or penalizes the individual based on the performance level.

Reasons for Performance Evaluation

Performance evaluations are done for three reasons: (1) to appraise a salesperson's past performance; (2) to develop a sales plan to increase the salesperson's future sales; and (3) to motivate salespeople to improve their performance. Sales managers' evaluations provide the basis for numerous decisions on salary, promotions, transfers, demotions, and dismissal.

Appraisal sessions involve giving face-to-face feedback to the salespeople on quality of performance, getting to know each other better, and gaining an understanding of what each person expects from the other.

Who Should Evaluate Salespeople?

The primary evaluator should be the salesperson's immediate superior because this person has direct knowledge about sales performance. The manager has actually worked with the salesperson. In some companies, the immediate superior completes the entire evaluation including recommendations for pay raises and promotions. The evaluations and recommendations are sent to the manager's immediate superior for final approval. The manager's superior accepts the recommendations without question. In the majority of organizations, several managers evaluate each salesperson. The simplest approach is for the district manager and the regional sales manager to arrive at an evaluation together. The other district managers in the region may also express their opinion when the region's entire management group get together periodically.

Many companies use the entire region's management group and a home office personnel specialist to evaluate salespeople's work, as shown in Figure 17.8. The specialist presents the home office viewpoint by making sure that the evaluation procedures are followed and that each person is treated fairly.

When Should Salespeople Be Evaluated?

Salespeople should be evaluated at the end of each performance cycle. A performance cycle is a period related to specific product goals and/or job activities. For example, consumer goods manufacturers typically have certain products they want to emphasize periodically. They may have six performance cycles during the year. Every two months, the sales force is given specific sales goals for five to ten different products. It is necessary to compare goals to results after each cycle. In addition, salespeople are monitored monthly in terms of the other products they sell.

These periodic performance evaluations provide the input for semiannual and/or annual performance evaluations. These performance evaluations provide important feedback to both management and salespeople. A minimum of one formal evaluation should be completed yearly for each salesperson.

Performance Criteria

Companies examine their salespeople's jobs; determine the important parts of the job; and develop performance criteria based on their findings. These performance criteria serve as the basis for evaluating a salesperson's performance. They are of two types—quantitative and qualitative.

Quantitative Performance Criteria. Of the two categories of performance criteria, **quantitative performance criteria** is best for effectively evaluating performance. This category represents end results or bottom-line objective data, such as:

- Sales volume:
  - —Percentage of increase.
  - —Market share.
  - —Quotas obtained.
- Average sales calls per day.

FIGURE 17.8 Possible management input into salesperson's performance evaluation

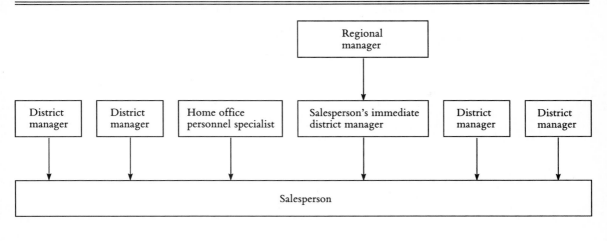

———— Direct input performance evaluation.

———— Indirect input performance evaluation.

- New customers obtained.
- Gross profit by product, customer, and order size.
- Ratio of selling costs to sales.
- Sales orders:
  —Daily number of orders.
- Total.
- By size, customer classification, and product.
- Orders-to-sales-call ratio.
- Goods returned.

Qualitative Performance Criteria. Many organizations use **qualitative performance criteria** because they represent the salesperson's major job activities and they indicate why the quantitative measures look as they do. Care should be taken to minimize the evaluator's personal biases and subjectivity in evaluating qualitative performance criteria. Examples of such criteria include:

- Sales skills:
  —Finding selling
  points.   —Obtaining participation.
  —Product knowledge.   —Overcoming objections.
  —Listening skill.   —Closing the sale.

- Territory management:
  - —Planning.
  - —Use of time.
  - —Records.
  - —Customer service.
  - —Collections.
  - —Follow-up.
- Personal traits:
  - —Attitude.
  - —Empathy.
  - —Human relations skills.
  - —Team spirit.
  - —Appearance.
  - —Motivation.
  - —Care of car.
  - —Capacity for self-improvement.

Evaluation Guidelines

Typically, the company sets up procedures for who will do the evaluation and how it will be done. The performance criteria for evaluation have been decided and materials, such as evaluation forms, are available. The following is a basic guideline for an effective performance evaluation.

Both Manager and Salesperson Should Be Prepared for the Interview. The manager should collect all information on the performance of the salesperson. The manager should then contact the salesperson and establish a time and place for the evaluation. The salesperson should be asked to review past performance using the evaluation forms, and to review the job description. This takes place before the formal meeting. Quantitative data should be used when possible.

Be Positive. It is extremely important that both manager and salesperson feel that the evaluation is a positive method of helping the salesperson do the job better. The salesperson may feel required to defend rather than explain past performance. Two examples may help to illustrate negative and positive approaches to evaluation:

MANAGER: Well, Lou, it's that time of the year again.

SALESPERSON: I'm looking forward to it!

MANAGER: I didn't have time to review your file, Lou, but I know you really messed up this year on the Goodyear account.

SALESPERSON: Well?

MANAGER: Well nothing! I really got chewed out by the regional manager over that.

SALESPERSON: Did you look at my total performance? Sales were up 5 percent above the district average.

MANAGER: All right, all right, so you're doing OK, but why did you lose the Goodyear account?

The manager is not prepared to talk to Lou. Lou is on the defensive from the beginning. It is no wonder neither of them looks forward to this confrontation. Compare this negative approach to a performance evaluation to a positive one:

MANAGER: Lou, it is great we can get together and discuss your achievements and your goals.

SALESPERSON: I'm looking forward to it!

MANAGER: You know I'm pleased with your sales. You're 5 percent above the district average, that's great! You're going a good job in managing your territory.

SALESPERSON: I'm glad you noticed. You know, I often feel I'm out there all by myself.

MANAGER: Well Lou, you're not! Is there anything I can do to help you?

SALESPERSON: Well, things are going good.

MANAGER: What about the Goodyear account?

SALESPERSON: I sure hated to lose them. My competitor got their business with a low price. But they aren't happy with the service or the products. I'll have that account back in my pocket before you know it!

MANAGER: I know you will. Lou, we are here today to develop ways to make you the best salesperson in the best district, and this is the best district the company has.

SALESPERSON: Sounds great to me. What can I do?

MANAGER: Did you use the forms I sent you to evaluate your performance?

SALESPERSON: Sure did.

MANAGER: What did you find out?

SALESPERSON: Well, there are a few areas I need to look at.

MANAGER: OK, but before we get to those, remember we are here to evaluate your performance to help you. You and I will work out a plan for this coming year that will allow you to continue to do the good job that you want to do. How does that sound?

SALESPERSON: In other words, ways I can make more money and maybe earn a promotion.

MANAGER: That's right. Ways for you to grow and prosper with our company.

These examples point to the need for both people to have a positive attitude toward the evaluation. The manager should believe in the positive effects this talk will have on Lou's future performance and attitude toward his job. The manager has sold Lou on the purpose of their meeting. The evaluation has been prepared for and its purpose agreed on by both the manager and the salesperson.

Actually Review Performance. Again, the manager should be sincere and positive in discussing each of Lou's performance criteria. There will be disagreements. Research has shown that people tend to evaluate themselves better than their superior does. It is important to:

- Freely discuss each performance criterion.
- Ask salespeople to discuss their performance.
- Ask salespeople to evaluate their performance.
- Give the manager's view of performance.

Finalize the Performance Evaluation. The manager should now review each performance area with the salesperson. It is preferable to begin by reviewing the high ratings and work down. The salesperson should understand clearly what has been decided. If there are disagreements, the manager should explain carefully why the salesperson receives a low evaluation in a particular performance area. Serious differences of opinion can occur when the salesperson does not fully understand what was expected.

Summarize the Total Performance Evaluation. The salesperson should be told how the manager views past performance. For example: "Susan, you have done above average work this year. You are continuing to improve year after year, and will receive a good raise. If you continue this level of performance, in a few more years you will be ready for a management position."

"Sam, this is the second year in a row your sales have decreased while the district's have increased. This has to change if you are to stay with the company. I don't want to do this, but you have six months to get your territory turned around."

Develop Mutually Agreed on Objectives. Performance and career objectives can be established now. Both manager and salesperson provide input.

Formalize Evaluation and Objectives. Immediately after the evaluation session is over, the manager should write a letter to the salesperson restating the results of the performance evaluation and the objectives. A copy is sent to the manager's superior to go into the salesperson's permanent personnel file.[6]

SUMMARY OF MAJOR SALES MANAGEMENT ISSUES

An important challenge of the sales manager is to motivate salespeople using financial and nonfinancial methods. Salary, commissions, contests, bonuses, and travel awards are common financial motivators. Achievement awards, challenging work assignments, recognition, leadership techniques, and performance evaluation are nonfinancial methods used as motivators.

Today, salespeople are paid by several methods, but most firms use a combination of salary and financial incentives rather than straight salary or straight commission plans. This provides the salesperson with a guaranteed salary and helps motivate them to reach their sales goals in order to earn commissions and bonuses or to win contests.

The sales manager needs to understand the principles of leadership and apply them to salespeople based on their individual personalities and territorial situations. It is important to be people-oriented and job-oriented toward salespeople to help them reach sales goals. This ultimately helps to reach the manager's goals.

The performance of sales personnel is evaluated by comparing their quotas and objectives to actual sales and job activities to determine their success. The salesperson's immediate manager implements periodic evaluations each year using both quantitative and qualitative performance criteria.

To effectively evaluate salespeople, managers should develop procedures to assure fair treatment. By being prepared for the interview and having a positive attitude, the salesperson will be receptive to the manager's critique. The manager should evaluate each performance criterion and explain the evaluation to the salesperson. A discussion of the salesperson's past performance concludes the interview.

Future performance quotas and objectives can now be established to serve as goals to reach for the upcoming sales period.

This chapter concludes the discussion of the challenging fundamentals of selling and sales management.

N O T E S

CHAPTER 1

1. John Hancock Mutual Life Insurance Corporation.

2. "Tomorrow's Jobs," *Occupational Outlook Handbook* (Washington D.C.: U.S. Department of Labor, Bureau of Labor Statistics, April 1988), p. 12.

3. Adapted from William A. O'Connell, "A 10-Year Report on Sales Force Productivity," *Sales & Marketing Management,* December 1988, pp. 33–38; "Survey of Selling Costs," *Sales & Marketing Management,* February 17, 1989; *Occupational Outlook Quarterly,* Spring 1989; "1989 Sales Force Compensation," *Dartnell's 24th Biennial Survey,* Chicago, 1988; and Charles Futrell, *Survey of America's Top Sales Forces,* 1989.

4. *Occupational Outlook Quarterly,* Spring 1989.

5. Also see Myron Gable and B. J. Reed, "The Current Status of Women in Professional Selling," *The Journal of Personal Selling and Sales Management,* May 1987, pp. 33–39; Darrell D. Muehling and William A. Weeks, "Women's Perceptions of Personal Selling: Some Positive Results," *The Journal of Personal Selling and Sales Management,* May 1988, pp. 11–20.

6. *Occupational Projections and Training Data* (Washington, D.C.: U.S. Department of Labor, Bureau of Labor Statistics, April 1988).

7. For further background on sales job classifications, see William C. Moncrief III, "Selling Activity and Sales Position Taxonomies for Industrial Salesforces," *Journal of Marketing Research,* August 1986, pp. 261–70.

8. Adapted from a survey of CEOs of Fortune 500 companies by Heidrick and Struggles, an executive search firm, as reported in *USA Today,* August 16, 1986, p. 1B; and "Marketing Newsletter," *Sales & Marketing Management,* February 1987, p. 27.

9. For examples, see William Keenan, Jr., "Executive Pay: Are You Falling Behind?" *Sales & Marketing Management,* November 1988, pp. 46–54.

10. For current information, the magazine *Sales & Marketing Management* publishes their "Salespeople's Average Annual Compensation" survey results in the February special issue each year.

11. Robert L. Shook, *Ten Greatest Salespersons* (New York: Harper & Row, 1978), p. 34.

12. "How They Make It to the Top," *Sales & Marketing Management,* September 14, 1986, p. 57.

13. Shook, *Ten Greatest Salespersons,* p. 65.

14. Xerox Corporation sales literature.

CHAPTER 2

1. William J. Stanton and Charles Futrell, *Fundamentals of Marketing* (New York: McGraw-Hill, 1987).

2. For further discussion, see Thomas L. Powers, Warren S. Martin, Hugh Rushing, and Scott Daniels, "Selling Before 1900: A Historical Perspective," *The Journal of Personal Selling & Sales Management,* November 1987, pp. 1–7.

3. Thomas J. Peters and Robert H., Waterman, Jr., *In Search of Excellence: Lessons from America's Best-Run Companies* (New York: Harper & Row, 1982); and Thomas J. Peters and Nancy Austin, *A Passion for Excellence: The Leadership Difference* (New York: Random House, 1985).

4. *Sales & Marketing Management,* February 17, 1989, pp. 57, 104–5.

5. Donald W. Jackson, Jr., Janet E. Keith, and Richard K. Burdick, "The Relative Importance of Various Promotional Elements in Different Industrial Purchase Situations," *Journal of Advertising* 16, no. 4 (1988), pp. 25–33.

6. Adapted from Stanton and Futrell, *Fundamentals of Marketing.*

CHAPTER 3

1. Robert L. Shook, *Ten Greatest Salespersons* (New York: Harper & Row, 1978), p. 25.

2. James F. Engel, Roger D. Blackwell, and Paul W. Miniard,

Consumer Behavior (Hinsdale, Ill.: Dryden Press, 1986).

3. Abraham Maslow, "A Theory of Human Motivation," *Psychology Review* (1943), pp. 370–96; and *Motivation and Personality* (New York: Harper & Row, 1954).

4. For a different definition of a feature, advantage, and benefit, see Neil Rackham, *SPIN Selling* (New York: McGraw-Hill, 1988), pp. 99–108.

5. Engel, Blackwell, and Miniard, *Consumer Behavior*, pp. 321–23.

6. Developed by Professor John C. Hafer of Kent State University.

7. Engel, Blackwell, and Miniard, *Consumer Behavior*, p. 321.

8. For a further discussion of the need-recognition stage, see Gordon C. Bruner II and Richard H. Pomazal, "Problem Recognition: The Crucial First Stage of the Consumer Decision Process," *The Journal of Consumer Marketing*, Winter 1988, pp. 53–63.

CHAPTER 4

1. Gerhard Gschwandtner, *Nonverbal Selling Power* (Englewood Cliffs, N.J.: Prentice-Hall, 1985), p. 3.

2. Ibid.

3. Text of figure reproduced from the sales training course, "The Languages of Selling," by Gerhard Gschwandtner & Associates, Falmouth, Va.: photos courtesy of Richard D. Irwin, Inc.

4. Also see David W. Steward, Sid Hecker, and John L. Graham, "It's More Than What You Say: Assessing the Influence of Nonverbal Communication in Marketing," *Psychology & Marketing*, Winter 1987, pp. 303–22.

5. Adapted from Tony Alessandra, Phil Wexler, and Rich Barrera,

Nonmanipulative Selling (Englewood Cliffs, N.J.: Prentice-Hall, 1987), pp. 58–66.

CHAPTER 5

1. James F. Bender, "Training and Developing Sales Personnel," in *Handbook of Modern Marketing*, ed. Victor P. Buell (New York: McGraw-Hill, 1986), pp. 12–44.

2. For further discussion and research findings on knowledge requirements for salespeople, see David M. Szymanski, "Determinants of Selling Effectiveness: The Importance of Declarative Knowledge to the Personal Selling Concept," *Journal of Marketing*, January 1988, pp. 64–77; Harish Sujan, Mita Sujan, and James R. Bettman, "Knowledge Structure Differences Between More Effective and Less Effective Salespeople," *Journal of Marketing Research*, February 1988, pp. 81–86; and Richard F. Beltramini, "High Technology Salespeople's Information Acquisition Strategies," *The Journal of Personal Selling and Sales Management*, May 1988, pp. 37–44.

3. For industry examples of cooperative advertising, see the special supplement, "Co-op Advertising," *Sales & Marketing Management*, May 1988, pp. 62–70.

4. R. Craig Endicott, "Philip Morris Surpasses P & G: Top 10 National Advertisers," *Advertising Age*, September 26, 1988, p. 3.

5. For recent information on premiums and incentives, see the magazine *Incentive Marketing*.

6. Paul W. Farris and John A. Quelch, "In Defense of Price Promotion," *Sloan Management Review*, Fall 1987, pp. 63–69.

7. For a discussion on the advantages and disadvantages of

using PCs in the sales force, see Thayer C. Taylor, "PCs Are Paying Off, But . . . ," *Sales & Marketing Management*, September 1988, pp. 82–85.

CHAPTER 6

1. Al Paul Lefton, Jr., "The Lucky Seven: How to Roll Leads into Sales," *Business Marketing*, August 1987, pp. 86–89.

2. Donald L. Brady, "Determining the Value of an Industrial Prospect: A Prospect Preference Index Model," *The Journal of Personal Selling and Sales Management*, August 1987, pp. 27–32.

3. "Trade Shows: Creating Sales Leads," *Marketing Communications*, November 1987, pp. 36–40.

4. Also see Hebert E. Brown and Roger W. Brucker, "Telephone Qualifications of Sales Leads," *Industrial Marketing Management*, August 1987, pp. 185–90.

5. Also see Kate Reilly and Eric Baron, "Teaching Salespeople the Five W's and H of Sales Call Planning," *Business Marketing*, August 1987, pp. 62–66.

CHAPTER 7

1. Adapted from G. M. Grikscheit, H. C. Cash, and W. J. E. Crissy, *Handbook of Selling: Psychological, Managerial, and Marketing Bases* (New York: John Wiley & Sons, 1981).

2. Example provided by Professor Richard D. Nordstrom, California State University–Fresno.

3. Adapted from Grikscheit, Cash, and Crissy, *Handbook of Selling*.

4. Ibid.

5. Example provided by Professor Richard D. Nordstrom, California State University–Fresno.

6. Adapted from Tony Alessandra, Phil Wexler, and Rich Barrera, *Nonmanipulative Selling* (Englewood Cliffs, N.J.: Prentice-Hall, 1987).

7. For 18 concession strategies useful during sales negotiations, see Homer B. Smith, "How to Concede—Strategically," *Sales & Marketing Management,* May 1988, pp. 79–80.

8. For a complete discussion, see Neil Rackham, *SPIN Selling* (New York: McGraw-Hill, 1988).

9. Dennis DeMaria, "Keep Quiet and Get the Order," *Personal Selling Power* 3, no. 2, March–April 1983, p. 17.

CHAPTER 8

1. Stan Moss, "What Sales Executives Look For in New Salespeople," *Sales & Marketing Management,* March 1986, p. 47.

2. For further discussion, see Michael F. Smith and James M. Hunt, "Disconfirmation of Expectations: A Method for Enhancing the Effectiveness of Customer Communications," *The Journal of Personal Selling and Sales Management,* May 1987, pp. 9–19; Mark H. McCormack, "What Makes a Great Salesman?" *The Wall Street Journal,* June 20, 1988, p. 10; Arthur Bragg, "Are Good Salespeople Born or Made?" *Sales & Marketing Management,* September 1988, pp. 74–78; Jeanne and Herbert Greenberg, "Why Do Top Salespeople Succeed Where Others Just Get By?" *Personal Selling Power,* November–December 1988, p. 20; and Donald J. Moine, "How Superachievers Outperform Their Peers," *Personal Selling Power,* November–December 1988, p. 11.

3. For a discussion on using proof statements to increase sales, see

Ronald E. Milliman and Douglas L. Fugate, "Using Trust-Transference as a Persuasion Technique: An Empirical Field Investigation," *The Journal of Personal Selling and Sales Management,* August 1988, pp. 1–7.

4. For a discussion on the reasons for including the negative with the positive information in the sales presentation, see James M. Hunt and Michael F. Smith, "The Persuasive Impact of Two-Sided Selling Appeals for an Unknown Brand Name," *Journal of the Academy of Marketing Service,* Spring 1987, pp. 11–18; and Michael F. Smith and James M. Hunt, "Disconfirmation of Expectations: A Method for Enhancing the Effectiveness of Customer Communications," *The Journal of Personal Selling and Sales Management,* May 1987, pp. 9–19.

CHAPTER 10

1. John L. Johnston, *Works of Mark Twain* (New York: Harper & Row, 1989), p. 133.

2. Mike Radick, "Training Salespeople to Get Success on Their Side," *Sales & Marketing Management,* August 15, 1983, pp. 63–65. Also see Neil Rackham, *SPIN Selling* (New York: McGraw-Hill, 1988).

CHAPTER 11

1. Also see A. Parasuraman, "Customer-Oriented Corporate Cultures Are Crucial to Services Marketing Success," *Journal of Services Marketing,* Summer 1987, pp. 39–46.

2. Robert L. Shook, *Ten Greatest Salespersons* (New York: Harper & Row, 1978), p. 95.

3. Ibid., p. 155.

4. Ibid., p. 67.

5. Also see Richard T. Garfein, "Guiding Principles for Improving Customer Service," *Journal of Services Marketing,* Spring 1988, pp. 37–41.

6. Courtesy of State Farm Insurance Companies.

7. John Firestone, "When You Don't Make the Sale," *Purchasing,* February 1989, pp. 12–16.

8. For an interesting discussion, see Robert E. Krapfel, Jr., "Customer Complaint and Salesperson Response: The Effect of the Communication Source," *Journal of Retailing,* Summer 1988, pp. 181–98; and Patricia Sellers, "How to Handle Customers' Gripes," *Fortune,* October 24, 1988, pp. 88–100.

9. Joe Gaston, "Don't Commit These Sins," *Purchasing,* January 1989, pp. 15–18.

10. Reprinted with permission of BJ-Hughes, Inc.

CHAPTER 12

1. 1988 *Census of Retail Trade* (Washington D.C.: U.S. Department of Labor, 1988).

2. Reprinted by permission from Delbert J. Duncan, Charles F. Phillips, and Stanley C. Hollander, *Modern Retailing Management* (Homewood, Ill.: Richard D. Irwin, 1972), p. 184.

3. "Retail Pay: Surprisingly Better," *Career Paths,* January 1988, p. 11.

4. Adapted from "The Top Fifty," *Forbes,* May 30, 1988, pp. 124–50.

5. Adapted from Stanley Marcus, "Fire a Buyer and Hire A Seller," *International Trends in Retailing,* Fall 1986, pp. 49–55.

6. Robert L. Shook, *Ten Greatest Salespersons* (New York: Harper & Row, 1978), pp. 7–24.

7. Ibid., pp. 135–54.

8. Arch G. Woodside and Taylor J.

Sims, "Retail Sales Transactions and Customer 'Purchase Pal' Effects on Buying Behavior," *Journal of Retailing* 52, 1986, pp. 57–64.

9. Adapted from Stanley Marcus, "Fire a Buyer and Hire a Seller," *International Trends in Retailing,* Fall 1986, pp. 54–55.

10. Adapted from information provided by Professor Richard D. Nordstrom, California State University–Fresno.

CHAPTER 13

1. Adapted from "Strange Tales of Sales," *Sales & Marketing Management,* June 3, 1985, p. 42.

2. *Standard Industrial Classification Manual* (Washington, D.C.: U.S. Government Printing Office, 1988).

3. Courtesy of International Business Machines Corporation.

4. Also see Richard N. Cardozo, Shannon H. Shipp, and Kenneth J. Roering, "Implementing New Business-to-Business Selling Methods," *The Journal of Personal Selling & Sales Management,* August 1987, pp. 17–26.

5. Richard M. Hill and the National Association of Purchasing Management.

CHAPTER 14

1. Robert L. Shook, *Ten Greatest Salespersons* (New York: Harper & Row, 1978), p. 79.

2. Charles M. Futrell, *Survey of America's Top Sales Force* (Working papers, Texas A&M University, 1989).

3. Harish Sujan, Barton A. Weitz, and Mita Sujan, "Increasing Sales Productivity by Getting Salespeople to Work Harder," *The Journal of Personal Selling and Sales Management,* August 1988, pp. 9–19.

4. For a technical discussion, see Andris A. Zoltners and Prabhakant Sinha, "Sales Territory Alignment: A Review and Model," *Management Science,* November 1983, pp. 1237–56.

5. Alan J. Dubinsky and Thomas N. Ingram, "A Portfolio Approach to Account Profitability," *Industrial Marketing Management,* February 1984, pp. 33–41.

6. For an industry example of developing customer classifications, see Raymond W. LaForge and Clifford E. Young, "A Portfolio Model to Improve Sales Call Coverage," *Business,* April–June 1985, pp. 10–16.

7. Paul H. Schurr and Bobby J. Calder, "Psychological Effects of Restaurant Meetings on Industrial Buyers," *Journal of Marketing,* January 1986, pp. 87–97.

8. John S. Wagle and Peter F. Kaminski, "Applying Territoriality to Steps in the Buyer-Seller Process," *Industrial Marketing Management,* February 1984, pp. 1–10.

9. For a technical discussion, see Edward K. Baker, "An Exact Algorithm for the Time-Constrained Traveling Salesperson Problem," *Industrial Marketing Management,* July 1983, pp. 179–92; and Shelby H. McIntyre and Adrian B. Ryans, "Task Effects on Decision Quality in Traveling Salesperson Problems," *Organizational Behavior and Human Performance,* December 1983, pp. 344–69.

10. For a more complete discussion, see Mel Mandell, "Car Phones: Should You Pick Up Now?" *Sales & Marketing Management,* September 1988, pp. 44–51.

CHAPTER 15

1. Peter F. Drucker, "The New Meaning of Corporate Social Responsibility," *California Management Review,* Winter 1984, pp. 53–63; and Donald P. Robin and R. Eric Reidenbach, "Social Responsibility, Ethics, and Marketing Strategy: Closing the Gap between Concept and Application," *Journal of Marketing,* January 1987, pp. 44–55.

2. Kenneth E. Aupperle, Archie B. Carroll, and John D. Hatfield, "An Empirical Examination of the Relationship Between Corporate Social Responsibility and Profitability," *Academy of Management Journal,* June 1985, pp. 446–63.

3. For a summary of various views on corporate social responsibility, see Van R. Wood, Lawrence B. Chonko, and Shelby D. Hunt, "Social Responsibility and Personal Success: Are They Incompatible?" *Journal of Business Research* 14 (1986), pp. 193–212.

4. For an in-depth discussion, see Gene R. Laczniak and Patrick E. Murphy, *Marketing Ethics* (Lexington, Mass.: Lexington Books, 1985); and Lawrence B. Chonko and Shelby D. Hunt, "Ethics and Marketing Management: An Empirical Examination," *Journal of Business Research* 13 (1985), pp. 339–59.

5. Adapted from "Strange Tales of Sales," *Sales & Marketing Management,* June 3, 1985, p. 46.

6. Lawrence B. Chonko and John J. Burnett, "Measuring the Importance of Ethical Situations as a Source of Role Conflict: A Survey of Salespeople, Sales Managers, and Sales Support Personnel," *The Journal of Personal Selling and Sales Management,* May 1983, pp. 41–47.

7. S. A. Youngblood and G. L. Tidwell, "Termination-at-Will: Some Changes in the Wind," *Personnel,* May–June 1981, p. 24.

8. *Fair Employment Report* (New York: Zenith Employment Publishers, Inc., August 2, 1982), p. 123.

9. "White Collar Crime Cost Increases," *USA Today,* January 8, 1987, p. A1.

10. Jeffrey A. Gadiman, "A Traveler's Guide to Gifts and Bribes," *Harvard Business Review,* July–August 1986, pp. 122–36.

11. Adapted from Steven Mitchell Sack, "Legal Puffery: Truth or Consequences," *Sales and Marketing Management,* October 1986, pp. 59–60.

12. "Trade Regulation Rule: Cooling-Off Period for Door-to-Door Sales," 16 C.F.R. Part 429 (Washington, D.C.: Federal Trade Commission, 1982).

13. For an excellent reference, see Louis W. Stern and Thomas L. Eovaldi, *Legal Aspects of Marketing Strategy: Antitrust and Consumer Protection Issues* (Englewood Cliffs, N.J.: Prentice-Hall, 1984), pp. 447–74.

14. O. C. Ferrell and Larry G. Gresham, "A Continguency Framework for Understanding Ethical Decision Making in Marketing," *Journal of Marketing,* Summer 1985, pp. 87–96.

CHAPTER 16

1. For a complete discussion on the many facets of sales management, see Charles Futrell, *Sales Management* (Hinsdale, Ill.: Dryden Press, 1988).

2. Harvey B. Mackay, "Humanize Your Selling Strategy," *Harvard Business Review,* March–April 1988, pp. 36–47.

3. Used with permission of Compute Corporation, Houston, Texas.

4. Used with permission of Alarm System, Inc., Kansas City, Missouri.

5. Used with permission of Textron Chemical Corporation, Houston, Texas.

6. Used with permission of Electro Corporation, Denver, Colorado.

7. Used with permission of Transtex Automotive Supply Corporation, Columbus, Ohio.

8. For a review of the subject, see James M. Comer and Alan J. Dubinsky, *Managing the Successful Sales Force* (Lexington, Mass.: Lexington Books, 1985). Also see Arthur Bragg, "Are Good Salespeople Born or Made?" *Sales & Marketing Management,* September 1988, pp. 74–78; Jeanne and Herbert Greenberg, "Why Do Top Salespeople Succeed Where Others Just Get By?" *Personal Selling Power,* November–December 1988, p. 20; and Donald J. Moine, "How Superachievers Outperform Their Peers," *Personal Selling Power,* November–December 1988, p. 11.

9. Richard Kern, "IQ Tests for Salesmen Make a Comeback," *Sales & Marketing Management,* April 1988, pp. 42–46.

10. For the student's viewpoint on recruiting, see Jack Falvey, "The Old College Try: Tricks to Recruiting Successfully on Campus," *Sales & Marketing Management,* May 1988, pp. 44–48; and Arthur Bragg, "Grads Give Recruiters Low Grades," *Sales & Marketing Management,* May 1988, pp. 48–49.

11. For a discussion on improving sales training effectiveness, see Thomas W. Leigh, "Cognitive Selling Scripts and Sales Training," *The Journal of Personal Selling and Sales Management,* August 1987, pp. 39–48.

CHAPTER 17

1. Adapted from "Facts Update," *Incentive Marketing,* February 1989, p. 45.

2. "The Beauty of It All: Jafra Incentives Spur Sales, Recruiting," *Incentive Marketing,* October 1986, pp. 59–62.

3. For a discussion of a direct selling organization, see John C. Crawford and Barbara C. Garland, "A Profile of a Party Plan Sales Force," *Akron Business and Economic Review,* Winter 1988, pp. 28–37.

4. Charles M. Futrell, *Survey of America's Top Sales Force* (Working papers, Texas A&M University, 1989).

5. Robert Tannenbaum and Warren H. Schmidt, "How to Choose a Leadership Pattern," *Harvard Business Review* 8 (Fall 1986), pp. 5–11.

6. Bill Kelly, "How to Manage a Superstar," *Sales & Marketing Management,* November 1988, pp. 32–34.

INDEX

Other BUSINESS ONE IRWIN Titles of Interest to You

MARKETING TO HOME-BASED BUSINESSES
Jeffrey P. Davidson

Over 34,000,000 Americans are performing some or all of their work at home. Jeffrey P. Davidson shows marketers how to identify this often elusive segment of customers and gain their business. He helps you acquire the knowledge, strategies, and techniques to effectively market to home-based businesses.
$39.95 ISBN: 1-55623-475-9

SAY IT WITH CHARTS
The Executive's Guide to Successful Presentations in the 1990s
Second Edition
Gene Zelazny

The Second Edition of *Say It With Charts* brings the task of choosing and using charts into the 1990s. Gene Zelazny expands his ideas on how to select the right chart for your presentation and shows you how to take advantage of new advances in computer graphics to create quality visuals for business presentations to small and large audiences.
$34.95 ISBN: 1-55623-447-3

IT'S SHOWTIME!
How to Plan and Hold Successful Sales Meetings
John K. MacKenzie

A creative reference for planning, staging, structuring, and holding a successful sales meeting. Details how improved sales supervision can bolster your company. Includes hundreds of ideas for staging humor, speeches, awards, and motivational modules.
$27.50 ISBN: 1-55623-238-1

MARKETING TO THE AFFLUENT
Dr. Thomas Stanley

A 1989 business book award finalist! Dr. Stanley shows you how to get the true demographics, psychographics, buying, and patronage habits of the wealthy. Includes in-depth interviews with some of the nation's top sales and marketing professionals to help you pinpoint your best prospects.
$55.00 ISBN: 1-55623-105-9

SELLING TO THE AFFLUENT
The Professional's Guide to Closing the Sales that Count
Dr. Thomas Stanley

Improve your closing percentage...and income. Dr. Stanley shows you how to approach wealthy prospects at the moment they are most likely to buy. In *Marketing to the Affluent* he tells you how to find them. Here he tells you how to sell them.
$55.00 ISBN: 1-55623-418-X

Prices quoted are in U.S. currency and are subject to change without notice.
Available in fine bookstores and libraries everywhere.